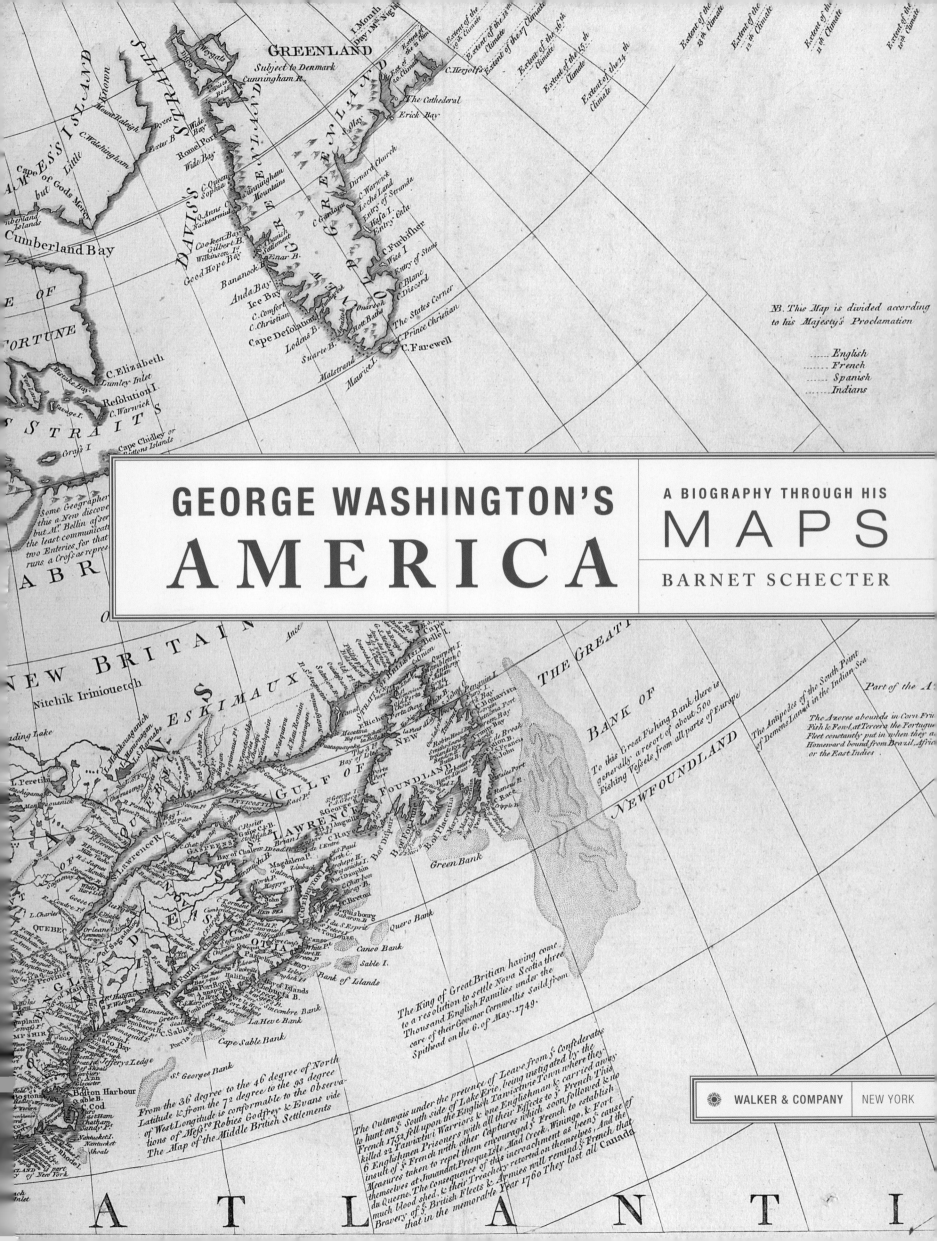

GEORGE WASHINGTON'S AMERICA

A BIOGRAPHY THROUGH HIS MAPS

BARNET SCHECTER

WALKER & COMPANY · NEW YORK

BY THE SAME AUTHOR

The Battle for New York: The City at the Heart of the American Revolution

The Devil's Own Work: The Civil War Draft Riots and the Fight to Reconstruct America

Published by Walker Publishing Company, Inc., New York

All papers used by Walker & Company are natural, recyclable products made from wood
grown in well-managed forests. The manufacturing processes conform to the environmental
regulations of the country of origin.

LIBRARY OF CONGRESS CATALOGING-IN-PUBLICATION DATA HAS BEEN APPLIED FOR.

ISBN: 978-0-8027-1748-1

Visit Walker & Company's Web site at www.walkerbooks.com

First U.S. edition 2010

1 3 5 7 9 10 8 6 4 2

Designed by **Think Studio, NYC**
Printed and bound by Imago in China

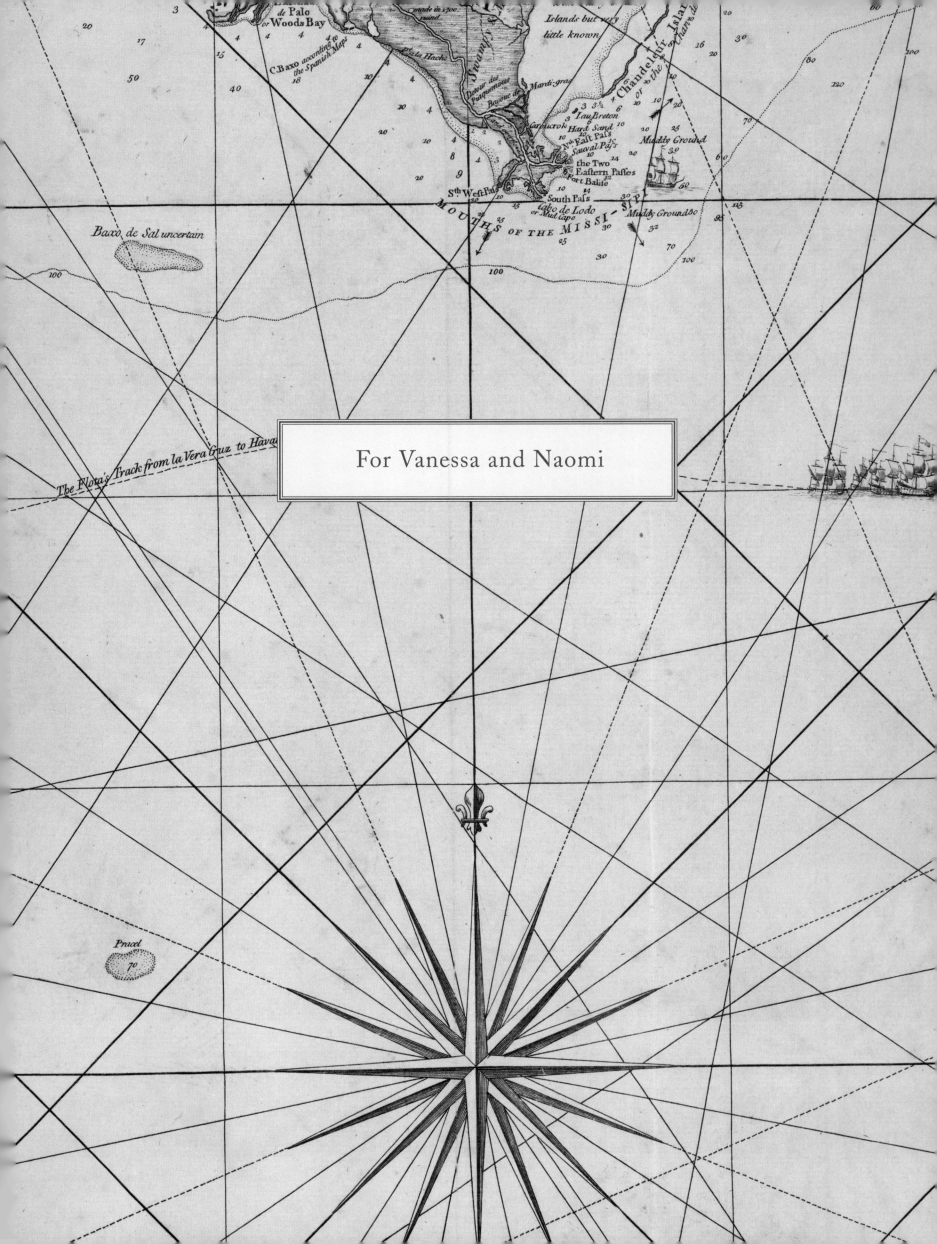

For Vanessa and Naomi

CONTENTS

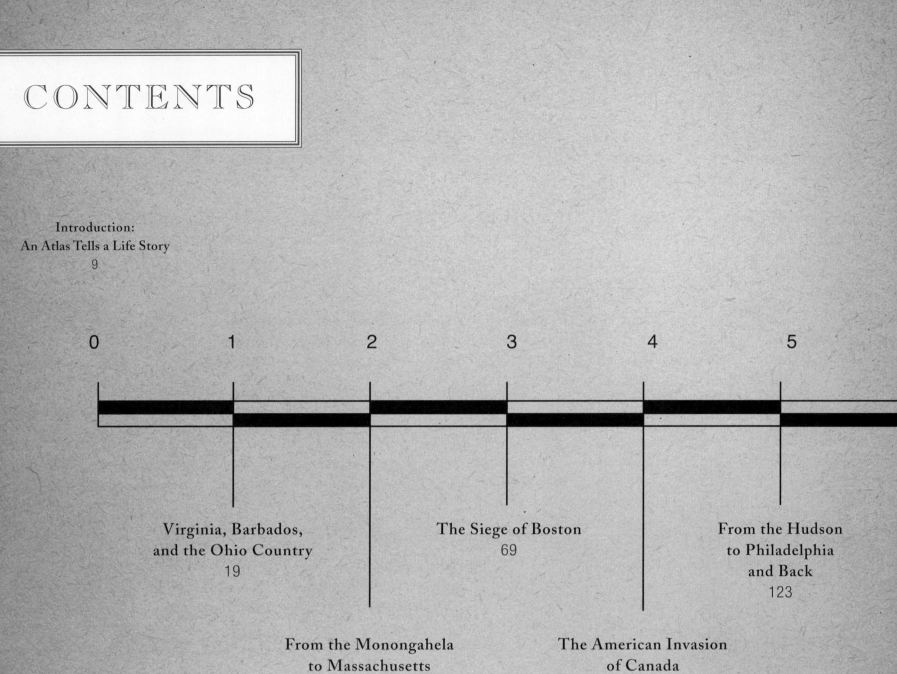

N
W —◇— E
S

INTRODUCTION

AN ATLAS TELLS A

LIFE STORY

"The old Indian with me spoke of a fine piece of land and beautiful place for a house, and in order to give me a more lively idea of it, chalked out the situation upon his deer skin," George Washington recorded in his diary on a trip to the Ohio Valley in 1770. The house would be atop a high hill, overlooking a vast stretch of flat land with a creek running through it. Around the house lay fertile land and a spring with many roads leading to it, worn by the herds of buffalo that came to drink. The creek ran parallel to the Ohio River and was surrounded by "large bodies of level, rich land."[1]

Like the rudimentary map sketched out on animal hide, the elaborate published maps of North America that Washington collected give us "a more lively idea" of his life story. These visual images, along with maps he drew himself, place us at the scene of his youthful ambition and his later battles—in the landscapes and on the waterways that were the theater of war in Britain's North American colonies, and that sparked the imagination and desires of the preeminent founder of the United States. After the Revolution, these maps, combined with Washington's travels through the new nation, shaped his vision of America as "a rising empire in the New World."

OPPOSITE: *Page from George Washington's expense account in 1776:* Here Washington recorded an expenditure, on June 4, 1776, "To Mr. Sparhawk for a collection of maps and a cover to the book, 14 pounds 18 shillings." A receipt reveals that this "collection" was a single atlas, indicating that such works were not always sold with a cover and suggesting that the Yale atlas could have been a single published work, not a collection of individual maps.

PAGE 8: George Washington, by Charles Willson Peale.

According to the inventory compiled after Washington's death in 1799, his library at Mount Vernon contained more than ninety maps and atlases. Among them was an atlas of eastern North America consisting of forty-three map sheets (some of them the northern or southern half of a pair) that was later passed down through four generations of Washington's nephews as part of the Mount Vernon library. Along the way, the maps were arranged in geographical order—from Canada, down the eastern seaboard, and west to Louisiana—and bound (sometime in the nineteenth century) between two marbleized covers. In 1876 this atlas was sold at auction to a prominent Connecticut family, and purchased finally by Yale University in 1970.*

Yale's *George Washington Atlas*, in the Map Collection at Sterling Library in New Haven, Connecticut, presents something of a historical mystery. The atlas is unusual because it is apparently a composite work, consisting of maps that Washington collected individually and that were only later bound into a single volume to preserve them—unlike the standard works of the day that Washington owned, like Thomas Jefferys's *American Atlas* and *General Topography of North America* or William Faden's *North American Atlas*, which were compiled by a cartographer, publisher, or engraver. However, the Yale atlas fits the pattern of the published atlases by Jefferys and Faden: It contains at least a dozen of the same maps and presents a complete picture of eastern North America. Whoever assembled the Yale atlas was clearly following the model of the published atlases, but with a tighter focus on Canada and the future United States. Moreover, published atlases in the eighteenth century were not always sold with a cover, as Washington's expense account shows. Is the Yale atlas a published atlas that is simply missing its title page? A comparison of the contents of the Yale atlas with published atlases of the period does not produce a match, and until such identification is made, it is fair to assume that Washington collected the maps individually.†

In the absence of a title page, the inventory of Washington's library does not clearly identify the Yale atlas. One scholar has speculated that the item "Military Plans of the American Revolution" refers to this group of forty-three map sheets.[2] This may well be the case, since many of the maps date from 1775 and a few depict details of the Revolution in addition to the North American landscape. The maps depicting the French and Indian War remained relevant in the Revolution, because they presented terrain and cities where new battles were to be fought. Thus, the Yale atlas contained vital intelligence that Washington needed as he led the Continental army against the British.

It is also possible that the Yale atlas was assembled later from another item, "9 Maps of different Parts of Virginia and Carolina, and also a Number of loose Maps." Valued at fifty-two dollars, it was one of the few most expensive items listed among the maps and atlases, suggesting that it contained enough material for two or more atlases. While the Yale atlas does make sense as a tool for the Revolutionary War, it furnishes enough material to tell Washington's entire life story, which is inseparable from that of the geographic evolution of the thirteen colonies into a unified, expanding nation and the preservation of American independence after the war.

Whatever its precise identity as an artifact, the Yale atlas reflects Washington's interests and concerns, bringing his experiences and his vision of America into sharp focus. Combined here with some additional maps from his library, a few maps he drew himself, some created for this book, and a narrative enriched by his diaries and papers, the Yale atlas enables us to look over Washington's shoulder, accompanying him as he journeyed through these landscapes, or struggled to direct his generals and monitor their campaigns in distant theaters of battle.

* Washington had no children of his own and bequeathed part of Mount Vernon, including his library, to his nephew Bushrod Washington. When he died in 1829, part of the library, including this atlas, was passed down to his nephew John A. Washington. He willed it to his son, also named John A. Washington, who in turn passed it down to his son, Lawrence Washington. The collection of Washington's possessions sold in Philadelphia in 1876 was among the very few "so accurately identified by unbroken successions of devises" (Toner, 97).

† I am grateful to Edward James Redmond, an authority on George Washington and cartography in the Geography and Map Division at the Library of Congress, for his generous assistance in cross-checking the contents of the Yale atlas against various editions of the Faden and Jefferys atlases. I am also grateful to William Reese, of William Reese Company in New Haven, an expert on eighteenth-century Americana, for his observations about the Yale atlas.

1776	8	Penn.ª			Lawful		
April	To amount bro.ᵗ forward £479.9.8	1886	10	8			
	Deduct 25 ⅌ C.ᵗ to re-duce Penn.ª to Lawful 95.17.11						
					303	11	9
	York Cy.						
25	To the Expences of myself & party reconnoitring the Landing places &c.ª on Staten Island 16:10						16
May 11	To Rob.ᵗ Porter £7.5.						
	To Ben. Hardeson 13.11.6	16	13	2			
	To Exp.ˢ of a Tour on & reconnoitring of Long Island 26.8.6						17
	To washing &c.ª 8.3.4						
	To M.ʳ Plunket Fleesons acc.ᵗ £64.2.6 Penn.ª eq.ᵗ to 51.6.0						
28	To M.ʳ Jn.º G. Frazer for a Trunk to pack my Papers in 2.16.—						
June 4	To M.ʳ Sparhawk for a Collection of Maps, and a Cover to the Book £14.18. eq.º 11.18.6						
	To the Exp.ˢ of myself and suit to, at, & from Phil.ª p.ʳ M.ʳ Harrison's acc.ᵗ 87.18.8						
	To washing, and other acc.ⁿ paid by myself amounting p.ʳ Bills to 10.5.—						18
14	To George Baylor Esq.ʳ 35.3.5						
26	To Ab. Dupee 7.16.6						
	To Exp.ˢ in Recony. the Chan-nel Landings on both sides the N.º River as high as Tar-ry Town to fix upon the de-fences of the River 10.18.						19
	To am.ᵗ carr.ᵈ forw.ᵈ £157.9.—	2398	4	4			

And we can follow Washington with a fair degree of precision, even though we do not know exactly when he acquired the maps in the Yale atlas. For some of the maps, evidence from Washington's papers pinpoints when he owned a copy—even if it was not this identical print. A receipt dated June 4, 1776, from Philadelphia bookseller John Sparhawk identifies the collection of maps Washington purchased on that date as *A General Topography of North America and the West Indies*, an atlas of

Sources of the Chaudiere, Penobscot, and Kennebec Rivers); and "A French Map of the Carolinas" (probably Henri Mouzon's *An Accurate Map of North and South Carolina*, also in the Yale atlas). Washington also mentioned some of these maps and others in his correspondence.

These maps and the Yale atlas are some of the finest products of the cartographer's skill and artistry in the eighteenth century—and many of them were republished for decades (some with improvements, and some without).

ninety-three maps published by Thomas Jefferys, which includes a dozen of the same maps as the Yale atlas (with some differences because they are from different editions, printed in different years). These maps will be identified as they appear in the narrative to document that Washington owned a copy of essentially the same map after June 4, 1776.

Additionally, the inventory of Washington's library at the time of his death confirmed that he owned loose copies of certain maps that are crucial to telling his life story. These include Joshua Fry and Peter Jefferson's *Map of Virginia* (also in the Yale atlas); Thomas Hutchins's *Map of the Western Parts of Virginia, Maryland, Pennsylvania and North Carolina*; William McMurray's *Map of the United States*; and Abraham Bradley's *Map of the United States*. Others were identified less specifically, but an educated guess can be made: "A Map of New England" (probably *A Map of the Most Inhabited Part of New England*, by Braddock Mead, alias John Green, also in the Yale atlas); "Map of Kennebec River" (probably John Montresor's

However, for Washington's purposes the information they provided was often limited and imperfect. He depended on these maps for a broad view of a province or region and for whatever detail they could provide, but he often complained that they were too general. He regularly sought out more accurate local maps—and sketched some himself—while urging Congress to commission new surveys in areas where he expected to conduct sustained military operations. Indeed, Washington created a map-making department of the Continental army in 1777 and appointed Robert Erskine as geographer and surveyor to the Army of the United States, to lead it.

Nonetheless, despite any limitations or distortions that impacted the demanding military user, these maps, many of them published in London and obtained through French sources during the American Revolution, were part of the basic vocabulary shared by the eighteenth-century Atlantic world for visualizing North America—when fighting colonial wars, redrawing imperial boundaries, and witnessing the birth of a new nation. At each stage

Receipt for A General Topography of North America and the West Indies: Washington purchased the *General Topography* from John Sparhawk on June 4, 1776. While the expense account entry suggests that the *General Topography* consisted of loose maps, it seems clear that the *General Topography* was not split up to create or contribute to the Yale atlas, because the *General Topography* was also auctioned in 1876, and the catalog says it contained ninety-three maps, i.e., it was complete.

of Washington's life, we can see the topography of America through the same lens that he did: through his own written observations and sketches and those that were sent to him—and through the medium of these great maps in his personal collection. And since Washington's life was from his early years until his death intimately bound up with the land, the maps tell a great deal about the man and his times.

When the Yale atlas was sold in 1876, it had not only the marbleized binding, but an inscription in the front stating that it was "From the Library of General Washington," and an "Index" (table of contents) listing the maps as they were bound.* They were arranged geographically, starting with *A General Map of North America* and then proceeding from north to south, from Canada down the Atlantic seaboard to Florida and Louisiana. The sequencing, and the fact that Washington collected all of these maps, which together present a portrait of the American colonies, and then the United States in Washington's time, provides an apt metaphor of his achievement. His leadership helped pull thirteen colonies together politically and militarily, see them through an eight-year war, and then keep the hostile European powers at the northwestern and southwestern borders from blocking the growth of the new republic or shearing parts of it off.

To tell Washington's life story, I have selected twenty-five of the forty-three map sheets—nineteen complete maps—from the atlas. Chapter 1 explores Washington's early years, from his birth in 1732 through the beginning of his military career in 1753, chiefly through four maps, three of which were published only later. While they are not all maps he used during those years, they are the best maps of the mid-eighteenth century showing the territory covered by the youthful Washington, and he would use all of these maps later in life.

Washington's two half brothers inherited most of their father's estate, and he was determined that by acquiring manners and land—and through distinguished military service—he would thrust himself into the front ranks of Virginia's gentry.† These maps allow us to follow Washington in great detail on his first expedition as an adjutant general of Virginia and also clarify the bewildering array of Indian tribes, their territories, and their complex and shifting alliances, with which Washington grappled on his mission.

In chapter 2, the same maps tell the story of Washington's second journey to the Ohio country, in 1754, and his earliest battles, which helped precipitate the French and Indian War. The bounty lands in the West that Washington received for his service or bought from other veterans would have a profound impact on the rest of his life. His vested interest in the West would help shape his vision for the United States after independence: an expanding nation and empire united from east to west by improved navigation on the many rivers with which it was blessed by divine Providence. Clearing obstacles from the Potomac River and building canals to make it a major commercial artery, connecting the Ohio Valley with the Atlantic seaboard at Chesapeake Bay, though interrupted by the Revolution, was an idea that would capture Washington's imagination for the rest of his life.

Some additional maps also give a clear picture of British campaigns during the French and Indian War, from Nova Scotia to the Ohio Valley, especially General Edward Braddock's expedition of 1755 in which Washington's composure and courage under fire during the battle on the banks of the Monongahela River made him a hero throughout the colonies, despite the disastrous outcome for the British forces. It was little known or simply disregarded that Washington had urged Braddock to divide his force so the advance column could travel with less baggage and reach Fort Duquesne before it was reinforced from Canada—advice that contributed to the failure of the mission.

The British would remain on the defensive for the next three years, until 1758, when the leadership of William Pitt helped the British turn the corner to victory. Washington took part in the successful campaign of General John Forbes to retake Fort Duquesne at the Forks of the Ohio that year, during which the troops of the First Virginia Regiment, trained by Washington, showed outstanding professionalism. Remarkably, however, Washington hectored Forbes about changing the army's route and never fully absorbed the lesson of the general's slow but sure victory. Washington retained an impulsive and impatient streak as a military leader, favoring a daring attack over the thorough, time-consuming logistical preparation which he eventually mastered and which proved to be the key to his own long-term success. This courage and combativeness would serve Washington well on important occasions, but would also cost him dearly on others during the Revolution and even as president and commander in chief in the 1790s.

Topography and maps played an important role in Washington's transformation from British subject to

* For a list of all the maps in Yale's *George Washington Atlas*, see the appendix.

† His half brothers, Lawrence and Augustine, were Augustine senior's sons from his first marriage.

American revolutionary in the wake of the British victory in the French and Indian War in 1761. Washington's hunger in 1770 for "large bodies of level, rich land" points to his growing dissatisfaction with the Crown and its attempts to confine the colonists east of the Appalachians with the Proclamation Line of 1763 in order to reduce conflict with the Indians.

As Washington acquired real estate and advanced into the top tier of Virginia planters and slaveholders, he had to order all of the luxury items that befit his station from England, and his resentment of mercantilist policies grew apace. Exorbitant prices for manufactured goods and low prices for tobacco put the Virginia planter in an endless cycle of debt and dependency. Owning real estate went hand in hand with inheriting, breeding, and buying slaves to work the land. And while Washington had shown callousness in punishing and selling slaves in the past, when he spoke out against English oppression, his rhetoric revealed a growing abhorrence of chattel slavery while implying that blacks were not inherently inferior, but rather had been degraded by captivity and forced labor.[3]

Passage of the Tea Act in 1773 and the Boston Tea Party that followed plunged the colonists and British authorities deeper into conflict. Washington attended the First Continental Congress and a year later was named commander in chief of the Continental army. Suddenly, his bounty lands in the Ohio Valley took on a new meaning. Washington told Congress he would give the war his all, but no one could deny that American defeat was possible, even likely. To protect his reputation, Washington asked every delegate to mark his words: He did not consider himself equal to the task before him. To protect his life, Washington looked westward: If the Revolution failed and he was hunted down by the British to be hanged for treason, he would flee to the wilderness in the West.[4]

In chapter 3, the first map, *The Seat of War in New England*, dramatically illustrates the fateful opening weeks of the Revolutionary War. The second map, *Boston Harbor*, while focusing on the waters around the city, also reveals key details of the British position within Boston. That Washington owned this British military map is testament to the thriving trade in maps between British and French dealers, which continued throughout the war despite the enmity between the two governments—and created a French connection for the Americans to acquire this cartographic intelligence.[5]

A Map of the Most Inhabited Part of New England graphically shows why the Hudson River became the focus of British strategy as early as August 1775, during the siege of Boston: By sending two armies, one down from Canada and another up from New York City, the British hoped to control the entire length of the river, creating a cordon to isolate New England from the rest of the colonies and starve Washington's army at Cambridge of provisions and supplies.

To prevent this scenario, the Americans launched an invasion of Canada in August and September of 1775, which is described in chapter 4. Maps depicting the French and Indian War, in which major battles were fought along the Hudson River–Lake Champlain corridor and at Quebec, would now serve Washington well as he tracked Philip Schuyler and Richard Montgomery's slow progress to Montreal and Benedict Arnold's tortured march through the Maine wilderness to besiege Quebec. Maps of the Maritime Provinces surrounding the mouth of the St. Lawrence River would also help Washington as he launched the fledgling American navy to capture British supply ships heading for Quebec and Boston. Indeed, Washington's preoccupation with the vital northern theater of the war, so evident in his papers, is confirmed in the Yale atlas by the nineteen map sheets (out of forty-three) that depict this region.

While chapters 1 through 3 present a continuous narrative, chapters 4 and 5 describe portions of the Revolutionary War that overlapped the events in chapter 3 and chapter 6: The American invasion of Canada began during the siege of Boston but ended about six months after it was over, during the campaign of 1776 in New York, described at the beginning of chapter 5.

After the British retreated from Boston to Halifax in March 1776, they regrouped and prepared to strike a decisive blow at the mouth of the Hudson. Anticipating this move against the river, the city, and the colony that John Adams had called a "key to the whole continent," Washington brought the army down to New York and, with the help of Montresor's detailed map of Lower Manhattan, fortified the city and its environs against a British attack. Montresor's astonishingly detailed *A Map of the Province of New York*, along with Lewis Evans's indispensable *A General Map of the Middle British Colonies*, helps to illuminate the struggle for the Hudson that unfolded between June and November 1776, the loss of New York City and its environs to the

British juggernaut, the American retreat through New Jersey to the Delaware River, and the victories at Trenton in December and Princeton in January 1777 that revived the American cause, allowing Washington to hole up with the remnants of the Continental army in the mountains of central New Jersey through the spring and into the summer of that year.

Montresor's large map of the province that became New York State also shows the terrain of John Burgoyne and Barry St. Leger's invasion from Canada in the summer and fall of 1777, which culminated in the pivotal British surrender at Saratoga in October. William Howe's misguided decision to head south in July to capture Philadelphia had unhinged the British grand strategy, which called for him to go up the Hudson and meet Burgoyne at Albany. Henry Clinton's capture of the Hudson Highlands forts and the burning of Kingston by General John Vaughan in October were not enough to save Burgoyne from his fate. Maps had helped to encourage and deceive the British in this fiasco. They conveyed the potential for a Hudson strategy, showing the 315-mile river neatly severing the Mid-Atlantic region from New England. At the same time, maps oversimplified the task, failing to convey adequately the vastness of the dense wilderness to be crossed by a heavily encumbered army.[6]

William Scull's map of Pennsylvania helps to illuminate Washington's maneuvers to defend Philadelphia against General William Howe's advancing army in the late summer and early fall of 1777, the siege of the city after the British captured it, and the American retreat to winter quarters at Valley Forge for the brutal winter of 1777–78. The spring and summer of 1778 brought the formal French alliance, and the well-drilled Continental army's strong stand at the Battle of Monmouth after Washington insisted on engaging the British army on its way back from Philadelphia to New York City under its new commander in chief, Sir Henry Clinton—events that can be traced on Montresor's map of the Province of New York. The first joint operation between Washington and a French fleet was stymied by the sandbars at Sandy Hook and was shifted in August to dislodge the British from Newport, Rhode Island, where the thwarted allied attempt can be visualized on *A Map of the Most Inhabited Part of New England*.

As the war in North America settled into a stalemate around the mouth of the Hudson in 1778–79, the British stepped up their attacks on the western frontiers of New York, Pennsylvania, and Virginia, employing irregular troops, Loyalist refugees, and Indian allies. Washington struck back in the summer of 1779 by sending a large expeditionary force under Major General John Sullivan on a scorched-earth campaign against the Iroquois tribes that had sided with the British. His path of destruction—across the terrain on Evans's map of the Middle British Colonies—reduced at least forty villages and vast quantities of crops to ashes, just before one of the worst winters on record. Along with the capture of British posts on the upper Mississippi and Wabash rivers by George Rogers Clark's expedition in 1778–79, Sullivan's devastation of the Iroquois confronted the British with a humanitarian crisis, threw them on the defensive in the Northwest, and opened the door to the westward expansion of the United States after the Revolution.

Faced with these setbacks in the Northwest, and declarations of war by both France and Spain, the British attempted to shift some of the burden of combat to Loyalists in the South, whose numbers had been exaggerated in overly optimistic reports to London. Sir Henry Clinton's capture of Charleston, South Carolina, in May 1780 established a major new base of operations for the British and soon helped to escalate the bitter partisan warfare between Whigs and Loyalists in the South, ongoing since 1775, to greater extremes of brutality.

Chapter 6 tells this overlapping story of the war in the South (which began during the siege of Boston and continued after Yorktown) through Washington's eyes and through some of the maps from the Yale atlas. Though he did not return to the South—to his native Virginia—until the Yorktown campaign in 1781, correspondence with his generals and maps of the region enabled Washington to monitor, and sometimes manage, the war in Virginia, the Carolinas, Georgia, and Florida. From his headquarters on the Hudson, Washington directed threatening maneuvers against the British in New York City, forcing them to dilute their strength in the South. The Franco-American victory at Yorktown in October 1781 did not end the war, and Washington returned to the Hudson early in 1782 to resume his vigil outside British-occupied New York. His plans to reinvade Canada and to recapture New York City with the help of a French fleet never materialized, and by November, provisional articles for a peace treaty with Britain had been signed in Paris.

While waiting for the Treaty of Paris to be finalized in 1783, Washington began exploring the frontiers of New York State, which he had never seen firsthand. Chapter 7 reveals how Washington's postwar vision for the nation's westward expansion evolved along with his patient strategy for dispossessing the Indians of their land. Washington also became a proponent of improving inland navigation—clearing rivers and building canals—in order to unite the eastern states and the western territories by bonds of common commercial interest.

In addition to his desire for a stronger central government and ratification of the Constitution, Washington's two main concerns in these years, which he pursued simultaneously, were his renewed efforts to develop the Potomac River as a route to and from the West and to secure and settle his bounty lands in the Ohio River Valley. In this postwar era, Washington began using a newer set of maps, not in the Yale atlas, which defined the borders of the new nation and provided a more detailed and accurate picture of the western territories.

Chapter 8 chronicles Washington's first term as president, showing how territorial issues—and therefore maps—were at the top of his agenda. With Spain and England both inciting Indian attacks and contesting the new nation's borders in the Southwest and the Northwest, and with France plunging into its own Revolution and on the brink of war with its European neighbors—war that threatened to engulf the United States—Washington's vision of the new nation's unique geographical position bolstered his policy of neutrality, enabling him to steer a course that prevented European domination. While his administration's diplomatic efforts triumphed in relations with the European powers, Washington ultimately resorted to war against the northwestern Indians, launching two disastrous campaigns in an attempt to conquer and pacify the region and appointing Anthony Wayne to lead a third one.

Washington's second term unfolds in chapter 9 with the beheading of King Louis XVI in Paris, the threat of war in Europe becoming a reality, and French ambassador Citizen Edmond Charles Genet attempting to drag the United States into the conflict by commissioning American vessels to prey on British shipping and mustering disgruntled inhabitants of the South and West to attack the Spanish in the Floridas and Louisiana. Washington's policy of neutrality was sorely tested as he faced the possibility that portions of the western territories would break away from the Union.

Amid these crises, Washington found time to begin planning for the emancipation of his own slaves, a scheme in which he envisioned renting out Mount Vernon's farms to individuals who would then hire the slaves as free laborers. Washington's own survey of the Mount Vernon plantation helped him pitch the idea to a prominent agriculturalist in England, and illustrates the various parts of his beloved estate over which he now prepared, for the sake of his plan, to relinquish direct control.

Regional tensions over the excise tax on whiskey erupted into a full-blown rebellion in western Pennsylvania in the middle of Washington's second term, bringing him back to the terrain of his early military career as he inspected the army that would restore order. During this trip, Washington learned that Wayne had been victorious in the Northwest, finally giving the United States control of the region.

Two diplomatic triumphs soon capped Washington's presidency: John Jay's treaty with Britain, leading to the withdrawal of British troops from posts on American soil along the Canadian border, and Thomas Pinckney's treaty with Spain, opening the navigation of the Mississippi River to American commerce. In his Farewell Address, Washington pointed to these achievements as proof that the federal government had worked in the interests of all Americans. He urged the people in turn not to be misled by demagogues who would focus on regional differences to stir local passions, but rather to pull together as one nation.

Washington had steered clear of entanglements with Britain and Spain, but in the process he had infuriated the French, who felt the alliance that had rescued the Americans during the Revolutionary War had been betrayed by the concessions to the English in the Jay Treaty. The mounting tensions with France as Washington left office in 1797 would become the responsibility of the second president, John Adams, but the threat of war would pull Washington back from retirement at Mount Vernon into a public role, as commander of American forces. Washington's selection of the top generals, his organization of the new army, and his strategy for a war with France all reflected his keen sense of geography, with all of its military and political ramifications.

When the diplomacy of President Adams averted war with France, Washington settled back into his routine at Mount Vernon. His own survey of the eight-thousand-acre plantation shows its five farms, the terrain that Washington rode on horseback every day during the last months of his life. This map not only depicts the land to which Washington was so firmly rooted, sentimentally and through his ancestors, it also reveals Washington's legacy, which he spelled out in his will. In writing the will and describing the portions of the plantation each heir would receive, Washington summoned for the last time the skills he had learned as a young surveyor and had used throughout his life. But he also made a radical new departure: Thwarted in his several attempts to free his slaves during his lifetime, Washington emancipated them in his will, an act which put him well ahead of his peers in this regard.

The map Washington drew of Mount Vernon is therefore a kind of self-portrait, revealing the wellspring of his energy and greatness, as well as his limitations as a product of his times. It shows the home that he created in his quest to become a wealthy gentleman, which was also his retreat amid his long labors as a public servant. But this is also the site of Washington's greatest missed opportunity. Had he emancipated his slaves as president, Mount Vernon would have become a great experiment in human freedom, like the new nation itself, and Washington's example might well have put the institution of slavery on the road to extinction much sooner.

Had this happened, Washington would have headed off his greatest fear, which materialized sixty years after his death, when the "*geographical* discriminations" he had warned of in his Farewell Address, "*Northern* and *Southern*," caused the dismemberment of the Union, and the Potomac, the river Washington had labored so quixotically to establish as the tie that would bind the Atlantic to the West, became the great divider in the eastern theater of the Civil War. The War Between the States would call forth the transcendent powers of another indispensable man, suited to his own times and destined, unlike Washington, to be the Great Emancipator. Washington had been transcendent in his own time, liberating the nation from the yoke of colonialism, laying the foundations of republican government, and rising above the fray to preserve the great experiment from ruin at the hands of political factions within and foreign powers at the borders. Here are the maps that accompanied Washington on this journey, informing his decisions, and inspiring his vision of America's future.

CHAPTER ONE

VIRGINIA, BARBADOS, AND

THE OHIO COUNTRY

"I, reposing special trust and confidence in the ability, conduct, and fidelity of you . . . George Washington, have appointed you my express messenger," wrote Governor Robert Dinwiddie of Virginia, on October 30, 1753. "I have received information of a body of French forces being assembled in a hostile manner on the River Ohio, intending by force of arms to erect certain forts on the said river, within this territory and contrary to the peace and dignity of our sovereign the King of Great Britain." Thus, twenty-one-year-old George Washington's military career was set in motion, with a commission from Dinwiddie and instructions to deliver the governor's letter to the French commanding officer, demanding the withdrawal of his forces from the Ohio country. This diplomatic exercise was also cover for a reconnaissance mission: Washington was to bring back not only a reply from the French, but intelligence on the size and disposition of French forces, their forts, and their lines of communication from Canada. (See *A General Map of North America*, page 20, and *Detail #1*, opposite.)

The map contains the following cartouche text:

A
GENERAL MAP OF
NORTH AMERICA;
In which is Exprefs'd
The feveral New Roads, Forts, Engagements, &c.
taken from Actual Surveys and Observations
Made in the Army employ'd there,
From the Year 1754, to 1761:
Drawn by the late JOHN ROCQUE, Topographer to
His MAJESTY.

CARTES GENERALES DE
L'AMERIQUE SEPTENTRIONALE;
En les quelles font exprimés
Les Nouvelles Routes, Forts, Battailles, &c. d'après
les Observations qui on ete fuites depuis
l'An 1754, jusqu'à l'An 1761:
Recuellies par feu JEAN ROCQUE, Topographe de
Sa MAJESTE BRITANNIQUE, &c.

ABOVE: *A General Map of North America* (southern half): Published in London by John Rocque in 1762, Washington used it later, but it nonetheless shows the extent of European knowledge about North America in this decade from 1751 to 1761 and how the continent was viewed by the British and Americans. (For the northern half, see pages 2–3.)

PAGE 18: *A General Map of North America, Detail #1:* French territory in North America, controlled through settlement or through Indian alliances, extended from the Gulf of St. Lawrence (upper right), down through the Great Lakes, the Ohio Valley, and the Mississippi Valley to the Gulf of Mexico (upper left to lower left). The British colonists, between the Atlantic seaboard and the Appalachian Mountains, viewed the Mississippi as their western border, as mapped in their founding charters (center to lower left).

TOP: George Washington at age twenty-five, by Charles Willson Peale.

ABOVE: Thomas, Lord Fairfax.

OPPOSITE, TOP: *A Map of the Most Inhabited Part of Virginia, Detail #1*: Mount Vernon (labeled *Washington*) is just south of Little Hunting Creek (up the Potomac River from Chesapeake Bay, north of the Occoquan River). Belvoir (not labeled) was on the neck of land south of Dogney Creek and north of the Occoquan River.

OPPOSITE, BOTTOM: *A Map of . . . Virginia, Detail #2*: The Northern Neck Proprietary extended northwest from the Chesapeake, ending at the western border of Maryland, where the North Branch of the Potomac converges with the straight line labeled *Lord Fairfax his Boundary Line* (upper left, where the source of the Potomac is labeled *Springhead*). The Rapidan and Rappahannock rivers (bottom) form the rest of the southern boundary line. Washington was appointed surveyor of Culpeper County (bottom center) but did most of his surveying in Frederick County, across the Blue Ridge, in the Shenandoah and Cacapon valleys (top left and center).

PAGES 24–25: *A Map of the Most Inhabited Part of Virginia:* This map in Yale's *George Washington Atlas* is dated 1775, indicating that he acquired it during the Revolution. (He purchased another copy in 1776 as part of the *General Topography*.) However, earlier versions, published in 1751 and 1753, were available to Washington at the end of his surveying career and for his early military expeditions.

Washington's mission in 1753, and his larger expedition to the frontier the following year, would stir up the smoldering territorial competition between France and Britain in the Ohio River Valley and help ignite a momentous contest for empire, the French and Indian War. For the first time a colonial war beginning in North America would spread to Europe—where it was called the Seven Years' War—and ultimately across the globe to Africa, India, and the Philippines. While victorious over the French and their Indian allies, the British would incur a staggering war debt, leading to efforts to tax the American colonies—and ultimately to the American Revolution.[2]

Governor Dinwiddie's selection of Washington for a critical and dangerous mission in October 1753 was the product of powerful family connections, combined with Washington's vigorous efforts on his own behalf. Having just secured appointment, with an aggressive letter-writing campaign, as one of Virginia's four adjutant generals, the hardy Major Washington had then volunteered for the five-hundred-mile journey to and from the frontier in the rain and snow of the oncoming winter. His physical strength, confidence, and ambition made his lack of diplomatic experience, or fluency in French, or even a proper British education, seem unimportant.

Washington's half brothers, Lawrence and Augustine, were members of the Ohio Company of Virginia, a consortium of twenty wealthy planters speculating in land on the frontier, which had given Washington surveying work a few years earlier and had given Dinwiddie a share in the company, a welcome gift, considering his meager salary. (Technically, he was lieutenant governor; the absentee governor collected the large salary in England and paid Dinwiddie to do his job in America, a common arrangement in the British colonies.) The company welcomed the governor's attentiveness to its interests, which were now his own.[3]

After their father died in 1743, when George was eleven, Lawrence treated him like a son. Lawrence married Ann Fairfax, daughter of Colonel William Fairfax, of Belvoir on the Potomac. William was the agent for his cousin Thomas, Lord Fairfax, who owned the Northern Neck Proprietary, a vast grant from the Crown—roughly the size of Massachusetts—of all the land between the Potomac and Rappahannock rivers from Chesapeake Bay to the crest of the Appalachian Mountains. From his youth, Washington was a frequent visitor at Belvoir with Lawrence, who had inherited the estate a few miles north, on Little Hunting Creek, which he named Mount Vernon, after Admiral Edward Vernon, his commander on the disastrous British expedition against the Spanish at Cartagena in 1741. (See *A Map of the Most Inhabited Part of Virginia*, pages 24–25, and *Detail #1* and *Detail #2*.)[4]

Born on February 22, 1732, George Washington was the first of Augustine and Mary Washington's six children and grew up on Ferry Farm, across the Rappahannock River from Fredericksburg, Virginia. (His siblings were Betty, Samuel, John Augustine, Charles, and Mildred, who died in infancy.) George was a fourth-generation American, his paternal great-grandfather having emigrated from England and settled at Bridges Creek on the Potomac River (southeast of Fredericksburg and directly east of Port Royal). When Augustine died in 1743, he also owned a larger plantation at Pope's Creek, which included the Bridges Creek property, and which he willed to the second surviving son of his first marriage, George's half brother Augustine Washington. George ultimately inherited Ferry Farm, three lots in Fredericksburg, ten slaves, half of a tract of land on Deep Run Creek (the other half going to his brother Samuel), and a one-fifth share of his father's remaining property. George's mother was to live on the Deep Run tract, northwest of Fredericksburg. (See *A Map of . . . Virginia, Detail #1*.)[5]

A MAP of
the most INHABITED part of
VIRGINIA
containing the whole PROVINCE of
MARYLAND
with Part of
PENSILVANIA, NEW JERSEY AND NORTH CAROLINA
Drawn by
Joshua Fry & Peter Jefferson
in 1775.

To the Right Honourable, George Dunk Earl of Halifax, First Lord Commissioner
and to the Rest of the Right Honourable and Honourable Commissioners for Trade and Plantations
This Map is most humbly Inscribed to their Lordships,
By their Lordships
Most Obedient & most devoted humble Servt. Thos. Jefferys

The Line between Virginia and North-Carolina from the Sea
to Peters Creek was Surveyd in 1728. by the Honble Willm Byrd,
Willm Dandridge and Richard Fitzwilliams, Commissioners;
and Mr Alexander Irvine and Mr Willm Mayo, Surveyors.

Printed for Robt. Sayer at No 53 in Fleet Street, & Thos. Jefferys at the Corner of St Martins Lane, Charing Cross, London.

A conjectural rendering of George Washington's birthplace.

Washington was introduced to his first profession, and to the wilderness, at the age of sixteen, when he accompanied William Fairfax's son, twenty-four-year-old George Fairfax (another member of the Ohio Company), on a surveying trip for Lord Fairfax, which took them across the Blue Ridge to the Shenandoah Valley and beyond. Washington was undoubtedly impressed that two years earlier George Fairfax had helped survey the boundary line of the Northern Neck, and had proudly carved his initials in a tree at the source of the Potomac. (See *A Map of . . . Virginia, Detail #2*, page 23.) The two Georges would remain friends for the next forty years. They set off from Belvoir on March 11, 1748. (See *A Map of . . . Virginia, Detail #3*.) On the third day, as they rode westward toward Lord Fairfax's home, Washington began recording his love affair with the land. "We went through most beautiful groves of sugar trees and spent the best part of the day in admiring the trees and richness of the land," he wrote in his diary.[6]

Washington learned the trade of surveying: walking a tract of land, determining its boundary lines, and reading their bearings from the dial of a circumferentor, a magnetic compass mounted on a tripod. Two chainmen accompanied the surveyor and measured the boundaries using long chains, while a marker carved notches in trees to establish these lines. In his field notes, the surveyor recorded the boulders, trees, or other features that defined the corners of the tract, and he produced a plat, a small map that was part of the final survey document.[7]

Washington also got a taste of the rugged frontier conditions he would encounter in far greater doses in the future. After a night on a bed of straw full of lice and fleas, he resolved to sleep outdoors by the campfire. A night in Frederick Town on "a good feather bed with clean sheets" made him appreciate the comforts of civilization, while the journey built up his naturally strong constitution. They moved north to the Potomac and saw the "Famed Warm Springs" before crossing the swollen river in canoes while their horses swam. On the Maryland side they traveled "all the day in a continued rain to Colonel Cresap's right against the mouth of the South Branch." Thomas Cresap was a well-known frontiersman and one of the founders of the Ohio Company of Virginia. Their route, Washington complained, was "the worst road that ever was trod by man or beast." (*See A Map of . . . Virginia, Detail #4*, page 29.)[8]

Some thirty Indian warriors arrived at Cresap's with a scalp and performed a some-times "comical" war dance after the surveyors served them liquor. Washington was beginning to learn the customary ways of interacting with Indians—the gifts, liquor, and long speeches—that he would have to master in competing for their allegiance first

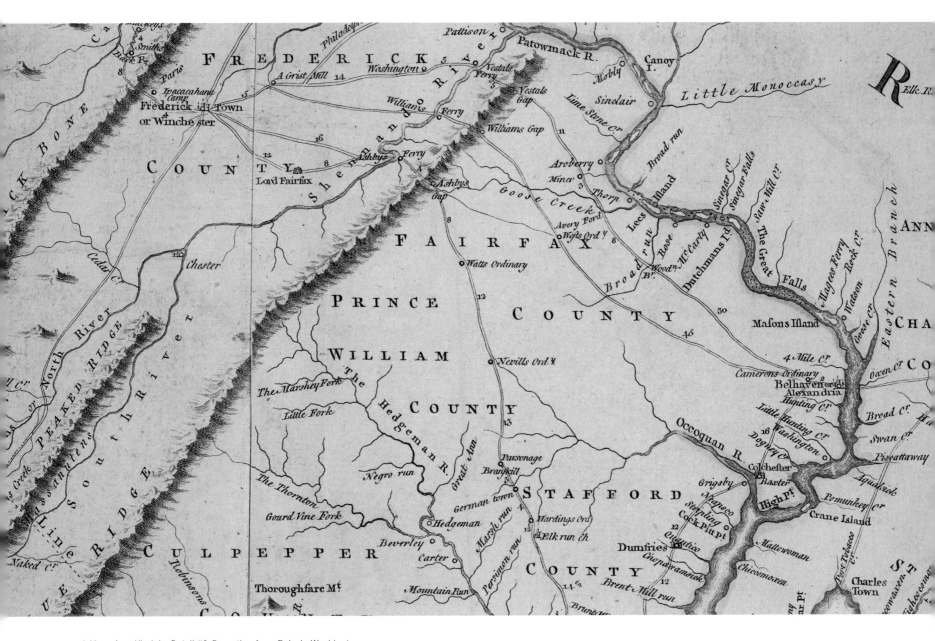

A Map of . . . Virginia, Detail #3: Departing from Belvoir, Washington and George Fairfax crossed the Occoquan River at the ferry before heading north and west to reach George Neville's Ordinary, a tavern in Prince William County (*Nevills Ord.y*) near the home of James Genn, an experienced wilderness surveyor, who joined them the next day. They proceeded across the Blue Ridge at Ashby's Gap and spent the night at Captain John Ashby's ferry house on the Shenandoah River. On the third day they rode westward to "his Lordships quarter" (the house labeled *Lord Fairfax*), where he would establish his residence a year later.

TOP: Gunter's chain, devised by Englishman Edmund Gunter in the early 1600s, remained the most widely used measuring instrument for surveyors in the eighteenth century.

ABOVE: American inventor, astronomer, mathematician, surveyor, and creator of scientific instruments David Rittenhouse made this surveying compass for George Washington.

against the French and twenty years later against the British. Moving west from Cresap's along the Potomac, the surveyors arrived at "the mouth of Paterson's Creek" before heading south to survey various lots all the way down to the Boundary Line of the Northern Neck. On March 31 Washington noted that he had surveyed a particular lot himself. The following night, Washington cheated death, as he would many times in his life, when the straw the men were sleeping on caught fire, and he was "luckily preserved by one of our men's waking" to warn the rest. [9]

Ten days later, Washington and Fairfax went hungry all day when their provisions ran out, and their supplier never arrived. It was a foretaste of one of Washington's greatest trials throughout his military career: struggling to feed his men in the face of countless logistical hurdles and disappointments with quartermasters. The next day the young surveyors headed home, traveling north and east for forty miles "over hills and mountains" to the Cacapon River and then to Frederick Town. They crossed the Blue Ridge at Williams Gap and stopped at West's Ordinary. The following day, after more than a month in the field, Washington wrote that "Mr. Fairfax got safe home and I myself safe to my brother's." (See *A Map of . . . Virginia, Detail #4*, and *Detail #3*, page 27.)[10]

Apparently through the patronage of Lord Fairfax, and through William Fairfax, a member of the governor's council, Washington was appointed surveyor for Culpeper County (in the Northern Neck) the following year, at the age of seventeen. Surveying was a respectable profession, practiced largely by Virginia gentlemen, in which Washington could earn more cash income than most planters, while working only a few months a year. The work of surveyors in the rest of Virginia was confined to the counties to which they were appointed, but Lord Fairfax allowed surveyors in the Northern Neck to make surveys anywhere within the Proprietary. And since Culpeper County was already largely settled, Washington made only one survey there before heading across the Blue Ridge to the Shenandoah and Cacapon valleys in Frederick County, where droves of settlers and speculators were in need of his services, and where he could acquire tracts of frontier land for himself.[11] (See *A Map of . . . Virginia, Detail #2*, page 23.)

When Lawrence was unable to shake off a persistent lung ailment, Washington accompanied him on repeated trips to the baths at Berkeley Springs in search of a cure. (See *A Map of Virginia, Detail #4*, upper right, labeled *Medicinal Springs*.) On these trips Washington was able to continue making surveys, including some for Lawrence, of land in the vicinity. "I hope that your cough is much mended since I saw you last," Washington wrote to Lawrence on May 5, 1749. "If so, likewise hope you have given over thoughts of leaving Virginia."

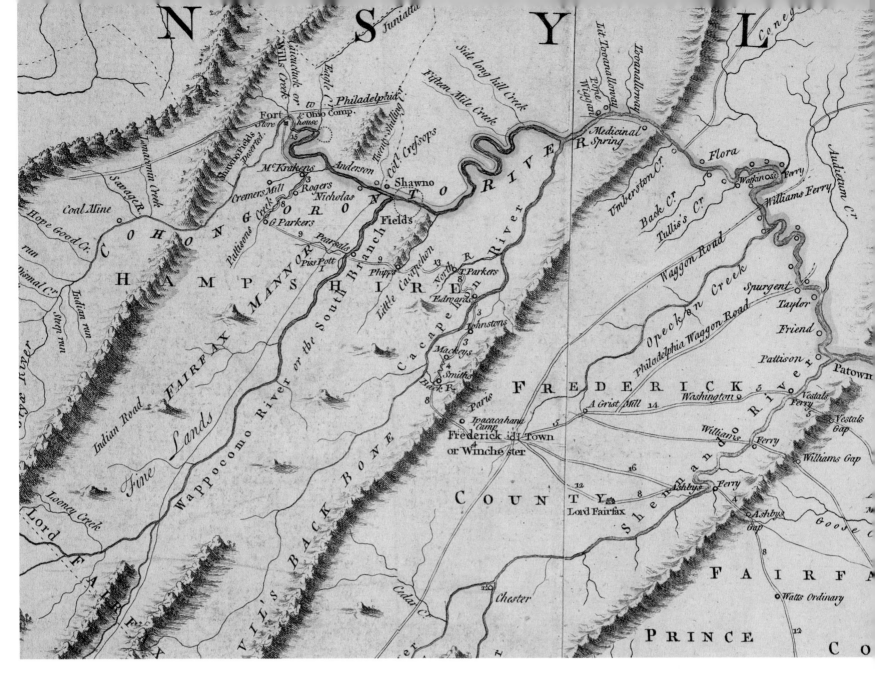

But Lawrence evidently had tuberculosis, and his condition did not improve. That summer he went to England to see more doctors. Advised to seek a change of climate, Lawrence returned to Virginia and then traveled to Barbados in the fall of 1751. Despite the financial sacrifice entailed in putting his lucrative surveying career on hold, Washington did not hesitate to go as Lawrence's companion.

On September 28, they embarked on a ship at the mouth of the Potomac, and spent more than a month at sea. Washington recorded his observations of the wind and weather and the ship's rigging in his diary, along with descriptions of the fish they caught for dinner. At last on November 2 came "the cry of land at four a.m.," Washington wrote. "We quitted our beds with surprise and found the land plainly appearing at about three leagues distance when by our reckonings we should have been nearly 150 leagues to the windward." Despite the captain's miscalculation of their course, by good fortune they did not bypass the island, which might have kept them at sea for another month. (See *A General Map of North America, Detail #2*, page 31.)[12]

They arrived in Bridgetown on November 3, and the following day had a visit from "an eminent physician" who assured Lawrence that his condition was curable and advised that he find lodging in the countryside, instead of in town. After leaving Bridgetown, Washington wrote rapturously in his diary about "the beautiful prospects which on every side presented to our view—the fields of cane, corn, fruit trees, etc. in a delightful green."

Washington's attraction to military affairs—and an inclination to view topography in that light—was already evident in several diary entries. "Dined at the fort with some ladies," he wrote, and went on to describe the thirty-six cannon mounted in the interior and the two fascine batteries outside, making a total of fifty-one guns. Washington also noted that all around the island "large entrenchments have been cast up wherever it's possible for an enemy to land." The island's hilly terrain favored the defenders, combining with the trenches to make Barbados "one entire fortification." Washington noted that the island had mostly extremes of rich and poor, with virtually no middle class, a situation reinforced by the legal requirement that the rich provide for the maintenance of one militiaman for every ten acres they owned. This feudal arrangement meant that these dependent individuals "can't but be very poor," Washington concluded. The proper way to raise, train, and maintain the militia in America would become a central concern for Washington throughout his career.

A Map of . . . Virginia, Detail #4: Traveling northwest from Lord Fairfax's home to Frederick Town (center) and then north to the Potomac, the surveying party visited Warm Springs (*Medicinal Spring*, upper right) before crossing the river to Maryland and heading west to the home of Colonel Cresap (*Col.l Cressops*) at the fork of the North and South branches of the Potomac (top center). In 1750 the Ohio Company would build a fort and storehouse at Wills Creek (*Fort and Ohio Comp. store house*, upper left), later the site of Fort Cumberland.

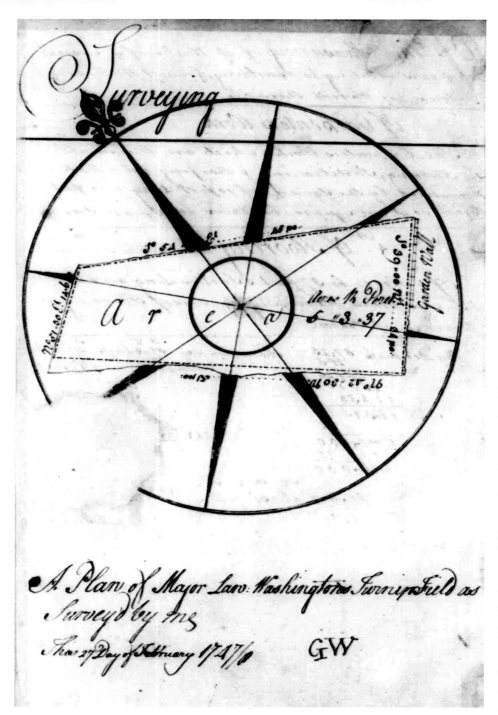

ABOVE: George Washington's survey of Lawrence Washington's turnip field, February 27, 1747.

After making the social rounds of the island's gentry for two weeks, on November 17 Washington wrote that he "was strongly attacked with the small pox," which kept him confined for almost a month—but gave him immunity for the rest of his life. A week after he recovered, Washington began packing up to go home to Virginia, and on December 22 he bid farewell to Lawrence. Since Lawrence's condition was not improving, he was advised to proceed to Bermuda, where the climate might be even more conducive to his recovery. Washington was to bring Lawrence's wife to join him there, assuming that he was in better health.[13]

Washington again spent almost five weeks at sea on the return voyage, enduring the turbulence of stormy weather and "mountainous" seas. Finally, at sunrise on January 26, 1752, the ship sailed past Cape Henry, reaching the mouth of the York River that night, where it was met by a pilot boat. Arriving in Williamsburg for the first time, Washington called on Virginia governor Robert Dinwiddie and presented him with letters from Barbados. "He inquired kindly after the health of my brother and invited me to stay and dine," Washington noted. This first encounter boded well for their relationship—which two years later would put Washington at the flashpoint of Britain's territorial contest with the French in North America.

Washington proceeded from Williamsburg to his half brother Augustine's home at Pope's Creek, before heading to Fredericksburg and then to Mount Vernon, where he delivered Lawrence's letters to his wife, Ann.[14] Lawrence remained in Barbados for three more months and then moved on to Bermuda, but his health continued to decline. By June he was back at Mount Vernon, where he died on the 26th. On his deathbed he signed a release "in consideration of the natural love and affection which he hath and doth bear unto his loving brother George Washington," giving Washington unrestricted title to the three half-acre lots in Fredericksburg. Two years later, Washington would inherit Mount Vernon as well.[15]

Having inherited ten slaves from his father, Washington received eighteen with Mount Vernon and proceeded to buy and rent still more. Like most Virginia slaveholders, he kept them in abject poverty, housing, feeding, and clothing them as cheaply as possible. And for the next twenty years, until his convictions began to change, Washington showed no compunction about buying and selling slaves or inflicting harsh punishments. In at least one case he combined the two, shipping a slave named Tom off to the West Indies for sale as punishment for being "both a rogue and a runaway." He would fetch a good price, however, Washington told the ship's captain, since he was "exceedingly strong and healthy and good at the hoe." The captain should keep Tom handcuffed until they were at sea, Washington advised. Having calculated Tom's value in goods from the Islands, Washington asked for a hogshead of molasses, one of rum, a barrel of limes, a pot of tamarinds, two of "mixed sweetmeats," and the rest in "good old spirits."[16]

Washington had resumed his career as a surveyor when he returned from Barbados but saw that his opportunities would eventually be limited by Lord Fairfax's control of the Northern Neck. While surveying would continue to play a role throughout Washington's life, he decided to leave it as a profession. Lawrence was a military man, and Washington was inspired to follow in his footsteps. In addition to going on the Cartagena expedition, Lawrence had been the adjutant general of Virginia, a post that conferred the rank of major and responsibility for the training of the colony's militia. In the months before Lawrence's death, Washington had learned that the post would be divided among four districts and promptly asked the governor for the Northern Neck assignment. Instead, he was given the southern district, the area below the James River. Commissioned a major in December 1752, with a handsome salary of one hundred pounds a year, Washington continued to lobby aggressively for the Northern Neck

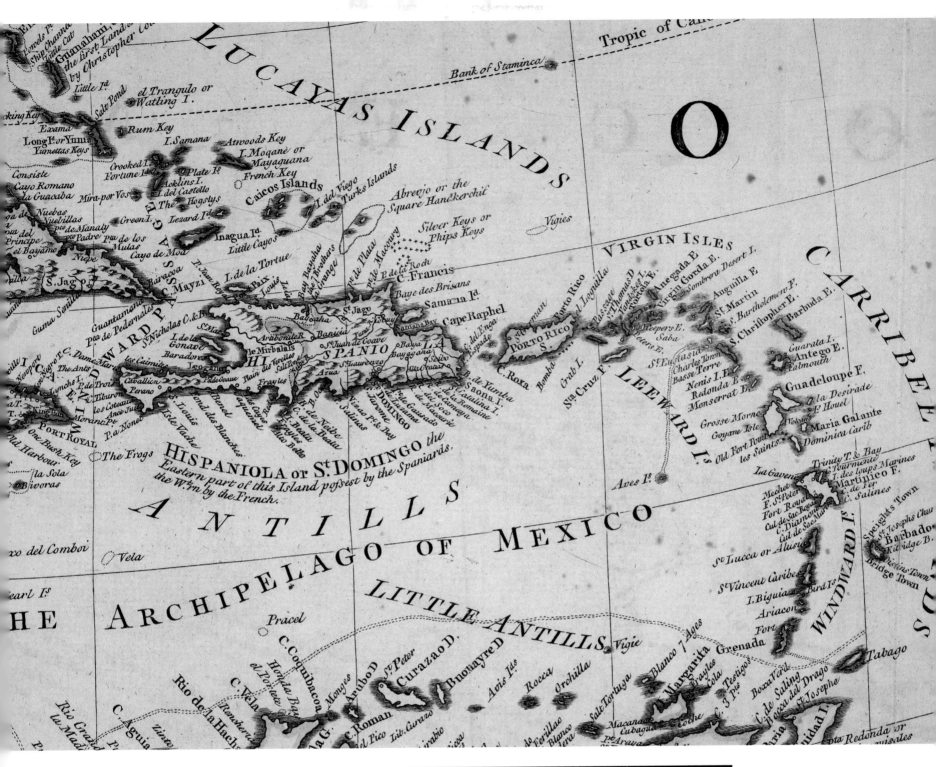

A General Map of North America, Detail #2: Washington and his half brother Lawrence arrived at Bridgetown, Barbados (*Barbadoes*, lower right) in early November 1751. The French islands are shown in green and the English in pink, their names followed by an *F* or an *E* accordingly. Spanish islands are in yellow. This was Washington's only trip abroad in his entire life. However, the West Indies would play a vital role in the American Revolution as a drain on British resources and a channel for supplies from the French and the Dutch to the Continental army.

RIGHT: Lawrence Washington.

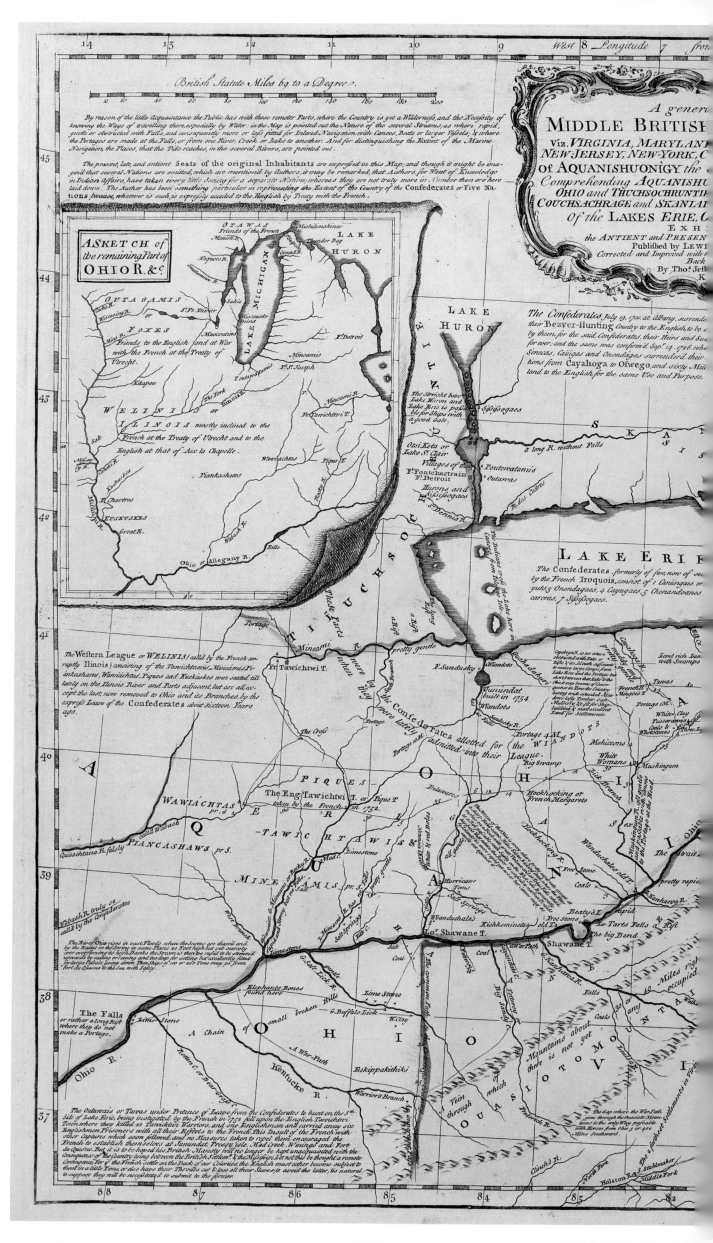

A General Map of the Middle British Colonies (1775): Lewis Evans published the first version of this map in 1755, in the midst of the French and Indian War and Washington's career as a Virginia Militia colonel, but too late for use in his earliest campaigns. (Washington evidently owned a copy of the 1755 edition, since he mentioned it in a letter to Adam Stephen on August 5, 1756.) This copy, in Yale's *George Washington Atlas*, is from the 1775 edition and apparently served Washington well during and after the Revolution. (In 1776 he purchased yet another copy, as part of the *General Topography*.)

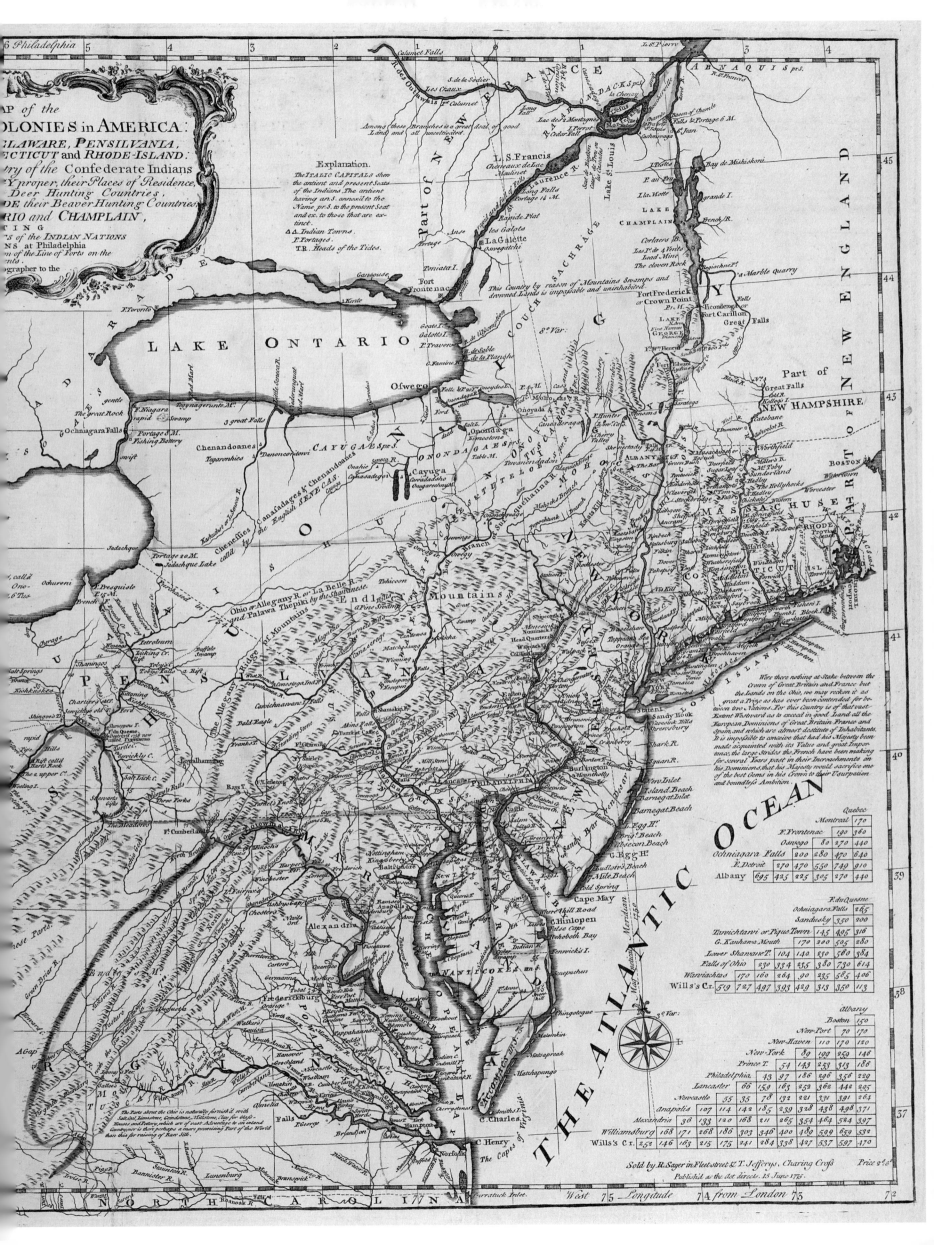

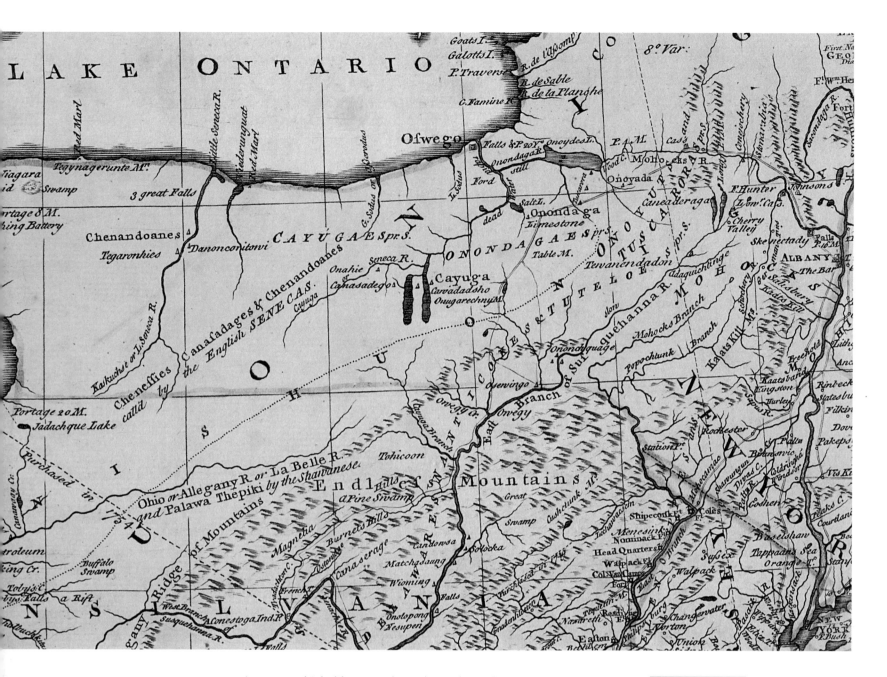

A General Map of the Middle British Colonies, Detail #1: The territory of the Six Nations is indicated by their names in capital letters south and east of Lake Ontario. From east to west: *MOHOCKS* (southeast of *Mohocks R.* and west of Albany); *TUSCARORAS* (the name curving upward across the Mohawk River); *ONOYUTS* (the Oneidas, southeast of *Onoydes L.* and the village of *Onoyada*); *ONONDAGAES* (south of the village and council fire at Onondaga, indicated by a triangular icon, for a teepee); *CAYUGAES*; and southwest of them the *SENECAS.*

appointment, which, like most things he set his sights on, he eventually received.[17]

In the summer and fall of 1753, Dinwiddie warned the Board of Trade in London about the French encroachments in the Ohio country. The new governor of Canada, the marquis de Duquesne, had drawn up plans the previous year to extend the French military presence southward with a series of forts that would dominate the Ohio River. Two thousand troops under Pierre Paul de la Malgue, sieur de Marin, had left Montreal early in 1753 and by midsummer had made significant progress in establishing a network of military and trading posts. The British asserted their own claim to the Ohio country on the basis of agreements concluded with the Iroquois League in 1744 and 1752. Acting on those agreements, the Ohio Company of Virginia had begun its own fortified posts on the Monongahela and at the Forks of the Ohio, thus provoking the belligerent French response. Through the secretary of state, the earl of Holderness, Dinwiddie received instructions to investigate the reports of French incursions and, if they were true, to demand that the French depart. If the invaders persisted, they were to be expelled "by force of arms."[18]

As Washington would soon learn firsthand, the contest for the Ohio Valley was not simply the clash of two European empires in the New World, but rather a delicate balance-of-power equation in which a third major power had been buffering the other two and, until now, sustaining a precarious peace. Washington was about to step into a complex, bewildering world of Indian alliances and agendas that he would have to struggle mightily to navigate and control in order to carry out his mission.

Direct French encroachment in the Ohio country was a recent development. For fifty years France had relied on a third imperial power, the Iroquois League, to keep the British out. Instead of sinking enormous resources into building forts and sustaining a military occupation, the French acknowledged Iroquois ownership of the area and profited from exclusive trading relationships with the local Indians. The League, also known as the Six Nations, was composed of the Mohawks, Oneidas, Onondagas, Cayugas, Senecas, and later the Tuscaroras, and was based in what is now upstate New York. However, by raiding distant Indian villages, the League at various times dominated the entire northeastern quarter of North America,

from the Midwest to northern New England and from Canada to South Carolina. (See *A General Map of the Middle British Colonies*, pages 32–33, and *Detail #1*.)[19]

During the colonial wars of the late 1600s, the Iroquois had found the English to be an undependable ally and the French a dangerous enemy, so in 1701 they signed separate treaties with each, making conflicting promises that avoided an exclusive alliance with either side. The Iroquois acted as a neutral party to the extent that it suited their interests; they also covertly aggravated tensions between the British and French, weakening these rivals while continuing to reap rewards from them—European-manufactured goods, firearms, ammunition, and other supplies. Geographically, the domain of Iroquoia, including the Ohio country, provided a buffer zone between New France and the English colonies; this, combined with the Iroquois' political maneuvering, ensured that during the first half of the eighteenth century neither the British nor the French gained a decisive military advantage in North America.[20]

At various times, the Iroquois had proved useful first to the Dutch and later to the British in putting down Indian uprisings in their colonies. Fearing unrest in Pennsylvania in the 1720s and '30s, as European settlers arrived in droves, James Logan, the agent of the Penn family, had Pennsylvania recognize the Iroquois as diplomatic spokesmen for the Delawares, Shawnees, and other Indians living in the province, effectively turning these independent tribes into feudal subjects of the League. This added layer of control also enabled William Penn's heirs to abandon their father's policy of fair-dealing with the local Indians and dispossess them of their land in short order.

The Iroquois sold the local Indians' land out from under them to the Penn brothers, who then resold it to white settlers at a princely profit. The League expected the Delawares and Shawnees to consolidate their settlements by moving from the eastern edge to the center of the province—from the Delaware Valley to the Susquehanna Valley—and many did so. Nearly three thousand of them, however, kept moving westward, beyond the

A General Map of the Middle British Colonies, Detail #2: In the Ohio country, the Shawnees who migrated from Pennsylvania established towns near the confluence of the Ohio and Great Kanawha rivers (*Shawane T.* and *Lower Shawane T.*, bottom left). The Delawares are indicated north of Lower Shawnee Town (halfway to Lake Erie), just west of the Scioto River. Northeast of the Delawares is a Mingo village (*Mingoes T.*, on the Cuyahoga River, south of Lake Erie).

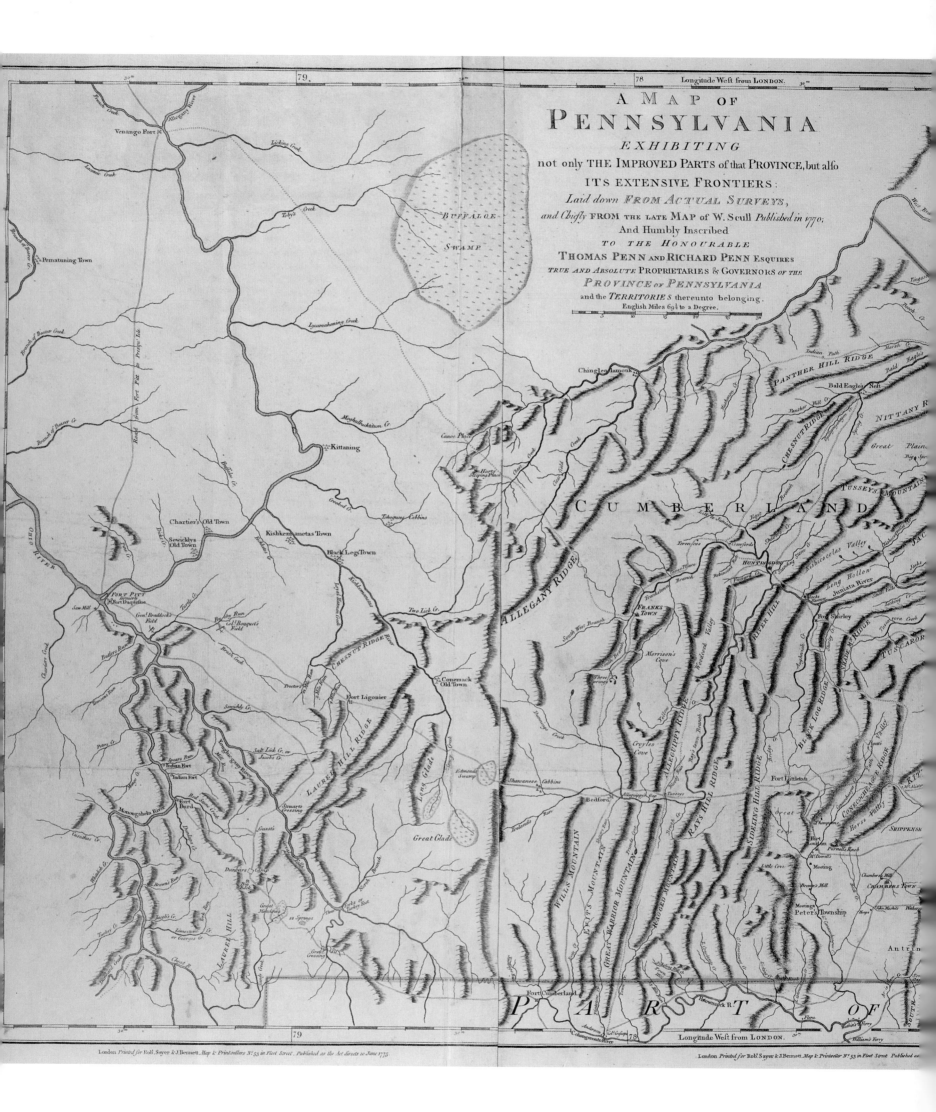

A Map of Pennsylvania: Based on William Scull's map of 1770, this map from
Yale's *George Washington Atlas* is dated 1775. While Washington did not acquire
it until the Revolution, it is helpful for understanding his early military career
because of its clear depiction of key points in western Pennsylvania.

Allegheny Mountains to the Forks of the Ohio (the future site of Pittsburgh). Delawares, Shawnees, and Mingos (western Senecas), they were seeking independence from the powerful chiefs of the Iroquois League and refuge from the wave of white settlement rolling through Pennsylvania. In the Ohio country they hoped to stake out neutral terrain that would give them autonomy both from the British to the east and from the French to the north and west. The Iroquois were initially content to let them go, since the presence of subject peoples in the Ohio country could be seen as confirmation of the League's dominion there. (See *A General Map of the Middle British Colonies, Detail #2*, page 35.)[21]

However, the exodus of Indians from Pennsylvania was soon followed by whites, eager to do business with them, trading for the abundant furs of deer, beaver, and bear in this newly settled area. Then, during King George's War (1744–48), the British capture of Louisburg, the French citadel town at the mouth of the St. Lawrence River, choked off the flow of French goods to their trading posts

in the interior, and traders from Pennsylvania aggressively expanded into the Ohio Valley to meet the demand. The most successful of them was George Croghan, an Irishman who established various trading posts, including one at Logstown, eighteen miles west of the Forks of the Ohio. These British posts attracted the Indians, drawing them away from the French post at Fort Detroit. Moreover, the Delawares and other Ohio Valley Indians began to show their independence from the Iroquois by initiating direct diplomatic relations with the Pennsylvania authorities. (See *A General Map of the Middle British Colonies, Detail #2*, page 35, upper right. The Forks of the Ohio is where the Allegheny and Monongahela rivers flow together to form the Ohio River.)[22]

The League knew it had to reassert its authority and stem the influx of British traders in order to forestall French military intervention in the Ohio Valley. They appointed a regent for the Ohio Indians, a special chief who was to act as their sole diplomatic representative. However, they immediately undermined his stature and

A Map of Pennsylvania, Detail #1: The Ohio Company built a fort and storehouse at Wills Creek, on the Maryland side of the Potomac just below the Pennsylvania border (lower right, labeled *Fort Cumberland*, built later) and a storehouse at Red Stone Creek on the Monongahela (center left, labeled *Fort Burd*, built later). Gist's plantation (*Guest's*) is east of the Monongahela at the head of Red Stone Creek.

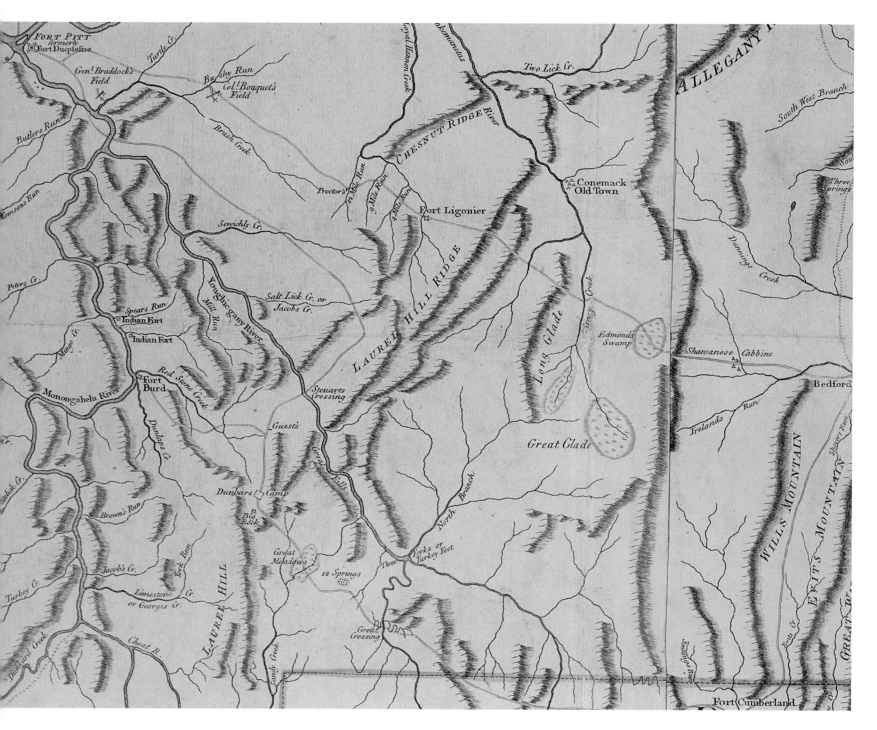

influence by insisting that any treaties he negotiated would have to be approved by the League Council at Onondaga. The regent's name was Tanaghrisson, but for his lack of full authority he would be known mockingly as "the Half-King." Further thwarting the League's plans was the fact that the Half-King needed a steady stream of trade goods to bestow on the Ohio Indian chiefs in order to win their loyalty, and the people best positioned to supply him with such gifts were British traders like Croghan from Pennsylvania, and a group from Virginia that had emerged in the last few years and posed a serious threat to the French: the Ohio Company of Virginia.

The Ohio Company was formed in 1744 by a group of prominent Virginia gentlemen and London merchants eager for land speculation and trade with the Indians in the upper Ohio Valley. Led by Thomas Lee, the charter members were mostly from northern Virginia, where Lord Fairfax's Proprietary forced them to seek lands further west. Throughout Virginia, pressure for westward expansion was also created by the cultivation of tobacco, which depleted the nutrients in the soil, and by the natural growth of the slave population, so the Ohio Company immediately faced opposition from other parts of the colony as well as from competing speculators in Maryland and Pennsylvania.

However, the company did have a stroke of luck in its first year: One of its members was appointed to the Virginia delegation attending a major conference with the Iroquois at Lancaster, Pennsylvania, where the League bartered away its remaining claims to land along the Allegheny Mountains. After the conference, the Virginians asserted the right to set up trading posts around the Forks of the Ohio and send families to settle the area.

The Ohio Company's immediate plans were put on hold by King George's War and by Governor William Gooch (Dinwiddie's predecessor) and his council, who rejected the company's first petition for royal support. John Hanbury, a London merchant and member of the company, appealed directly to the government in London, and in March 1749, the Privy Council instructed Gooch to grant the company two hundred thousand acres in the Ohio Valley. If the company fulfilled its promise to promote trade with the Indians and settle one hundred families on the land, an additional three hundred thousand acres would be granted. These half-million acres lay along the Ohio between the Kanawha and Monongahela rivers.

In 1750 the Ohio Company set to work, commissioning frontiersmen, including Christopher Gist and William Trent, to build storehouses at Wills Creek and Red Stone Creek and to cut a road through the woods that would connect them—and ultimately link Virginia to the Forks of the Ohio. The frontiersmen were also instructed to identify and survey sites for the settlers. Gist also built a plantation between Wills Creek and Red Stone Creek, which helped establish trade and diplomatic relations with

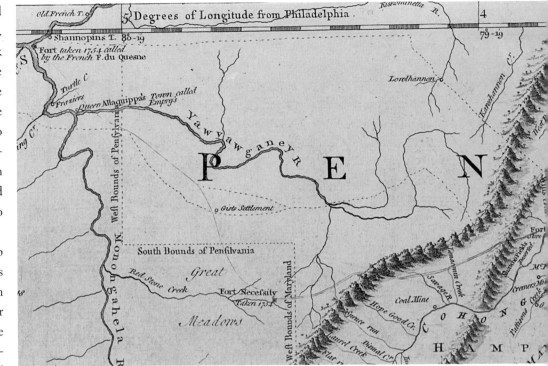

the Ohio Indians. The following year, Dinwiddie was appointed lieutenant governor. A staunch proponent of British authority and westward expansion, and a member of the Ohio Company, Dinwiddie became its most powerful advocate. In 1752 he helped arrange a conference at Logstown that secured permission from the Indians for the company to build a fort at the Forks of the Ohio. Under orders from Dinwiddie, Trent began work on the site. This British incursion at the Forks, combined with the construction of the fort at Red Stone Creek, convinced Duquesne it was time to secure the area with French troops and forts, provoking Dinwiddie to respond in turn. (See *A Map of Pennsylvania*, pages 36–37, and *Detail #1*.)[23]

On October 31, 1753, the day he received his orders from Dinwiddie, Washington set out from Williamsburg to deliver the governor's letter to the French commander. Stopping along the way to hire Jacob Van Braam (a Dutchman) as his French interpreter and to procure supplies for the expedition, Washington arrived at Wills Creek almost two weeks later, on November 14. There, Washington hired Christopher Gist as their guide, and four other men as servants. The following day, the party of seven men left the settled area behind and plunged into the cold, wet wilderness to the northwest, heading toward the home of John Frazier, a trader who lived on Turtle Creek. "The excessive rains and vast quantity of snow which had fallen prevented our reaching Mr. Frazier's" until the 22nd, Washington wrote. (See *A Map of . . . Virginia, Detail #5*.)

Arriving at the confluence of the Allegheny and Monongahela rivers, ten miles north of Frazier's, Washington judged the "land in the Fork" to be "extremely well situated for a fort, as it has the absolute command of both rivers." Shingiss, king of the Delawares, lived two miles from the Forks and accompanied Washington's party to Logstown for a meeting with other Indian leaders.

A Map of . . . Virginia, Detail #5: On October 31, 1753, Washington set out from Williamsburg. Traveling west and north to Fredericksburg, he proceeded northeastward to Alexandria (*Detail #1*, page 23). He then headed north and west, across the Blue Ridge to Winchester (*Detail #3*, page 27). Obtaining baggage and horses, he continued north and west to Wills Creek (on the road shown in *Detail #4*, page 29). His party pressed on, past Gist's Settlement (center) to John Frazier's trading post at the mouth of Turtle Creek, on the Monongahela (upper left).

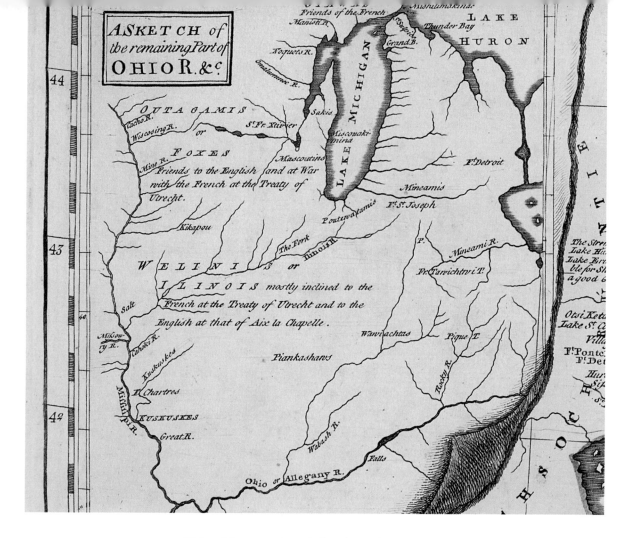

A SKETCH of the remaining Part of OHIO R. &c.

A General Map of the Middle British Colonies, Detail #3: The lower half of this inset shows how the French traveled between Canada and New Orleans. From the western end of Lake Erie, the Maumee River (*Mineami R.*) and one of its branches connected via a short portage (*P.*) to the St. Jerome River and the Wabash River, which flowed into the Ohio (bottom center). The Ohio flowed into the Mississippi (lower left), completing a continuous passage across French domains in North America.

Using his surveying skills along the way, Washington calculated that they had traveled seventy miles from Wills Creek to Gist's Settlement, another fifty to the Forks, and twenty more to Logstown. They were deep in the Ohio country, "at least 135 or 140 miles" from the last English settlements.[24]

Following Dinwiddie's orders, Washington immediately sought out Monakatoocha, an Oneida and Mingo chief who was also headman of the Logstown Shawnees. Through his Indian interpreter, John Davison, Washington explained his mission and that he "was ordered to call upon the sachems of the Six Nations, to acquaint them with it." Accepting a string of wampum and a twist of tobacco from Washington, Monakatoocha promised to send for the sachems in the morning. Dinwiddie's orders assumed that the Six Nations (the Iroquois League) were in charge in the Ohio Valley, exerting control—at a distance and through their regent, the Half-King—over the Delawares, Shawnees, and Mingos. Washington would gradually discover that this was not the case.[25]

Instead of the sachems, several French deserters came to town on November 25 and confirmed for Washington what the British suspected: The French were trying to strengthen their line of communication between New Orleans and Canada via the Mississippi River and the Ohio country. The deserters, who were part of a body of a hundred men sent from New Orleans, described the French forts all the way from the lower Mississippi to Illinois. They also mentioned a small fort on the Ohio at the mouth of the Wabash River about two hundred miles from the Mississippi. The Wabash, with its source near the western end of Lake Erie, "affords the communication

between the French on the Mississippi and those on the Lakes," Washington noted. (See *A General Map of the Middle British Colonies, Detail #3*, and *A General Map of North America, Detail #3*.)[26]

That afternoon the Half-King came to Logstown, and Washington asked him about his recent trip to see the French commander, Jacques Legardeur, sieur de Saint-Pierre, who had just replaced the sieur de Marin when he died. The Half-King recounted his exchange of speeches with the French commander: how he had protested the French incursion onto Indian land with towns and forts, and how the Frenchman had responded disdainfully that he would take the land as he pleased. The Half-King told Washington that the French had built two forts, "one on Lake Erie, and another on French Creek . . . and a large wagon road between." He gave Washington a plan of each fort that he had drawn himself. (See *A General Map of the Middle British Colonies, Detail #4*.)[27]

On November 26, Washington made a speech at the long house to a council of chiefs, describing his mission to the French commander at Fort Le Boeuf, and asking for an escort of young warriors and hunters. The Half-King promised to help, but asked Washington to wait a few days so he could summon his men and fetch the wampum and speech-belt that would be returned to the French commander to signal the break in relations and the Indians' alignment with the British. After a series of delays, Washington finally set out at nine A.M. on November 30 with Gist at his side and only four Indians—the Half-King, two other chiefs, and one hunter—as his escort.[28]

The embarrassing lack of support clearly indicated that the man mocked as the Half-King had no authority

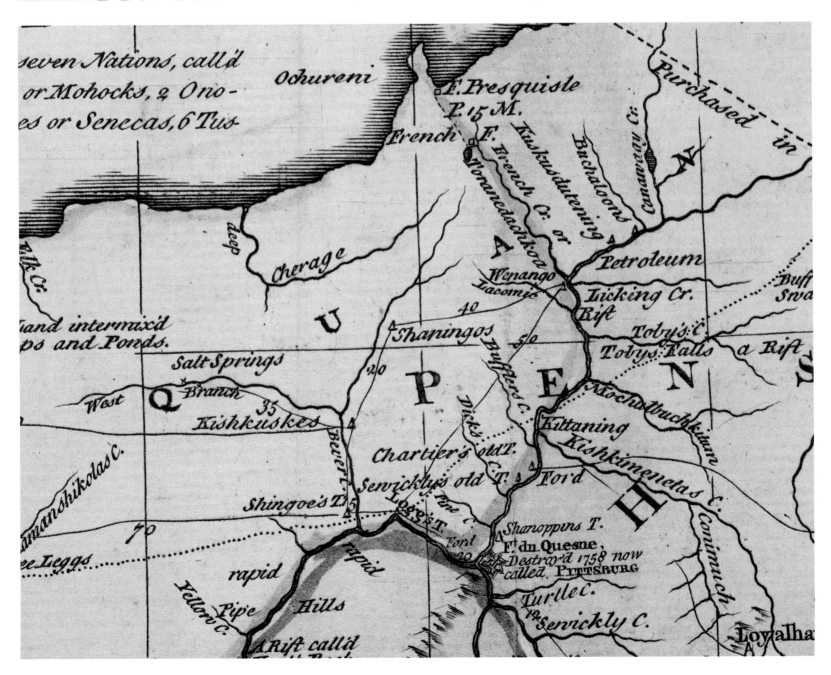

A General Map of North America, Detail #3: This detail extends the view in *A General Map of the Middle British Colonies, Detail #3*, continuing south and west. Below the confluence of the Ohio and Mississippi rivers (*The Fork*, top center), the French had a series of forts at frequent intervals down to New Orleans. Shown from north to south are Fort Prudhome, Fort del Assumption, Fort St. Francois, and Missionet Fort. At the bottom, near the confluence of the Mississippi and Yazoo rivers, another French post is indicated, as *F Fort*.

A General Map of the Middle British Colonies, Detail #4: From Fort Presque Isle (today's Erie, Pennsylvania) on the southern shore of Lake Erie (top center) the wagon road leads fifteen miles south to Fort Le Boeuf (*French F.*) on French Creek (near today's Waterford, Pennsylvania). To reach Fort Le Boeuf from Logstown (labeled *Logg's T.*, bottom center) via Venango (to the northeast), Washington's party used the road next to Beaver Creek (center) instead of the more direct road just to the east. The numbers on the map show that the direct route was sixty miles; Washington's route, he calculated, was more than seventy.

over the Ohio Indians, who had moved there precisely because they wanted to be free of Iroquois domination. The Ohio Indians had drifted into relations with traders from Pennsylvania and Virginia, but now that the French were making a strong show of force and looked like the probable winners of any military contest for the area, these Indians were prepared to drift back into their orbit. Washington, as instructed by Dinwiddie, was courting the wrong Indians if the British hoped to expel the French.[29]

To reach Fort Le Boeuf, by way of Venango at the southern end of French Creek, would take "five or six nights sleep, good traveling," according to the Half-King. Heavy rains and soggy ground meant they could not go by the "nearest and levellest way." They "traveled on the road to Venango," Washington wrote, "where we arrived the 4th of December" after enduring "a continued series of bad weather." (See *A General Map of the Middle British Colonies, Detail #4*, page 41.)

At Venango, the French flag had been raised over a house from which they had driven John Frazier (the trader now at Turtle Creek). "There were three officers," Washington noted, "one of whom, Captain Joncaire, informed me that he had the command of the Ohio, but that there was a general officer at the near fort, where he advised me to apply for an answer." Chabert de Joncaire, the son of a Frenchman and a Seneca woman, courteously invited Washington to supper. Joncaire and his fellow officers "dosed themselves pretty plentifully" with wine, Washington observed, which loosened their tongues and provided him with detailed intelligence.

"They pretend to have an undoubted right to the [Ohio] River, from a discovery made by one La Salle sixty years ago," Washington wrote. In 1682, René-Robert Cavelier, sieur de La Salle, had traveled from Canada down the Mississippi all the way to its mouth. Determined to keep the British from settling in the area, the French had a chain of forts stretching six hundred miles from Montreal to Lake Erie that could be traveled in four weeks in large boats or six weeks in canoes. (See *A General Map of the Middle British Colonies, Detail #5*.) The four forts closest to the Ohio were garrisoned with a total of six hundred men.[30]

During the next three days, foul weather delayed Washington's departure for Fort Le Boeuf, as did Joncaire, who got the Half-King and the other Indians drunk and tried to prevent them from going with Washington. With Gist's help, Washington prevailed, and the whole party left on December 7, escorted by three French soldiers and the French commissary of stores, Michel Pepin, better known as La Force.

"We passed over much good land since we left Venango," Washington wrote in his diary, "and through several extensive and very rich meadows, one of which I believe was near four miles in length and considerably wide in some places." The glowing descriptions of landscape in his youthful diaries were giving way to the more professional assessments of a surveyor and speculator turned soldier. The French threat was not simply a pretext for speculation as opponents of the Ohio Company claimed, but Washington's mission did enable him to scout out choice parcels of land while serving king and country.

Because of "excessive rains and snows and bad traveling through many mires and swamps," they did not reach the fort until December 11. The following day, Washington presented Dinwiddie's letter to the French commander, Legardeur. The French officers conferred privately about the letter and held a council of war the next day, which gave Washington time to make detailed observations about the strength of the fort and its garrison. Meanwhile, he had dispatched Gist and the others to count the French canoes—fifty of birch bark and 170 of pine, plus many more under construction—to gauge the size of the invasion force the British could expect in the spring.[31]

On the evening of the 14th Washington received the sieur de Saint-Pierre's reply, which rebuffed Dinwiddie's demand that the French retreat from the Ohio. Washington prepared to leave the next day, but once again the French plied the Half-King and the other Indians with liquor and gifts, hoping to split them off from Washington and gain their allegiance. Washington was in a hurry to return to Williamsburg, but he dared not leave the Indians behind. "I can't say that ever in my life I suffered so much anxiety as I did in this affair," he wrote in his diary. Washington shuttled between the French commander and the Half-King, pressuring each in turn, until finally on the 16th the Indians left with him as they had promised.

The French had provided canoes laden with provisions, but it took six exhausting days of paddling, wading, and portaging along the ice-choked creek to reach Venango. "This creek is extremely crooked," Washington declared. "I dare say the distance between the fort and Venango can't be less than 130 miles, to follow the meanders." On December 23, the party set off on horseback for the Forks of the Ohio, parting with the Half-King, who promised to meet them there. Over the next three days, as the temperature dropped and the snow became deeper, the horses grew weaker. Their progress was so slow that Washington decided he had to split off and make his way on foot to Williamsburg. Taking Gist with him, and leaving Van Braam in charge of the horses and baggage, Washington set out on the 26th.[32]

The next day, as they were about to "quit the path and steer across the country for Shannapins Town," Washington wrote, "we fell in with a party of French Indians who had lain in wait for us. One of them fired at Mr. Gist or me, not fifteen steps off, but fortunately missed." They seized their assailant and, after releasing him around nine P.M., marched all night to get ahead of their pursuers. They reached Piney Creek the next morning and kept walking all day, arriving at the Allegheny

CHAMPLAIN,

IAN NATIONS
elphia
Forts on the

Name, pr. S. to the present Seat
and ex. to those that are ex-
tinct.
△ △. *Indian Towns.*
P. *Portages.*
T.R. *Heads of the Tides.*

Toniata I.

Gancouse

Fort
Frentenac

△*Kente*

F. Toronto

L A K E   O N T A R I O

Goats I.
Galotts I.
P. *Traverse*

C. Famine R.

Red Marl

gentle
The great Rock

F. Niagara
rapid   *Swamp*

Tegynagerunte Mt.

Ofwego

Falls &.

Ochniagara Falls

3 great Falls

N

Ford

Portage 8 M.
Fishing Battery

swift

Chenandoanes

Tegaronhies

△*Danoncoritowi*

C A Y U G A E *Spr. S.*

dead

O N O N D

Cayuga
Cavvadadsho
Onugarechny M.

Onahie
Canasadego

Seneca R.

Cayuga

Canasadages & Chenandoanes
English SENE CAS.

O

U

ABOVE *A General Map of the Middle British Colonies, Detail #5:* In addition to Fort Le Boeuf and Fort Presque Isle, the French posts included Fort Niagara, at the portage around Niagara Falls (120 miles northeast of Presque Isle). Directly north of Fort Niagara on the shore of Lake Ontario stood Fort Toronto (upper left). At the northeastern corner of Lake Ontario, at the headwaters of the St. Lawrence River, stood Fort Frontenac, one of three additional French forts completing the line of communication back to Montreal. Fort Frontenac was almost directly north of the British fort at Oswego, on the southern shore of the lake, Washington noted.

LEFT: A blockhouse at Fort Le Boeuf.

"about two miles above Shannapins" well after dark. (See *A General Map of the Middle British Colonies, Detail #4*, page 41, bottom center.)

Gist and Washington had "but one poor hatchet" and spent an entire day fashioning a log raft, since this was the only way to cross the partially frozen Allegheny River. Large chunks of ice were coming down the river, and "before we were half way over, we were jammed in the ice, in such a manner that we expected our raft to sink and ourselves to perish," Washington recalled. Using a setting pole, he tried to stop the raft and let the ice pass by, but the swift current threw a chunk of ice against the pole and pitched him into ten feet of water. "I fortunately saved myself by catching hold of one of the raft logs," he wrote. This narrow escape from death, one of many such incidents in his life, undoubtedly reinforced his belief that a higher power, Providence he often called it, was preserving him for a special purpose.

Unable to get the raft to either shore, they abandoned it and made their way to a nearby island to spend the night. By morning, Gist's fingers and some of his toes were frostbitten, but the river's surface had frozen too, enabling them to walk off the island and make their way to Frazier's on Turtle Creek. While waiting there for horses to be found, Washington went on a diplomatic side trip to visit Queen Aliquippa of the Delawares near Frazier's at the mouth of the Youghiogheny River. She "had expressed great concern that we passed her in going to the fort. I made her a present of a matchcoat and a bottle of rum, which latter was thought much the best present of the two." (See *A Map of . . . Virginia, Detail #5*, page 39.)

On January 1, 1754, Washington left Frazier's and made his way, with Gist, back to Wills Creek. Along the way they met "seventeen horses loaded with materials and stores for a fort at the Forks of the Ohio, and the day after some families going out to settle." Sent by the Ohio Company, they were on a collision course with the French. Washington finally reached Belvoir on the 11th, "after as fatiguing a journey as it is possible to conceive, rendered so by excessive bad weather." He took a day's rest and then set out for Williamsburg, arriving there on the 16th. "I waited upon his Honor the Governor with the letter I had brought from the French commandant," Washington wrote, "and to give an account of the success of my proceedings."[33]

Maps played a significant role in that account: Dinwiddie sent Washington's journal of the expedition, a map he drew of the frontier, and a plan of Fort Le Boeuf to the Board of Trade in London. Washington's journal was also published as a pamphlet and in newspapers on both sides of the Atlantic, launching his long ascent to universal fame. On January 21, Dinwiddie presented the obstinate French reply to the council, which advised him to send Washington immediately with a hundred troops to the Forks of the Ohio to complete the Ohio Company's fort and fend off a French attack.[34]

George Washington and Christopher Gist poling across the Allegheny River.

OPPOSITE: *Washington's map of the frontier:* Washington's training as a surveyor enabled him to create this accurate map of his route on the western frontier. The Allegheny Mountains are shown across the bottom of the map, above the Potomac River. (Rotating the map counterclockwise, so the upper right corner is at the top—to the north—produces a more familiar orientation.) The Forks of the Ohio is just below and to the right of center. Northeast of the compass, Fort Le Boeuf and Fort Presque Isle are shown but not labeled, between the head of French Creek and the shore of Lake Erie.

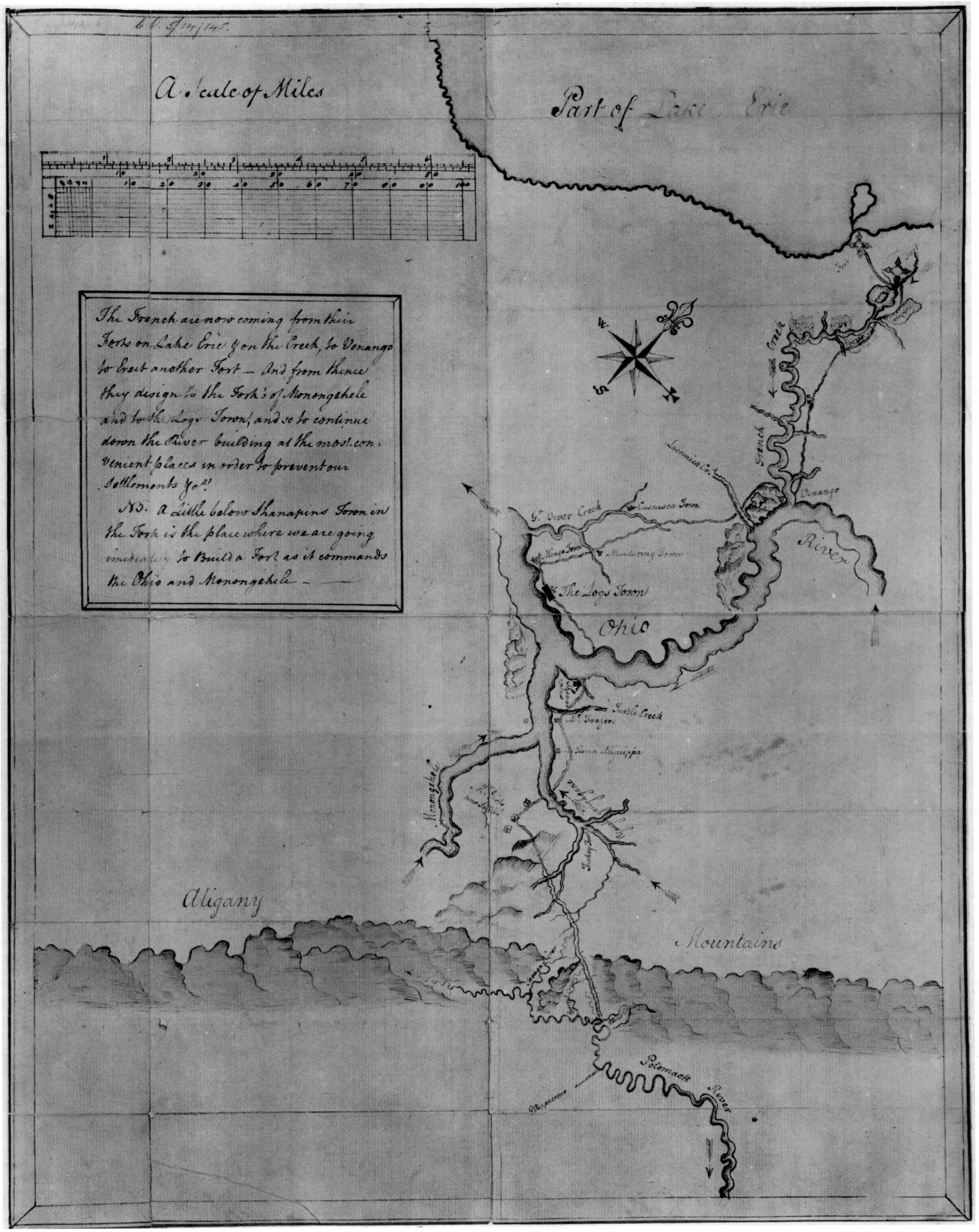

A Scale of Miles

Part of Lake Erie

The French are now coming from their
Forts on Lake Erie & on the Creek, to Venango
to erect another Fort — And from thence
they design to the Fork's of Monongehele
and to the Logs Town, and so to continue
down the River building at the most convenient places in order to prevent our
Settlements &c.[?]

N.B. A Little below Shanapins Town in
the Fork is the place where we are going
imediately to Build a Fort as it commands
the Ohio and Monongehele —

W S

Fort

French Creek

Jacomica Cr.

Gr. Bever Creek Cuscuscca Town

Mingo Town Murdering Town

The Logs Town

Venango

River

Ohio

Turtle Creek

Mr. Frazer.

Queen Aliquippa

Monongehele

Aligany

Mountains

Potomack River

Wills Creek[?]

CHAPTER TWO

0   1   2

FROM THE MONONGAHELA

TO MASSACHUSETTS

Washington's report on the French invasion "was yet thought a fiction," he later recalled, a "scheme to promote the interest of a private company (by many gentlemen that had a share in government) . . . These unfavorable surmises caused great delays in raising the first men and money." Dinwiddie had the backing of the royal council, but all appropriations originated in the House of Burgesses, where many members regarded the governor's plans as a shameless land grab for the Ohio Company. The burgesses did not meet until the middle of February and then appropriated only ten thousand pounds for military operations on the frontier—and that only with great reluctance.[1]

Amid these delays, Washington received frantic letters from Trent and Gist at the Forks, urging him to hurry to their defense. Trent, who had been working on the Ohio Company storehouse at Red Stone Creek, arrived at the Forks on February 17. Gist joined him, and they had tried to rally a crew of about eighty traders and Indians to put the fort in a defensible condition pending the arrival of Washington and his troops, along with other units to be raised by Dinwiddie. However, according to intelligence Trent and Gist gathered from the Indians—and threats issued by La Force, the French commissary of stores—the French were massing hundreds of troops who would arrive at the Forks in two weeks and slaughter the British.[2]

More hurdles, however, prevented Washington from rushing to their aid. Since it remained uncertain whether the Forks of the Ohio belonged to Virginia or to Pennsylvania, and since the militia could not be sent outside the colony, Dinwiddie had trouble drafting men from the counties to serve on the expedition. He resorted to the more expensive solution of recruiting volunteers by offering cash bounties and grants of land in the Ohio country.

Since the officers on the expedition were eligible for the largest land grants, Dinwiddie's offer would have a lasting impact on Washington's life. He would later become an advocate for the veterans as a group when they sought to take possession of these tracts, and he would also buy up warrants from cash-strapped veterans, amassing tens of thousands of acres in the West for himself.

Dinwiddie's aim was to assemble three hundred men at Alexandria by March 20 and have them bring cannon and supplies via Wills Creek to the Forks. The earl of Holderness had delivered on his promise to send thirty cannon and eighty barrels of gunpowder to Virginia, but the guns were "much too large to be transported so great a distance by land, and in bad roads," Dinwiddie told the Board of Trade. Nonetheless, he wrote, he would try to send ten of them to the Forks.[3]

By March 15, Washington had successfully lobbied his connections in Williamsburg for a promotion to lieutenant colonel—second in command—of the British expedition. The commander in chief would be Colonel Joshua Fry, just promoted from lieutenant of militia in Albemarle County. Educated at Oxford, Fry was a math professor at the College of William and Mary and tutored young Thomas Jefferson.* Alarmed by the warnings from Trent and Gist that the French were poised to strike sooner than expected, Dinwiddie ordered Washington to set out for the Forks immediately with whatever force he had managed to recruit, "Colonel Fry to march with the others as soon as possible." Dinwiddie also promised to send three independent companies of regular British troops, two on their way from New York and one from South Carolina.[4]

The governor's decision to rush an advance column forward—effectively dividing his force in the face of a more numerous enemy—violated the most basic precepts of eighteenth-century warfare. And Washington's detachment would pay the price. Remarkably, however, the lesson would not stick. This temptation to speed troops to the scene of battle, instead of consolidating a more powerful strike force and securing its route, was one that Washington himself would fall prey to a year later, and again as president and commander in chief after the Revolution during the fight against the Indians in this same region, by then called the Northwest Territory.

Washington set out from Alexandria at noon on April 2 with a little more than 150 men (see *A Map of . . . Virginia, Detail #3*, page 27.) They marched six miles the first day "and pitched our tents about four miles from Cameron" (*Cameron's Ordinary*, west of Alexandria), he noted. Marching through the Blue Ridge at Vestal's Gap, they crossed the Shenandoah at Vestal's Ferry to reach Winchester. Following the road to Wills Creek (see *A Map of . . . Virginia, Detail #4*, page 29), they stopped at Edwards's Fort (*Edwards*) on the Cacapon River and then at Pearsal's on the South Branch of the Potomac. There Washington received a message from Trent on the 19th, "demanding a reinforcement with all possible speed as he hourly expected a body of eight hundred French." The following day, after leaving the road and heading north across the Potomac to Cresap's, Washington received word that the French had captured the fort. Two days later he learned the details from Trent's ensign, Edward Ward.[5]

On the 17th, Ward had surrendered the unfinished fort to the French, under Captain Contrecoeur, who had come down the Allegheny from Venango to the Forks with sixty bateaux and three hundred canoes, carrying more than a thousand men and eighteen cannon. (Trent was absent from the fort, having left to procure more supplies in Virginia.) The thirty-three men of the garrison were allowed to leave. Ward also brought Washington a speech from the Half-King—who was present at the surrender—appealing for help in fighting the French. "If you do not come to our assistance now, we are entirely undone, and I think we shall never meet together again," the Half-King concluded. "I speak with a heart full of grief."[6]

ABOVE: Lieutenant Governor Robert Dinwiddie of Virginia.

OPPOSITE: Governor Dinwiddie's proclamation encouraging men to enlist.

* Fry had created **A Map of the Most Inhabited Part of Virginia** (see pages 24–25), with Peter Jefferson, Thomas's father.

Virginia, ſſ.

By the Hon. *ROBERT DINWIDDIE*, Eſq;
His Majeſty's Lieutenant-Governor, and Commander in
Chief of this Dominion.

A PROCLAMATION,

For Encouraging MEN to enliſt in his Majeſty's Service for the Defence and Security of this
Colony.

WHEREAS it is determined that a Fort be immediately built on the River *Ohio*, at the Fork of *Monongahela*, to
oppoſe any further Encroachments, or hoſtile Attempts of the *French*, and the *Indians* in their Intereſt, and
for the Security and Protection of his Majeſty's Subjects in this Colony; and as it is abſolutely neceſſary that a
ſufficient Force ſhould be raiſed to erect and ſupport the ſame: For an Encouragement to all who ſhall voluntarily enter
into the ſaid Service, I do hereby notify and promiſe, by and with the Advice and Conſent of his Majeſty's Council of this
Colony, that over and above their Pay, Two Hundred Thouſand Acres, of his Majeſty the King of *Great-Britain*'s
Lands, on the Eaſt Side of the River *Ohio*, within this Dominion, (One Hundred Thouſand Acres whereof to be conti-
guous to the ſaid Fort, and the other Hundred Thouſand Acres to be on, or near the River *Ohio*) ſhall be laid off and
granted to ſuch Perſons, who by their voluntary Engagement, and good Behaviour in the ſaid Service, ſhall deſerve the
ſame. And I further promiſe, that the ſaid Lands ſhall be divided amongſt them immediately after the Performance of
the ſaid Service, in a Proportion due to their reſpective Merit, as ſhall be repreſented to me by their Officers, and held and
enjoyed by them without paying any Rights, and alſo free from the Payment of Quit-rents, for the Term of Fifteen Years.
And I do appoint this Proclamation to be read and publiſhed at the Court-Houſes, Churches and Chapels in each County
within this Colony, and that the Sheriffs take Care the ſame be done accordingly.

Given at the Council-Chamber in *Williamsburg*, on the 19th Day of *February*, in the 27th Year of his Majeſty's
Reign, *Annoque Domini* 1754.

ROBERT DINWIDDIE.
GOD Save the KING.

Having reached Wills Creek, Washington held a council of war on April 23. (See *A Map of Pennsylvania, Detail #1*, page 38, lower right.) Since they did not have enough troops to challenge the French at the Forks, they decided instead to march north and west to the mouth of Red Stone Creek on the Monongahela River and build a fort (upper left, the site labeled *Fort Burd*). On the way there, they would clear a road "broad enough to pass with all our artillery and our baggage." They reasoned that the Ohio Company's storehouse on Red Stone Creek would provide them with a base, and that the proposed fort, less than forty miles up the Monongahela from the Forks, would make a good launch point for an attack later on: Instead of dragging their heavy guns all the way to the Forks, they could send them by water. Finally, the war council hoped that building the fort would help maintain morale within the expedition, while restoring confidence among their Indian allies.[7]

Washington had hoped to move nimbly with packhorses westward from Wills Creek, but the horses he had requested from Cresap and Trent never arrived; instead Washington had to procure wagons from the settlers on the South Branch of the Potomac (forty miles away) and clear a road substantial enough to accommodate them—along with the carriages of the ten heavy cannon that were to arrive with Colonel Fry. On May 9, Washington wrote to Dinwiddie from Little Meadows that after more than a week of "great difficulty and labor," they were still only twenty miles west of Wills Creek.

While Washington's troops toiled at this backbreaking task, he sent out a scouting party of twenty-five men toward Gist's Settlement to confirm reports that La Force and four French soldiers "under the specious pretence of hunting deserters, were reconnoitering and discovering the country." Washington's scouts were to find out where La Force was operating, and if possible to bring in a French prisoner for interrogation. Meanwhile, Washington told Dinwiddie, the Half-King reportedly was "much pleased with the speech I sent them, and is now upon their march with fifty men to meet us."[8]

More good news arrived on May 12, that Colonel Fry had reached Winchester and would soon join Washington with a hundred men. Colonel James Innes was also supposed to be on his way from North Carolina with three hundred and fifty men. And two hundred more were expected from Maryland. Pennsylvania would send money to pay the troops and had sent six hundred of its own to harass the French in Canada, which might draw them out of the Ohio country.

The bad news came from the other direction: The various traders fleeing the French onslaught knew the area well and told Washington that clearing a road for heavy wagons all the way to Red Stone Creek was an impossible task. However, there might be a way to get to the Monongahela by water. By May 18 Washington's men had improved the road from Wills Creek as far as the Great Crossing of the Youghiogheny River, a few miles north of the Maryland border in Pennsylvania. (See

ABOVE: A modern rendering of George Washington's headquarters at Wills Creek.

OPPOSITE: General Edward Braddock.

A Map of Pennsylvania, Detail #1, page 38, lower right.) Washington told Dinwiddie on the 18th that most of the traders "assure me that (except one place) water carriage may be had down this river [the Youghiogheny] which will be a most advantageous discovery if it proves so—as it will save forty miles land carriage over almost impassible roads and mountains."[9]

The one exception was the waterfall at Turkey Foot (also called Three Forks; today's Confluence, Pennsylvania), and Washington planned to set out in a canoe the next morning with an officer and five men "to inform myself concerning the nature and difficulty attending this fall." (See *A Map of Pennsylvania, Detail #1*, lower right.) A few days later he returned to the Great Crossing disappointed and wrote to Joshua Fry that the river could "never be made navigable." Having explored the river for thirty miles, he found that the fall "continued rough, rocky, and scarcely passable for two miles, and then fell, within the space of fifty yards, nearly forty feet perpendicular." (The map indicates the falls downstream from Turkey Foot.)[10]

Clearing a road to Red Stone Creek proved almost impossible, and on May 24, after three weeks of toil, Washington and his troops had advanced only as far as Great Meadows, some fifty miles west of Wills Creek. (See *A Map of Pennsylvania, Detail #1*, lower right.) A trader there confirmed a warning from the Half-King that the French had sent out "a strong detachment" from the fort at the Forks, so Washington "placed troops behind two natural entrenchments, and had our wagons put there also."

Three days later, there was no sign of the French at Great Meadows, but Gist arrived and reported that in his absence La Force had been at his plantation with fifty men, searching for the Half-King in a threatening manner. The French would have ransacked the house if the two Indians he left in charge had not talked them out of it. "I did not fail to let several young Indians who were in our camp know that the French wanted to kill the Half-King; and it had its desired effect," Washington wrote. "They immediately offered to accompany our people to go after the French" and "to incite their warriors to fall upon them."[11]

That evening, Washington received word from the Half-King that he knew where the French were hidden. Washington took forty men and marched all night through a heavy rain to join the Half-King and his dozen warriors. The next morning they surrounded the French encampment of some thirty-five troops, which was well hidden in a rocky glen. "We had advanced pretty near to them . . . when they discovered us," Washington recalled. "I ordered my company to fire." After ten or fifteen minutes of "sharp firing on both sides," the battle was over and the French were routed. The French commander, the sieur de Jumonville, lay dead, along with nine of his men, and twenty-one were taken prisoner, including La Force. The Half-King and his warriors scalped the dead Frenchmen. Washington lost only one man killed and three wounded.[12]

What Washington did not report was that the wounded Jumonville was calling for a cease-fire and protesting that he was on a diplomatic mission when the Half-King raised his hatchet, saying, "Tu n'es pas encore mort, mon Pere" (You're not dead yet, my father), and split the Frenchman's head open. Washington believed he had manipulated the Indians into attacking the French, but he had succeeded mainly because the Half-King was intent on getting the British to do the same. Realizing he had no influence over the Ohio Indians, the Half-King saw that his only means for expelling the French was to drag the British into an armed conflict with them.[13]

The French "pretend they were coming on an embassy," similar to his own mission to Fort Le Boeuf, Washington reported to Dinwiddie, "but the absurdity of this pretext is too glaring, as your Honor will see by the instructions and summons enclosed. Their instructions were to reconnoiter the country, roads, creeks, etc. to the Potomac, which they were about to do." Washington argued that their choice of a hidden campsite also proved they were spies, not diplomats. They were reconnoitering his camp to determine his strength, Washington asserted, and would have attacked as soon as they had adequate reinforcements. Dinwiddie congratulated him for showing the Indians "that the French are not invincible when fairly engaged with the British." (See *A Map of Pennsylvania, Detail #1*, page 38, center. The battle site, in a rocky glen where the French were camped—today called Jumonville Rocks, in Pennsylvania—was about halfway between Great Meadows and Gist's Settlement, labeled Guest's.)[14]

Remarkably, Washington came through his first experience of combat unscathed and exhilarated. "I fortunately escaped without a wound, though the right wing where I stood was exposed to and received all the enemy's fire and was the part where the man was killed and the rest wounded," Washington told his brother John Augustine. "I can with truth assure you, I heard bullets whistle and believe me there was something charming in the sound."

Anticipating an attack by a considerable French force in response to the Jumonville affair, Washington and his men built a small, circular stockade fort at Great Meadows, which he named Fort Necessity. "I shall not fear the attack of five hundred men," he told Dinwiddie on June 3.[15]

The following day, Dinwiddie wrote to Washington, commissioning him colonel of the Virginia Regiment to succeed Colonel Fry, who had died a few days earlier after falling from his horse. Fry had been on his way from Winchester to join Washington, and the troops with him, the rest of the Virginia Regiment, were brought forward to Great Meadows on June 9 by Major George Muse, now lieutenant colonel of the regiment. Dinwiddie also appointed Washington acting commander in chief of the expedition (pending the arrival from North Carolina of Colonel Innes, "an old experienced officer"). However, Washington's rank meant nothing to Captain James McKay, who arrived with his independent company of royal troops a few days after Muse and proceeded to establish a separate encampment. Like all officers in the regular British army, who were commissioned by the king, McKay refused to take orders, or let his men take orders, from any colonial officer, commissioned by a mere governor.[16]

On June 16, Washington took his own troops and struggled forward in broken wagons to continue clearing the road to Red Stone Creek. McKay said his men would not help clear the road unless they received extra pay, so Washington left them behind at Fort Necessity. Two days later, a delegation of Mingos from Logstown arrived at Washington's camp (at Gist's Settlement), insisting "that a council must be held." Over the next few days, Washington engaged in a series of conferences with the Half-King and other representatives of the Six Nations, as well as the Loups, Shawnees, and Delawares, among others. Washington's small force clearly did not inspire confidence that he could prevail over the French, and the negotiations ended without any commitment of support from the Indians. Indeed, Washington believed some of the Indians at the conference were spies for the French, and in response to their questions he gave false information to bring back to the fort at the Forks, now called Fort Duquesne.[17]

Washington did rely, however, on the advice of Monakatoocha, the Oneida and Mingo chief who had helped him at Logstown on the mission to Fort Le Boeuf the year before. Monakatoocha, who visited Fort Duquesne on June 26, warned Washington that the French had just received reinforcements from Canada and were preparing to attack with eight hundred troops and four hundred Indians. Washington intended to pull all of his men together at Gist's and build a stockade there to fend off the French. However, at a council of war on June 28, Washington and his officers "unanimously resolved that it was absolutely necessary to return to our fort at the Meadows."

Among the various reasons given, the most compelling concerned the local topography. The French could "come within five miles of Gist's house by water," via Red Stone Creek, but to reach Great Meadows, "thirteen miles further of bad road" stood in their way. The French lacked horses to carry provisions and supplies over this "hilly road formed naturally for ambushes," while Washington would be able to receive supply convoys more easily from Wills Creek, to the east. "While we lay at Gist's house, they might pass us unobserved by a different road from Red Stone [Creek] that lay about nine miles from us," the war council wrote, "but at the Meadows, both roads are united, and the bearing of the mountains makes it difficult for an enemy to come near or pass us without receiving advice of it." (See *A Map of Pennsylvania, Detail #1*, page 38. Gist's Settlement could be approached from several directions, while Great Meadows was shielded by Laurel Hill, the westernmost major ridge of the Allegheny Mountains.)[18]

Washington's troops traveled the rough mountain road back to Great Meadows, dragging nine swivel guns, supplies, and ammunition with the help of only a few horses. They were already tired from their labor at Gist's, and they were starved, having gone almost a week without bread or meat, since none had been sent by the quartermaster in Alexandria. Soon after they reached Great Meadows on July 1, a food convoy finally arrived but delivered only a few bags of flour. Too exhausted to retreat on foot to Wills Creek, Washington's men could only strengthen the unfinished stockade of Fort Necessity, and prepare to make a stand against the French.[19]

While Washington's council of war was meeting on June 28, a strong force under Jumonville's brother, Louis Coulon de Villiers, left Fort Duquesne and traveled up the Monongahela River to Red Stone Creek. The French marched to the site of Jumonville's death and then, informed of Washington's retreat by a British deserter, pursued him over Laurel Hill to Great Meadows, arriving there early on July 3. The battle began at about eleven in the morning as the French columns, numbering some seven hundred troops, approached Fort Necessity. (The Half-King, seeing that Washington could offer little resistance to the French, had departed, taking his warriors, along with some eighty Indian women and children, to safer ground.) "We continued this unequal fight," Washington reported to Dinwiddie, "with an enemy sheltered behind the trees, ourselves without shelter, in trenches full of water, in a settled rain, and the enemy galling us on all sides incessantly from the woods, till eight o'clock at night, when the French called to parley."[20]

Given the anger of the French over Jumonville's death, and the advantage they held, the terms were lenient. Washington had no choice but to sign the capitulation, which would allow his defeated force to "march away with all the honors of war" and retreat to Wills Creek. Only later would the world learn that the French had exacted a higher price for their lenience: In the articles of capitulation, translated verbally by Van Braam and signed on that dark, rainy night, Washington unwittingly confessed to the "assassination" of Jumonville. According to the French, Jumonville was on a diplomatic mission, and by international law, assassinating a diplomatic envoy was an act of war. A few months later the French published the articles of capitulation along with their own translation of Washington's journal, captured at Fort Necessity. The French had made their case—and given King Louis XV a justification to declare war on Great Britain.[21]

Buying time while modernizing their navy, the French delayed their declaration and instead proposed a demilitarized zone in the Ohio Valley. By contrast, the British reacted to the defeat at Fort Necessity with alarm. General Edward Braddock was sent to America as commander in chief of all British and colonial forces, and plans were laid for an ambitious campaign to capture or destroy key French forts from Nova Scotia to the Ohio Valley. Braddock would personally lead the expedition against Fort Duquesne and take Washington with him as a volunteer on his staff.

Royal officials in London privately criticized Washington for the defeat at Fort Necessity, but in Virginia, the governor and council made a grant of cash to thank the officers and men for their bravery, and the public mood as expressed in the press was sympathetic. The blame was laid on the other colonies for not sending troops in time. In the months leading up to Braddock's campaign, while troops were brought over from Europe and supplies stockpiled in a new fort at Wills Creek, Washington considered his options.

The British army's rules would not allow Washington, a provincial officer, to rank higher than any regular officer on the expedition, so he initially faced the prospect of demotion from colonel to captain (leading a company of provincial troops) if he wanted to participate. Instead he chose to forgo any pay, in exchange for the status and gentlemanly camaraderie he would enjoy performing the duties of a regular army captain in Braddock's military "family." If all went well, Washington could expect

Stobo's map of Fort Duquesne: Stobo's map was smuggled out of Fort Duquesne by the visiting Indian chiefs. Stobo and Van Braam were the two hostages taken by the French at the surrender of Fort Necessity as security for the prisoners Washington had taken in the skirmish with Jumonville and sent east under guard to Williamsburg.

Braddock to commission him as an officer in the regular army when a position opened up.

Washington immediately ingratiated himself with Braddock's most trusted aide, Captain Robert Orme, by sending him a map of the frontier, "which though imperfect and roughly drawn (for want of proper instruments) may give you a better knowledge of these parts." (The map, which has been lost, may have been similar to the one Washington drew the previous year of his route to Fort Le Boeuf. See page 45.)[22]

In May 1755, Braddock gathered his force at Wills Creek, where Fort Cumberland had been constructed in the fall and winter of 1754, across the Potomac from the Ohio Company's storehouse. (See *A Map of Pennsylvania, Detail #1*, page 38.) The fort was named for Braddock's political patron, the duke of Cumberland, King George II's favorite son and captain-general of the British army. Spurred by a hawkish faction in the cabinet, the duke used his influence to put Britain on a war footing in the wake of the surrender at Fort Necessity.

Between the two regular army regiments he had brought from Ireland and companies of provincials from Virginia, Maryland, and North Carolina, Braddock's massive column would consist of 2,400 troops, supported by some 500 civilian tradesmen and female camp followers. Washington assumed there would be little opposition from the French, since he expected, too optimistically, that they would be pinned down by British attacks in Nova Scotia and on the Great Lakes. The bigger challenge, he predicted, would be getting the artillery and wagons over the mountains.[23]

In the hope of obtaining intelligence about any French forces he might soon encounter, Braddock enlisted the help of George Croghan, the Pennsylvania trader, who invited Indian leaders to a meeting at Fort Cumberland. Tanaghrisson had died in October 1754, and was succeeded as Half-King by Monakatoocha, who arrived at the fort in late May with a delegation that included the Delaware chiefs Shingas and Delaware George and a Mohawk named Moses the Song. They were eager to help drive the French from the Forks, along with their Indian allies—the Potawatomis, Ottawas, Abenakis, and others—whose arrival was crushing the Ohio tribes' hopes for autonomy, which had brought them to the area in the first place.

The delegation presented Braddock with a map of Fort Duquesne drawn by Captain Robert Stobo, one of two hostages led away by the French after the surrender of Fort Necessity. In exchange for their support, the Ohio Indians wanted assurances that the British would not establish permanent settlements in the Ohio country after the French were expelled. Convinced that his disciplined, professional troops and their weaponry were virtually invincible, with or without Indian help, Braddock rebuffed their overtures, saying that "the English should inhabit and inherit the land." Convinced that they were better off with the French, the chiefs departed, leaving the British with only Monakatoocha at their side. He was able to muster only seven Mingo warriors to serve as scouts.[24]

Braddock's force, the largest the British had ever assembled in North America, would have been too cumbersome, with all of its baggage and artillery, had it marched through the wilderness and camped as a single body. So on May 29 he sent out an advance party of five hundred men to improve the road and establish a base twenty-five miles west of Fort Cumberland, and the rest of the force, in three divisions, followed separately, departing from Fort Cumberland on June 7, 9, and 10. After this first leg of the journey, the entire force was reconfigured to travel as two brigades.[25]

Pressured by Braddock and his quartermaster, the Pennsylvania authorities had sent a crew of some two hundred men to clear a new road from Shippensburg westward, through Raystown (later called Bedford), to Turkey Foot on the Youghiogheny River. This road was to connect with the road cut by Braddock's army, providing him with a line of supply—and of retreat if necessary—in Pennsylvania. However, as the army left Fort Cumberland, the Pennsylvania road was far behind schedule. (See *A Map of Pennsylvania, Detail #2*. Here called *Bedford*, center, west of Rays Hill Ridge, Raystown is shown on *A General Map of the Middle British Colonies*, page 32, center, as *Rays T.*)[26]

Braddock's expedition reached the Youghiogheny River at the Great Crossing on June 24. Crossing over that morning and marching all day, they were still four miles east of Great Meadows when they camped for the night. By the morning, three men had been silently killed and scalped by the Indians. With guards on its flanks, the column passed through Great Meadows that day and continued beyond the site of Fort Necessity to reach Gist's on the 27th and Stewart's Crossing on the 29th. However, the second brigade, eight hundred men led by Colonel Thomas Dunbar, had fallen far behind as they struggled with most of the army's baggage and provisions, with only enough horses for two thirds of their 150 wagons. (See *A Map of Pennsylvania, Detail #1*, page 38. Dunbar's camp is indicated slightly north and east of Great Meadows, about five miles south of Gist's.)[27]

The first brigade crossed the Youghiogheny at Stewart's and marched more than forty miles over the next eight days before camping near the mouth of the river, where it flowed into the Monongahela. Washington had been traveling with the slower units to get medical care because he was suffering from dysentery, but he caught up to Braddock at this camp on July 8. The French had their Indian scouts monitoring Braddock's march and firing occasionally from the woods, but they inflicted negligible damage on the British force. By July 9, the forward column had crossed and recrossed the Monongahela unopposed, and arrived about six miles southeast of Fort Duquesne. (See *A Map of Pennsylvania, Detail #3*.)[28]

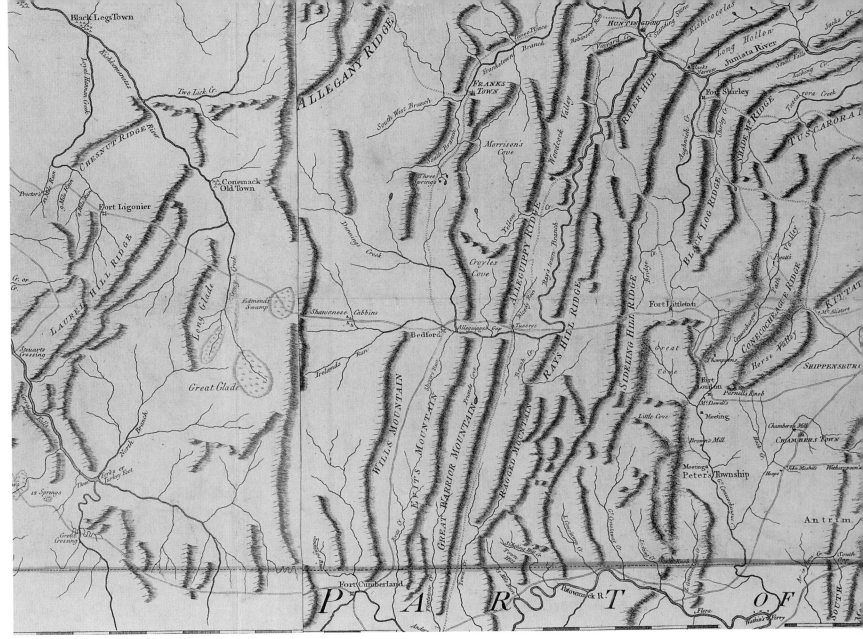

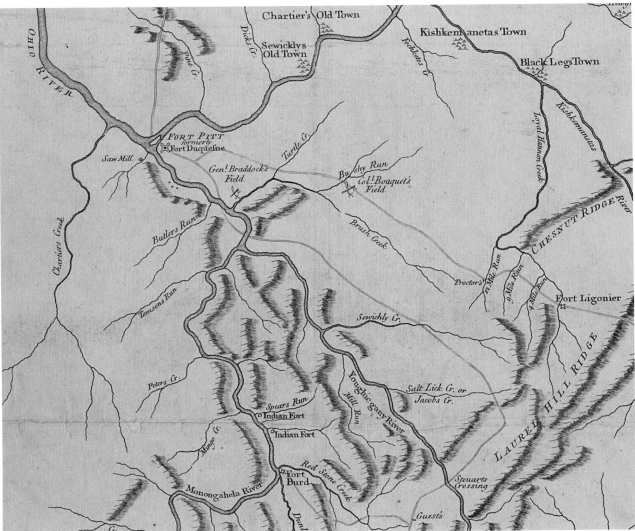

ABOVE: *A Map of Pennsylvania, Detail #2:* The road began in the middle of southern Pennsylvania at Shippensburg (right center) and continued westward across Sideling Hill Ridge but had yet to cross Ray's Hill Ridge. The road was not even halfway to its intended junction with Braddock's Road near Turkey Foot (lower left). The completed road shown on the full map is the one used by the Forbes expedition to Fort Duquesne three years later.

LEFT: *A Map of Pennsylvania, Detail #3:* From Stewart's Crossing (bottom right), Braddock's first brigade marched to the mouth of the Youghiogheny at the Monongahela (upper left). To avoid a possible ambush in the narrow gorge between the two rows of hills directly in their path, the British crossed the Monongahela twice, as indicated by the path of Braddock's Road, and arrived at the area (labeled *Gen.l Braddock's Field*, with crossed swords) where they encountered the French and Indian column.

Braddock began to think that the French might have abandoned the fort since they had not attacked when his troops were most vulnerable, as they crossed the river. Just then, his column collided head-on with a detachment of almost nine hundred Indians and French troops. The surprise encounter on the narrow path sowed panic and confusion on both sides. The British advance party retreated, slamming into the main body, which had lunged forward toward the sound of gunfire. The French commander was killed in the opening volley, and his troops broke ranks. However, more than two thirds of the French force consisted of their Indian allies—including Delawares, Shawnees, and Mingos—and they required no orders from a French officer. Amid the chaos they slipped into the forest on both sides of the road and fired into the mass of redcoats. Unable to see the Indians concealed in the trees, Braddock's troops fired back to little effect, hitting each other more often than the enemy.[29]

High in his saddle and heedless of the bullets flying around him, Braddock rode among his troops trying to restore order and discipline. Washington, still "very weak and low" from dysentery, had two horses shot out from under him and four bullets fired harmlessly through his coat and hat, but he continued to ride next to Braddock, unlike his other two aides, who had been wounded. Braddock remained in charge, and his troops kept fighting until, three hours later, two thirds of the 1,450 men and women of the British column had been killed or wounded.

Then, after a musket ball hit Braddock in the back and toppled him from his horse, the British broke ranks completely and began to flee "as sheep before hounds,"

The defeat of General Braddock and his troops.

Washington recalled. He had Braddock loaded onto a "small covered cart" and evacuated him across the Monongahela at the lower ford. Expecting the enemy to pursue them, Braddock, some officers, and a hundred troops prepared to make a stand. Washington was dispatched to stem the tide of fleeing troops at the upper ford, where he found Lieutenant Colonel Thomas Gage trying to rally the men without success. (Gage would become commander in chief of British forces in America from 1763 to 1775.)[30]

The Indians did not attempt to cross the river: They were celebrating their victory by breaking into the two hundred gallons of rum in the British supply wagons. Braddock nonetheless was abandoned by most of the troops at the lower ford and decided to retreat, carried on a stretcher. When Washington met up with him after sunset, the general ordered him to ride the fifty miles to Dunbar's camp and have food, medicine, and wagons for the wounded forwarded to Gist's, or even further north if possible. Washington rode all night and into the next morning, despite his illness. Along the way he was shocked by "the dead—the dying—the groans—lamentation—and cries along the road of the wounded for help." The "impervious darkness occasioned by the close shade of thick woods" increased the "gloom and horror" of this suffering, while forcing his two guides at times to grope on the ground looking for the path. The following night, Braddock arrived at Gist's and found the supplies and wagons from Dunbar; he reached Dunbar's camp late the next day. He died there on July 13, and Washington had him buried in the road so the

army would pass over the site, obliterating any trace and preventing the Indians from exhuming and mutilating the body.[31]

The remnants of the first brigade combined with Colonel Dunbar's amounted to more than thirteen hundred healthy soldiers, but they, and he, were too demoralized to rally and resume the offensive. Little did they know that, sated with plunder and captives, the warriors of the Ottawas and other northern tribes had gone home, abandoning the French and leaving Fort Duquesne without enough men to defend its ramparts. In a panic, Dunbar had the army destroy vast quantities of supplies, artillery, and ammunition so they could retreat all the faster. They fled all the way back to Philadelphia in disgrace, seeking winter quarters in the middle of July.[32]

Washington nonetheless returned home to a hero's welcome for his part in the campaign. His friends at Belvoir, relieved to finally learn that he had survived, could hardly wait to see him. "DEAR SIR,—After thanking Heaven for your safe return I must accuse you of great unkindness in refusing us the pleasure of seeing you this night," George Fairfax's wife, Sally, wrote on July 26 on behalf of the ladies at Belvoir. "I do assure you nothing but our being satisfied that our company would be disagreeable should prevent us from trying if our legs would not carry us to Mount Vernon this night, but if you will not come to us, tomorrow morning very early we shall be at Mount Vernon." As a young man Washington was passionately in love with Sally Fairfax, and he harbored that affection for the rest of his life.[33]

"I tremble at the consequences that this defeat may have upon our back settlers, who I suppose will all leave their habitations unless there are proper measures taken for their security," Washington told Dinwiddie in July. Because of his courage under fire, Washington had emerged from the disastrous Braddock campaign as a hero celebrated throughout the colonies, and in August Dinwiddie reappointed him colonel of the Virginia Regiment, reconstituted and based at Fort Cumberland. As Washington predicted, the failure to capture Fort Duquesne would make the worst English fears of Indian attacks come true and create an enormous refugee crisis. Over the next three years Braddock's Road became the route for Ohio Indian warriors to reach the backwoods settlements of Pennsylvania, Maryland, and Virginia and terrorize the inhabitants with frequent raids, sponsored by the French at Fort Duquesne. The frontier counties would lose 30 to 50 percent of their populations. In addition to plundering and burning settlements, the Indians took white captives, often selling the men into slavery as agricultural workers for the French and adopting the women and children into Indian families to sustain their own populations.

With its pacifist, Quaker government, Pennsylvania had no militia to protect its settlers, while the Maryland authorities abandoned Fort Cumberland and declared they would defend the frontier no further than Fort Frederick, forty-five miles west of Baltimore. In September, Washington put Lieutenant Colonel Adam Stephen in charge of the Virginia Regiment's twelve hundred troops at Fort Cumberland, and established his own headquarters at Winchester, which he deemed a better post for organizing the defense of the entire Shenandoah Valley, with its three-hundred-mile frontier.

By October, one of Washington's officers complained that he was barely able to travel from Alexandria westward across the Blue Ridge because so many refugees were clogging the passes, "flying [eastward] as if every moment was death." Indeed, in the final months of 1755 fifteen hundred settlers were killed and a thousand captured.[34] Virginia's burgesses ordered Washington to spread the regiment out and garrison eighteen small stockade forts. When this failed to secure the frontier, Washington argued that the Indian raids must be cut off at the source, by capturing Fort Duquesne.

For the next two years, however, the entire British war effort would remain largely on the defensive. Washington spent this time shaping the Virginia Regiment into a well-drilled, cohesive, and reliable force, while improving his own skills as a military leader and administrator. He learned to work with politicians, both locally and in Williamsburg, to secure uniforms, supplies, and provisions for his men. With these basics under control, he was able to focus on training and disciplining the unruly troops—mostly raw

George Washington as Colonel of the Virginia Regiment, by Charles Willson Peale, 1772

recruits and conscripts—resorting at times to floggings and executions to produce results. Washington also taught his officers to lead by example, instead of expecting obedience simply on the basis of their rank. In March 1757, he asserted to Dinwiddie that his men could perform as well as any British regulars in America. Indeed, Washington had transformed his provincial troops into a professional force—the first in American history.

However, as the regiment grew more robust, Washington's health deteriorated. Overworked and exhausted, he once again developed symptoms of dysentery and had to take time off to recover at Mount Vernon. Washington, like many colonists, was also frustrated by the course of the war and how the British were conducting it. To the north, the campaign against Fort Niagara had gotten no further than Fort Oswego before it sputtered to a halt because of desertions and logistical failures, while the British offensive against Fort St. Frédéric on Lake Champlain had been neutralized by a French and Indian counterattack. At this point the British built Fort William Henry at the foot of Lake George. Only the capture of the French forts on Nova Scotia's Shegnekto peninsula had succeeded, but the ethnic cleansing of Acadia—the British expulsion of French Catholics—would remain incomplete while the French continued to hold the fortress of Louisburg.

In August 1756, Major General Louis-Joseph de Montcalm had captured Fort Oswego from the British, and in June 1757, the British expedition against Louisburg got no further than Halifax. Then, in August, Montcalm captured Fort William Henry, and his Indian allies slaughtered the British after the surrender. (See ***A General Map of the Middle British Colonies, Detail #6***.) The war also spread to Europe, where the British, German, and Prussian alliance foundered against France, Russia, and Austria. [35]

Not until 1758, with Secretary of State William Pitt at the helm of the war effort, did the British regain the initiative. Instead of imperiously issuing orders to the colonial assemblies, Pitt motivated them to raise troops by offering incentives: Britain would pay for the troops' food and equipment and reimburse the colonies for certain other expenses, including enlistment bounties. Moreover, provincial officers would no longer be outranked by regular officers below their grade, and provincial troops would not be subject to the harsh code of martial law that governed the redcoats. The colonists, perceiving themselves now as equal partners in the common struggle to defend the British Empire, responded with an outpouring of loyalty and raised large numbers of troops. No longer afraid of bankrupting their province, Virginia authorities formed a second regiment, under Colonel William Byrd III, and increased pay for the troops. Instead of conscripting vagrants and convicts, Washington was now able to fill his regiment with volunteers. [36]

In North America, Pitt planned to renew the three original Anglo-American offensives under new commanders and with some modifications. The basic strategy, dictated as always by geography, remained the same. To cut off supplies and troops to New France via the St. Lawrence River, Lieutenant General Jeffrey Amherst would revive

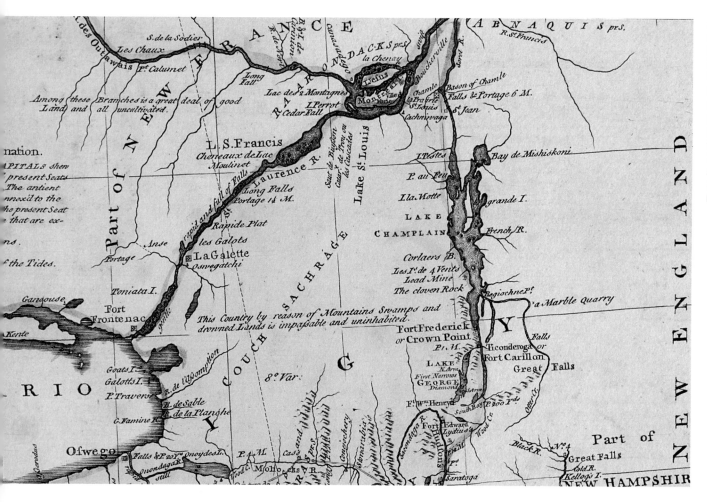

A General Map of the Middle British Colonies, Detail #6: Fort St. Frédéric, called Crown Point by the British, is indicated at the lower right of this view, near the southern end of Lake Champlain, on its western shore. Slightly to the south is Ticonderoga, called Carillon by the French. (These two names are east of the lake, but the fort was on the western shore.) Fort William Henry is indicated further south, just below Lake George.

William Pitt, secretary of state.

Lieutenant General Jeffrey Amherst.

Major General James Abercromby.

the attack against Louisburg that had fallen short the previous year. Major General James Abercromby, the new commander in chief, and Brigadier General George Augustus Howe would besiege Carillon, the French fort on the Ticonderoga peninsula guarding the Lake Champlain–Richelieu River water route leading to Montreal and Quebec on the St. Lawrence. Brigadier General John Forbes would march westward against Fort Duquesne by completing the road from Shippensburg begun by Pennsylvania authorities during the Braddock campaign.[37]

The first campaign of 1758 ended in disaster for the British, when Abercromby ordered his forces to storm the French lines at Carillon on July 8. Viscount George Howe, the eldest of the three Howe brothers, was killed. Amherst and his second in command, Brigadier General James Wolfe, were more fortunate at Louisburg, which they besieged, bombarded, and captured, also in July. Forbes's campaign against Fort Duquesne unfolded into the fall. Washington, who was on the expedition, received word from his friend Joseph Chew on September 11 "of Colonel Bradstreet's taking Fort Frontenac with all the vessels on Lake Ontario, two of which is loaded with furs, etc., just arrived from Niagara. This is a glorious stroke. Cuts off all communication with their western settlements and forts and will I hope make the conquest of Duquesne easy, of which I impatiently expect to hear." (See *A General Map of the Middle British Colonies, Detail #5*, page 43.)[38]

Brigadier General George Augustus Howe.

Washington and Byrd led the two thousand troops of the two Virginia regiments on the Forbes expedition, which also consisted of two regiments of British regulars and additional troops from Delaware, Maryland, North Carolina, and Pennsylvania for a total of five thousand. As the senior colonel, Washington had overall command of the two Virginia regiments. Forbes planned to avoid Braddock's two principal mistakes. First, for supplies, security, and communication, he would have substantial forts at fifty-mile intervals along his route and blockhouses between them no more than a day's march apart. Second, he would work hard to gain the allegiance of the Ohio Indians.[39]

He did not anticipate, however, the strenuous protests of Washington and Byrd against his plan to continue the road directly to the west instead of linking it to the old Braddock Road, thirty miles to the south. The Braddock Road already existed, the Virginians argued; continuing the Pennsylvania road from where it had stopped, only twenty miles west of Raystown, would take too long, and probably prevent the expedition from reaching Fort Duquesne before winter shut down the campaign. Forbes interpreted their opposition as venal self-interest: They wanted the Pennsylvania route discontinued in order to give Virginia's speculators and settlers an edge over Pennsylvanians in the competition for Ohio lands. Forbes chastised them for placing their provincial allegiance above "the good of the service," and took the advice of some Philadelphia officials to avoid Braddock's Road.[40]

During the first week of September, the advance guard of Forbes's expedition, a regiment of regulars under Colonel Henry Bouquet, began constructing Fort Ligonier, about halfway to Fort Duquesne from Raystown on the Pennsylvania route. (See *A Map of Pennsylvania, Detail #3*, page 55, right center.) On the 11th, Bouquet sent a detachment of eight hundred men toward the Forks of the Ohio, and three days later they were badly defeated by a French and Indian force from Fort Duquesne, suffering 300 casualties. The loss would have been far greater had it not been for the steadiness of 150 Virginia troops from Washington's regiment, led by Captain Thomas Bullitt, who held their ground at the rear, allowing others to escape past them when the battle became a rout. And Forbes's methodical approach was validated because the men were able to retreat to a nearby fort, preventing a full-blown disaster like Braddock's march. Nonetheless, combined with the horrendous defeat of Abercromby's force and Viscount Howe's death at Carillon in July, the setback near the Forks weighed heavily on Forbes. Washington became all the more convinced that this northern route had been a mistake, but he dutifully brought the rest of his regiment from Fort Cumberland to Raystown, as Forbes ordered, and the two men gradually repaired their relationship.[41]

Forbes moved his headquarters forward to Fort Ligonier, where he received news on November 7 that the Treaty of Easton (Pennsylvania)—which he had done much to foster by his diplomacy behind the scenes—had been concluded in late October. The Ohio tribes, represented by the Delaware chief Pisquetomen, agreed to stop their attacks and return English captives, while Pennsylvania governor William Denny promised to deal directly with the Delawares, formally recognizing their autonomy and independence from the Iroquois League. Pennsylvania traders would establish a post at the Forks after Fort Duquesne was captured from the French, but Denny promised on behalf of the Crown to contain white settlement east of the Alleghenies. The treaty would soon strip the French of their Indian allies in the Ohio Valley, who were already disgruntled about the dwindling supply of trade goods at Fort Duquesne. Forbes therefore expected little opposition on the last leg of his march to the Forks.[42]

Before word of the treaty had spread throughout the Ohio Valley, on November 12, the French and Indians made a final raid near Fort Ligonier, inflicting heavy casualties and destroying hundreds of horses and livestock. Forbes sent a detachment of the Second Virginia Regiment under Lieutenant Colonel George Mercer in pursuit of the attackers, and then dispatched Washington with a contingent from the First Virginia Regiment to provide support. In the darkness, Mercer's and Washington's men mistook each other for the enemy and opened fire. Despite the efforts of Captain Bullitt and Washington, who ran into the gauntlet of musketry shouting the order to cease fire and pushing the muzzles into the air, fourteen soldiers died and twenty-six were wounded. Washington, as usual, remained unscathed.[43]

After the French raid, Forbes received intelligence that they had few troops at Fort Duquesne and were preparing to abandon the Forks, so he pushed the expedition forward as fast as possible, without tents or baggage, and with only light artillery, clearing three to five miles of road a day through the woods. The French commander, meanwhile, had the fort's artillery rowed down the Ohio to the Illinois settlements, before torching the buildings on November 23 and leveling the walls with a gunpowder mine. Forbes's men heard the explosion and saw the smoke from several miles away.

"The enemy, after letting us get within a day's march of the place, burned the fort, and ran away (by the light of it) at night," Washington reported to Virginia's lieutenant governor, Francis Fauquier, after Forbes's column took possession of the Forks on the 25th. "The possession of this fort has been a matter of great surprise to the whole army, and we cannot attribute it to more probable causes than those of weakness, want of provisions, and desertion of their Indians." Forbes's "great merit" also had something to do with it, admitted Washington, who had pestered the

Brigadier General John Forbes.

general about Braddock's Road even during the final phase of the campaign. Forbes had attained Braddock's goal by assiduously avoiding his blunders.

With quiet restored on the frontier, Virginia's role in the war was essentially over. Washington returned to Mount Vernon in December 1758, resigned his commission, and looked forward to civilian life as a landowner, planter, elected official, and family man. In January 1759 he married Martha Custis, a wealthy young widow whose two children he adopted and cared for as his own. The nearly two hundred slaves that had been part of the dowry for her first marriage remained assets of the Custis estate, but many of them were brought from the Custis properties to work at Mount Vernon under Washington's management, as if they were his own. In February Washington took his seat in the House of Burgesses, representing Frederick County.[44]

Martha Dandridge Custis.

"The French are so well drubbed, and seem so much humbled in America, that I apprehend our generals will find it no difficult matter to reduce Canada to our obedience this summer," Washington wrote to a British merchant on August 10, 1760. The summer and early fall of the previous year, 1759, had seen a string of stunning British victories in North America that rolled back the borders of New France and penetrated to its core: the fall of Fort Niagara to Sir William Johnson's forces; Amherst's capture of Carillon and Fort St. Frédéric; and, after a long and brutal siege, Wolfe's triumph and martyrdom at Quebec.[45] The British campaigns through Iroquois territory into the heart of Canada were made possible by the League's decision to end its policy of neutrality and ally with the British (just as the Ohio tribes' shift to the British had made the Forbes campaign a success in 1758).

With the French driven from Fort Duquesne, and the Ohio Indians vigorously asserting their independence, the Iroquois were anxious to bring these once subordinate Indians back under control. A prophetic spiritual movement that began a decade earlier among the Delawares of the Susquehanna Valley when they were displaced by the Iroquois had spread to the West, where its denunciation of the white man's corrupt ways (alcohol, firearms, cattle, and all manner of trade goods) was uniting the various tribes of the region against the Six Nations as well. Warning the British that the Delawares and Shawnees secretly planned to rejoin the French, the Iroquois offered to help defeat their schemes. In exchange for large gifts of weapons and supplies, the Iroquois pledged to keep the Ohio country in British hands—a promise that would soon prove impossible to keep. For a similar price, the Iroquois would indeed help the British make their next campaign to conquer Canada a success, by sending envoys to the French-allied tribes along the St. Lawrence River and the Great Lakes and convincing them to remain neutral.[46]

After the loss of Quebec, the French had retreated toward Montreal for the winter and hoped to retake Quebec from the small British garrison as soon as reinforcements and supplies arrived from France in the spring. However, a British naval victory in Europe broke up the relief convoy, and Amherst, now commander in chief, launched an ambitious three-pronged campaign in 1760, with Iroquois support, which succeeded as planned by early September: British ships at Louisburg brought troops to enlarge the garrison at Quebec and pushed on to Montreal, where two additional British forces converged from the south—one from Oswego and down the St. Lawrence, and the other along the Lake Champlain–Richelieu River axis.[47] Even as Canada fell to the British, however, the Seven Years' War continued in Europe and around the globe, ultimately reaching the Caribbean, Africa, India, and the Philippines. Washington's triumphant tone in the summer of 1760 was tempered by worry about Britain's allies. "We are in pain here for the King of Prussia," he wrote, "and wish Hanover safe, these being events in which we are much interested."

When the Definitive Treaty of Peace was finally signed in Paris in 1762 and ratified in 1763, the French lost all of their territory in North America east of the Mississippi River (except New Orleans) to the British. France's ally, Spain, had lost Havana to the British during the war and recovered it in exchange for Spanish Florida—the peninsula and the Gulf Coast as far west as the Mississippi. The French regained the bulk of their captured sugar islands in the West Indies, while returning the territory they had taken in Hanover, Hesse, Brunswick, and Westphalia to the German princes. A separate treaty between Prussia, Austria, and Russia restored their prewar boundaries.[48]

"Another tempest has arose upon our frontiers, and the alarm spread wider than ever," Washington wrote to his friend Robert Stewart on August 13, 1763. "In Augusta County many people have been killed, and numbers fled, and confusion and despair prevails in every quarter." In May the Ottawa war chief, Pontiac, joined by Potawatomi and Wyandot bands, had led a raid on the British garrison at Fort Detroit, igniting a string of surprise attacks by Shawnees, Delawares, and other Ohio tribes who joined

Pontiac preaching to tribal chiefs.

the rebellion across the western frontiers. Still in retirement from the military, Washington kept abreast of events, but was now merely an observer. He noted that his former second in command, Adam Stephen, had been dispatched by the governor and council at the head of five hundred militiamen to meet the emergency on the frontier.

Pitt's spending spree had won the war but left the British government with enormous debt, and vast new territories that would be expensive to occupy and administer. When the War Office reduced Amherst's budget in North America, he cut back on gifts to the Indians (with the exception of the Six Nations), including ammunition and alcohol. The Indians felt doubly betrayed because the British, who had promised at Easton in 1758 to build only trading posts and to curb westward settlement, were instead maintaining forts in Indian country, seemingly as an entering wedge for the white population that was rapidly spilling beyond the Appalachian Mountains.[49]

By July only three frontier forts—Detroit, Niagara, and Pitt—remained in British hands. (See *A General Map of the Middle British Colonies, Detail #7*.) Amherst sent Colonel Henry Bouquet with five hundred troops to lift the Indians' siege of Fort Pitt. "At this instant a calm is taking place, which forebodes some mischief to Colonel Bouquet," Washington wrote. The Indians had retreated, he thought, probably to gather their forces and attack Bouquet's column on its march along Forbes's Road through Pennsylvania to the frontier. Indeed, they attacked Bouquet near the head of Bushy Run. After a fierce two-day battle with heavy casualties on both sides, Bouquet drove away the Indians and proceeded to Fort Pitt. (See *A Map of Pennsylvania, Detail #3*, page 55, the site labeled *Bouquet's Field* and marked with crossed swords.) By the time Amherst was recalled to London in the fall, some four hundred troops and two thousand settlers had been killed or captured, while "Pontiac's War" raged on.

In October, King George III issued the Proclamation of 1763, reaffirming the Treaty of Easton and the British pledge to contain white settlement east of the Appalachians. This served as the basis for talks the following year, in which Sir William Johnson negotiated the return of most white captives in exchange for resuming diplomatic gifts and the trade in ammunition and rum. By 1765 the Proclamation Line had improved Indian relations with the British and helped pacify the frontier, but Pontiac's War and its resolution deprived many settlers and traders like William Trent of lands they had acquired in the Ohio country. Trent became a leader of the "Suffering Traders," who petitioned the Crown, seeking compensation.[50]

Similarly, over the next two decades Washington became an advocate for the veterans who had received warrants for land in the Ohio country as bounties when they enlisted in 1754 and marched with him there. Washington was primarily looking out for his own interests since, as a colonel, he was entitled to twenty thousand of the two hundred thousand acres promised by Governor Dinwiddie. A captain was to receive nine thousand acres, while a private could claim only four hundred. Enough of these men were strapped for cash that Washington was able to buy up warrants entitling him to a total of thirty-three thousand acres. On top of Dinwiddie's proclamation of 1754, the Royal Proclamation of 1763 awarded land to officers who had served in the French and Indian War. However, since the king had simultaneously halted westward expansion, none of the land covered by either proclamation would be granted for years to come.[51]

Just as the frontier settled down in 1765, the cities of the eastern seaboard erupted in rioting. A painful downturn in the economy following the boom years of the war had already set the colonists on edge when the Stamp Act unleashed their fury. The new tax reached into every

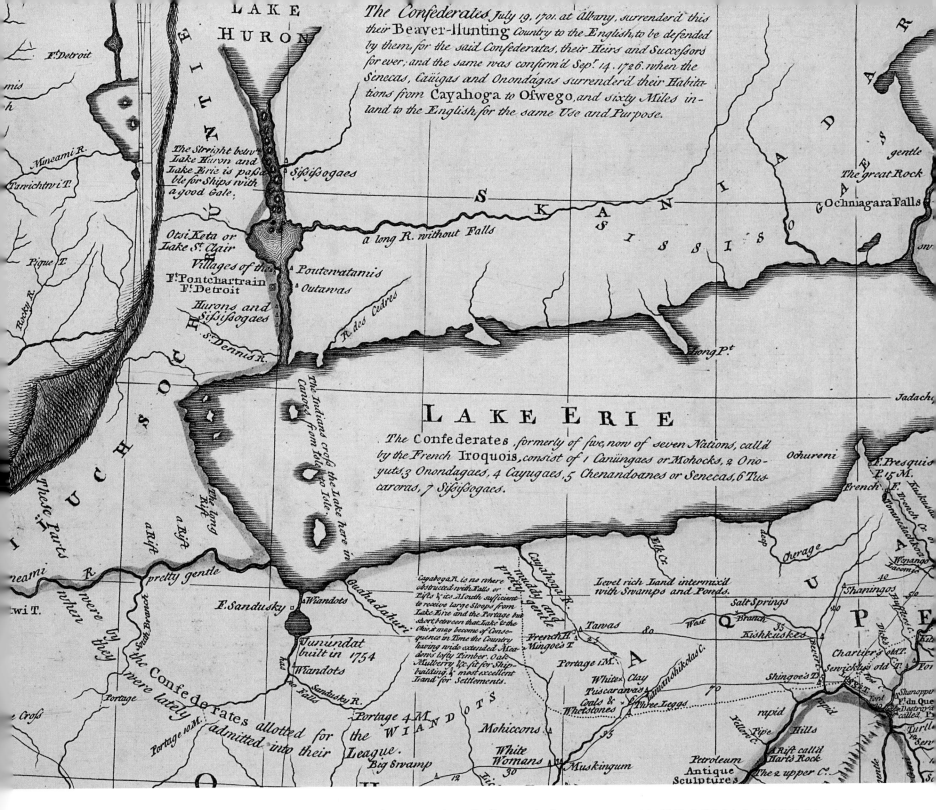

The following text appears on the map:

LAKE HURON

The Confederates July 19. 1701. at Albany, surrender'd this their Beaver-Hunting Country to the English, to be defended by them, for the said Confederates, their Heirs and Successors for ever: and the same was confirm'd Sep.t 14. 1726. when the Senecas, Caiügas and Onondagas surrender'd their Habitations from Cayahoga to Oswego, and sixty Miles inland to the English, for the same Use and Purpose.

LAKE ERIE

The Confederates, formerly of five, now of seven Nations, call'd by the French Iroquois, consist of 1 Canüngaes or Mohocks, 2 Onoyuts, 3 Onondagaes, 4 Cayugaes, 5 Chenandoanes or Senecas, 6 Tuscaroras, 7 Sisisogaes.

household, requiring the purchase of stamps for everyday transactions. Parliament had taken a first step to making the colonists share the burden of the war debt. Washington at first discussed the issue with pragmatic detachment, writing to a relative that while some colonists viewed this "unconstitutional method of taxation as a direful attack upon their liberties, and loudly exclaim against the violation," he viewed the act as one of several "ill judged measures" that would disrupt Britain's mercantilist system. Washington predicted that "the advantage accruing to the Mother Country will fall greatly short of the expectations of the Ministry, for certain it is, our whole substance does already in a manner flow to Great Britain and that whatsoever contributes to lessen our importations must be hurtful to their manufacturers." If Parliament tried to squeeze the colonists, they would become more frugal and industrious, Washington observed. They would learn to do without British luxuries and produce goods of their own.[52]

By 1767, however, Washington was characterizing the Stamp Act as "an act of oppression," and was glad that it had been repealed the previous year. Yet, in writing to London merchants, he still focused on the idea that allowing the colonies to thrive commercially was wise because it would ultimately benefit the Mother Country. Ever the surveyor, he used the compass as his metaphor: "The money therefore which [the colonists] raise would centre in Great Britain, as certain as the needle will settle to the poles."[53]

A General Map of the Middle British Colonies, Detail #7: Potawatomis and Wyandots joined the initial attack on Fort Detroit, and Fort Sandusky was also captured (just north and just south of the western end of Lake Erie). Forts Presque Isle, Le Boeuf (*French F.*), and Machault (at Venango) were also taken (lower right). See *Detail #3,* page 40, for Michilimackinac, on Lake Huron, also captured, as were other posts on Lake Michigan, the Wabash River, and the Miami River.

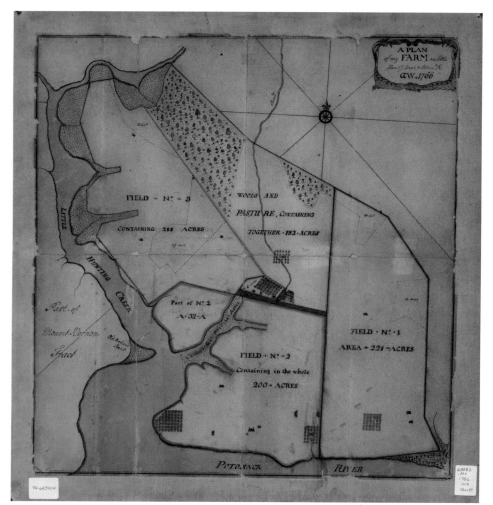

George Washington's 1766 plan of his farm on Little Hunting Creek and the Potomac River, part of Mount Vernon.

especially when those Indians consent to our occupying those lands. Any person who neglects hunting out good lands, and in some measure marking and distinguishing them for his own, in order to keep others from settling them will never regain it.

Crawford, a Pennsylvania surveyor, lived at Stewart's Crossing on the Youghiogheny River and, along with other settlers, had secured land grants in the area (today's Fayette County, Pennsylvania). Washington proposed a partnership in which Crawford would scout out choice parcels and Washington would secure ownership, bearing the cost of surveying and patenting the land.

"By this time it will be easy for you to discover that my plan is to secure a good deal of land. You will consequently come in for a handsome quantity," Washington wrote. He warned Crawford to "keep the whole matter a secret, rather than give the alarm to others or allow [yourself] to be censured for the opinion I have given in respect to the King's Proclamation." If Crawford were questioned, Washington advised, he should say that his trips to the wilderness were to hunt game. "I will have the land surveyed and keep others off and leave the rest to time and my assiduity."

Crawford promised to "examine all the creeks from the head of the Monongahela down to the Fort, and in the Forks of the River Ohio and New River, or as far as time will allow me between this and Christmas. You may depend upon my losing no time."[54] Within weeks Crawford had identified some fine tracts near Fort Pitt, and by the following year Washington had secured title to his first piece of land west of the Alleghenies—on the Youghiogheny thirty-five miles southeast of Fort Pitt. The two men enjoyed a lucrative partnership for the next fifteen years.[55]

"At a time when our lordly masters in Great Britain will be satisfied with nothing less than the deprecation of American freedom, it seems highly necessary that something should be done to avert the stroke and maintain the liberty which we have derived from our ancestors," Washington wrote to his neighbor George Mason in 1769, when the two men were discussing Virginia's non-importation agreement, written by Mason. While repealing the Stamp Act in 1766, Parliament had passed the Declaratory Act, affirming its right to tax the colonies. With the Townshend Act of 1767 Parliament again attempted to raise revenue from the colonies through taxes on a wide variety of goods. The colonies reacted with non-importation agreements aimed at slashing the profits of British merchants and having them in turn pressure the government to repeal the taxes. "Addresses to the throne, and remonstrances to Parliament" having proved futile, Washington wrote, the boycotts should be given a chance; resorting to arms should be a last resort after all other avenues of resistance had been exhausted.[56]

Like most Americans, who had viewed themselves as full partners with the Mother Country in the great victory over the French in the Seven Years' War, Washington remained loyal to the king and only gradually came to regard the interests of Britain and the American colonies as fundamentally incompatible. The colonists asserted the right to tax themselves; the British government countered that Parliament had the sole power to impose taxes and its sovereignty could not be divided—its power could not be shared with the colonial assemblies.

In addition to his political principles, Washington's desire to break out of his perpetual indebtedness to British merchants and his determination to acquire land in the Ohio country helped erode his reverence for the Crown. Since the Proclamation of 1763 had suspended the veterans' land grants, Washington would eventually choose to disregard its authority. In September 1767 in a letter to William Crawford, a boyhood friend who had served as an officer in his regiment during the Forbes campaign, Washington confided:

I can never look upon the Proclamation in any other light (but this I say between ourselves) than as a temporary expedient to quiet the minds of the Indians. It must fall, of course, in a few years,

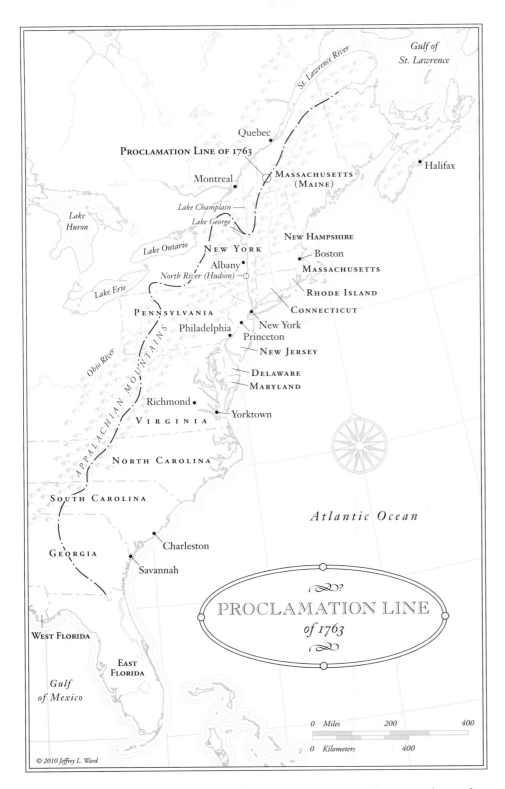

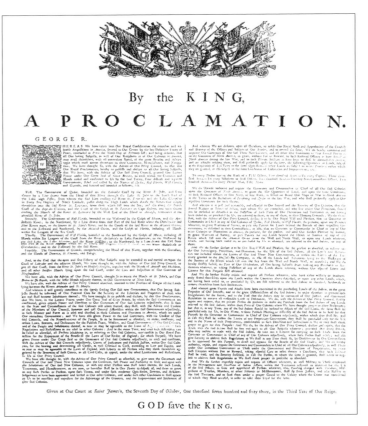

ABOVE: George III's Proclamation Line.

RIGHT: George III's proclamation forbidding settlement west of the Appalachian Mountains.

Since Pennsylvania had been allowing traders and settlers to claim land west of the Alleghenies, in December 1769 Washington found Virginia's governor and council eager to keep up when he petitioned them for the two hundred thousand acres promised by Dinwiddie fifteen years earlier. Two recent treaties had vacated Indian land south and east of the Ohio River, which the council now awarded to the veterans, including Washington. During a month-long trip in the fall of 1770 Washington and Crawford traveled two hundred miles down the Ohio River, from Fort Pitt to the mouth of the Great Kanawha River, selecting some two hundred thousand acres, which Crawford later surveyed as twenty-five tracts of various sizes. Over the next two years, Washington supervised Crawford's work, collected money from the veterans to cover their share of the surveying expenses, and assigned parcels to them or their heirs. Including the land he bought from other veterans, Washington amassed ten thousand acres on the Ohio River and twenty-three

thousand acres—forty continuous miles—along the Great Kanawha. (See *A General Map of the Middle British Colonies, Detail #8*, page 66.)[57]

At the same time, Washington was lobbying officials in Maryland and Virginia to turn the Potomac River into a water highway between these western lands and the Atlantic seaboard. The river, he wrote, was to be "the channel of commerce between Great Britain and that immense territory which is unfolding to our view," conveying "the extensive and valuable trade of a rising empire." The Potomac was to be connected to the Ohio by Braddock's Road and the Youghiogheny and Monongahela rivers. Two years later, he would help get a bill passed by Virginia's General Assembly to raise money for making the Potomac navigable between Fort Cumberland and Chesapeake Bay. The ambitious project would soon be interrupted by war with England, but Washington would return to it with renewed zeal after the Revolution. Washington readily admitted that the plan had clear advantages for him personally, linking his twelve thousand acres of Tidewater property with his much larger western holdings and enhancing their value. However, with the winning of American independence, Washington would also come to see the commercial development of the Potomac as essential to cementing the union of the eastern and western states.[58]

For the moment, however, Washington envisioned an expanded British Empire, and in the struggle with Parliament he remained a moderate. While the boycotts

A General Map of the Middle British Colonies, Detail #8: Washington's bounty lands, in the area along the Ohio River between the Great Kanawha and Little Kanawha (lower left), were separated from the Potomac River (right center) by the Allegheny Mountains (running from lower left to upper right). Connecting the headwaters of the Potomac to the Ohio country would remain a tantalizing dream for the rest of Washington's life.

had allowed the Virginia gentry to start weaning themselves of the luxuries that kept them in debt, when the new prime minister, Frederick, Lord North, repealed all but one of the Townshend duties in 1770—keeping the one on tea to show Parliament's authority—Washington and other moderates were happy to resume importing British goods.[59] The economy pulled out of the postwar recession, and by the middle of 1771, non-importation had been dropped throughout the colonies.

In the fall, John Murray, Lord Dunmore, became Virginia's new governor and soon developed a good rapport with Washington, since both men were eager for development of the Ohio country and regarded the Proclamation of 1763 as a temporary expedient. Washington volunteered to take the governor on a tour of the Ohio Valley in the summer of 1773. The death of Washington's stepdaughter, Patsy Custis, prevented him from making the trip, but Dunmore went on his own. Finding that the land around the Forks was already settled—illegally—by some ten thousand whites, Dunmore proceeded to claim the land for Virginia by incorporating it into Augusta County and issuing land patents to the settlers. Pennsylvania authorities also claimed the area and fought back by organizing it as Westmoreland County. Tensions between the settlers from the two competing colonies threatened to boil over into civil war.[60]

At the same time, passage of the Tea Act in 1773 renewed the struggle between Parliament and the colonies. An attempt to bail out the ailing British East India Company by giving it a monopoly on tea sales in the colonies inflamed colonists' resentment, since they perceived it to be a stealthy way of imposing the tea tax

retained, in principle, three years earlier. In the Boston Tea Party on December 16, 1773, protesters dressed as Mohawks raided the East India Company's ships and dumped large amounts of tea into the harbor. Lord North and his ministers reacted with a set of harsh measures, which the colonists soon dubbed the "Intolerable Acts." The Massachusetts charter was revised to reduce the colonists' rights, and the governor was replaced by the commander in chief of British forces in America, Lieutenant General Thomas Gage, who arrived from New York to occupy Boston with four thousand troops and shut down the port.[61]

As outrage spread through the thirteen colonies, Washington voted with his fellow Virginia burgesses on May 24, 1774, for a day of prayer and fasting for Boston's plight. If the Americans submitted quietly to the British, Washington warned, "custom and use shall make us as tame and abject slaves as the blacks we rule over with such arbitrary sway." Intentionally or not, Washington had revealed his growing aversion to human bondage by equating Americans' rights with those that were denied to black slaves. He effectively denounced his own and his fellow planters' "arbitrary" treatment of their slaves and implied that their servile condition was due to "custom and use" rather than any natural inferiority. Washington had stopped buying slaves two years earlier, and the subsequent growth of the slave population at Mount Vernon was primarily the result of new births.[62]

When Governor Dunmore punished the burgesses by dissolving the House, they met at a tavern to form the Virginia Convention and invite the other colonies to a Continental Congress. Hoping to pry Virginia loose from this burgeoning Continental movement, Dunmore raised a volunteer force to launch a military campaign against the Shawnees in the Ohio Valley, ostensibly in retaliation for the murder of three traders. In fact Dunmore was getting a head start on claiming the entire southern half of the Ohio Valley, a move that was sure to please his colony's gentry, who coveted the lands south of the river that the Shawnees clung to tenaciously as their hunting grounds.[63]

In September and October, while Washington attended the First Continental Congress in Philadelphia as a Virginia delegate, Dunmore led his 2,400 troops west and attacked the Shawnees. Dunmore hoped to sabotage the meeting in Philadelphia by removing a major grievance of the colonists: the restrictions on western expansion imposed by the Proclamation of 1763. He might be reprimanded or dismissed by the Crown for his recklessness, but he might instead emerge as a conquering hero, thanked by London and the colonies alike, and he was willing to take the risk. On October 10, after a battle with the Indians at the confluence of the Ohio and Great Kanawha rivers (today's Point Pleasant, West Virginia), Dunmore declared victory. The Shawnees agreed to an armistice and a suspension of hunting south of the river, with final terms to be determined at a peace conference the following spring. Back in Williamsburg, the gentry applauded Dunmore's apparent success. In March 1775 a second Virginia Convention met to pick delegates for the Second Continental Congress but also issued a resolution extolling Dunmore's virtues and giving thanks for his "expedition against our Indian enemy."[64]

Having gained the goodwill of the gentry, Dunmore tried in vain to bring them firmly under his control and disrupt their resistance to the Crown. Apparently to give Washington second thoughts about returning to Philadelphia for the next meeting of Congress, Dunmore threatened to declare "null and void" the patents granted to Washington and the other veterans for their bounty lands in the West, on the specious grounds that William Crawford, who had laid off the tracts, was not a qualified surveyor. Washington wrote to Dunmore on April 3 that the news of his action "appearing altogether incredible, I gave little attention to it," until he confirmed the report and learned that "all the patentees . . . were exceedingly distressed and at a loss, to know what to think of it, or how to act in a case so uncommon." Washington restated the veterans' case, quoting from Dinwiddie's proclamation of 1754, and asking, after everything the men had been through, if it would not "be exceedingly hard then, my Lord . . . to declare that the surveys are

invalid?" Washington also mentioned that he was writing to learn the facts because he was to "leave home the first of May," clearly indicating that he still planned to attend the Second Continental Congress.[65]

Two weeks later, Dunmore infuriated Virginians everywhere by transferring Williamsburg's gunpowder supply to a British warship—just when a slave revolt was expected to erupt in the James River Valley. Into this maelstrom of anger and fear came reports, a week later, that the British army's attempt to seize the colonists' gunpowder outside Boston had triggered clashes with the militia at Lexington and Concord on April 19. Both sides suffered heavy casualties, but the Americans had driven the British regulars back into Boston, where they were now besieged by militiamen from all over New England.

In May Washington attended the Second Continental Congress dressed in the blue-and-buff uniform he had designed for the Fairfax Independent militia company, but he gave no other indication that he wanted to command the troops around Boston. Charles Lee, a British officer who had come over to the American side during the tea crisis, appeared to be the candidate with the most professional military experience. On the other hand, Artemas Ward, a provincial colonel in the French and Indian War, and John Hancock, the wealthiest Whig in New England, were both from Massachusetts, the epicenter of the conflict. Washington's military exploits, while seventeen years in the past, had given him a name recognition throughout the colonies that the other candidates lacked, and he was a vocal advocate of Continental unity. Unlike Hancock and Lee, Washington did not lobby for the appointment, and thus assuaged the other delegates' fear of a standing army led by an ambitious usurper of civilian authority. John Adams of Massachusetts nominated Washington as commander in chief, and by putting a Virginian at the head of New England troops, Congress took the first step in forging a national army, making the plight of Boston the cause of every American, from Georgia to the Canadian border.[66]

"I have been called upon by the unanimous voice of the colonies to the command of the Continental Army," Washington wrote from Philadelphia on June 19, 1775, to a relative in Virginia. Washington fervently believed in the justice of the American cause and was ready to focus completely on the task at hand, which he would carry out "with the strictest integrity," he wrote. Nonetheless, the prospect was daunting. "I am now embarked on a tempestuous ocean, from whence, perhaps, no friendly harbor is to be found."[67]

John Murray, Lord Dunmore.

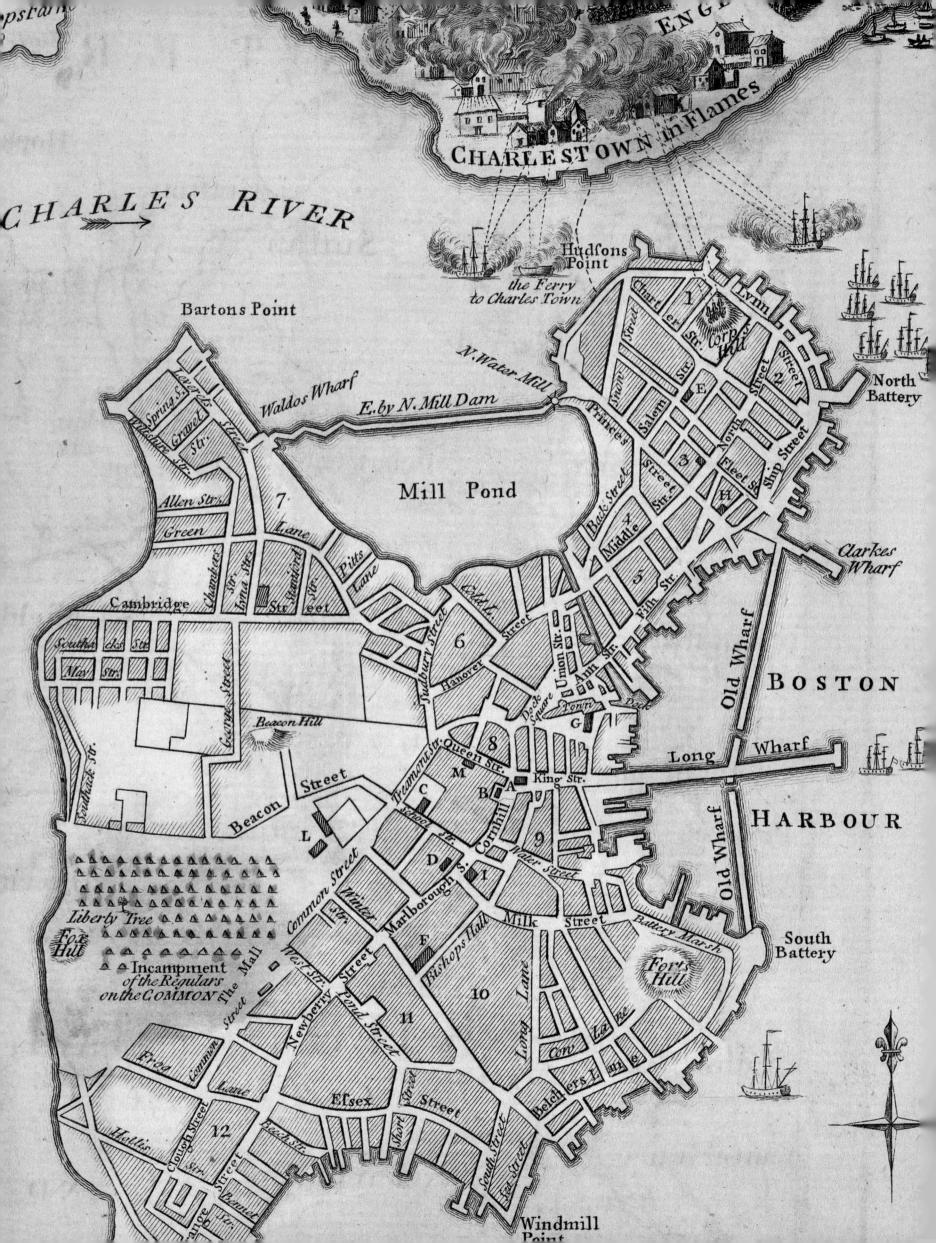

ENG[...]

CHARLESTOWN in Flames

CHARLES RIVER

Hudsons Point

the Ferry to Charles Town

Bartons Point

N. Water Mill

E. by N. Mill Dam

Waldos Wharf

Mill Pond

North Battery

Spring L.

Laurel St.

Gravel Str.

Wheeten Str.

Allen Str.

Green

Cambria

Chambers

Str. Str.

Lynn Str.

Lane

Pitts Lane

Str. Stanford Str.

7

Prince's

Salem

Charter Str.

Simon

Lynn

1

E

North Street

2

Street

Corp'l Hill

Street

3

H

Fleet St.

Ship Street

Clarkes Wharf

Back Street

Middle

Str.

5

Wm. Str.

Cambridge

Southacks Str.

May Str.

George Street

Beacon Hill

Cold L.

6

Hanover

Street

Sudbury Street

Union Str.

Ann Str.

Dock Square

Jenn

G

Denn

Bell

BOSTON

Old Wharf

Beacon Street

Beacon Street

Treamont St.

Queen Str.

8

M

A

King Str.

Long Wharf

HARBOUR

L

C

B

Cornhill

9

Water Street

Old Wharf

School St.

D

I

Common Street

Winter Str.

Marlborough

Bishops Hall

Milk Street

Battery Marsh

South Battery

Liberty Tree

Incampment of the Regulars on the COMMON

F

10

Lords Lane

Con Lane

Forts Hill

Fox Hill

The Mall

West Str.

Pond Street

11

Newberry Street

Belchers Lane

Frog Lane

Common Lane

Efsex

Street

Short Str.

Hollis Str.

Clough Str.

12

Canoe Str.

Bennet Str.

South Street

Windmill Point

N
W · E
S

CHAPTER THREE

0   1   2   3

THE SIEGE OF

BOSTON

On June 20, 1775, as Washington set out from Philadelphia to Cambridge, where American forces were gathered, a messenger arrived with news that a battle had been fought on the Charlestown peninsula, north of Boston, but reports were still sketchy as to casualties on each side. In New York, Washington's hosts urged him to open a sealed dispatch addressed to Congress that had just arrived from Massachusetts, since he might have to act upon the contents. He hesitated and then broke the seal.

The Americans had sent twelve hundred men to fortify "a small hill, south of Bunker's Hill," Washington read. The British "marched up to our entrenchments, from which they were twice repulsed, but in the third attack [seized] them . . . At this time, the buildings in Charlestown appeared in flames in almost every quarter, kindled by hot balls, and is since laid in ashes. Though this scene was almost horrible and alto-gether new for most of our men, yet many stood and received wounds by swords and bayonets before they quitted their lines. At five o'clock the enemy were in full possession of all the posts within the isthmus."

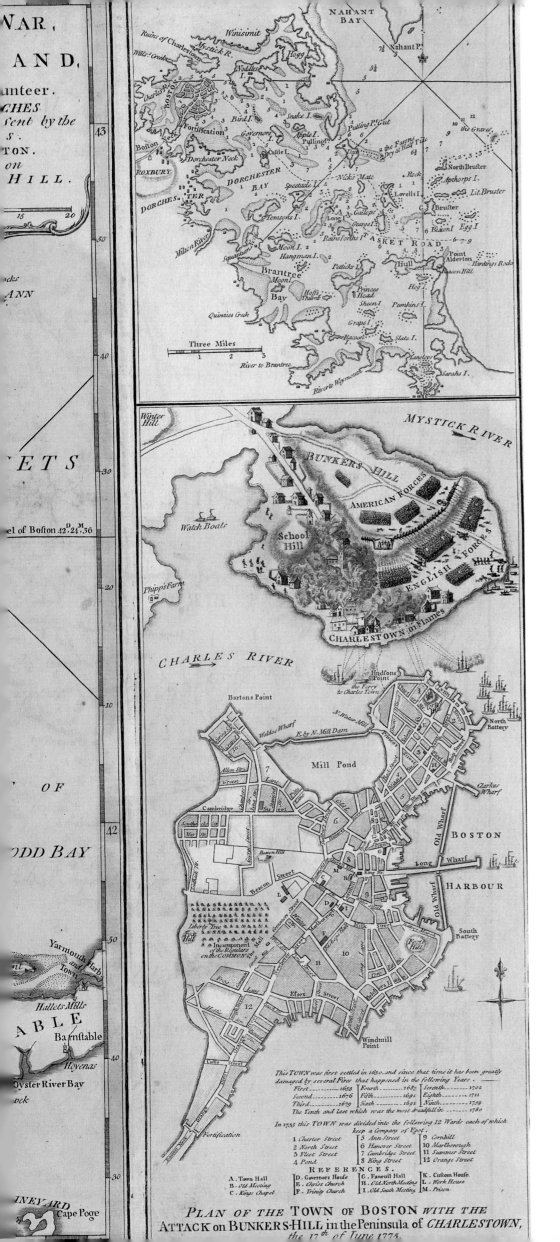

PLAN OF THE TOWN OF BOSTON WITH THE
ATTACK on BUNKERS-HILL in the Peninsula of CHARLESTOWN,
the 17ᵗʰ of June 1775.

The Seat of War in New England: Printed in London, on September 5, 1775, the map probably made its way into Washington's hands from French map dealers, who continued to trade with their colleagues in London throughout the war. An unusual feature of the main map is the depiction of citizen-soldiers from all over New England moving along their various routes as they converge on Cambridge. At left center, Washington's entourage approaches from the west (see also *Detail #1,* page 72). Further along his route, the skirmish at Concord's North Bridge is noted with the date and a pair of crossed swords.

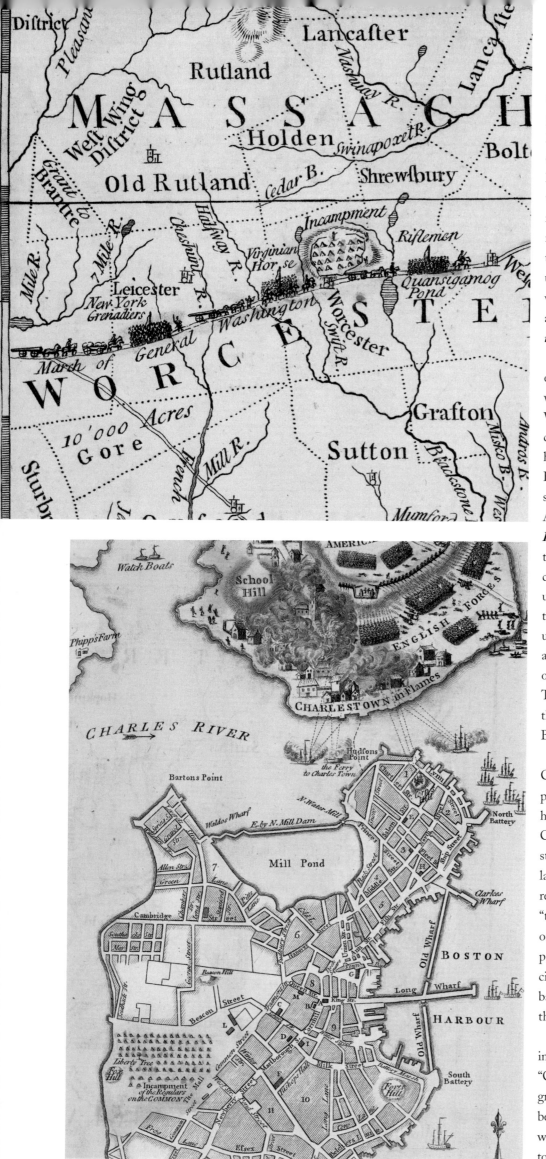

Calling for Congress to send gunpowder and a commander in chief, if he had been named, the dispatch portrayed a defeat in which the Americans had lost sixty or seventy killed and missing and possibly one hundred wounded.[1] Gradually the world would learn that the Battle of Bunker Hill had been a victory for the British only in name. They had driven the rebels from a trench on Breed's Hill, but at the cost of more than a thousand casualties. Though he was anxious to be on his way, Washington did not reach Cambridge until July 2, having been delayed by cheering crowds and welcoming committees—"the successive civilities which accompanied me in my whole route." (See **The Seat of War in New England**, pages 70–71, and **Detail #1**.)[2]

"Upon my arrival, I immediately visited the several posts occupied by our troops, and as soon as the weather permitted, reconnoitered those of the enemy," Washington reported to John Hancock on July 10. After capturing Breed's Hill three weeks earlier, the British had pushed further west and dug in firmly on Bunker Hill in order to dominate the narrow neck of the peninsula, positioning themselves to break out and attack the Americans at Cambridge. (See **The Seat of War in New England, Detail #2**.) The British had three floating batteries anchored near the mouth of the Mystic River, which could be moved upstream to attack the New Hampshire units in trenches at Winter Hill. Next to them, the position at Prospect Hill, manned by Connecticut troops under Major General Israel Putnam, was also vulnerable, with "the enemy's camp in full view at the distance of little more than a mile," Washington told Hancock. The Americans' "advanced guard" was even closer, with the sentries "almost near enough to converse" with the British.[3] (See **The Seat of War in New England, Detail #3**.)

Just south of these posts, Massachusetts troops in Cambridge under Major General Artemas Ward comprised the main encampment, and Washington had his headquarters there in a vacant private home. From the Charlestown peninsula down to Brookline, Washington strengthened "such intermediate points as would admit a landing" by the British. Just south of Boston, Washington reported, General John Thomas's division at Roxbury had "thrown up a strong work . . . which, with the brokenness of the ground and great numbers of rocks, has made that pass very secure," preventing a British breakout from the city. Thomas's men had recently forced some British scouts back into Boston by torching the houses near Roxbury that they had been using as an observation post.

The remaining seven hundred troops were deployed in small towns along the coast to prevent British attacks. "Considering the great extent of the line and the nature of the ground," Washington wrote, "we are as well secured as could be expected in so short a time and under the disadvantages we labor." The army needed more engineers and more tools to fortify the ground, and more troops to defend the works.

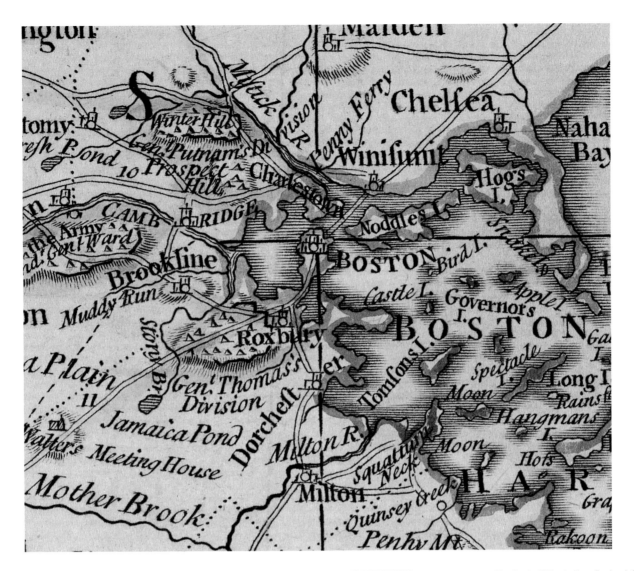

OPPOSITE, TOP: *The Seat of War in New England, Detail #1:* The "March of General Washington" shows men with cannon and horses and identifies their functions or units: "Piquets, Riflemen, Virginian Horse, New York Grenadiers." The "incampment" between Shrewsbury and Worcester is illustrated with an earthen wall around a campground with tents and a guard. Towns are indicated uniformly by an icon of a church façade.

OPPOSITE, BOTTOM: *The Seat of War in New England, Detail #2:* The Battle of Bunker Hill and the burning of Charlestown by the British are depicted in extraordinary detail. Two months into the siege, the Americans believed the British were preparing to capture the Charlestown peninsula, and preempted them by digging in on Breed's Hill. Most maps, including this one, presented Bunker Hill as a single elevation and did not distinguish between Breed's Hill, in the center of the peninsula, and Bunker Hill, near the neck. Therefore, the engagement on June 17, 1775, came to be known as the Battle of Bunker Hill.

ABOVE: *The Seat of War in New England, Detail #3:* General William Howe's troops were concentrated at the necks of the Charlestown and Boston peninsulas, fending off the Americans, while attempting to break out of the siege. The Americans had encamped and dug in at Winter Hill, Prospect Hill, Cambridge, Brookline, and Roxbury, as well as points along the shore of this crescent where the British were likely to land.

LEFT: Major General Israel Putnam.

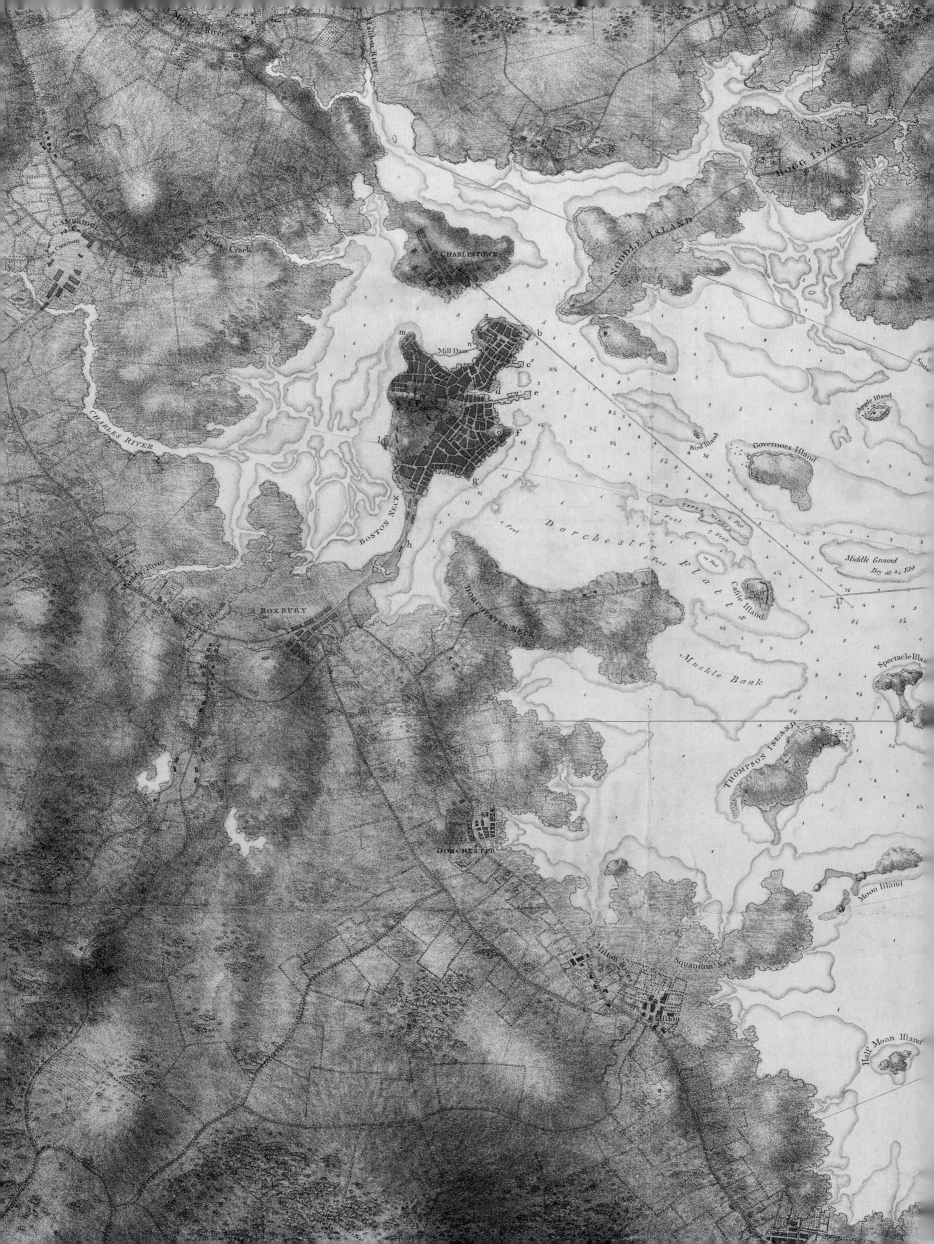

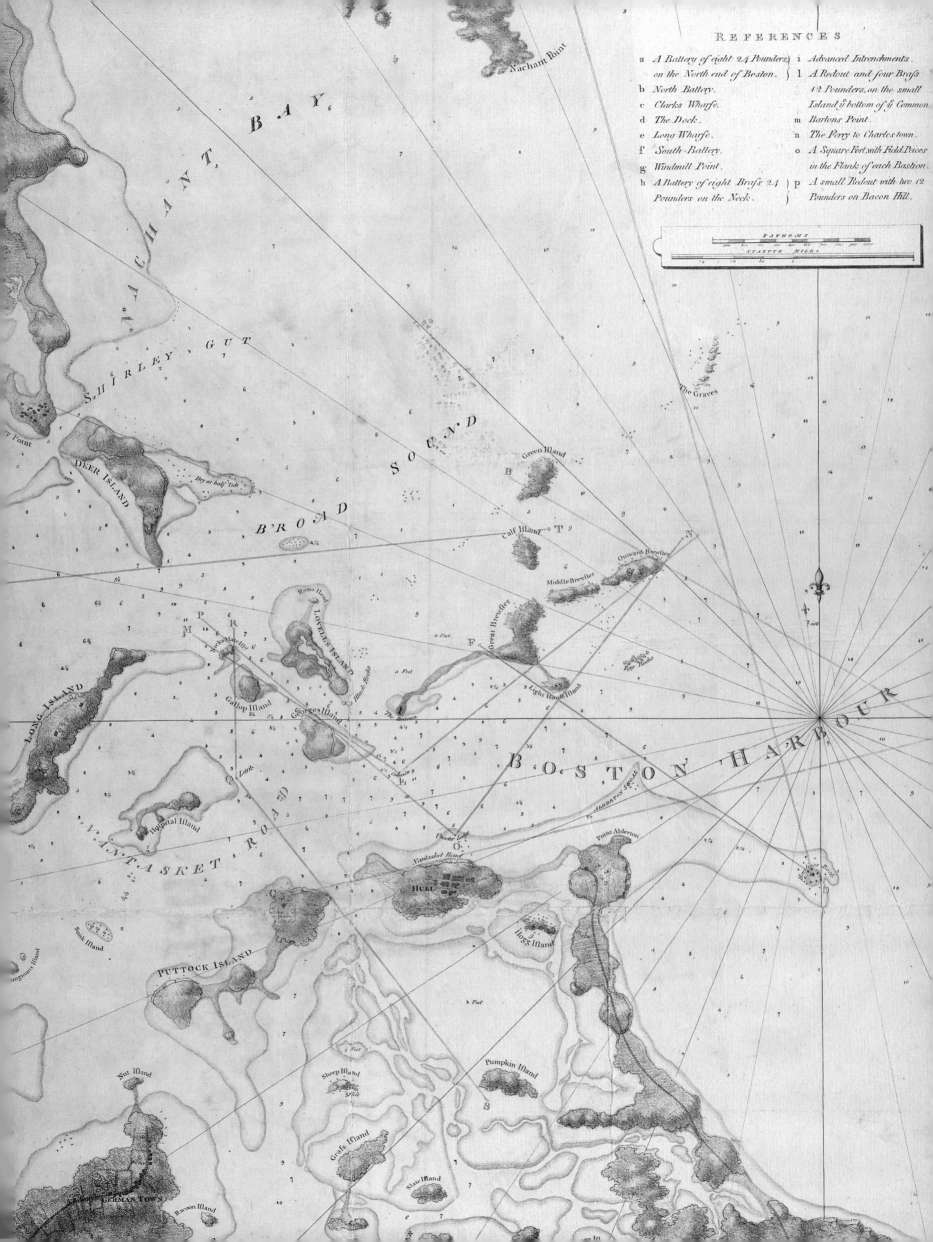

REFERENCES

a A Battery of eight 24 Pounders,
   on the North end of Boston.
b North Battery.
c Clarks Wharfe.
d The Dock.
e Long Wharfe.
f South-Battery.
g Windmill Point.
h A Battery of eight Brass 24
   Pounders on the Neck.

i Advanced Intrenchments.
l A Redout and four Brass
   12 Pounders, on the small
   Island, ÿ bottom of ÿ Common.
m Bartons Point.
n The Ferry to Charles town.
o A Square Fort with Field Pieces
   in the Flank of each Bastion.
p A small Redout with two 12
   Pounders on Bacon Hill.

NACHANT BAY

Nachant Point

SHIRLEY GUT

DEER ISLAND

Dry at half Tide

BROAD SOUND

Green Island

BROAD

Calf Island

Outward Brewster

Middle Brewster

Rams Head

Great Brewster

LOVELLS ISLAND

Sculps Mate Isld

Black Rocks

Nicks Mate Isld

Gallop Island

The Beacon

Georges Island

Light House Island

LONG ISLAND

Lark

Cohasset

BOSTON HARBOUR

Hospital Island

NANTASKET ROAD

Charter Leds

Point Alderton

Nantasket Head

HULL

Sunk Island

Langmans Island

Hogg Island

PUTTOCK ISLAND

Nut Island

Sheep Island

Pumpkin Island

GERMAN TOWN

Bacon Island

Grass Island

Slate Island

The Graves

Despite the shortage of manpower at Cambridge, Washington convinced his generals to ban African Americans from the army. Like most southerners he had an abiding fear of arming slaves, lest they attack their masters, and had been alarmed by the sight of blacks in the ranks, some of whom had fought at Bunker Hill. Warned that these blacks would go over to the British, Washington agreed to allow veterans to re-enlist. As the war continued, and Washington spent more time in the North, he eventually opposed the segregation of blacks in separate units there and favored his aide John Laurens's plan to free southern slaves in exchange for serving in black units under white officers. Washington also expressed a desire, later in the war, to do without slave labor at Mount Vernon, but he could not yet envision how the plantation would make the economic transition to a system of free labor.[4]

Washington mentioned to Hancock that the British had "a battery on Copp's Hill on the Boston side which much annoyed our troops in the late attack," at Breed's Hill. The British had installed the powerful battery of eight 24-pounders on the north end of Boston in April and used it to support the troops advancing against Breed's Hill. This battery is shown on another map that would soon be available to Washington. (See **Boston Harbor**, pages 74–75, and **Detail #1**.)[5]

A few weeks after his arrival, Washington summed up the challenge posed by the topography of Boston and its environs in a letter to his brother John Augustine. "We have a semicircle of eight or nine miles to guard, to every part of which we are obliged to be equally attentive, whilst they, situated as it were in the center of that semicircle, can bend their whole force (having the entire command of the water) against any one part of it with equal facility . . . However, by incessant labor (Sundays not excepted) we are in a much better posture of defense now than when I first came."

Washington sketched a map of the Boston area and included it with the letter. "The enclosed, though rough, will give you some small idea of the situation of Boston and Bay on this side, as also of the posts they have taken in Charlestown Neck, Bunker Hill, and our posts." To offset the British advantage, Washington had ordered ten horses "ready saddled" to be kept "at several posts in order to bring the most speedy intelligence of any movement of the enemy."[6]

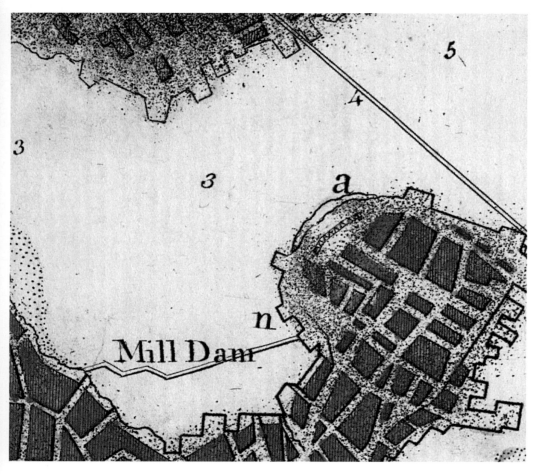

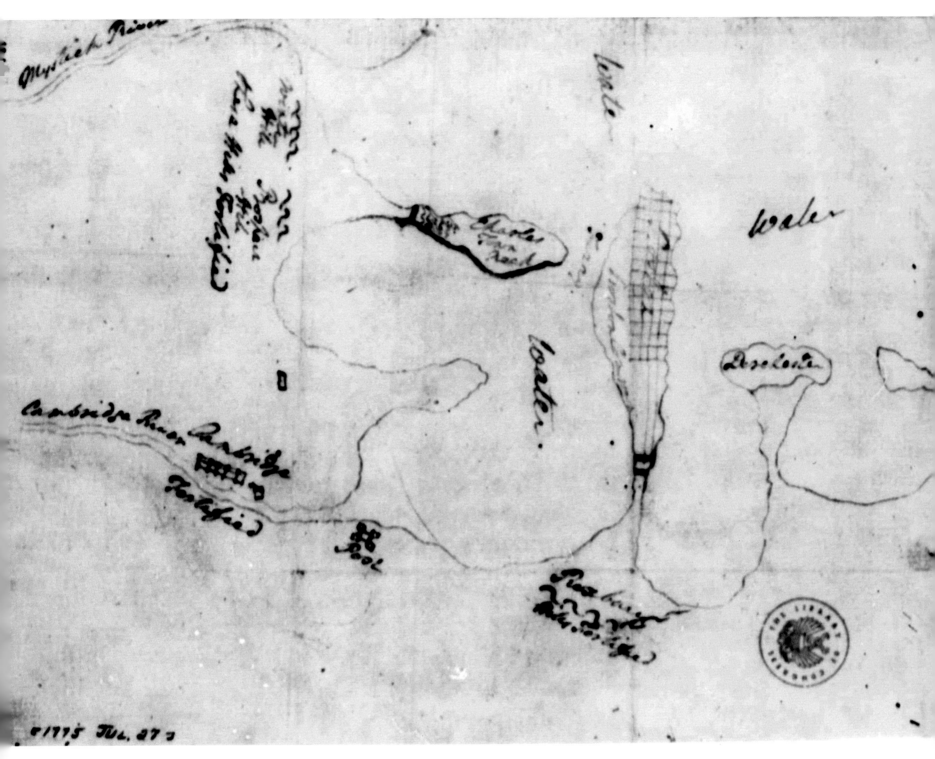

Washington tried to contest the British command of the waterways by deploying some three hundred whaleboats. Small, light, and swift, these vessels were well suited to patrols and raids amid the many islands of Boston Harbor and could escape pursuing British ships by fleeing into areas of shallow water and by operating on calm days or nights, when the American oarsmen had the advantage over enemy sailing craft. Washington asked for the names of the men in each regiment who were the "most expert in the management of whale boats." He then "ordered all the whale boats along the coast to be collected, and some of them are employed every night to watch the motions of the enemy by water," to prevent a surprise attack on the American lines.[7]

Washington also used the whaleboats to deprive the British of provisions from the islands in the harbor. On July 11, Major Benjamin Tupper led four hundred men in whaleboats on a raid of Long Island (southeast of Boston and northeast of Milton, Squantum Neck, and Moon Island; see *Boston Harbor, Detail #2*, page 78). Under the cover of night, the Americans seized twenty cows and a few sheep and captured some fifteen workers hired to mow hay for the British. The next day a smaller force—137 men in ten whaleboats—returned to complete the work of burning the houses and seventy tons of hay, bundled and ready for transfer to Boston. This time, however, they were spotted by the British. "A number of armed cutters immediately surrounded the island," Abigail Adams reported to her husband, John, from Braintree, where the townspeople had gathered to watch. The Americans "came off with a hot and continued fire upon them, the bullets flying in every direction and the Men of War's boats plying them

with small arms." Firing at close range, the British cursed the Americans and ordered them to surrender, but they all escaped across the half-mile strait to Moon Island.[8]

A week later, another detachment of four hundred Americans raided the Nantasket peninsula, removing a thousand bushels of barley and a large amount of hay to keep it out of British hands. The peninsula forms the southern half of the gateway to Boston Harbor. (See ***Boston Harbor, Detail #3***.) Moving northward across the channel in half a dozen whaleboats, the Americans burned the lighthouse, provoking a counterattack from several British vessels.[9]

Just when the British had almost rebuilt the lighthouse at the end of July, Tupper struck with three hundred men in whaleboats and burned every building on the island while killing several marines and taking three dozen British and Loyalist prisoners. "Being detained by the tide, in his return he was attacked by several boats," Washington

reported to Hancock, "but he happily got through with the loss of one man killed and another wounded." Washington praised the operation, saying that the taking of prisoners showed the Continental army "will be as famous for their mercy as for their valor."

The British stuck back by trying to overwhelm the American post at Roxbury "but they being apprised of it by a deserter, had time to prepare," Washington wrote. The British did manage to burn the George Tavern at Roxbury "and have every day since been cannonading us from their lines both at Roxbury and Charlestown" but with little effect. Trying to conserve gunpowder, "we have made little or no return."[10]

On the same night as the second lighthouse raid, the Americans at Prospect Hill, facing Charlestown Neck, were woken up by an alarm: "Turn out,—for God's sake, turn out." The soldiers manned the lines, and for most of

Boston Harbor, Detail #2: The map shows the many shallow areas, like Dorchester Flatts (top center), where American whaleboats could maneuver beyond the reach of British warships. Washington ordered whaleboat crews not only to patrol the shoreline against a surprise attack but to carry out raids that deprived the British of provisions. After the July 12 raid on Long Island (right center) the Americans barely escaped to nearby Moon Island, to the southwest, under heavy fire from British vessels.

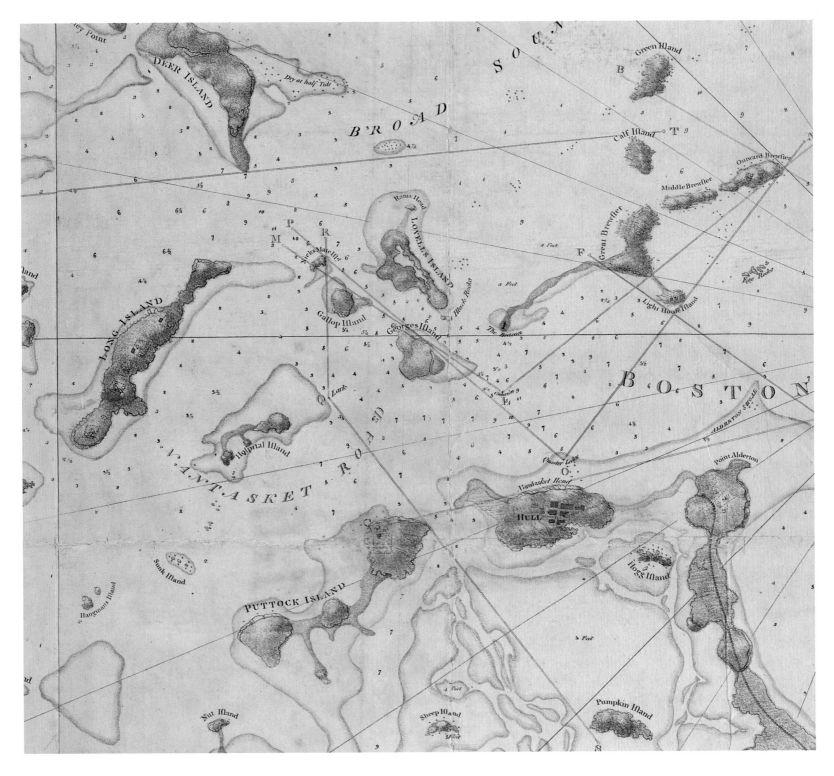

the night "the air was filled with the roaring of cannon and the cracking of small arms upon all sides," Lieutenant Paul Lunt recalled. Washington had suspected the British "were extending their lines at Charles Town" and had "ordered some of the riflemen down to make a discovery or bring off a prisoner," he told Hancock. "They were accidentally discovered sooner than they expected by the guard coming to relieve, and obliged to fire upon them," which set off the frenzy of firing on both sides. The riflemen carried off two prisoners and suffered no losses.[11]

Washington was puzzled by the lack of aggressive action by the British, since "their strength is lessened every day by sickness, desertions, and little skirmishes."[12] Maintaining the siege was a crushing financial burden for the Americans, so Washington began to receive advice on how to end it decisively. Richard Henry Lee wrote from Philadelphia on August 1:

We understand here that batteries may be constructed at the entrance of the Bay of Boston so as to prevent the egress and regress of any ships whatever. If this be fact, would it not Sir be a signal stroke to secure the fleet and army in and before Boston so as to compel a surrender at discretion? While I write this, I assure you my heart is elated with the contemplation of so great an event. A decisive thing that would at once end the war and vindicate the injured liberties of America. But your judgment and that of your brave associates will best determine the practicability of this business.

The idea of mounting cannon at Lighthouse Island and Point Alderton to control the gateway to Boston Harbor had been pitched to John Adams a few weeks earlier by Josiah Quincy, who lived on the shore near Squantum

Boston Harbor, Detail #3: The Nantasket peninsula extends from the lower right corner of the map and, together with Lighthouse Island to the north, forms the outer gateway of Boston Harbor. At Point Alderton, the peninsula turns ninety degrees to the west, and the end is labeled *Nantasket Head.*

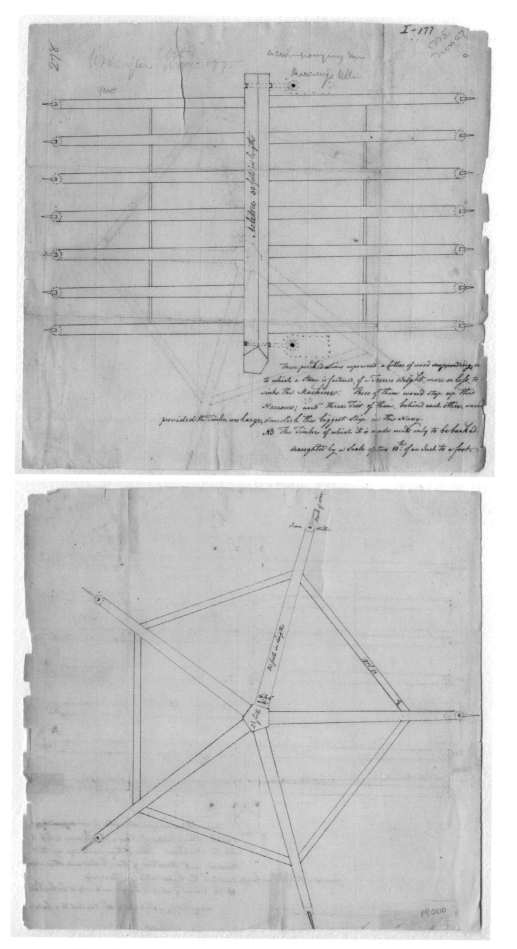

Josiah Quincy's diagrams of devices for blocking the entrance to Boston Harbor.

Neck. Adams politely dismissed the idea as impractical, so Quincy refined his plan and presented it to Washington in the coming months.[13]

Washington rejected all such schemes, explaining that the critical shortage of gunpowder in the Continental army would make it impossible to bombard ships in that channel even if he somehow managed to mount heavy cannon at these two outposts. Moreover, he was unwilling to detach men from his lines around Boston for a mission so unlikely to produce results. He had information that another channel, north of Lighthouse Island, would enable all but the largest British vessels to come and go from Boston, even if the main channel were blockaded. Instead, Washington focused on obtaining gunpowder from every possible source, from Nova Scotia to Bermuda.[14]

Not averse to taking risks, Washington believed bold plans could surprise the enemy because they were so improbable. "Enterprises which appear chimerical often prove successful for that very circumstance," he wrote when asking Nicholas Cooke, the acting governor of Rhode Island, for two ships to send to Bermuda. "Common sense and prudence will suggest vigilance and care where the danger is plain and obvious but where little danger is apprehended the more the enemy is found unprepared and consequently there is the fairer prospect of success."[15]

In early August, Washington wrote to Hancock that "a gentleman of my [military] family, assisted by a deserter who has some skill in fortification, has by my direction sketched out two draughts of our respective lines at Charlestown and Roxbury, which with the explanations will convey some idea of our situation." Washington enclosed two sketches by John Trumbull (the youngest child of Connecticut governor Jonathan Trumbull), who was trained as an artist and later became America's most famous painter of Revolutionary scenes. Trumbull's older brother Joseph was the quartermaster general of the Continental army and had advised John to make some drawings of the fortifications as a way to win the notice of the commander in chief. John crawled through the tall grass to get close to the British lines undetected, and his observations were later supplemented by the deserter.

Indeed, shortly after the sketches were submitted, Washington asked to see John and made him an aide-de-camp, part of the general's military family. Washington clearly liked to grasp his military situation and convey it to others in a visual medium: He had sent his own rough sketch of the Boston area to his brother and valued Trumbull's artistic ability.[16]

Behind the British lines, conditions in Boston were dismal, with food scarce and prices high, so the British were allowing some residents to leave by ferry to Winisimmet and Chelsea. (See *The Seat of War in New England, Detail #3*, page 73, where the ferry is indicated by a double line across the water—a continuation of the interstate roadway, the Boston Post Road.) British warships landed troops on

Noddle Island, where they dug a trench and threw up a breastwork commanding the ferry route. Washington began to face the possibility that the British would evacuate Boston altogether—and perhaps put America's third largest city to the torch when they left.[17]

With the British inactive in Boston, Washington also began to speculate that their next move would be to head south and capture New York City. He wrote to Governor Jonathan Trumbull of Connecticut to recall the troops he was sending to Cambridge and hold them in reserve to defend New York. At the same time, Washington vetoed a proposed invasion of Nova Scotia. He was working on a broad geographical canvas, balancing the siege of Boston with the risk of an attack on New York City, and trying to anticipate British cattle raids on Block Island, Gardiner's Island, and Montauk, on Long Island Sound. To the north, Washington tracked British movements and intercepted supplies from Halifax while weighing action there.[18]

Regarding the details of transporting supplies across the Northeast, Washington claimed ignorance but knew exactly what he wanted. Writing to Trumbull, he asked that the governor take charge of a supply of lead from Ticonderoga on its way to Boston to be made into bullets. "I am not sufficiently master of the geography of the country to know the easiest and safest conveyance," the Virginian told the New Englander. "But from the time in which letters have come this way through your hands, I apprehend Connecticut must be the best and most expeditious." Washington urged Trumbull to use caution if the shipment was to travel parts of the route by water where there was any danger from the British navy.[19]

In late August, the American lines of defense were nearly complete, and Washington summed up the stalemate at Boston to his cousin Lund Washington, who was managing Mount Vernon in his absence. Since the British would not attack, "and it is almost impossible for us to get to them, we do nothing but watch each other's motions all day at the distance of about a mile; every now and then picking up a straggler when we can catch them [outside] their entrenchments." Sporadic British cannon fire did little damage to the American lines—"the waste of a considerable quantity of powder to themselves which we should be very glad to get."[20]

The inactivity of the British encouraged Washington to consider detaching a thousand men under Colonel Benedict Arnold to assist in the American invasion of Canada, approved by Congress at the end of June. Washington was also spurred by a letter forwarded by Governor Trumbull from an American officer in Canada. "Now sir is the time to carry Canada," Major John Brown wrote, but the invasion was stalled "notwithstanding the season far advanced and a fine opportunity presents of making ourselves masters of the country with the greatest ease which I fear may cost us much blood and treasure if delayed."

Finally, on August 28, General Richard Montgomery embarked his army at Ticonderoga and sailed north on Lake Champlain to capture St. Johns from the British. Two weeks later, Arnold's expedition began leaving Cambridge for Maine, creating a second prong of the American invasion. Arnold's mission was to capture Quebec, or create a diversion that would facilitate Montgomery's advance. Control of Canada, Congress and Washington hoped, would shut the Hudson River corridor from the north, the probable route of a British invasion aimed at isolating New England from the rest of the colonies and cutting off the supply lines of the army at Cambridge.[21]

On August 25, General Ward warned Washington that the British might be planning to seize and fortify Dorchester Heights, overlooking Boston Neck and the southern part of the city. If they succeeded, their guns would bear down on "a very considerable part of our works." Ward did not mention the advantages for the Americans of seizing this high ground first: American guns could be pointed directly at Boston at close range.[22]

Major General Artemas Ward.

"As we have now completed our lines of defense, we have nothing more, in my opinion, to fear from the enemy, provided we can keep our men to their duty and make them watchful and vigilant," Washington wrote to Richard Henry Lee at the end of August.[23] Indeed, the main worry for Washington was not a British attack but rather the enormous expense of maintaining the siege on the one hand, and on the other the danger that the siege

ABOVE, LEFT: General
Thomas Gage.

ABOVE, RIGHT: John Hancock.

OPPOSITE: *A Map of the Most
Inhabited Part of New England:*
The British believed the Hudson
River, stretching from Ticonderoga
to New York City on the left
side of the map, was the key to
crushing the American rebellion.
Once controlled by the British,
the river could be used to isolate
New England from the colonies
to the west and south and starve
Washington's army at Cambridge.
This map from the Yale atlas
dates from 1774, and Washington
bought another copy as part of the
General Topography in 1776.

would evaporate at year's end when the soldiers' enlistments expired.

On September 8 Washington wrote to his generals, proposing to end the siege by attacking the British in Boston "by means of boats, co-operated by an attempt upon their lines at Roxbury." With winter coming on, Washington warned, the expense of building barracks for the men, clothing them, and feeding them would be astronomical. And every stick of wood—even houses—from the surrounding country would have to be consumed for fuel. If the army would not re-enlist, new troops would have to be raised, and two armies would have to be paid at once, "or, by disbanding one set before you got the other, expose the country to desolation, and the cause perhaps to irretrievable ruin."

Washington acknowledged that the consequences would also be dire if the attack failed, and a few days later his council of war voted that an attack was too risky.[24] "The enemy and we are very near neighbors," Washington wrote in frustration. "We see everything that passes, and that is all we can do, as they keep close on the two peninsulas of Boston and Charlestown, both of which are surrounded by ships of war, floating batteries, etc. and the narrow necks of land leading into them fortified in such a manner as not to be forced without a very considerable slaughter, if practicable at all."[25]

In late September, Washington warned Congress that the army was on the verge of collapse. Many of the men had no blankets, winter was coming, and their enlistments would expire in a matter of weeks. Most of the troops were ready to mutiny.[26]

Washington assumed that the British knew all of this and were planning to drag out the siege until the

Continental army disintegrated. Moreover, while the British were besieged, they were not completely entrapped, because they had access to the harbor and to the Atlantic Ocean. A key element of their strategy in the coming weeks would be to threaten or destroy American towns along the coast both to weaken American resistance and to pry some of Washington's forces away from Cambridge. Washington refused to take the bait. He would not divert men or gunpowder from the siege to fend off British ships up and down the Atlantic seaboard, even if townspeople and their elected officials cried out for help.[27] John Glover's regiment of mariners at Beverly was an exception to this policy.[28] And Washington did begin outfitting half a dozen armed vessels to protect the coast and harass enemy ships.[29]

In early October, as Washington prepared the army for winter, he received word of British reinforcements coming to America, including some "twenty thousand Hessians and Hanoverians"—auxiliaries hired from the king's German relatives. Any chance of an accommodation with the British seemed to be fading, Washington told Hancock, as the ministers in London were "determined to push the war to the utmost." The British commander in chief, General Gage, was recalled to England and replaced by General William Howe. The coming year would reveal that while boosting their troop strength in America, the British had appointed a leader whose ambivalence about crushing the American rebellion would have a decisive impact on the outcome of the war.[30]

On October 5, 1775, Hancock passed along intelligence to Washington that revealed the British grand strategy: By capturing New York City and controlling the Hudson

A MAP of
the most INHABITED part of
NEW ENGLAND
containing the PROVINCES of
MASSACHUSETS BAY and NEW HAMPSHIRE
with the COLONIES of
CONECTICUT AND RHODE ISLAND.
Divided into Counties and Townships.
The whole compofed from Actual Surveys and its Situation adjusted by
ASTRONOMICAL OBSERVATIONS.

A PLAN of BOSTON HARBOR from an Accurate SURVEY.

A PLAN of the TOWN of BOSTON

River all the way up to Canada, they planned to make incursions eastward into New Hampshire, Massachusetts, and Connecticut, while cutting off the supplies Washington was receiving through Connecticut from New York, New Jersey, Pennsylvania, and points south. (See *A Map of the Most Inhabited Part of New England*, page 83.)[31]

A more immediate British stratagem, Washington suspected, was to release residents from Boston, where smallpox had broken out. These refugees could spread the disease among the Continental soldiers and across the countryside. Since their route out of Boston was the ferry to Winisimmet, Washington had it stopped with orders to fire on any boat attempting to land.[32] (See *The Seat of War in New England, Detail #3*, page 73, upper right.)

"We are obliged to submit to an almost daily cannonade without returning a shot from our scarcity of powder, which we are necessitated to keep for closer work than cannon distance whenever the red coat gentry pleases to step out of their entrenchments," Washington wrote to his brother John Augustine in the middle of October. In summing up the siege thus far, Washington expressed hope that the invasion of Canada was progressing as planned. He was confident that the privateers he was outfitting would soon be capturing British supply vessels, "some of which have already fallen into our hands laden with provisions."[33]

Congress too was growing impatient with the siege, and had urged Washington to consider taking the offensive and driving the British out. However, at a council of war Washington's generals again voted against an assault, since the British were so well entrenched in Boston and at Bunker Hill. Nonetheless, Washington began laying the groundwork for victory in the stalemate. In late October Washington asked Congress if he was authorized to destroy Boston in the course of bombarding the king's troops. "Artillery of different kinds will be wanted," he continued. "How is it to be got, and where?"

Washington was also looking ahead, predicting the next phase of the war. "Suppose troops should be landed at New York," he asked Congress, "is it expected that any part of the army before Boston (whilst the ministerial troops remain there) are to move that way?"[34]

The British meanwhile displayed few qualms about targeting civilian settlements. On October 18, 1775, British warships destroyed the town of Falmouth (now Portland, Maine), escalating the Revolutionary War to a new level of brutality.[35] In early November, Washington pressed for an end to the siege, telling his generals it might be necessary to "destroy the ministerial troops in the town of Boston, before they can be reinforced in the spring, even if it should be by bombarding and firing the town." He asked if it was "advisable to erect any kind of works upon Dorchester Point, before frost sets in, and what kind?" Washington was referring to Dorchester Heights and Nook's Hill, which overlook Boston from the southeast—commanding ground from which to threaten

the city with artillery. However, if the ground was frozen solid, the Americans would not be able to dig trenches and throw up breastworks.[36]

With provisions dwindling in Boston, on November 9 the British sent a party of some five hundred men to steal cattle from Lechmere's Point, east of Cambridge and below Willis Creek. Striking at high tide, when the point was an island, the British thought they were protected by water on all sides. However, two regiments of Americans waded across a causeway, submerged to their waists, to drive off the cattle-raiders, forcing them "to embark under cover of a man of war, a floating battery, and the fire of a battery on Charlestown Neck," Washington reported to Hancock. Two Americans were seriously wounded by grapeshot from the warship, and two British soldiers were killed.

"This little maneuver of the enemy is nothing more than a prelude," Washington told Joseph Reed. The Americans started building a battery on Lechmere's Point and expected a major British offensive any day: A traitor had just defected to the British, reporting that the American troops were unwilling to re-enlist and their lines were weak. Meanwhile, Washington ordered all the livestock on Shirley Point, on Pulling Point, and in Chelsea driven back, out of the enemy's reach. (See *Boston Harbor, Detail #4*.)[37]

On November 16, Washington took a step that would prove decisive in ending the siege. He ordered Colonel Henry Knox to take stock of the army's artillery and ammunition and then set out "in the most expeditious manner" to procure what he could from the authorities in New York City and from General Schuyler at Ticonderoga, Crown Point, St. Johns—or even Quebec, if it was in American hands.[38]

Meanwhile, Washington warned his officers that "the bay between us and Boston" was likely to freeze over soon: The city, in effect, would no longer be on a peninsula, and the British would probably attack, since "any movement upon the ice" would be "as easy as if no water was there." Moreover, General Howe was expecting reinforcements and would be eager "to relieve himself from the disgraceful confinement in which the ministerial troops have been all this summer." In addition to bolstering the American lines with new gun batteries, Washington hoped to launch a surprise attack on Castle William with a thousand men in whaleboats to capture the garrison and its provisions. Castle Island and its fortress would soon become a focal point in the endgame of the siege.[39] (See *Boston Harbor, Detail #5*.)

Unable to obtain heavy cannon from New York, in late November, Knox reported to Washington that he was heading north to Ticonderoga. Arriving on December 4, Knox wrote that it would take at least ten days to get the heavy guns across Lake George and ready for the trip to Cambridge. Then he would need a sufficient layer of snow to cover the rutted roads and enable teams of oxen to pull the cannon on sledges.[40]

ABOVE: *Boston Harbor, Detail #4:* Chelsea is indicated at the top center of the map, with the name and a cluster of red buildings. On the peninsula extending southward from Chelsea, Pulling Point (not labeled) is the knob of land directly east of Noddle Island. Shirley Point is the fishhook-shaped extension southeast of Pulling Point, which forms the end of the peninsula. With Deer Island to the southeast, it forms the strait called Shirley Gut.

LEFT: *Boston Harbor, Detail #5:* Castle William stood on Castle Island, just east of Dorchester Heights. In addition to the main fortress with its four bastions, the map reveals a circular fort at the island's north end. Evidently, the extensive works on the east side, defending Boston against invading ships, were not calculated to contend with a rebellion on the mainland, such as the British confronted in 1775.

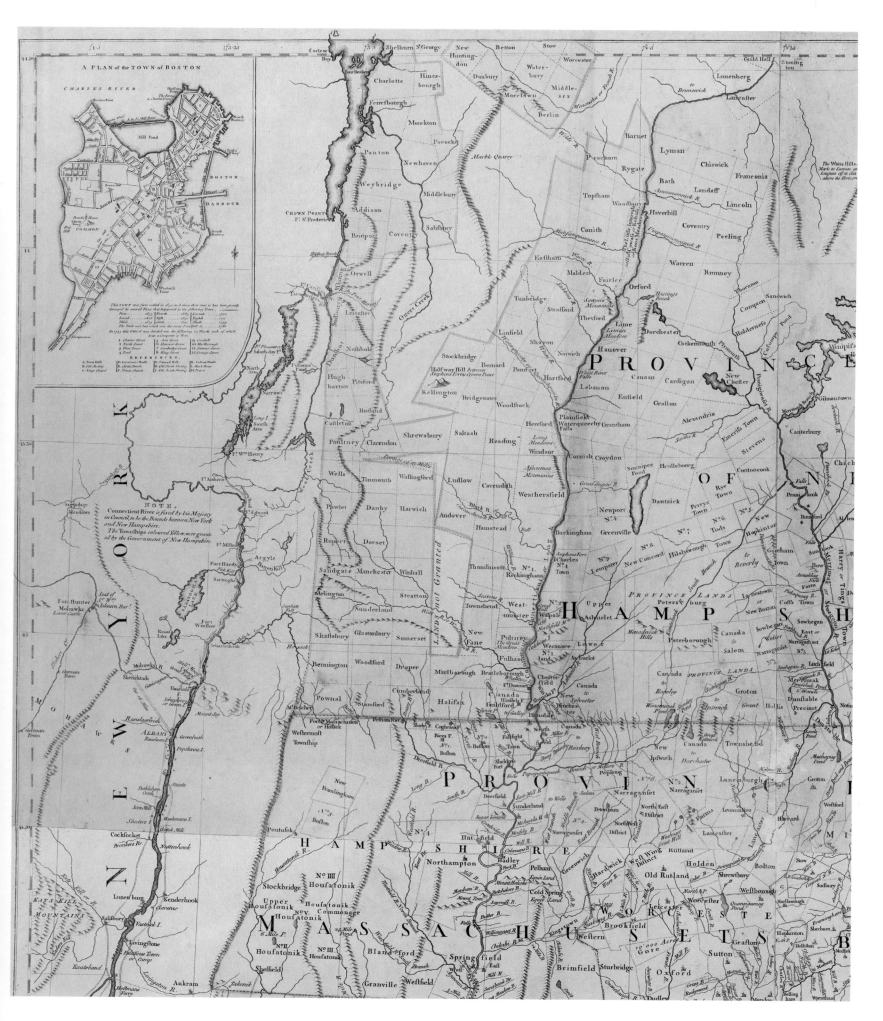

A Map of . . . New England, Detail #1: Knox took the guns from the southern end of Lake Champlain by boat to the southern end of Lake George just before it froze (upper left, below and to the right of the inset of Boston). With forty-two sleds pulled by oxen, Knox headed south along the frozen Hudson to Albany (lower left) and then southeast to Springfield, Massachusetts (bottom center). From Springfield he could follow a single road eastward to the outskirts of Boston.

In Cambridge, Washington's staff was busy recruiting a new army to replace the troops who would be leaving by the end of December when their enlistments expired. The vulnerability of the American lines during this transition had, Washington wrote, "increased my vigilance and induced me to fortify all the avenues to our camps to guard against any approaches upon the ice." The grinding siege was taking a heavy toll on the civilian population, as the temperature dropped and the Continental army consumed vast quantities of wood and hay from local farms. Inside Boston conditions were desperate. The British were running out of provisions, and the officers were reduced to dining on horse meat.[41]

On December 17, Knox wrote that he had brought the guns to the southern end of Lake George and had made "forty two exceeding strong sleds and have provided eighty yoke of oxen to drag them as far as Springfield, where I shall get fresh cattle to carry them to camp." (See *A Map of . . . New England, Detail #1*.) In two and a half weeks, he hoped "to present your Excellency a noble train of artillery."[42]

The timing was critical. Washington needed the cannon to comply with the wish of Congress, voted on December 22, that he bombard and capture Boston, even if it meant destroying the city.[43] However, Washington faced the danger that by the time the cannon arrived, his army might be dissolved, and the new one was growing with discouraging slowness. A week later, Washington called on his troops not to leave abruptly when their enlistments expired, but rather to stay until the end of January. If they should leave, and disaster strike "before the new army gets greater strength, they not only fix eternal disgrace upon themselves as soldiers, but inevitable ruin perhaps upon their country and families."[44]

As a precaution, Washington called for militia reinforcements and asked the new Continental army recruits to join their regiments a few days early, at the end of December, to ensure the American lines would not be empty during the transition. On January 1, 1776, when thousands of men from the old army left for home, the strength of Washington's forces dropped dramatically. Fewer than ten thousand men had signed up to replace the seventeen thousand whose terms had expired; this was less than half of the twenty thousand troops authorized for the new army.[45]

Remarkably, over the next few days there was no sign of a British attack, and Washington wrote to Hancock in amazement and relief:

> It is not in the pages of history, perhaps, to furnish a case like ours; to maintain a post within musket shot of the enemy for six months together, without [gun-powder] and at the same time to disband one army and recruit another within that distance of twenty-odd British regiments, is more probably than ever was attempted. But if we succeed as well in the last as we have heretofore in the first, I shall think it the most fortunate event of my whole life.[46]

Knox had hoped to be in Cambridge by January 5, but instead he was at Albany waiting for colder weather so he could move the guns across the frozen Hudson, after which, he told Washington, he could reach Springfield in eight or nine days. From there the road was good enough that he would no longer be dependent on sleds and snow. On January 7, Schuyler wrote from Albany that Knox was on his way: "Yesterday a frost came on and this morning I had the satisfaction to see the first division of sleds with cannon cross the river."[47]

The good news was welcome amid the challenges that faced Washington at every turn. "We are now without any money in our treasury, powder in our magazines, arms in our stores," Washington complained to Joseph Reed, about the failure of Congress to focus on the army's needs. "I no longer entertain a hope of completing the army by voluntary enlistments, and I see no move, or likelihood of one, to do it by other means."

The predicament of the army "produces many an uneasy hour when all around me are wrapped in sleep," Washington confided to Reed. "I have often thought how much happier I should have been if . . . I had taken my musket upon my shoulder and entered the

Artillery expert Colonel Henry Knox became a major general by the end of the Revolutionary War.

ranks, or, if I could have justified the measure to posterity and my own conscience, had retired to the back country and lived in a wigwam." The only hope now was that the British might not discover and exploit the weakness of Washington's forces: If they could make it through the month, Washington told Reed, "I shall most religiously believe the finger of Providence is in it, to blind the eyes of our enemies."[48]

The disadvantages of the Americans made it all the more imperative that they attack Boston before the British could be reinforced in the spring. Surmounting every obstacle, Knox completed his arduous mission and arrived in Cambridge on January 18. The cannon were left at Framingham, some twenty miles away, until they could be brought into action.

Two days later, General William Howe's second in command, General Henry Clinton, slipped out of Boston Harbor aboard a small fleet with transports and some three hundred troops. After stopping in New York City, he would continue southward to rendezvous at Cape Fear, North Carolina, with a much larger expeditionary force coming from England to capture Charleston, South Carolina. The first battle of the American Revolution in the South would erupt when Loyalists marching from the backcountry to the coast to join this British expedition were ambushed at Moore's Creek Bridge, northwest of Cape Fear.

Toward the end of the month, Washington was waiting for the bay to freeze and create "a bridge" of ice that would enable his forces to storm Boston after an American bombardment.[49]

As the bay began to freeze near Roxbury, Washington focused on fortifying the commanding ground of Lechmere's Point, but on February 11, Rufus Putnam, the army's chief engineer, called his attention to the importance of fortifying Dorchester Heights, overlooking Boston from the southeast. Washington toured Dorchester Heights the same day, but work did not begin for another three weeks. Washington and his engineers faced the problem of fortifying frozen ground that, during the day, was in plain view of the enemy.[50] By taking Dorchester Heights, Washington told Hancock, "we shall be able to command a great part of the town and almost the whole harbor." This threat of bombardment would force the British to come out from Boston and fight a battle, Washington hoped, giving the Americans a chance to end the siege victoriously.

However, the British showed every sign of retreating instead. Reports from Boston indicated they were loading cannon and provisions onto their ships. "Whether they really intend to embark, or whether the whole is a feint, is impossible for me to tell," Washington told Hancock. "If they do embark, I think the possessing themselves of [New York] and the North River is the object they have in view, thereby securing the communication with Canada,

and rendering the intercourse between the Northern and Southern United Colonies exceedingly precarious and difficult. To prevent them from effecting their plan is a matter of the highest importance." (See *A Map of . . . New England*, page 83.) If the British did set sail, Washington promised, he would "detach part of the light troops to New York and repair thither myself if the circumstances shall require it."[51]

Putnam, meanwhile, had been leafing through an English translation of a French manual for military engineers and had stumbled upon a way to fortify the frozen ground of Dorchester Heights—and to do it quickly. Since it was impossible to dig trenches and pile up the excavated earth to create defensive walls, Putnam proposed to move prefabricated walls, called chandeliers, to the heights. Over the next two weeks, these heavy timber frames were assembled, ready to be packed tightly with long bundles of brushwood, called fascines, and with bundles of hay held together by long wooden screws.[52] On the night of Saturday, March 2, Washington unleashed an all-night bombardment on Boston with cannon and mortars and repeated the barrage on the next two nights. The artillery diversion worked as planned, Washington told Joseph Reed, "for though we had upwards of three hundred teams in motion at the same instant carrying on our fascines and other materials to [Dorchester Heights] and the moon shining in its full luster, we were not discovered till daylight on Tuesday morning."[53]

On March 5 British engineer Archibald Robertson was flabbergasted by the sight of the American fortifications, "a most astonishing night's work" that "must have employed from 15 to 20,000 men." General Howe immediately ordered 2,400 troops to rendezvous on Castle Island, just east of Dorchester Heights, and drive the rebels from their works that night. Instead, Washington told Reed, "a violent storm which arose in the afternoon of that day and continued through the night" forced the British to return to Boston. Unable to dislodge the Americans from the heights, Howe decided to evacuate the city.[54]

Section of a prefabricated fascine.

RIGHT: Colonel Rufus Putnam, the Continental army's chief engineer.

BELOW: View of Boston from Dorchester Heights.

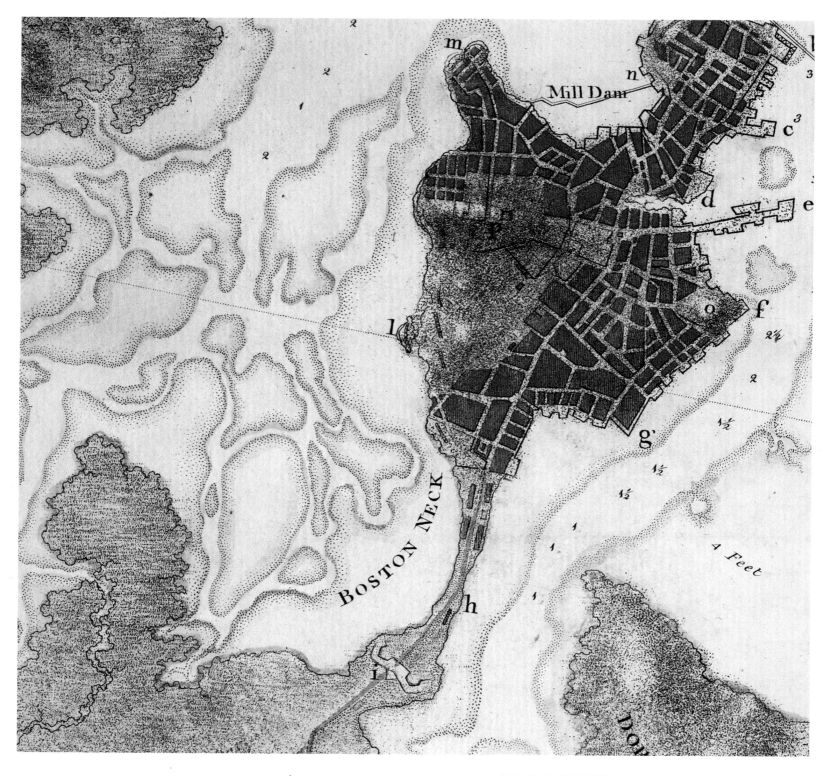

Boston Harbor, Detail #6: Expecting the British to attack the new American works on Dorchester Heights on March 5, 1776, Washington had a detailed plan in place to capture Boston from the west at the same time. Several key points in the plan can be found on the map: Beacon Hill (*P*), Barton's Point (*m*), and the gates and works at the Neck (*h* and *i*). The Powder House (not shown here) was located on the Common, the open area south of Beacon Hill.

The disruption of the British attack by the storm was a great disappointment to Washington because he had hoped to capture Boston with an amphibious assault from the west while Howe's forces were occupied on Dorchester Heights. Responding to a signal given from Roxbury, Washington explained to Hancock, four thousand Americans "were to have embarked at the mouth of the Cambridge River in two divisions . . . The first division was to land at the Powder House and gain possession of Beacon Hill and Mount Whoredom—the second at Barton's Point or a little south of it, and after securing that post, to join the other division and force the enemy's gates and works at the Neck for letting in the Roxbury troops. Three floating batteries were to have preceded and gone in front of the other boats and kept up a heavy fire on that part of the town where our men were to land." (See **Boston Harbor, Detail #6**.)[55]

After seizing Dorchester Heights, the Americans were well positioned to fortify "Nook's Hill and the points opposite the south end of Boston," Washington told Hancock on March 7. These points would place American guns at close range to the enemy, making them "of much importance and great service to us."[56] (See **Boston Harbor, Detail #2**, page 78, upper left. Nook's Hill, not labeled, formed the northwest corner of Dorchester Heights, labeled *Dorchester Neck*.)

The following day, Washington received word from Boston's selectmen that General Howe had "no intention of destroying the town" unless his troops were "molested during their embarkation or at their departure" by the American forces. Nonetheless, Washington planned to use the topography of the entire harbor to harass the retreating ships. "I shall order lookouts to be kept upon all the headlands to discover their movements and course," Washington told Hancock, "and moreover direct Commodore Manly and his little squadron to dog them as well." He hoped to capture any vessels that became separated from the convoy. And to keep the British out once they had left, Washington thought of "fortifying the entrance into the harbor," despite his earlier rejection of such proposals from Josiah Quincy and others.[57]

From their posts near the city, American guards could hear a "great noise of carriages in Boston, and frequent firing of small arms," all through the night. Then at 4:00 A.M. on March 9, "the bells rang in Boston" and the British were seen moving ammunition and cannon from Bunker Hill to the ferry. Washington put his troops on high alert against any deceptive maneuvers by the British, in case their preparations for a full retreat were merely a feint. Washington was also ready to send a detachment of Continental riflemen to the mouth of the Hudson. "Notwithstanding the report from Boston that Halifax is the place of their destination," he had told Hancock, "I have no doubt but that they are going to the southward of this, and I apprehend to New York." The riflemen were ordered "to hold themselves in readiness, to march at an hour's warning."[58]

Washington reasoned that if he was wrong and the British were heading to Halifax instead, so they could sail up the St. Lawrence River to reinforce General Guy Carleton at Quebec, the American troops dispatched to New York could be redeployed to Canada via the Hudson River more quickly than they could be from Cambridge. (See *A Map of . . . New England*, page 83.)[59]

That night, during an attempt to fortify Nook's Hill, four Americans were killed after they unwisely lit a fire and stood around it, making themselves a mark for British gunners. The campfire provoked "a continual roar of cannon and mortars, from the Castle and lines on Boston Neck" all evening and night, to which the Americans responded from their batteries at Roxbury and Lechmere's Point. American control of Nook's Hill would have to be postponed for a week.[60]

On March 12, when it appeared the British might be ready to evacuate Boston by the following morning and throw open the gates on the Neck, Washington gave strict orders that no one was to enter, lest the American troops contract smallpox or loot the town. Washington also dispatched patrols to guard against a possible British landing at the nearby towns of Milton, Braintree, Hingham, and Cohasset and as far south as Plymouth along the Atlantic coast. (See **The Seat of War in New England, Detail #4**.) By March 14, the British ships were starting to leave for Nantasket Roads. (See **Boston Harbor, Detail #3**, page 79.)[61]

After the riflemen left for New York on March 15, Washington felt ready to give the enemy a final push to dislodge them from Boston. The Americans succeeded in fortifying Nook's Hill on March 16, and the following day

The Seat of War in New England, Detail #4: As the British prepared to evacuate Boston in the middle of March 1776, Washington was concerned that their retreat might be a feint, and that the fleet might try to land at one of the nearby towns, such as Milton, Braintree, Hingham, or Cohasset, which appear on the map along the harbor to the south and east of Boston. Cohasset, just outside Boston Harbor, is labeled *Konohasset*. Washington also wanted the Atlantic coast patrolled as far south as Plymouth, visible on the full map just west of "Cape Codd Bay."

the British completed their evacuation. Washington wrote to Joseph Reed that American possession of Dorchester Heights had put the British "into a most violent fury to embark, which was still further precipitated . . . by our breaking ground on Nook's Hill (the point nearest the town.)"[62]

Washington's letter to Hancock announcing the glorious end of the eleven-month siege was more formal but brimmed with hard-won satisfaction. "It is with the greatest pleasure I inform you that on Sunday last, the 17th instant, about 9 o'clock in the forenoon, the ministerial army evacuated the town of Boston, and that the forces of the United Colonies are now in actual possession thereof. I beg leave to congratulate you Sir, and the honorable Congress on this happy event." Washington sent a thousand men, who had had smallpox and were therefore immune, to enter the city.[63]

In their hasty retreat the British had left behind a massive amount of provisions, equipment, ammunition, and heavy cannon. They tried to destroy their baggage, wagons, and carts by throwing them into the water. Seeing them wash up on the shores of Boston, Washington was reminded of another British defeat, during the French and Indian War. "In short, Dunbar's destruction of stores after General Braddock's defeat affords but an imperfect idea of what was seen here," he wrote to Landon Carter in Virginia. Without boasting, Washington seemed to suggest that the scale of his triumph at Boston redeemed the disaster in western Pennsylvania in 1755 on the ledger of his military career.[64]

A week later, however, the British fleet remained in the harbor, even though the wind and weather allowed for their departure, Washington reported to Hancock. The British destroyed all the fortifications and buildings on Castle Island, and the fleet had departed gradually from "below the Castle, extending themselves to Nantasket Road, about nine miles." Remaining vigilant, Washington sent only five regiments to New York, on the heels of the riflemen, and kept the army at Boston on high alert.[65] He also ordered "a large and strong work to be thrown up on Fort Hill, a post of great importance, as it commands the whole harbor and . . . will greatly annoy any fleet the enemy may send against the town." In case the British should recapture Boston, Washington had the fortifications destroyed on the Neck and on the western side of

the city, "facing the country." (See **Boston Harbor, Detail #6**, page 90. Fort Hill, in the middle of the eastern shore of the city, is labeled with the letter *O* and identified in the References as "A Square Fort with Field Pieces in the Flank of each Bastion.")[66]

While the British lingered inexplicably, the daring and relentless Benjamin Tupper led a detachment in some twenty whaleboats from Dorchester Heights to Thompson's Island, where they hauled a cannon to the northern end and harassed British work parties on Spectacle Island as well as some troop transports anchored nearby. (See **Boston Harbor, Detail #2**, page 78.) Tupper also had plans, never carried out, to launch flaming rafts toward the British warships at Nantasket Roads to set them on fire. Weary of the prolonged finale to the siege, Washington briefly endorsed the plan, to be "attempted in a windy or dark night. I think this would discover their designs if no other good effect resulted from it."[67]

Washington suspected that the British might attack "around Pulling Point Gut and along the back of the islands to Chelsea," moving into these concealed, shallow waters at high tide. (See **The Seat of War in New England, Detail #5**.) In response he called for increased patrols in these areas and ordered a battery built on Charlestown Point.[68]

Instead, the British fleet finally left Boston Harbor on the afternoon of March 27. Washington sent six more regiments to New York and prepared to go there himself with the rest of the army, leaving only a few regiments to protect Boston. The siege had been nearly bloodless, and the city remained largely intact. At a dinner for Washington and his generals on the 28th, the grateful members of the Massachusetts General Court presented an address that concluded with both lavish praise and a gentle reminder that Americans detested standing armies and military dictators:

And (the deliverance of your country being effected), may you in retirement enjoy that peace and satisfaction of mind which always attends the good and great, And may future generations in the peaceful enjoyment of that freedom, the exercise of which your sword shall have established, raise the richest and most lasting monuments to the name of *Washington*.[69]

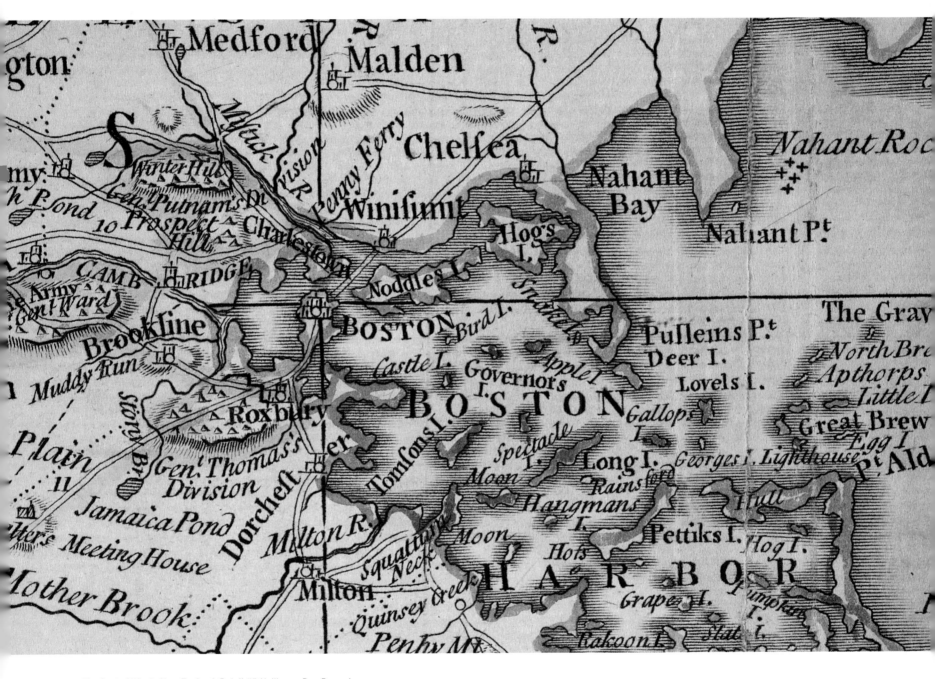

The Seat of War in New England, Detail #5: Unlike on Des Barres's map, *Boston Harbor*, Shirley Point here is labeled *Pulleins Pt.* (Pulling Point), and the strait was called Pulling Point Gut. Washington suspected that if the British attempted to launch an attack instead of leaving the harbor, they would come up from Nantasket Roads, using the small islands for cover, and come through Pulling Point Gut into the concealed waters around Hogg Island and Noddle Island and land at Chelsea, just to the north.

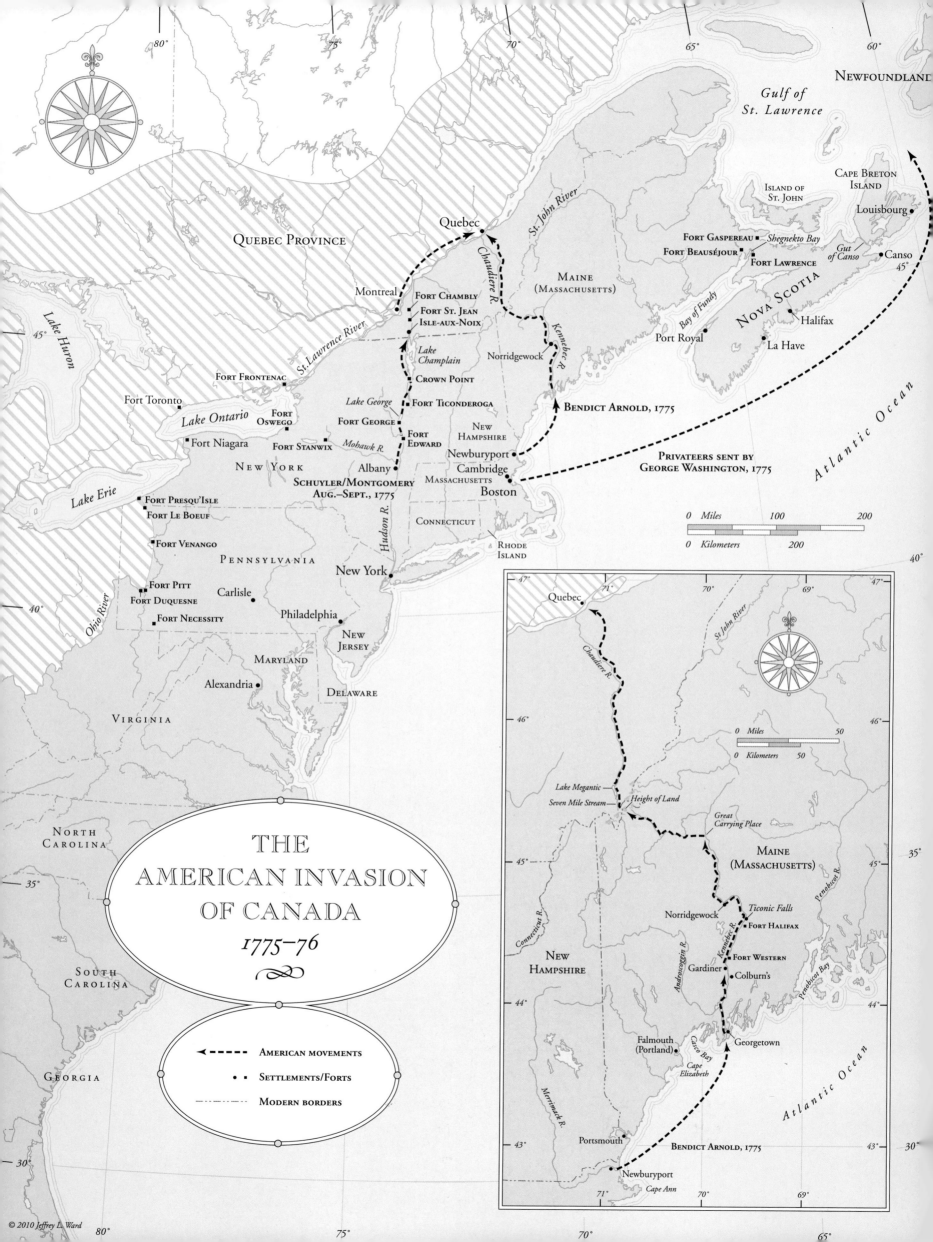

THE
AMERICAN INVASION
OF CANADA
1775–76
෴

━ ┅ ┅ ━ AMERICAN MOVEMENTS

● ● ● ● ● SETTLEMENTS/FORTS

─ ∙ ─ ∙ ─ MODERN BORDERS

© 2010 Jeffrey L. Ward

CHAPTER FOUR

THE AMERICAN INVASION

OF CANADA

"You are entrusted with a command of the utmost consequence to the interest and liberties of America," Washington had written to Colonel Benedict Arnold on September 14, 1775. "Upon your conduct and courage and that of the officers and soldiers detached on this expedition, not only the success of the present enterprise and your own honor, but the safety and welfare of the whole continent may depend."[1] With these words, the commander in chief dispatched Arnold and a thousand men from Cambridge northward through the wilderness of Maine and Canada to capture Quebec. The maps they used concealed as much as they revealed, and would not prepare them for the punishing journey along a river that wound through the rugged landscape like a rattlesnake; for the rapids, waterfalls, and long portages; for fatigue, starvation, and the bitter cold of the approaching Canadian winter.[2] This was the second thrust of an American invasion of its northern neighbor that began with a resolution by Congress on June 27, 1775, and the advance of a contingent under Generals Philip Schuyler and Richard Montgomery on August 28 from Ticonderoga, New York. Washington meant for Arnold's expedition to "take possession of Quebec if possible, but at all events to create a diversion in favor of General Schuyler," whose forces were marching northward to that stronghold on the St. Lawrence River via Lake Champlain, St. Johns, and Montreal.[3] (See *The American Invasion of Canada, 1775–76*.)

When Samuel de Champlain explored the St. Lawrence River for France almost two centuries earlier, in 1603, the Algonquin Indians had a settlement on the steep rocky hill they called Kebec, "where the river narrows," jutting into the St. Lawrence where it is fed by the St. Charles River. Naturally fortified against attack, and dominating a region of numerous smaller rivers flowing into the deep, navigable St. Lawrence, Quebec was marked by the French for a future city. It would facilitate transportation and trade locally as well as export to Europe. Native American trade routes extended from the St. Lawrence as far as the southern coast of Maine, and in 1606 Champlain learned about the Kennebec-Chaudiere trail that Arnold now planned to use. The Kennebec had been a major trade and transportation route and source of food for Native Americans for thousands of years. The Frenchman had been told by natives that the route went from Maine to Quebec "some fifty leagues, without passing more than one portage of two leagues." It would not be the last time that locals described the route while downplaying its numerous obstacles.[4]

The paramount importance of the invasion, in Washington's eyes, was to secure a friendly neighbor to the north, preventing the British from moving down the Hudson River Valley to divide the colonies, and from descending into the Ohio River Valley to stir up local tribes to attack the Americans on their western frontier. On one hand, the eighty thousand French Canadians—abandoned to English rule by the French withdrawal from North America after their defeat in 1763—hated Americans for helping the British win the French and Indian War. On the other hand, Washington hoped they might now be eager to help the Americans defeat the British. So far they had remained neutral.

With the Quebec Act of 1774—counted by infuriated Americans as one of the "Intolerable Acts" that punished Boston for the Tea Party—the British had established a government in Canada without a representative assembly and bound to be dominated by the Crown. They combined French civil law (without trial by jury) and British criminal law and extended the southern border of the sprawling province to the Ohio River. Creating a repressive Catholic neighbor to the north and west—larger than the thirteen American colonies combined—seemed part of the British design to subjugate the American colonies.[5] (See *The American Invasion of Canada, 1775–76*, page 94, showing the borders of Quebec Province.) The American invasion had to win over the Canadians and deprive the British of new recruits. "If these expeditions succeed," Washington wrote with a rare touch of sarcasm to his brother Samuel, "the Ministry will make a glorious figure with their Canada Bill, and the regiments they proposed to raise in that government for the purpose of deluging our frontier settlements in blood."[6]

During the Revolution, most of the published maps of Canada available to Washington commemorated the battlefields of the French and Indian War, but in the summer of 1775, these elegant depictions were suddenly of more than historical or artistic interest: The strategic objectives of twenty years earlier—the same waterways, forts, and cities—had become the targets of the ambitious American offensive.

The Americans hoped to control Canada in 1775, just as the English had fought to wrest it from the French in the 1750s, finally succeeding in 1760. The St. Lawrence River penetrated from the Atlantic all the way to Lake Ontario, which made the river a major water highway for transporting troops and supplies to forts and cities deep inside the continent. By establishing forts on the Great Lakes, the French were able to press southward and contest the Ohio River Valley while linking up with their forces ascending the Mississippi River from New Orleans. Control of the trans-Appalachian West promised to hem in British expansion, while giving the French a lock on the lucrative fur trade with native tribes on the Great Lakes. (See *La Nouvelle France, ou Le Canada*, page 98.)

Similarly, in 1775, British control of Canada provided the means of containing and attacking the rebellious American colonies from the north and west. Extending the Canadian border to the Ohio River was one stratagem. Another would be to send British forces down from Canada via the Richelieu River, Lake Champlain, and Lake George to control the Hudson River Valley all the way down to New York City. Mastery of this

QUEBEC, *The Capital of* NEW-FRANCE, *a Bishoprick, and*
Seat of the Soverain COURT.

1. The Citadel. 2. the Castle. | 7. Cathedral of Our Lady. | 11. S.¹ Charles River. | 14. The Bishop's H. se. 15. The
3. Magazine. 4. § Recolets. | 8. The Palace 9. § Seminary. | 12. The Common Hospital. | Parish Church of the Lower Town.
5. Ursulines. 6. Jesuits. 7. | 10. The Hôtel Dieu. | 13. The Hermitage of the Recolets. | 16. The Upper Town 17 § Lower Town.
| | | 18. The Platform & Battery of Cannon
| | | 19. The Isle of Orleans. 20. Point Lievi.

ABOVE: An early depiction of Quebec, showing the upper and lower towns
and significant locations.

PAGE 94: *The American Invasion of Canada, 1775–76:* During the siege
of Boston, in August and September 1775, the Americans launched a
two-pronged invasion of Canada. Montgomery and Schuyler moved up the
Hudson-Champlain axis (center) while Arnold's force (to the east) trekked
through the Maine wilderness, along the Kennebec and Chaudiere rivers.
Washington also sent privateers to the Gulf of St. Lawrence (upper right)
to intercept British supply ships headed for Quebec.

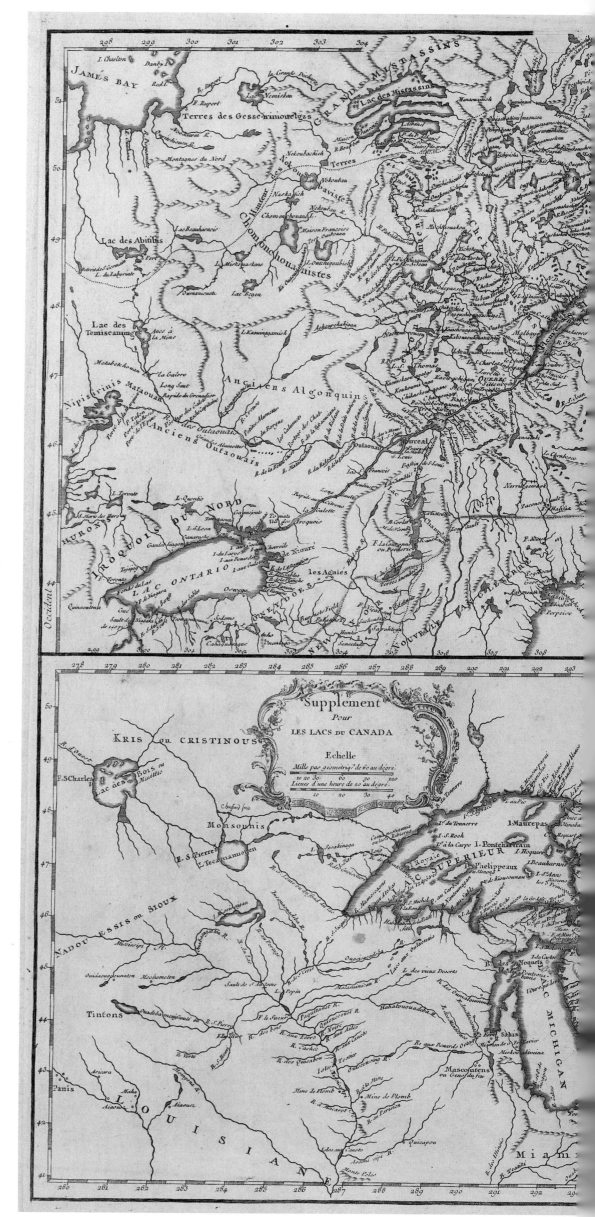

La Nouvelle France, ou Le Canada: Published in 1755, as the British were thrown on the defensive in the French and Indian War, this is the only French map in the Yale *George Washington Atlas*. In 1776, the map provided Washington with a comprehensive view of Canada. On the left, center, the St. Lawrence River flows from Lake Ontario out to the Atlantic Ocean (top center), creating a water route to and from the interior of the continent—especially the Great Lakes—shown in detail in the inset, lower left.

PARTIE DE
L'AMÉRIQUE SEPTENT.le
qui comprend
LA NOUVELLE FRANCE
OU LE CANADA,
Par le Sr. Robert de Vaugondy Géog.
Ordinaire du Roy.
Avec Privilege, 1755.

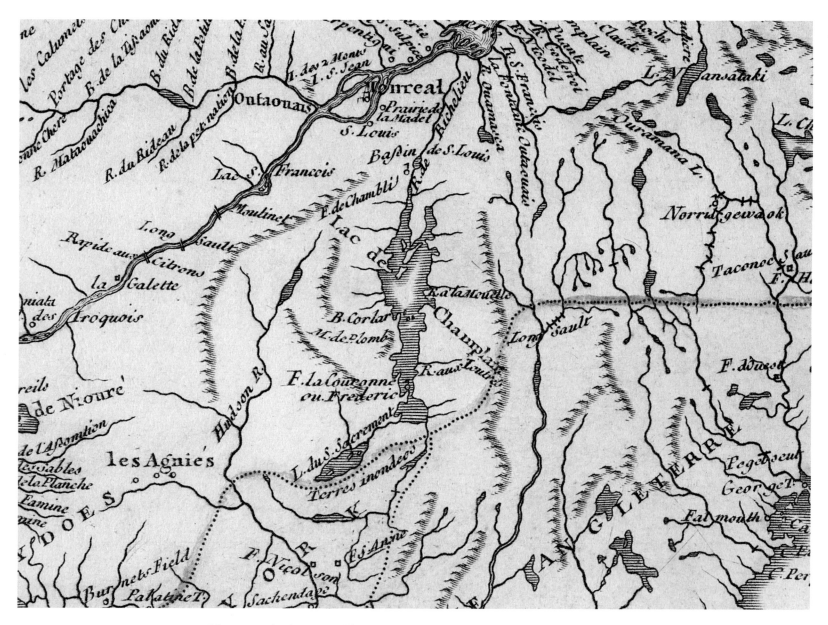

ABOVE: *La Nouvelle France,
ou Le Canada, Detail #1:* The
Richelieu River (called the Sorel
River by the English), flowing
from Lake Champlain into the
St. Lawrence River northeast of
Montreal, formed the first section
of a veritable water highway from
Canada to New York City via the
Hudson River. (See *A Map of the
Province of New York* for the rest
of the route.)

OPPOSITE: *A Map of the Province
of New York:* John Montresor's
map of 1774, from the Yale atlas,
shows the Hudson River as the
dominant feature of the colony and
illustrates the potential for British
control of this corridor to divide
New England from the Mid-Atlantic
colonies and the South.

second key water highway would split New England from the Mid-Atlantic and southern colonies. Combined with a naval blockade of the seacoast, this presumably would strangle the American rebellion. See *La Nouvelle France, Detail #1*, and *A Map of the Province of New York*.)

"The Ministerial dependence on Canada is so great, that no object can be of greater importance to North America than to defeat them there," Richard Henry Lee wrote to Washington from Philadelphia. "It appears to me, that we must have that country with us this winter cost what it will." The Indians in the Ohio River Valley were slow to take sides, he reported. They were waiting to see the outcome in Canada, before siding with the victor.[7]

Schuyler and Montgomery embarked their invasion force from Fort Ticonderoga at the end of August 1775. The fort dominated the connection between Lake Champlain and Lake George, establishing a critical point of control along the Hudson-Champlain axis. Like Louisburg, the citadel on Cape Breton Island guarding the Gulf of the St. Lawrence River, Ticonderoga was commonly known as "the key to a continent." (See *A Map of the Province of New York, Detail #1*, page 102.)[8]

In order to protect the Hudson River corridor and gather more cannon and powder for the Americans, Ethan Allen and the Green Mountain Boys and Arnold

had surprised the British and seized Fort Ticonderoga a few weeks after Lexington and Concord, on May 10, 1775. Two days later they moved north and seized Crown Point. To prevent a British counteroffensive, Arnold sailed all the way up to St. Johns and captured the only British vessel in the area that would have enabled them to transport a sizable force southward.

Having launched his own raid deep into Canada, and concluded that the Native Americans and Canadians were likely to side with the Americans against the British, on June 13 Arnold wrote to Congress proposing a full-scale invasion to take St. Johns, Montreal, and Quebec. Two weeks later, Congress resolved to invade Canada and informed Washington the following day.[9] When it was clear that Washington and Congress had settled on Schuyler, the commander of the Northern Department, to lead the invasion, Arnold headed back to Cambridge. In early August, he met with Washington and proposed the second prong, the Kennebec-Chaudiere expedition.[10] Washington liked the idea but had only basic information about the route. (See *La Nouvelle France, Detail #2*, page 103.) He needed much more detailed information in order to approve the mission.

In mid-August, Washington met with Reuben Colburn, a shipbuilder who had lived on the banks of the

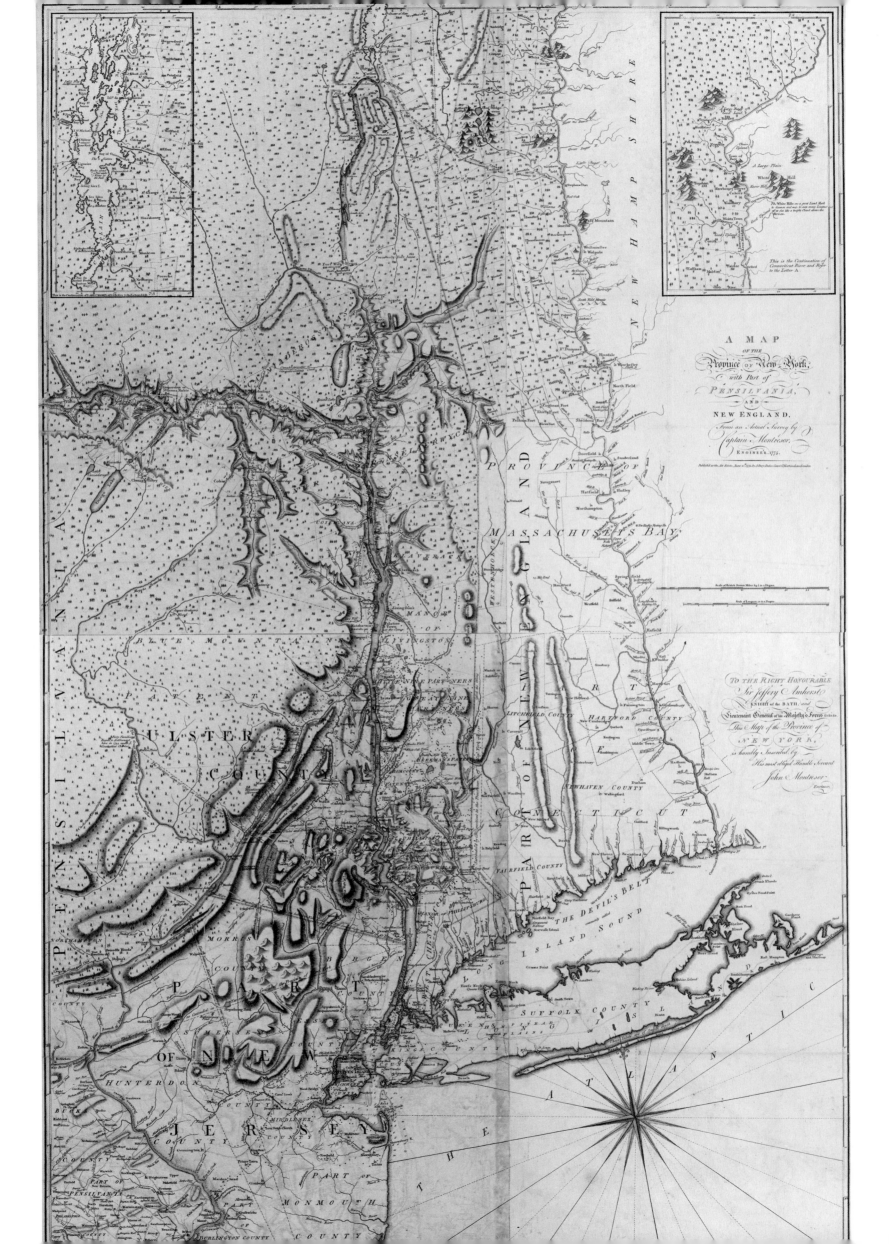

A MAP
OF THE
Province of New York,
with Part of
PENSILVANIA,
AND
NEW ENGLAND,
From an Actual Survey by
Captain Montresor,
ENGINEER 1775.

TO THE RIGHT HONOURABLE
Sir Jeffery Amherst,
KNIGHT of the BATH, and
Lieutenant General of his Majesty's Forces &c &c &c
This Map of the Province of
NEW YORK,
is humbly Inscribed by
His most obliged Humble Servant
John Montresor
Engineer.

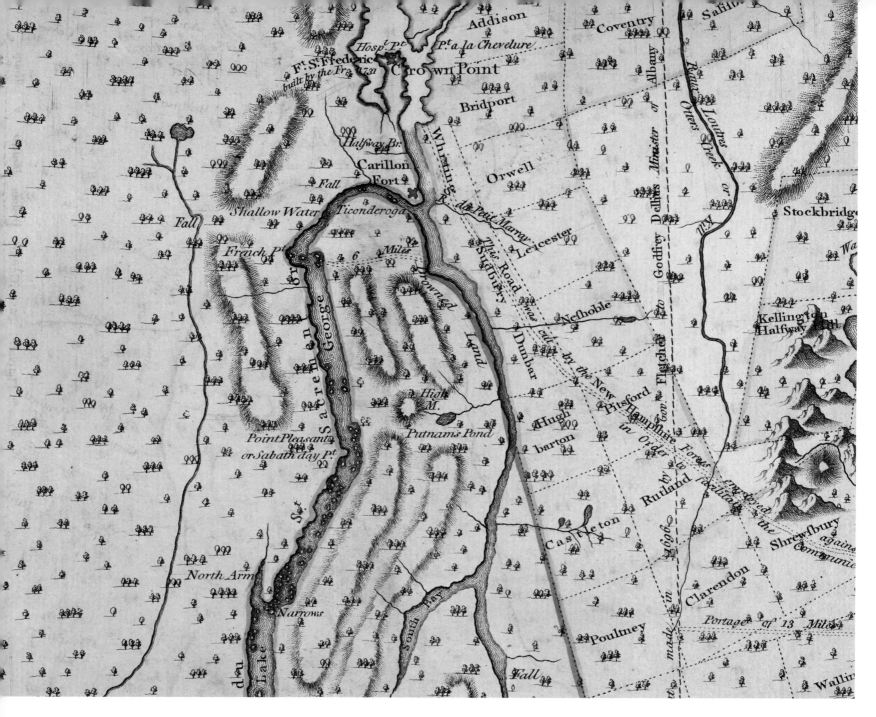

ABOVE: *A Map of the Province of New York, Detail #1:* While the French called it Carillon, suggesting that the adjacent waterfall (to the west, marked *Fall*) flowing from Lake George into Lake Champlain sounded like chimes, Ticonderoga was a Native Amer can name meaning "the place where two waters meet." Crown Point is shown at the top of the map on Lake Champlain, which connects to Lake George at Ticonderoga. Parallel to Lake George is the southern extension of Lake Champlain.

LEFT: Colonel Benedict Arnold became a general later in the war.

Kennebec for more than ten years. In addition to providing the commander in chief with intelligence reports, Colburn had previously brought representatives of the local tribes to meet him in Cambridge. Washington took a first concrete step by issuing money to Colburn with orders to start sawing planks for the wooden boats Arnold would need. Washington then sent Colburn to nearby Watertown to see Arnold, recently commissioned as a colonel in the Continental army.

Arnold asked Colburn how fast he could build two hundred boats to hold six or seven men each plus their baggage and barrels of flour and salted pork. Could his blacksmiths produce enough nails for the job? How many portages were there on the route, and how long were they? How deep was the water in the rivers at this time of year? Was there any British naval presence near the mouth of the Kennebec to hinder the start of the expedition?

At the end of August Colburn went back to Maine to start answering these questions.[11] He enlisted the help of Samuel Goodwin, who owned an inn and general store in the courthouse at Pownalborough (now Dresden, Maine) and was also a surveyor. "I think I know as much of this country as anyone as I have been traveling, surveying, and settling this part ever since the year 1750," Goodwin wrote to Washington. Following Washington's verbal orders, passed through Arnold and Colburn, Goodwin spent three weeks gathering and making maps for the expedition. By his account, these included the seacoast from Cape Elizabeth to Penobscot and the Kennebec River, the passes and carrying places along the rivers all the way to Quebec, and several small, detailed plans for each section of the route. (Goodwin's maps have not been found.)

Goodwin also gave Arnold a copy of British army engineer Lieutenant John Montresor's journal from 1761, "which represented all the quick water and carrying places

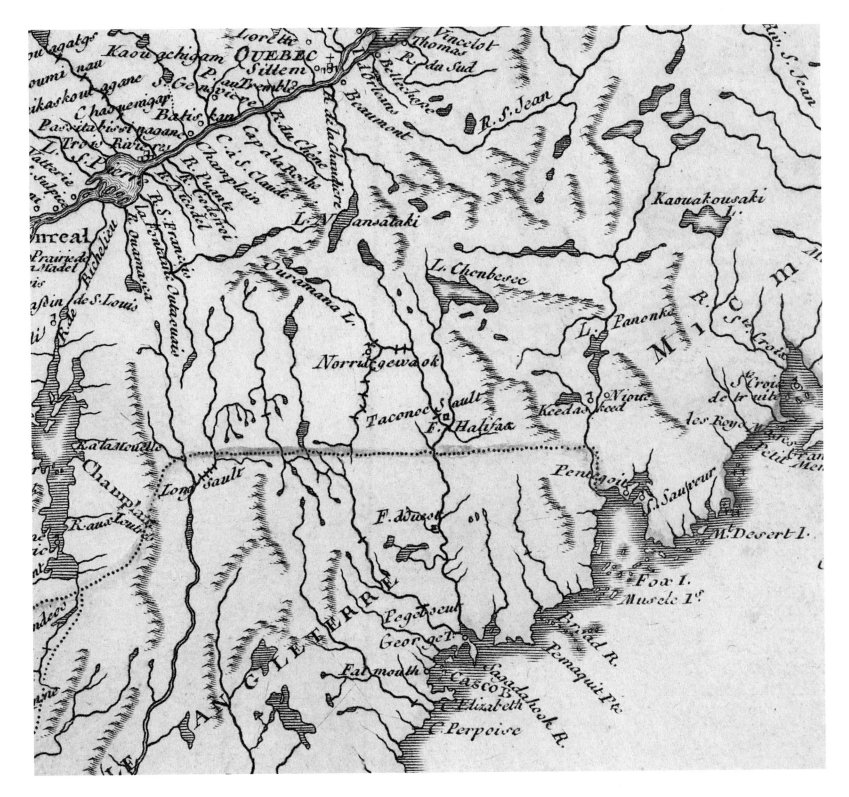

ABOVE: *La Nouvelle France, Detail #2:* From the Maine coast (bottom center) the route went north to Fort Western (*F. d'Ouest*), Fort Halifax, Ticonic Falls (*Taconoc Sault*), and Norridgewock. Here the portage called the Great Carrying Place, a short line with two stitches across it, leads to the western branch of the Kennebec known as Dead River because of its calm surface (marked *Ouramana Lake*). Next, a series of ponds leads to the Height of Land, a line of hills pointing the way to Lake Megantic (*Lake Nansalaki*) the source of the Chaudiere River (*R. de la Chaudiere*), which flows into the St. Lawrence near Quebec (top, left of center).

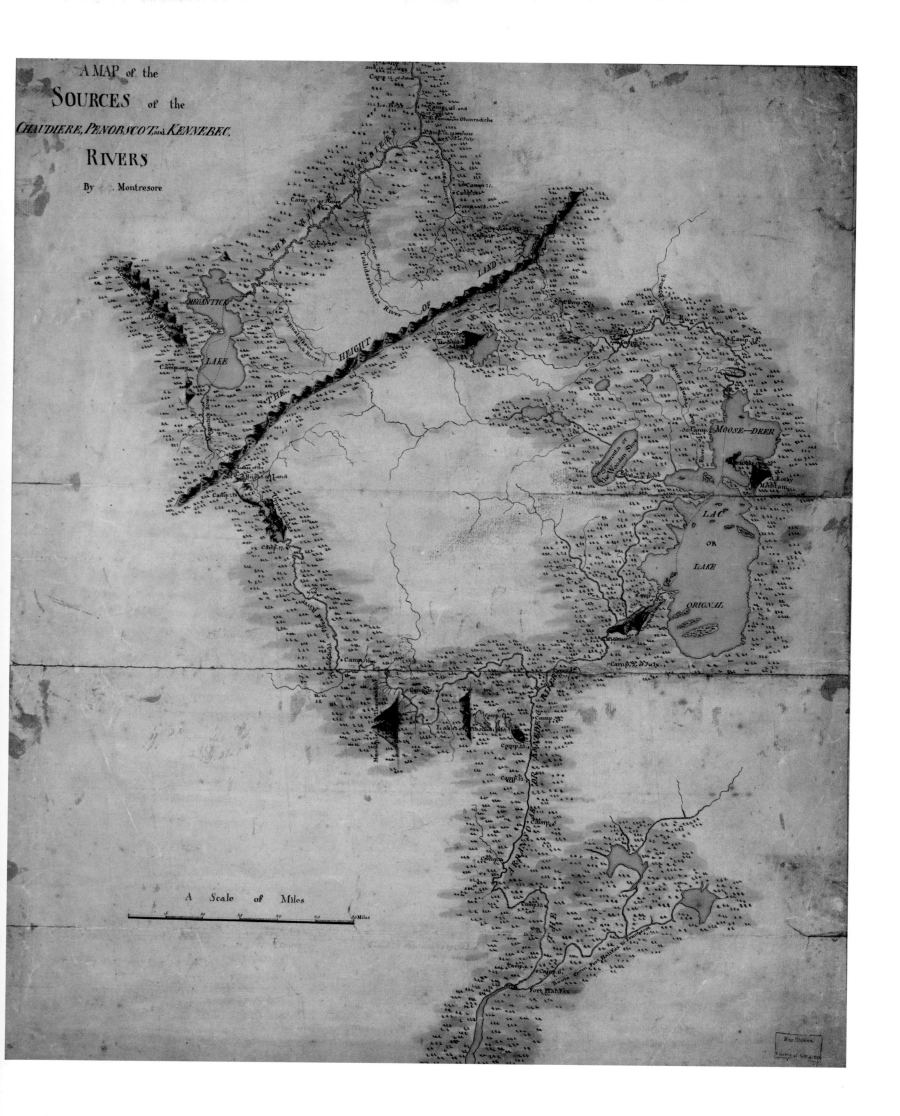

A MAP of the

SOURCES of the

CHAUDIERE, PENOBSCOT, and KENNEBEC,

RIVERS

By Montresore

A Scale of Miles

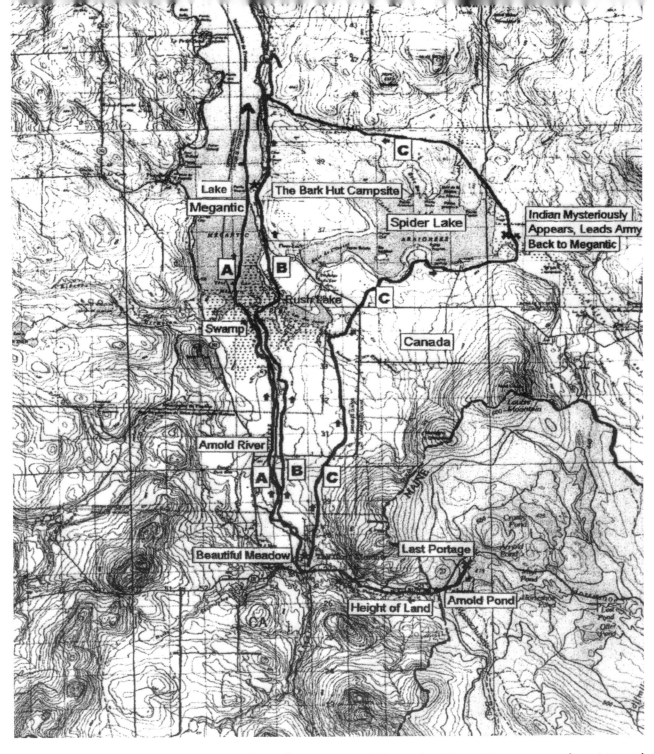

OPPOSITE: *Sources of the Chaudiere, Penobscot, and Kennebec Rivers:* Goodwin gave a copy of this map to Arnold, but Washington owned at least one map of the area, possibly a copy of this one. The inventory of Mount Vernon lists a "Map of Kennebec River, &c." In Montresor's map, the Height of Land stretches from left center to upper right. The omitted features are shown on the *Map of Lake Megantic and the Height of Land Border Country.*

RIGHT: *Map of Lake Megantic and the Height of Land Border Country:* In this modern map, the Height of Land is shown by topographical lines (from the bottom center to the right center) along the border between Maine and Canada. The false mouths of Seven-Mile Stream led to the swamp (center left) just south of Lake Megantic. Rush Lake and Spider Lake are shown northeast of the swamp.

to and from Quebec both ways, viz. east and west," wrote Goodwin.[12] In 1761, when major combat in the French and Indian War had ended with the British in possession of Quebec, they wanted a route to the New England coast. Montresor mapped the route and created the journal.[13]

There were several problems with Montresor's map and journal, however. (See *Sources of the Chaudiere, Penobscot, and Kennebec Rivers*.) First, many of the distances had been left blank in the journal in order to make it less useful if it fell into the hands of the enemy. Moreover, Montresor's map of the Dead River–Lake Megantic region omitted Rush Lake, Spider Lake, and the treacherous false mouths of Seven-Mile Stream.[14] (See *Sources of the Chaudiere, Penobscot, and Kennebec Rivers* and *Map of Lake Megantic and the Height of Land Border Country*.) Finally, Montresor was traveling in the opposite direction from Arnold, in a milder season, and with a far smaller party—not a thousand-man army and all of its supplies.

Goodwin did not mention the journal's defects, but he did express doubt that maps alone would facilitate the mission. He wrote to Washington that "if there was a road cut,

it would be much easier carrying an army and provision and would shorten the way much, and then you might have a post to pass once a week or ten days," to get supplies and provisions. He offered to "lay out a road and see it cleared," adding that Washington should have "a copy of said plan, etc. and then you would be a judge of what would be best to be done." He said he would make a copy if he received orders to do so. Washington thanked Goodwin for supplying Arnold with "the plans for his route to Quebec" and said he would keep in mind his offer to lay out a road.[15]

There was a strong irony in Washington's decision to follow Montresor's journal for Arnold's march—and in hurrying forward without cutting a road first. Montresor first came to America in 1754 as ensign and chief engineer with General Braddock.[16] Washington's expeditions to the Ohio Valley in 1754 and 1755 involved hacking a road through the wilderness. Recollecting the defeats at Fort Necessity and on the banks of the Monongahela might have made Washington more cautious in 1775—or perhaps superstitious—about tying his fortunes in Canada to Braddock's engineer.

In addition to tapping Goodwin's expertise, Colburn sent a scouting party of local men with a Native American guide to reconnoiter the Kennebec-Chaudiere route as far as Lake Megantic. He then returned to Cambridge to report on his preparations. Satisfied with the news from Maine, Washington gave his approval for Arnold's expedition to proceed. In a letter of September 3, 1775, he authorized Colburn to hire men, build the wooden boats, and procure barrels of corn, flour, pork, and beef for Arnold and his troops.[17]

As plans for Arnold's march progressed, Washington revealed his excitement in a letter to Schuyler, describing "a plan of an expedition which has engrossed my thoughts for several days . . . The land carriage by the route proposed is too inconsiderable to make an objection . . . It would make a diversion that would distract Carlton and facilitate your views." Lacking more detailed maps, Washington would remain under the mistaken impression that the portages would be manageable—that the "land carriage" was "inconsiderable." It was August 20, and Washington was anxious to put the plan in motion as soon as possible, and to get Schuyler's expedition moving too, given the onset of fall and winter in Canada.[18]

Schuyler had been at Ticonderoga for a month, waiting for reinforcements and supplies from New York while building enough wooden boats for the invasion. He had taken a trip south to Albany when Montgomery received intelligence at Ticonderoga that the commanding British general in Canada, Guy Carleton, was preparing to launch his own vessels on Lake Champlain. Montgomery decided not to wait for Schuyler's approval and set out a week later, on August 28, with a force of twelve hundred men to capture St. Johns, just north of the lake on the Richelieu River. Montgomery first planned to occupy Ile-aux-Noix and use a log boom at this narrow point in the river to prevent Carleton's vessels from reaching the lake. Schuyler joined Montgomery near Ile la Motte on September 4, and they proceeded to Ile-aux-Noix the same day. They covered the twenty miles to St. Johns on the 5th.[19]

See *A General Map of the Middle British Colonies, Detail #6*, page 58. Moving north from Ticonderoga— sailing and rowing by day as the winds allowed, and going ashore at night—Montgomery's fleet reached Crown Point on the western shore on August 29. The expedition then waited on a sandy beach just beyond Ile la Motte (off the northwestern shore of the largest island, Grand Ile), where Schuyler caught up with it on September 4, and they proceeded to Ile-aux-Noix (not shown) and St. Johns (*St. Jean*), just north of Lake Champlain on the Richelieu River (here called by its English name, the Sorel River).

During the next week, the Americans made three attempts to attack the fort, but each time the inexperienced troops panicked and retreated under fire both real and imagined, unaware that they outnumbered the two

Major General Philip Schuyler.

General Richard Montgomery.

hundred defenders inside the walls. Schuyler became so ill that he put Montgomery in charge and left the expedition on September 16. The following day, Montgomery rallied his troops and began laying siege to the fort by digging trenches and building gun batteries. Back at Ticonderoga, Schuyler forwarded supplies and reinforcements to Montgomery, whose strength grew to seventeen hundred men. However, some six hundred were sick and the rest were poorly trained and mutinous. Struggling with swampy terrain, cold weather, and supply shortages, they were incapable of storming the fort.[20] Montgomery wrote Schuyler, saying he needed more men and provisions, and that the Canadians were not coming to his side because his expedition appeared weak.[21]

As Montgomery became literally bogged down, Arnold's expedition set off from Cambridge with high hopes on September 11, 1775. Washington wrote detailed instructions to Arnold, focusing on the need for discipline among the men in treating the inhabitants, and their religion, with respect.[22] Washington also provided Arnold with some propaganda to distribute. In his "Address to the Inhabitants of Canada," Washington appealed to the Canadians to make common cause with America against the tyranny of Britain. He trumpeted the news that the Americans were besieging the mighty British army inside of Boston, and suggested that God was smiling on the efforts of the United Colonies.[23]

A week later, Arnold and his troops sailed from Newburyport, Massachusetts, and arrived at the mouth of the Kennebec River the following day. (See *The American Invasion of Canada, 1775–76*, page 94, and *The Lower Kennebec*.) They disembarked at Georgetown, on one of the islands that divides the river from the Sheepscot. (See also *La Nouvelle France, Detail #2*, page 103, where Georgetown is labeled *GeorgeT*.) Joined by some volunteers, they moved up the river as far as ships could travel, to Colburn's home and sawmills at Gardiner, Maine, where they found their two hundred wooden boats waiting for them on the shore. Each of these bateaux, as they were called, was twenty-two feet long and weighed four hundred pounds, taxing the strength of four men to carry it. Canoes would have been a better choice for such a journey, but the maps and descriptions of the route suggested the portages would be few and not very long.[24]

Not until September 21 did Washington inform Congress of Arnold's expedition. "I made all possible inquiry as to the distance, the safety of the route, and the danger of the season being too far advanced, but found nothing in either to deter me from proceeding," he told Hancock. Washington enclosed "a copy of the proposed route."[25] This verbal description was probably the work of Goodwin and is surprisingly accurate as to overall distance. It was deceptive, however, in its brevity and simplicity, making the journey sound straightforward, noting that the

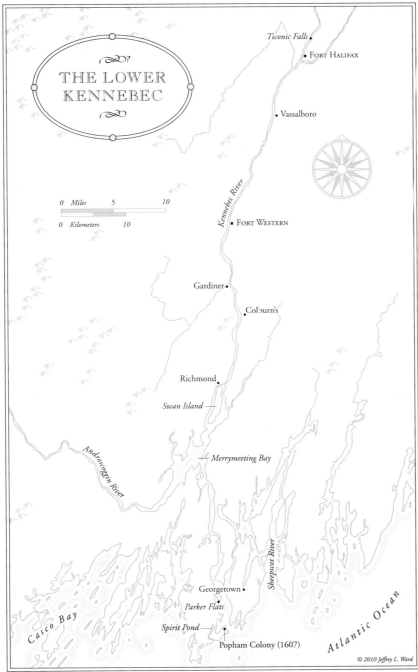

THE LOWER
KENNEBEC

Ticonic Falls

Fort Halifax

Vassalboro

0 Miles   5   10

0 Kilometers   10

Kennebec River

Fort Western

Gardiner

Colburn's

Richmond

Swan Island

Androscoggin River

Merrymeeting Bay

Sheepscot River

Casco Bay

Georgetown

Parker Flats

Spirit Pond

Popham Colony (1607)

Atlantic Ocean

© 2010 Jeffrey L. Ward

ABOVE: At the end of August 1775, Montgomery embarked his troops for the journey northward on Lake Champlain. Washington hoped that Arnold's expedition, which arrived at the Lower Kennebec some three weeks later, would go on to capture Quebec or at least draw the British away from Montgomery's advancing army.

Captain Daniel Morgan, later a colonel and brigadier general.

General Sir Guy Carleton, governor of British Canada.

distance "from the mouth of Kennebec River to Quebec on a straight line is 210 miles." The travel would be on anything but a straight line: The rough terrain and foul weather would turn the expedition into a six-week ordeal covering 350 miles of wilderness.[26]

Colburn's scouts had returned and reported that Carleton had stationed Native Americans and British soldiers at several points along the route to inform him of an American invasion. While the scouts had returned safely, Arnold was setting off on the same route several weeks later in the season, and the impending cold would make for harsher conditions. At the end of September, it took three days to get the men and provisions into the boats and up the river several miles north of Gardiner to Fort Western, the launch point for the expedition. Arnold did not know that to reach Quebec he would cover a distance almost twice as long as his maps and guides projected.[27]

On September 24, Arnold sent out a scouting party, followed by a team with a "surveyor and pilot to take the exact courses and distances to the Dead River." Since Goodwin was known to have Loyalist leanings, Arnold may have wanted to confirm the information he had provided at Colburn's request. Goodwin did not supply false data; he was apparently cultivating both the British and the Americans, waiting to see which side would prevail. Moreover, he must have known that Arnold could check his work with other local residents on the expedition who had traveled the route.[28]

Despite the fact that he was moving a thousand-man army with all its supplies and provisions upstream in heavy boats, Arnold predicted to Washington on September 26 that "by the best information I can procure, we shall be able to perform the march in twenty days—the distance about 180 miles," leaving the commander in chief to believe he would be at the walls of Quebec by mid-October.[29]

As the siege of St. Johns dragged on, Carleton was able to send reinforcements, boosting the regulars in the fort from 200 to 500, plus another 225 militia and other recruits. With a total of only 800 regulars in Canada, Carleton had decided to concentrate most of them at St. Johns and Chambly to delay the American advance. If he could not defeat the more numerous invaders, he wanted to stall them until winter set in and thwarted their drive to Montreal and Quebec.[30] Ethan Allen hoped to speed the invasion by splitting off with a contingent of forty men to attack Montreal on September 25 but was taken prisoner in the failed assault.[31]

Washington became concerned when he learned that Schuyler was sick and General David Wooster was to replace him. Believing Wooster was not a man of action and initiative, Washington feared this thrust would be called off and Arnold abandoned. On October 6, Washington urged Schuyler to make sure Arnold had sufficient notice that he was on his own, and to keep Carleton's attention fixed so he did not turn on Arnold before he had time to retreat. Arnold expected to be in Quebec "in 20 days from the 26th September," Washington wrote, "so that I hope you will have no difficulty in regulating your motions with respect to him."[32]

A week later, Washington revised that estimate. "Our last accounts from Colonel Arnold are very favorable," he told Hancock. "He was proceeding with all expedition, and I flatter myself, making all allowances, he will be at Quebec the 20th, where a gentleman from Canada (Mr. Brice) assures me he will meet with no resistance."[33]

While Arnold appeared to be making progress to the east, Montgomery decided to bypass St. Johns temporarily in order to take Fort Chambly, which fell to the Americans on October 18, lifting their spirits and enabling them to prevent two British detachments from crossing the St. Lawrence to rescue the garrison at St. Johns. (See *A General Map of the Middle British Colonies, Detail #6*, page 58. Chambly, labeled *Chamle*, is shown northwest of St. Johns, across the Sorel River.)[34]

Just as Montgomery's advance toward Montreal accelerated, Arnold's expedition ran into trouble. Even with two advance parties leading the way from Fort Western, and three rifle companies under Captain Daniel Morgan cutting a wide road through the woods for the divisions behind them, Arnold's men struggled mightily, since they were moving northward against the river's current. Rowing and wading upstream or hauling their boats on land for eighteen miles, they reached Fort Halifax. Next came the carrying place around Ticonic Falls, where it was impossible to paddle. (See *La Nouvelle France, Detail #2*, page 103, center, just north of the border between New England and Canada.)

"You would have taken the men for amphibious animals," Arnold told Washington, "as they were a great part of the time under water." With falling temperatures, it took only a day before many of the soldiers fell ill from the cold and from being wet constantly. Lacking sufficient clothing and equipment, they suffered from fatigue, diarrhea, and dysentery.[35] With the first frost in the last few days of September, the men awoke with wet clothing frozen onto their bodies. Men who got sick needed to be sent back, and the force to storm Quebec grew smaller.

They faced a cascade of problems. With their boats battered or destroyed by rocks in the rapids, they lost weapons and ammunition, while water seeped in and destroyed their provisions. With fewer boats they had to carry fewer provisions, yet the longer the trek took the more food they would need. At the same time, they were moving into higher, more barren country without game and fish in the same abundance as on the lower reaches of the Kennebec.

Portage of bateaux on Arnold's expedition.

On October 5, the expedition made the portage around Norridgewock Falls slowly and painfully despite the help of oxen. Almost a week later, on October 11, Arnold and the vanguard of his force were only at the beginning of the Great Carrying Place, well named by the Native Americans, as it confronted the expedition with eight miles of portage and four miles of rowing across three ponds in order to reach the Dead River. Arnold wrote to Washington on the 13th describing the hardships they had endured, but declared that "as the men are in high spirits, I make no doubt of reaching the Chaudiere River in eight or ten days."

Another thirty miles of rowing upstream brought them to the Height of Land, but not before they were drenched by heavy rains and a ferocious hurricane. The plateau required another four miles of carrying to Seven-Mile Stream, with its many false mouths, before they arrived at Lake Megantic.[36] Montresor's map did not indicate the almost impassible swamps at the mouth of Seven-Mile Stream, which nearly finished off several parties of Arnold's expedition.[37] (See **Map of Lake Megantic and the Height of Land Border Country**, page 105. Route A indicates the progress of Arnold's party and two other companies; Route B shows two companies that became mired in the swamp; and Route C is the path of the six remaining companies, some 350 men, who got lost near Rush Lake, veered off course to the northeast, and were saved by an Indian, who guided them to Lake Megantic.)[38]

On October 25, with the men starving and exhausted, Arnold decided to take a detachment ahead in search of provisions for the main body of troops, hoping they would join him in about ten days. He also ordered the rear guard to send forward only a body of men that could be supplied with two weeks' rations. Lieutenant Colonel Roger Enos decided that the order authorized him not only to send the sick back to Cambridge, as Arnold specified, but to turn back with some three hundred men under his command as well. Arnold's invasion force had lost about one third of its original strength.[39]

A few days later, Arnold wrote to Washington that "excessive heavy rain and bad weather have much retarded our march." He explained the loss of provisions and the departure of those too sick or weak to proceed. Still, he told Washington, he would try to make a surprise attack on Quebec if possible with his forward units, and if not he would wait for the whole expedition and cut off the city's communication with Carleton at Montreal. "Our march has been attended with an amazing deal of fatigue, which the officers and men have borne with cheerfulness. I have been much deceived in every account of our route, which is longer, and has been attended with a thousand difficulties I never apprehended. But if crowned with success, and conducive to the public good, I shall think it but trifling."[40]

Still unaware of this worrisome report, Washington assumed no news was good news and Arnold should be at Quebec soon if he was not there already. Adding to Washington's anticipation, American privateers had captured a brig headed from Quebec to Boston; he had received an intercepted letter saying that Quebec was packed with the arms and ammunition so badly needed for the siege of Boston, and that the Canadians were ready to welcome the Americans as liberators. He told Schuyler to keep Carleton occupied: "If Quebec should be attacked before Carleton should throw himself into it, there will be a surrender—without firing a shot."[41]

While launching a two-pronged land invasion, Washington also focused on capturing British supply ships bound for Boston and Quebec. In addition to starving the British out of Boston, while gaining ammunition for the Continental forces, Washington and Congress were trying to starve Quebec of supplies that might thwart the American invasion of Canada.

Since there was no Continental navy at this time, Washington decided to recruit soldiers with seafaring experience and use them to man armed vessels. Salem, Marblehead, Beverly, and other towns on the Massachusetts coast provided such men. Colonel John Glover's regiment, dubbed the "Marblehead mariners," would play a decisive role later in the war, manning the boats that carried the army to safety after the Battle of Brooklyn, and across the Delaware River for the attack on Trenton. In the fall of 1775, these regiments of sailors and fishermen supplied the crews for a fledgling American fleet of six armed vessels.

On September 5, the schooner *Hannah* had set sail under Captain Nicholson Broughton, who soon made the first capture ever by a Continental vessel. The *Unity*, bound for Boston carrying naval supplies and lumber, was taken off Cape Ann and brought into Gloucester, Massachusetts.[42]

Following orders from Congress, on October 16 Washington also moved to cut off supplies to Quebec through the St. Lawrence River. Intelligence reports revealed that two ships from England bound for Quebec were "laden with 6,000 stand of arms, a large quantity of powder, and other stores," Hancock told Washington, who instructed Captain Broughton and Captain John Selman, commanding the *Franklin*: "You are hereby directed to make all possible dispatch for the River St. Laurence and there to take such station as will best enable you to intercept the above vessels." If the British ships had already entered the river, the Americans were to "keep the station as long as the season will admit," Washington wrote, "as there is a great probability that Quebec will fall into our hands in a very short time. It may be expected that not only the above ordnance vessels but others from Quebec and Montreal may come down and fall into our hands."[43] (See *A Chart of the Gulf of St. Laurence*.)

A Chart of the Gulf of St. Laurence: This map from the Yale atlas depicts the mouth of the river, where Washington told the captains to lie in wait for the British cargo ships. Printed in London on March 25, 1775, the map could have reached Washington by October, through a French map dealer.

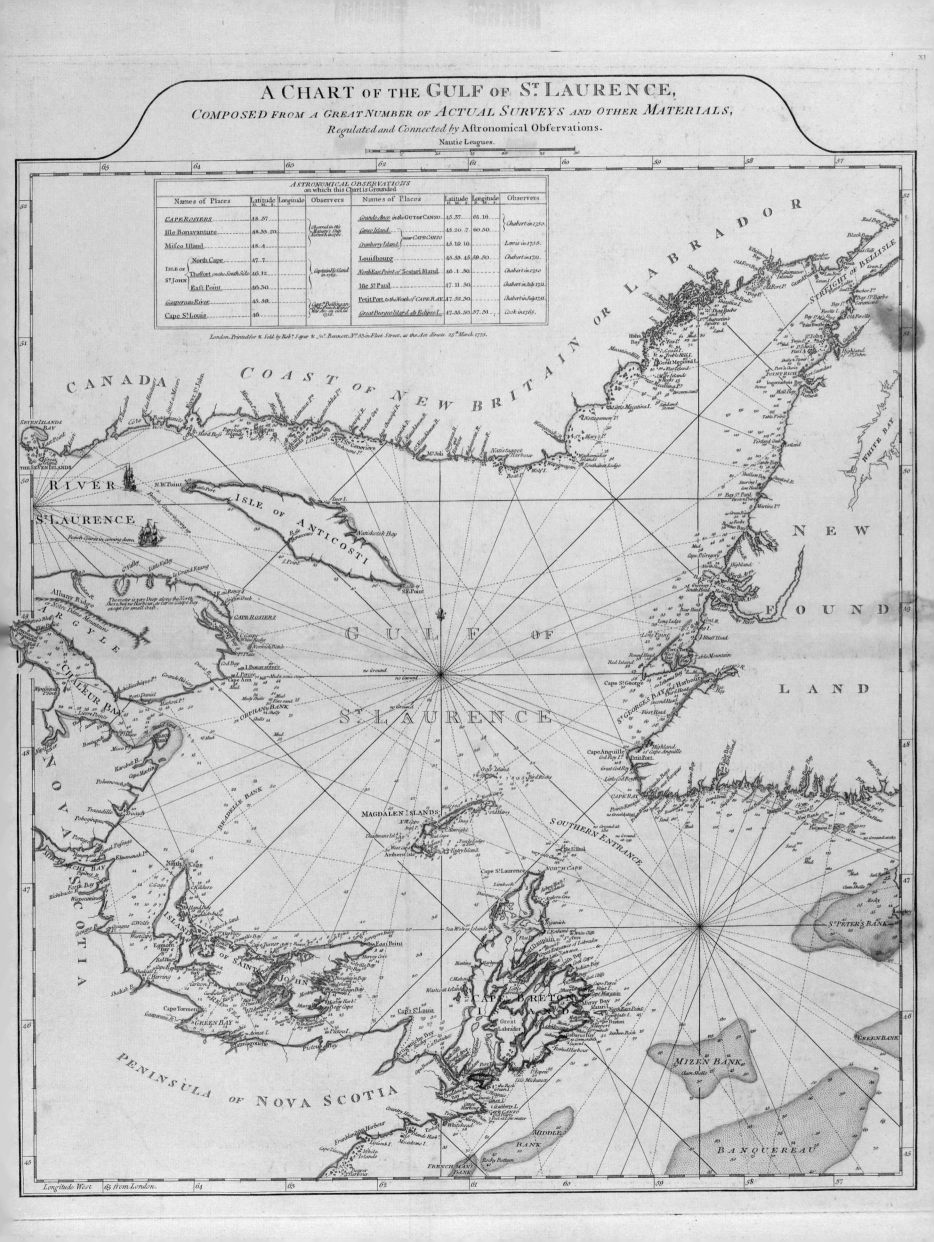

A CHART OF THE GULF OF ST. LAURENCE,

COMPOSED FROM A GREAT NUMBER OF ACTUAL SURVEYS AND OTHER MATERIALS,

Regulated and Connected by Astronomical Observations.

Nautic Leagues.

CANADA COAST OF NEW BRITAIN OR LABRADOR

ISLE OF ANTICOSTI

GULF OF ST. LAURENCE

RIVER ST. LAURENCE

CHALEUR BAY

ARGYLE

NOVA SCOTIA

ISLAND OF SAINT JOHN

MAGDALEN ISLANDS

BRADELLE BANK

ORPHANS BANK

CAPE BRETON ISLAND

NEW FOUND LAND

STREIGHT OF BELLISLE

WHITE BAY

ST. GEORGES BAY

CAPE RAY

SOUTHERN ENTRANCE

ST. PETERS BANK

GREEN BANK

MIZEN BANK

BANQUEREAU

PENINSULA OF NOVA SCOTIA

"As there may be men-of-war at Newfoundland you are so to conduct as to prevent being discovered by them or any intelligence given of your station," Washington continued. "Whatever vessels you may meet bound in and out of the River St. Laurence which you have reason to believe are in the service of the ministerial army or conveying any stores to them of provision or of any other nature, you are to endeavor to seize." As an incentive, the captains and their crews, privateers, would receive one third of the value of the ships and cargo they captured.

On October 26 Schuyler wrote to Washington that Chambly had fallen to Montgomery and St. Johns should soon follow. When Wooster arrived with more troops, he agreed to cede to Montgomery's authority even though he outranked him. Schuyler hoped "the next accounts I receive will announce the arrival of Colo. Arnold (whose success seems now certain) and the reduction of St. Johns . . . As I can easily conceive that Your Excellency's anxiety must be extreme, I shall forward what intelligence I receive by express."[44]

On November 3 St. Johns at last fell to Montgomery's forces. Carleton lost half of his regular troops, but his costly strategy was working. The siege had cost the Americans nearly two months, allowing Carleton's deputy to prepare the defenses of Quebec for an American assault

that would have to be launched, with great difficulty, in the dead of winter, since British warships would arrive with reinforcements from England in the spring as soon as the St. Lawrence River thawed.[45]

Schuyler wrote to Washington on the 7th with the good news about St. Johns. The next day, Washington reported to Hancock that he had not heard from Arnold since his letter of October 13 and concluded that "he must be in Quebec. If any mischance had happened to him, he would, as directed, have forwarded an express." Washington added that he had no word of the privateers sent to the mouth of the St. Lawrence either, but he was confident they would intercept the British supply ships either "inward or outward bound." A week later, Washington wrote to William Ramsay that he had not heard from Arnold, "which, although it may be considered in a favorable point of view, keeps me in a very disagreeable state of suspense."[46]

Washington replied to Schuyler on November 16 that "the surrender of St. Johns is a pleasing presage of the reduction of Quebec" and he hoped Arnold would be there to help storm the walled city. Revealing his careful attention to the details of Arnold's route, Washington continued: "The last account of him is dated 13th October at the second portage from Kennebec to the Dead River [at the Great Carrying Place], from whence he had

A Chart of the Gulf of St. Laurence, Detail #1: Whitehead is indicated at the bottom center. The captains were undoubtedly referring to a river feeding into Spanish Bay between Coal Cove and Coal Cape on the northeastern part of Cape Breton Island, due north of Louisburg.

dispatched an express to you and expected your answer at Chaudiere Pond [Lake Megantic], where he hoped to be in eight or ten days. By your not mentioning to have heard from him I apprehend the express has been intercepted."[47]

Three days later, Washington received Arnold's discouraging letter of October 27, written from Lake Megantic. Forwarding a copy to Hancock along with a letter from Colonel Enos, Washington wrote that "notwithstanding the great defection, I do not despair of Colonel Arnold's success." However, Washington added that Arnold's task would have been much easier "if he had been a fortnight sooner," since Carleton would now have time to gather all of his forces inside the walls of Quebec to make a final stand.

Washington again told Hancock that he had no word from the armed vessels sent to the St. Lawrence.[48] Broughton now commanded the armed schooner *Hancock* and Selman remained at the helm of the *Franklin*. They had written to Washington on November 2, with the dateline "White Head 5 Leagues West of Canso In Nova Scotia." They had captured a ship and gained some intelligence. No warships were reported at Quebec. They were going to intercept a large brig that was loading up with coal "at Spanish River on the Island of Loisburgh" and bound for Boston; "three or four score Boston men were digging coal there for the ministerial army for the season," they reported.[49] (See *A Chart of the Gulf of St. Laurence, Detail #1.*)

Broughton and Selman proved to be overzealous, capturing several ships that were later released by American authorities, since their captains were not pro-British and they were not carrying arms for the king. On November 6, Selman and Broughton had written to Washington again, this time from the Gut of Canso, the narrow strait between Nova Scotia and the southern end of Cape Breton Island, "just at the entrance of the Gulf of St. Laurence," as the captains explained in the dateline. They complained that heavy storms had hampered their operations, and they had not made it to Spanish River to capture the coal brig. However, they were now in a favorable position and boldly declared that "no vessel passes this season to Boston, Halifax, or to any part of America from Quebec but must pass within gunshot of us."[50]

To the southwest, most of Arnold's men had escaped the icy swamps at the false mouths of Seven-Mile Stream and found their way to Lake Megantic. The expedition had then regrouped on the Chaudiere River on October 31. They had only a few boats left, and no food, and had resorted to eating shaving soap, hair grease, lip salve, and boiled leather from their shoes and cartridge boxes. Arnold had gone ahead with a detachment that arrived at some Canadian settlements further along the river and sent back food that reached the main body of troops on November 2. A week later, Arnold and his advance party arrived at Point Levy, across the St. Lawrence River

from Quebec.[51] (See *An Authentic Plan of the River St. Laurence . . . with the Operations of the Siege of Quebec*, pages 114–15, and *Detail #1.*)

There Arnold "waited three days for the rear to come up and in preparing scaling ladders," he told Washington. The weather and the terrain had given the expedition a

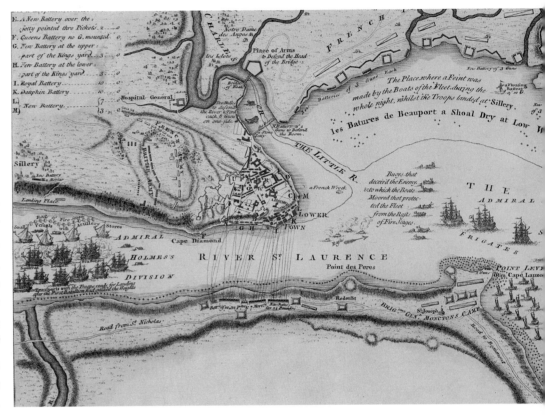

beating in the six weeks and 350 miles since it left Fort Western on the Kennebec, and of the original 1,100 men, only 675 remained. Nonetheless, they were in sight of Quebec and were eager to complete their mission. On the night of November 13, the day Montreal fell to Montgomery, Arnold moved most of his men across the St. Lawrence in canoes, completing the operation the following night. They landed at Sillery, just upriver from Quebec, where the British commander General Wolfe had landed his troops in 1759. (See *An Authentic Plan of the River St. Laurence, Detail #1.*)[52]

Low on ammunition, and lacking artillery, Arnold and his officers reluctantly decided not to storm the walls right away; they would cut off supplies to the city and wait for Montgomery, expected soon from Montreal.[53] Instead, Carleton arrived on the 19th, having escaped from Montreal on an armed sloop "disguised *en Canadien* and accompanied by six peasants." Expecting the British to sally from the walled city with a superior force, Arnold pulled his troops back to Point aux Trembles twenty miles up the St. Lawrence.[54] (See *An Authentic Plan of the River St. Laurence, Detail #2*, page 116.)

With operations in the Province of Quebec hovering between success and failure, Congress had Washington send a pair of spies to gather intelligence in Nova Scotia, to assess the military strength of that colony and how inclined the inhabitants might be to side with the

An Authentic Plan of the River St. Laurence, Detail #1: After leaving the Chaudiere River, Arnold had crossed the Etchemin River (bottom left) to reach Point Levy (bottom right). Three curving lines of text in the St. Lawrence River across from Point Levy note that the British fleet placed some decoy vessels here while Wolfe landed his troops at Sillery (left center). From the *Landing Place* a path leads diagonally up the steep riverbank to the Heights of Abraham. The lines across the river (bottom center) indicate British batteries firing on Quebec from the opposite shore.

PAGES 114–15: *An Authentic Plan of the River St. Laurence . . . with the Operations of the Siege of Quebec:* The British captured Quebec from the French on September 13, 1759, after William Howe led his troops up the steep slope to the plateau outside the city walls (left center). The British succeeded because the French left the safety of the city to fight on the Heights of Abraham. The British would not repeat that mistake in 1775. (This map was part of the *General Topography* that Washington bought in 1776, but he may have had this copy, from the Yale atlas, much earlier, since it was originally published in 1759.)

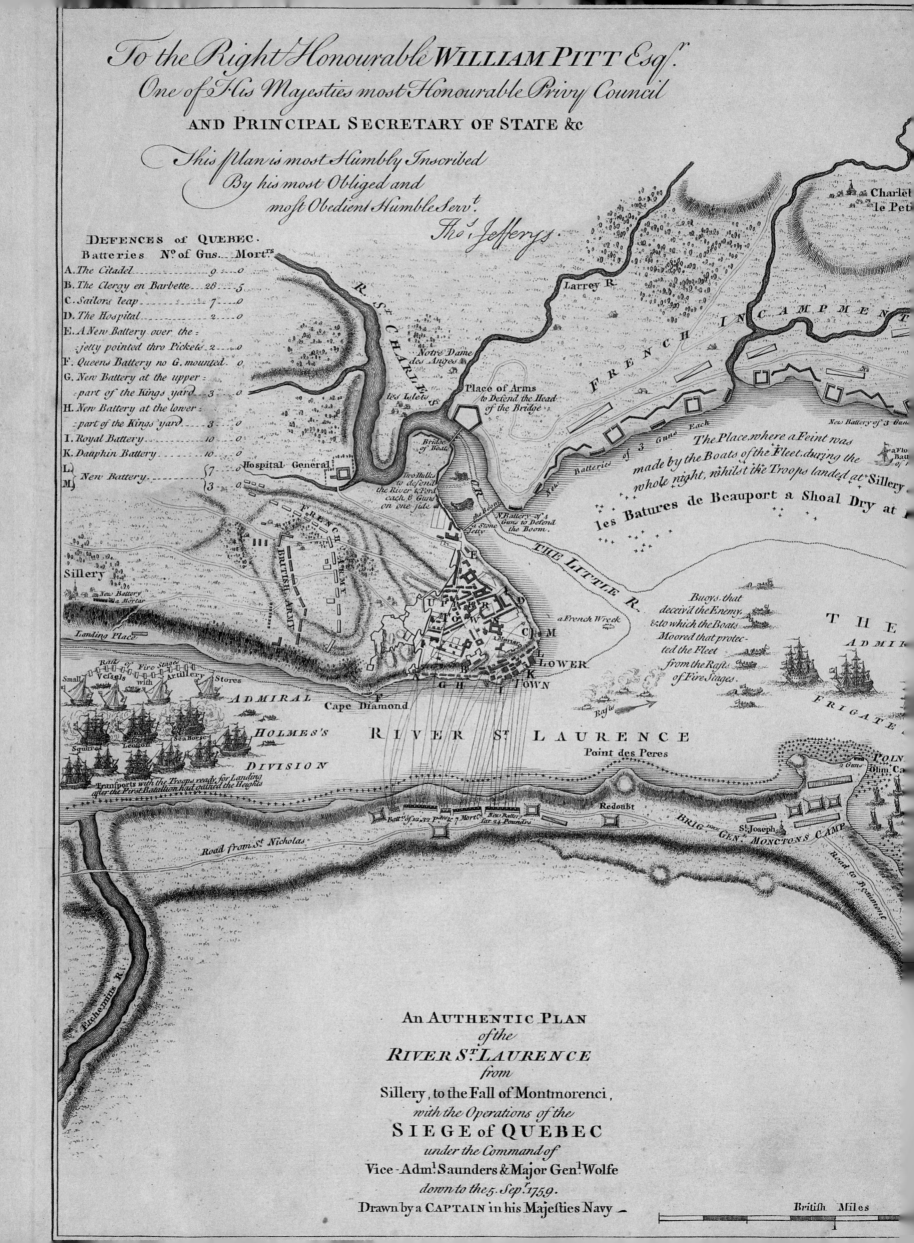

To the Right Honourable WILLIAM PITT Esqʳ.
One of His Majesties most Honourable Privy Council
AND PRINCIPAL SECRETARY OF STATE &c

This plan is most Humbly Inscribed
By his most Obliged and
most Obedient Humble Servᵗ.
Thoˢ Jefferys.

DEFENCES of QUEBEC.

Batteries	Nᵒ of Guˢ.	Mortˢ
A. The Citadel	9	0
B. The Clergy en Barbette	28	5
C. Sailors leap	7	0
D. The Hospital	2	0
E. A New Battery over the jetty pointed thro Pickets	2	0
F. Queens Battery no G. mounted	0	
G. New Battery at the upper part of the Kings yard	3	0
H. New Battery at the lower part of the Kings yard	3	0
I. Royal Battery	10	0
K. Dauphin Battery	10	0
L. New Battery	7	0
M.	3	0

An AUTHENTIC PLAN
of the
RIVER Sᵗ. LAURENCE
from
Sillery, to the Fall of Montmorenci,
with the Operations of the
SIEGE of QUEBEC
under the Command of
Vice-Admˡ Saunders & Major Genˡ Wolfe
down to the 5. Sepʳ. 1759.
Drawn by a CAPTAIN in his Majesties Navy

British Miles

Part of the
Upper River of
S!ˢ LAURENCE.

Montmorenci
Fall
Beauport
Isle of
Orleans
Charlesbourg
QUEBEC
Sillery
Pt Tremp.
Rouge Cap
S! Augustin
Newville
Bequencourt
S! Nicholas
Tilli
Chaudiere
Falls
De Chamband
Richilieu Falls
S! Goix
Chaudiere R.

British Leagues.
1   2   3   4   5

A VIEW of the
ACTION gained by the ENGLISH
Sep.ʳ 13. 1759. near
QUEBEC.
Brought from thence
By an OFFICER of Distinction

R. S! Charles

Hospital
General

THE HIGHTS OF
ENGLISH   ABRAHAM
ARMY

FRENCH   ARMY

B. G. Townshend
Light Inf.
Royal
Americans
Light
Inf.
Anstruthers
Highlanders
Lascelle's
Kennedy's
Bragg
GEN! WOLF
Louisbourg
Grenad.

Sillery
4 G Batt.
Passage in
the Mountain
Landing Place
Royal American

St Laurence R.

Beauport
Batteries
2 Guns Each
Rafts
of Fire Stages
Water

FRENCH   INCAMPMENT
Intrenchments commanding the Redoubts   & Batteries   within Musquet Shot
a Mortar

Falls of
Montmorenci
300 F! High

GENERAL WOLF'S
CAMP

Point a l'Essay
New Battery
of 3 Guns
the Place
of Attack July
30.
New Battery
of 5 Guns
the Ford
4 Guns

the Centurion's Station
for covering the Troops
at the Attack

BASON

SAUNDERS'S ON

NORTH   CHANNEL

DIVISION   POINT of ORLEANS
2 Guns

Admiral's   Ship

MAJOR HARDY'S   POST

Transports
laid ashore
to clean

Road to S! Pierre

ISLE

Road to S! Laurence

OF

Part of the

Transports at Anchor

ORLEANS

Part of the Upper River of St. LAURENCE.

An Authentic Plan of the River St. Laurence, Detail #2: On November 19, Arnold retreated to Point aux Trembles (labeled *Pt. Trempe,* today's Neuville) next to Neuville at the center of this small inset from the top of the main map.

Americans. In his instructions to Aaron Willard and Moses Child on November 24, Washington wrote that "as the season is late, and this a work of great importance, I entreat and request that you will use the utmost dispatch, attention, and fidelity" and act "with a proper degree of caution and secrecy." (See *A Large and Particular Plan of Shegnekto Bay*.) Halifax was a port of enormous strategic value for the British, as would be demonstrated by their retreat from Boston the following spring and what Washington suspected might be their preparations for capturing New York City. Situated on the shortest route across the northern Atlantic, Halifax was a vital stopover for troop and supply ships sailing between England and the American colonies.[55] (See *The American Invasion of Canada, 1775–76,* page 94, upper right. Halifax is shown halfway down the eastern coast of Nova Scotia.)

Washington's errant privateers, Broughton and Selman, had meanwhile gotten into more trouble. In mid-November they arrived at Charlottetown, the capital of the Island of St. John (now Prince Edward Island) off the northern coast of Nova Scotia. (See *A Chart of the Gulf of St. Laurence,* page 111. Charlottetown is just north of the large harbor on the southeastern shore of the island.) Acting on faulty intelligence, they broke up "a nest of recruits intended to be sent against Montgomery" to thwart his march on Quebec. Broughton and Selman captured the acting governor, along with two other prominent figures. After looting their homes and drinking their liquor, the privateers headed back to Cambridge with the prisoners, leaving their wives and scores of new immigrants who depended on them without support or provisions for the winter.[56]

"By the last accounts from the armed schooners sent to the River St. Lawrence, I fear we have but little to expect from them," Washington told Hancock. Low on provisions, they were giving up their vigil, "which at this time is particularly unfortunate" since "if they choose a proper station, all the vessels coming down that river must fall into their hands," Washington fumed. "The plague, trouble and vexation I have had with the crews of all the armed

vessels is inexpressible. I do believe there is not on earth a more disorderly set."[57] When they arrived in Cambridge, Washington reprimanded the privateers and released the prisoners, telling Hancock, "I have thought it but justice to discharge these gentlemen, whose families were left in the utmost distress."[58]

Others of the six privateers did better. As Washington told Arnold, "We have taken several prizes, to the amount it is supposed of 15,000 pounds sterling—one of them a valuable store ship (but no powder on it) containing a fine brass mortar 13 inch—2,000 stand of arms—shot, etc., etc." This was the brig *Nancy,* captured on November 28 by the armed schooner *Lee* under Captain John Manley.[59]

"All I can learn of Colonel Arnold is that he is near Quebec," Washington wrote to Hancock on November 28. "I hope Montgomery will be able to proceed to his assistance. I shall be very uneasy until I hear they are joined." To Schuyler, Washington wrote that Colonel Enos had returned to Cambridge with most of his men, leaving Arnold too weak to attack Quebec without Montgomery's help. "I hope he will be able to give it to him, and by taking that city finish his glorious campaign."[60]

Dressed in rags after their wilderness march, Arnold and his men had to wait two weeks to be reinforced and resupplied by Montgomery, who arrived at Point aux Trembles with three hundred men on December 3 and assumed overall command. Two days later, Montgomery and Arnold moved downriver to Quebec and resumed the American blockade of the city.

Arnold assured Washington that inside was "a wretched motley garrison of disaffected seamen, marines and inhabitants, the walls in a ruinous situation, and cannot hold out long."[61] Montgomery told Schuyler he planned to distract Carleton with a feigned frontal attack on the main gates but actually intended "to insult the works, I believe towards the lower town, which is the weakest part."[62]

At this point, Washington had just received Arnold's letter from Point Levy and was thrilled he had made it so

far. "It is not in the power of any man to command success, but you have done more—you have deserved it." By now, Washington hoped, Arnold had "met with the laurels which are due to your toils, in the possession of Quebec. My thanks are due and sincerely offered to you for your enterprising and persevering spirit. To your brave followers I likewise present them." To Schuyler, Washington wrote of Arnold that "the merit of this gentleman is certainly great and I heartily wish that fortune may distinguish him as one of her favorites."[63]

On December 31, after weeks of waiting, Washington finally learned that Montgomery had joined Arnold at Point aux Trembles and they were preparing to storm Quebec. Indeed, on that very day the enlistments expired for many of the expedition's troops, and with their force rapidly dwindling, Montgomery and Arnold had decided to attack that night. Montgomery from the south and Arnold from the north, each led a column toward the Lower Town, expecting to meet there for an assault on the Upper Town. But Carleton anticipated their strategy. His troops lay in wait, and despite the moonless night and the snowstorm, they saw the Americans coming.

Montgomery was killed instantly, along with several of his officers and men, by a blast of grapeshot from a log house commanding that route. The rest of his column turned back. Arnold's column, approaching from the northern suburbs, encountered a barricade where Arnold's leg was shattered by a bullet, and he was evacuated to the hospital. His troops stormed the barricade but were thrown back at a second one and trapped by a detachment of Carleton's troops in their rear. In the daring attempt, some four hundred Americans were captured. (See *A Plan of Quebec*, page 118.)[64]

Washington had not heard of the defeat, and wrote to Schuyler: "I confess that I am much concerned for General Montgomery and Colonel Arnold . . . However, I trust that their distinguished conduct, bravery, and perseverance will meet with the smiles of fortune, and put them in possession of this important fortress."[65]

The following evening he received the news. "I wish I had no occasion to send my dear general this melancholy account," Schuyler wrote. "My amiable friend and gallant Montgomery is no more. The brave Arnold is wounded and we have met with a severe check, in an unsuccessful attempt on Quebec."[66]

Washington responded that he was "heartily sorry" and offered his condolences "upon the unhappy fall of the brave and worthy Montgomery and those gallant officers and men who have experienced a like fate . . . I am much concerned for the intrepid and enterprising Arnold and greatly fear that consequences of a most alarming nature will result from this well intended but unfortunate attempt."[67]

Arnold's phenomenal determination displayed itself again after the assault, with his decision to carry on the blockade of Quebec with a mere six hundred men.[68] Washington found this "a most favorable circumstance" which "exhibits fresh proof of Arnold's ability and perseverance in the midst of difficulties." Two days after Washington learned of the defeat, Congress voted to send reinforcements to

A Large and Particular Plan of Shegnekto Bay: This map from the Yale atlas shows the French forts in Nova Scotia captured by the British during the French and Indian War. In November 1775, Washington relayed instructions from Congress to Willard and Child to investigate "the condition of the fortifications, docks, yards, the quantity of artillery and warlike stores, and the number of soldiers, sailors and ships of war there, and transmit the earliest intelligence." (Washington bought another copy of this map in 1776 as part of the *General Topography*.)

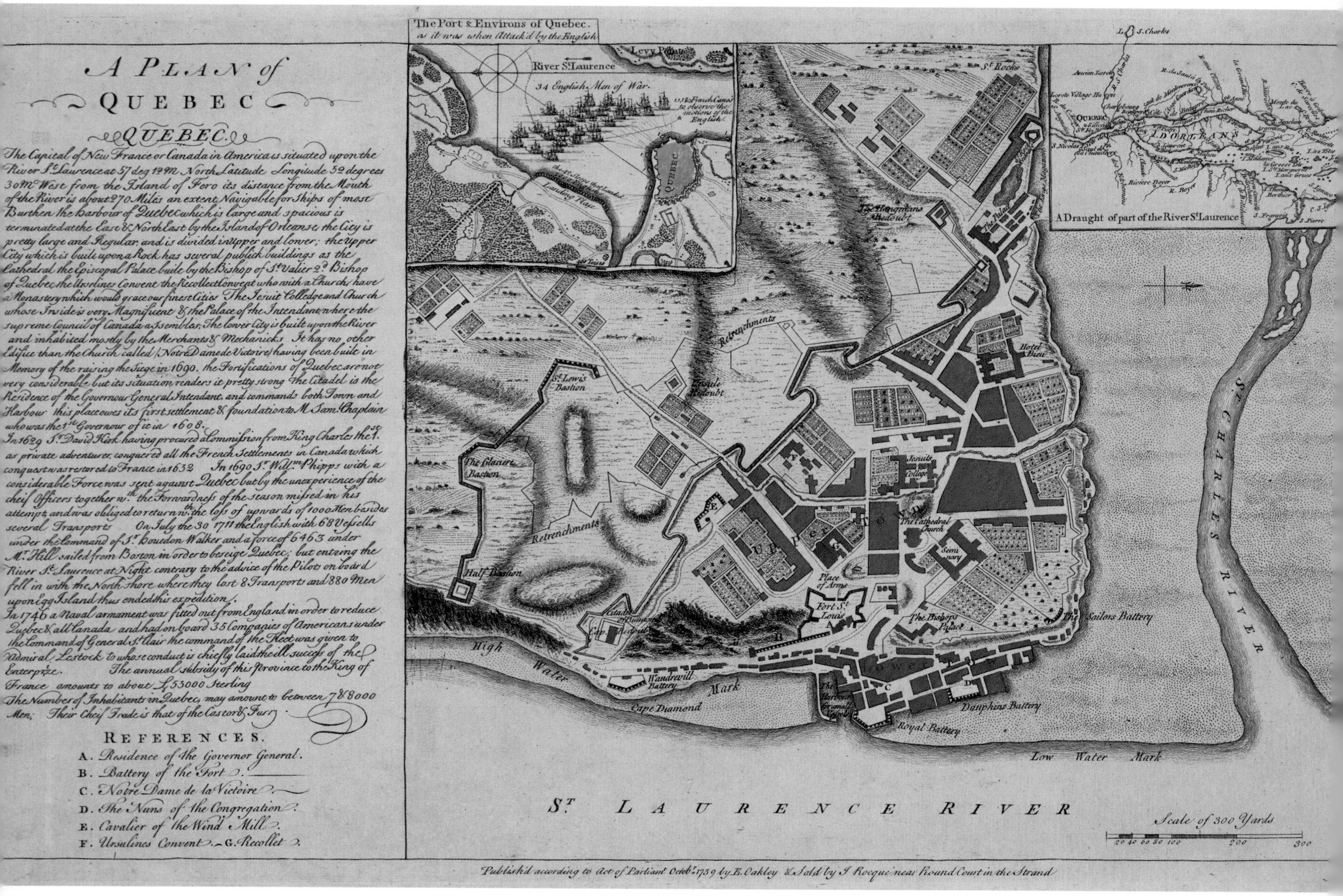

A PLAN of QUEBEC

QUEBEC

The map contains extensive handwritten engraved text describing the history of Quebec, as well as numerous place labels.

REFERENCES.
A. Residence of the Governor General.
B. Battery of the Fort.
C. Notre Dame de la Victoire.
D. The Nuns of the Congregation.
E. Cavalier of the Wind Mill.
F. Ursulines Convent. G. Recollet.

Scale of 300 Yards

The Port & Environs of Quebec. as it was when Attack'd by the English.

A Draught of part of the River St. Laurence.

ST. LAURENCE RIVER

ST CHARLES RIVER

Publish'd according to Act of Parliam't Octob 1759 by E. Oakley & Sold by I. Roque near Round Court in the Strand

A Plan of Quebec: This map from the Yale atlas was published in October 1759, before news reached London that the city had fallen to the British on September 13. The text on the left gives a history of various failed attempts to capture the city over the previous two centuries. On the night of December 31, 1775, Arnold's column approached through the suburbs of St. Roch (*St. Rocks*) and Palais (*The Palace*)—shown at the top center, next to the upper right inset—attempting to rendezvous with Montgomery's troops in the Lower Town (bottom center).

Arnold. Washington displayed his own indomitable cast of mind when he managed to find a silver lining in the defeat at Quebec. "The reinforcement ordered to him will, I hope, complete the entire conquest of Canada this winter; and but for the loss of the gallant chief [Montgomery] and his brave followers I should think the rebuff rather favorable than otherwise." Had the attack succeeded with so few men, the British would easily retake Quebec in the spring. Instead, with the defeat "our eyes will now, not only be open to the importance of holding it, but the numbers which are requisite to that end."[69]

To Arnold he wrote of the defeat at Quebec: "This unhappy affair affects me in a very sensible manner, and I sincerely condole with you upon the occasion." He then turned to the bright side and what had to be done. He was sending reinforcements, he told Arnold, and impressed on him the importance of Canada:

I need not mention to you the great importance of this place and the consequent possession of all Canada in the scale of American affairs—you are well apprized of it—to whomsoever it belongs, in their favor probably will the balance turn. If it is in

ours, success I think will most certainly crown our virtuous struggles. If it is in theirs, the contest, at best, will be doubtful, hazardous, and bloody. The glorious work must be accomplished in the course of this winter. Otherwise it will become difficult, most probably impracticable. For, [the British], knowing that it will be impossible ever to reduce us to a state of slavery and arbitrary rule without [Canada], will certainly send a large reinforcement there in the spring.

Capturing Quebec would add "the only link wanting in the great chain of Continental union."[70]

By the end of 1775 none of the six armed vessels Washington had dispatched remained in service. The men had not been paid their share of the prizes and would not re-enlist, and one of the ships had been captured by the British.[71] However, between January and March 1776, all six privateers had been sent out again.[72] On January 25 Washington thanked Manley for capturing two British ships on their way from Whitehaven, Nova Scotia, to Boston.[73] On February 9 Washington told Hancock that American privateers had captured a brig carrying firewood and other supplies to Boston from La Have, Nova Scotia, just south of Halifax. Washington also gained valuable intelligence: The captain of the brig said he was at Halifax in January, when two regiments had arrived from Ireland. The British were starting to amass the expeditionary force that would capture New York City.[74]

Less successful was the mission of Willard and Child to assess the attitude of Nova Scotia's inhabitants toward the American cause and determine their military strength. "They have not answered the purposes of their commission by any means," Washington told Hancock on February 14, "as they only went but a little way into that country and found their intelligence upon the information of others." Disgusted with their excuses, Washington enclosed their report.

They explained that they had gone to "Campobello about twenty or thirty miles into the Province aforesaid, but could not cross the Bay of Fundy for no vessel could be hired or procured except we purchase one, as every vessel even to a boat that crossed the bay was seized as soon as they came into port except cleared from Halifax. And we could not travel any further into the country by reason of Governor Legge establishing martial law and issuing several proclamations" warning the inhabitants against any contact with rebels. The report must have made Washington all the more grateful for Arnold, who seemed to surmount every obstacle, scraping together enough canoes to sneak hundreds of men across the St. Lawrence under the guns of two British warships in the dead of night.[75]

At the end of February, Arnold wrote to Washington from Quebec that smallpox had "crept in among the troops." Nonetheless, against all odds and with a mere five hundred men fit for duty, Arnold maintained the siege through the winter.[76]

At the beginning of April, Washington wrote to Arnold from Cambridge conveying the good news of the British evacuation on March 17, and warning that the ice-covered St. Lawrence River would soon thaw:

Major General [John] Thomas will long before you receive this have informed you of the success of our operations here. The enemy have quitted this harbor last week. We have no certain accounts of their destination. It is generally believed they are gone to Halifax. If true, it is probable they will attempt to penetrate Canada on the opening of the St. Lawrence. I hope before that happens you will be in full possession of Quebec and have its avenues well secured, upon which depends the fate of this campaign in these parts.[77]

General David Wooster and Arnold had just traded places: Arnold, promoted to brigadier general in January but still convalescing from his leg wound, took charge in Montreal, while Wooster assumed command of an expanded force of some two thousand men at Quebec. At the same time, Congress sent a team of three envoys—Benjamin Franklin, Charles Carroll, and Samuel Chase—who arrived in Montreal on April 29 to urge the Canadians to become the fourteenth colony: to break with England, establish their own government, and send delegates to Congress.[78]

Washington had moved the army down to New York City to defend against the expected British invasion, and from there he dispatched some two thousand troops under General William Thompson up the Hudson to Canada.[79] At the end of April, Washington confided to his brother John Augustine: "It was thought best to strengthen that quarter at the expense of this. But I am afraid we are rather too late in doing of it."[80]

A few days later, on May 1, Major General Thomas arrived at Quebec, filling the role of the late Montgomery as overall commander, now with 2,500 men. The following day, with the melting of the ice in the St. Lawrence, news reached Thomas of British warships sailing toward Quebec to relieve the garrison and inhabitants. He began pulling his troops back toward Montreal. More reinforcements arrived in Canada from New Jersey, Pennsylvania, and New York, including the regiments sent by Washington, for a total of almost seven thousand troops. However, expiring enlistments, desertions, and disease whittled away at the force relentlessly. Smallpox now spread through the ranks and became an epidemic.[81]

After the first ships arrived at Quebec, Carleton sallied from the city on May 6 with almost a thousand troops and four fieldpieces, putting the remaining American troops to flight. Left behind were their sick and wounded along with artillery and supplies. Carleton then waited for the rest of the fleet carrying more troops under Major General John Burgoyne. Carleton now had some thirteen thousand troops including 4,300 Hessians.[82] Harried by British ships, Thomas and his troops collected themselves at Deschambault, forty miles upriver from Quebec, before retreating to Sorel, where they arrived on May 17.

Several days later, Washington wrote to Schuyler that "our troops cannot make a stand at De Chambeau as I had hoped." (See "De Chambaud" on *An Authentic Plan of the River St. Laurence, Detail #2*, page 116, lower left.) "I wish it were practicable, for most certainly the lower down the river we can maintain our post, the more important will be the advantages resulting from it . . . But unacquainted as I am with the country, I cannot undertake to say where it should be. Not doubting and hoping that everything for the best will be done."[83]

Washington was more forceful in a letter to Thomas two days later, saying his retreat from Quebec had given "a sad shock to our schemes in that quarter and blasted the hope we entertained of reducing that fortress and the whole of Canada to our possession . . . But nevertheless it is hoped that you will be able to make a good stand yet."

Major General John Thomas.

Washington had met that day with members of Congress, and they had resolved that the forces in Canada should focus their efforts "on the St. Lawrence below the mouth of the Sorel" (the English name for the Richelieu River). The committee that met with Washington also reported that "it is of the highest importance that post be taken at Dechambeau, and that the same be fortified; that works be likewise erected on the islands in the River St. Lawrence at the mouth of the River Sorrel, as well to keep open the communication between Dechambeau and St. Johns."[84]

However, Thomas was already proceeding southward to St. Johns, where he met Major General John Sullivan on June 1. Sullivan took over from Thomas, who died the following day from smallpox. Wooster was recalled by Congress on June 6.[85] Sullivan reported that the army was in chaos and utterly demoralized, but he intended to rally. Washington had fortified New York and was in Philadelphia to consult with Congress when Sullivan wrote to him on June 5–6, saying he was "extremely happy to find that I have anticipated the wishes of Congress . . . for, it was my fixed determination to gain post at Dischambeau which I mean to fortify . . . This commands the channel, secures the country, destroys the [enemy's] communication and affords a safe retreat, if we are obliged to make one." Sullivan had dispatched General Thompson for that purpose, and he was now at Three Rivers just downstream from De Chambeau. (Three Rivers is labeled *Trois Rivieres* on **La Nouvelle France, Detail #2**, page 103, upper left corner.) The British ships were thus upstream from Thompson, but if he secured Three Rivers, the British would be forced to fall back, Sullivan wrote, and the Americans would then advance on Quebec "as fast as possible."[86]

Ignoring Sullivan's grandiose plans, on June 6 Arnold wrote to Schuyler from Montreal that he was preparing to evacuate the city. He painted a picture of defeat on every front and the probable loss of Canada to the British, while forming a plan for a last stand at St. Johns or Ile-aux-Noix. "The want of a little attention in time has lost us this fine country. I hope for better things on your side and that in the rotation of fortune, something better will turn up for us here."[87]

Though the Americans were defeated at the Cedars some forty miles southwest of Montreal on May 18, their morale was nonetheless boosted by reinforcements and supplies. (See *Cedar Falls* on **A General Map of the Middle British Colonies, Detail #6**, page 58, top center.) Then their last hopes for the fourteenth colony were dashed with the defeat of Thompson's vastly outnumbered force at Trois Rivieres on June 8. The following day, Arnold and the garrison at Montreal fled across the St. Lawrence to Longueil, and then to St. Johns. Arnold directed the rear guard while his men packed themselves and supplies into bateaux and headed south to Crown Point. Sullivan ordered a retreat to Lake Champlain and moved most of

his troops out of Sorel in bateaux on June 14 just before the British arrived. In the midst of the retreat, on June 17, Congress designated Major General Horatio Gates as commander of American forces in Canada. With Sullivan on Lake Champlain and Schuyler in Albany, it was unclear which of them Gates was succeeding. Two days later, all of Sullivan's men had reached Ile-aux-Noix, where they were struck by dysentery.

All the Americans had reached Crown Point by July 2. The Americans had set out ten months earlier to liberate Canada from the British, with Montgomery leading the way from Ticonderoga. The invasion had cost them five thousand casualties, and another eight thousand were either in need of a hospital or otherwise unfit for duty.[88]

On July 5, Schuyler, Gates, and Sullivan held a war council at Crown Point and decided, over many objecting voices, to evacuate this strong position and drop down to make a stand at Ticonderoga where they could be more easily resupplied. On July 8, Congress resolved the ambiguity and Gates officially became Schuyler's second in command. Sullivan was furious. The Americans started rebuilding the defenses at Ticonderoga.[89]

Carleton remained at St. Johns, building a fleet to dominate Lake Champlain and transport his large army southward. The Americans tried to keep up, building a fleet of their own during the summer. With Arnold commanding the American squadron and patrolling the northern end of the lake, the two sides fought the Battle of Valcour Island on October 11, 1776. Though greatly outnumbered, the Americans fought bravely before retreating at nightfall. Over the next two days the British chased down the American vessels, and the fighting continued as they scattered and tried to escape. Most of the American commanders were able to run their boats aground on the shore and flee with their crews.[90]

Ten days after the Battle of Valcour Island, Washington wrote to Schuyler: "From my remote situation and my ignorance of the country in which the army under your command to the northward is to act, it is impossible for me to give peremptory orders, or scarcely my opinion . . . I am confident your own good sense, zeal, and activity will suggest to you the most probable means of making amends for the heavy loss we have sustained by the destruction of General Arnold's fleet upon Lake Champlain." Nonetheless, Washington offered some advice that predicted the turn of events that winter.

I have been informed that Ticonderoga, properly garrisoned and supplied with provisions and ammunition, is almost impregnable . . . I would advise a collection of as much provision as could possibly be got together, which if sufficient for nine thousand effective men . . . I should imagine you could keep Carleton and Burgoyne at bay until the rigor of the season would oblige them raise the siege, not only

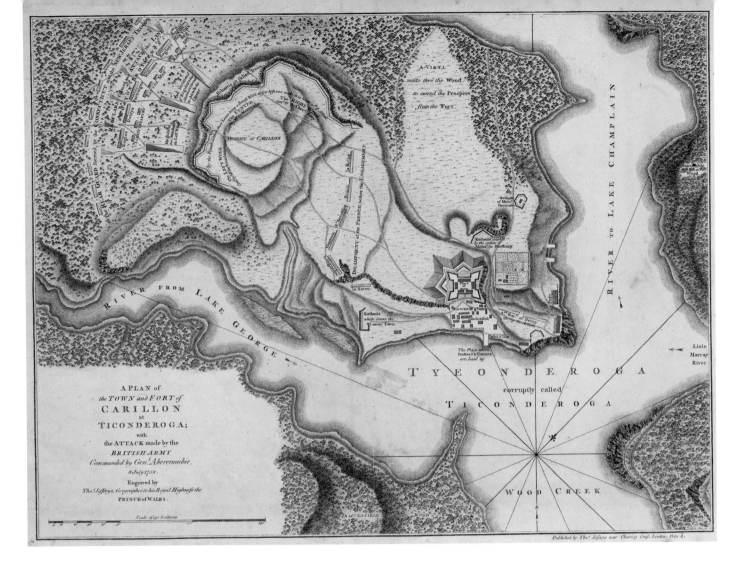

for want of conveniencies to lay in the field, but for fear the freezing of the lake should make their return impracticable.[91]

Carleton was at Crown Point with his army and fleet on the evening of October 26 when Gates wrote from Ticonderoga that "an attack may hourly be expected here—The wind is now against the enemy's fleet, as it providentially has been for this week past, and it is to be wished it may continue so." On the morning of the 28th Carleton's forces were finally able to approach the outer defenses of Ticonderoga by land and water, but they withdrew late in the afternoon without attacking. Schuyler commented to Washington that "if General Carleton does not mean to attack, he must soon return [to Quebec] as the inclemency of the season will not suffer him to remain long encamped." The following day, Schuyler predicted that Carleton would not attack Ticonderoga, "nor can any of his army penetrate to the Mohawk River" without being detected by American scouts "incessantly traversing the country from Ticonderoga to Fort Stanwix."[92]

By November 6, Carleton had completely evacuated Crown Point and moved his forces to St. Johns for the winter. Gates remarked that the Americans' retreat all the way to Ticonderoga had indeed been wise. Had they remained at Crown Point, Carleton could have cut off their supplies after defeating Arnold's fleet by placing his own vessels south of Crown Point.

Arnold wrote that the British "give out their intention is to return to Canada and pay us a visit in the spring. I wish it may not be a feint to put us off our guard and to return the first fair wind. As the season is so far advanced, I am rather inclined to think they are in earnest to return." Several days later, Washington congratulated Hancock and Congress "upon the news from Ticonderoga and that General Carleton and his army have been obliged to return to Canada without attempting anything."[93]

Thus the invasion of Canada in 1775–76 ultimately served a crucial purpose: It delayed the British invasion of the Hudson River Valley for a year, setting the stage for Burgoyne's surrender at Saratoga in October 1777 at the hands of a better prepared Continental army—a resounding defeat that proved to be the great turning point of the American Revolution.

Washington's admiration of Arnold's bravery and perseverance under the worst of conditions suggests that he may have seen the younger man as an alter ego, a reminder of his own exploits in the wilderness some twenty years earlier. The Kennebec-Chaudiere expedition may have echoed in his mind his several journeys from Virginia to the Ohio River Valley, missions that were critical in their timing and involved punishing battles against the elements as well as the enemy. Washington possessed the same "enterprising and persevering spirit" that he praised in Arnold—an audacity, toughness, and willingness to take risks that created its own luck. The hardship and sacrifice endured by the Americans in Canada paved the way for success, drawing "the smiles of fortune," to the American cause.[94]

A Plan of the Town and Fort of Carillon at Ticonderoga: This map from the Yale atlas (also included in the *General Topography*) depicts the disastrous defeat in 1758 of British and provincial forces under General Abercromby (upper left) by the French, who had protected themselves on three sides by "abbattis or felled Trees" around the Height of Carillon. The British succeeded in capturing the fort (center right) in 1759, when the French blew up the ramparts and abandoned the site. Thus, while the map did not present an accurate picture of the rebuilt fortifications in 1775, it gave Washington a detailed view of the surrounding landscape.

A PLAN of the CITY of NEW-YORK & its ENVIRONS to Greenwich, on the North or Hudsons River, and to Crown Point, on the East or Sound River, Shewing the Several Streets, Publick Buildings, Docks, Fort & Battery, with the true Form & Course of the Commanding Grounds, with and without the Town.

Survey'd in the Winter, 1775.

Sold by A. Dury, Dukes Court St Martins Lane.

To the Honble. Thos. Gage, Esqr. Major General and Commander in Chief of his MAJESTY'S Forces in North America, and Colonel of the 22d. Regiment of Foot. This PLAN is Most humbly Inscrib'd, by his Obedient Servant, John Montresor, Engineer.

A CHART, of the Entrance to NEW YORK, from Sandy Hook, shewing the proparest Channel, for Sailing with the Banks and Depths of Water.

NEW JERSEY

PART OF LONG ISLAND

PART OF STAATEN ISLAND

West Bank

East Bank

PART OF THE OCEAN

NEW JERSEY

NORTH OR HUDSONS RIVER

GREENWICH

CROWN POINT

EAST OR SOUND RIVER

References.

A. Fort George.
B. Batteries.
C. Military Hospital.
D. Secretaries office.
E. Powder Magazines.
F. Soldiers Barrack.
G. Wharfs and Keys.
H. Ship Yards.
I. City Hall.
K. Exchange.
L. Goal.

M. Workhouse.
N. Colledge.
O. Markets.
P. Trinity Church.
Q. St Georges Chapel.
R. St Pauls Church.
S. Old Dutch Church.
T. New Dutch Church.
U. Lutheran Church.
W. Calvinistic Church.
X. French Protestant Church.

Y. Quakers Meeting.
Z. Presbyterian Meeting.
1. Jews Synagogue.
2. Baptist Meeting.
3. Moravian Meeting.
4. New Lutheran Meeting.
5. Ruins of Alderman Romeve Battery.
6. Fresh Water Engine from whence the Town is supplied.

New York.

CHAPTER FIVE

0   1   2   3   4   5

FROM THE HUDSON TO PHILADELPHIA

AND BACK

"The consequences of the enemy's possessing themselves of New York have appeared to me so terrible that I have scarcely been able to sleep," Washington's second in command, Major General Charles Lee, wrote to him in Cambridge on January 5, 1776. An eccentric Englishman who had resigned his commission in the British army to join the American cause, Lee was gifted with a flair for language and the power of persuasion. He had written a highly influential piece of American propaganda in the run-up to the war, and now he urged Washington to send him through Connecticut to recruit a regiment of volunteers that would "effect the security of New York—and the expulsion or suppression of that dangerous banditti of Tories who have appeared on Long Island . . . Not to crush these serpents before their rattles are grown would be ruinous."[1]

ABOVE: Major General Charles Lee.

PAGE 122: *A Plan of the City of New-York:* The inset (upper left) shows that New York's waters provided a connection—the channel at Sandy Hook—between the Atlantic Ocean and the interior of Canada via the Hudson. This copy of Montresor's map, from the Yale atlas, was published in June 1775 and thus would have been available to Washington as Lee fortified New York some eight months later. (It was also in the *General Topography.*) The claim in the cartouche that the map was surveyed in 1775 is misleading, however: Montresor did the work in 1766, and it was simply republished with the new date in 1775.

Leery of Lee's mercurial temperament and careful not to overstep his own authority, Washington consulted with John Adams, who assured him in a letter from Watertown, Massachusetts, the following day that as commander in chief he did not need further authorization from Congress to send Lee into New York at the head of a regiment. Moreover, Adams declared, New York was the greatest strategic prize in North America. The city, the province, and the Hudson River flowing through it were of "vast importance," he wrote, forming "the nexus of the northern and southern colonies, as a kind of key to the whole continent, as it is a passage to Canada, to the Great Lakes, and to all the Indian nations. No effort to secure it ought to be omitted." (See *A Plan of the City of New-York*, page 122.)[2]

In his instructions to Lee two days later, Washington wrote that if the British captured the city and controlled the river "they will thereby command the country and the communication with Canada. It is of too much consequence . . . to hazard such a post at so alarming a crisis." (See *A Map of the Most Inhabited Part of New England,* page 83, for the Hudson from New York City to Lake Champlain, and *A General Map of the Middle British Colonies, Detail #6*, page 58, for the rest of the route to Canada.) Washington kept the pressure on the British in Boston while he dispatched Lee to fortify New York City and its environs. "Should they get that town and the command of the North River, they can stop the intercourse between the southern and northern colonies, upon which depends the safety of America," Washington told another general. "My feelings upon this subject are so strong that I would not wish to give the enemy a chance of succeeding."[3]

Lee would be Washington's eyes and ears in New York until Boston was safe and the commander in chief could bring the whole army down from Cambridge. Arriving in New York on February 4, Lee soon reported that the citizens there had cheerfully helped him remove the cannon from the batteries to the Common for safekeeping. (See *A Plan of the City of New-York*, page 122, and *Detail #1*.) "To do them justice, the whole show a wonderful alacrity, and in removing the cannon, men and boys of all ages worked with the greatest zeal and pleasure." For the most part, Lee concluded, the people of New York were as sympathetic to the patriot cause "as any on the continent."[4] Following Washington's orders to suppress the Loyalist population, Lee soon reported that the two British warships and the merchantman carrying the royal governor of New York, which had been provisioned by the city under an uneasy truce, had now retreated from the city to less threatening positions. "The *Asia* lies betwixt Nutten's and Bedloes Island" and "the *Duchess of Gordon* with his Excellency Governor Tryon is under her stern," he wrote. "The *Phoenix* is stationed a league below the Narrows." (See *A Plan of the City of New-York, Detail #2*, page 126.)

"We have taken strong hold of Hell Gate, so that the passage betwixt Long Island and the Continent is absolutely blocked up to the enemy," Lee wrote to Washington from New York on February 19.[5] Hell Gate was the rocky passage (spanned today by the Triborough Bridge) where Long Island Sound became the East River. This was the back door to New York's waters, the front gate being the channels through the network of sandbars between Sandy Hook and Coney Island. These two entrances were the only access for the British navy from the Atlantic. Rocks and whirlpools made Hell Gate hazardous for ships, as sandbars did at Sandy Hook. Since the British warships would have to enter in single file, these were the best places to begin confronting their fleet. While Lee had begun to fortify Hell Gate as a choke point to bombard enemy ships, he had neglected Sandy Hook. (See *A Map of the Province of New York, Detail #2*, page 127.)

Lee was waiting for more troops, he told Washington, before digging trenches and building fortifications "on Long Island opposite to the city . . . This I think a capital object, for should the enemy take possession of New York when Long Island is in our hands, they will find it almost impossible to subsist."[6] Control of the area opposite the city (today's Brooklyn Heights) would enable the Americans to cut off the flow of farm goods to Lower Manhattan by stopping the ferries. Not only would Howe's army be deprived of provisions, they would be forced out of the city by American cannon pointing down at them from this high ground across the East River, just as they had been

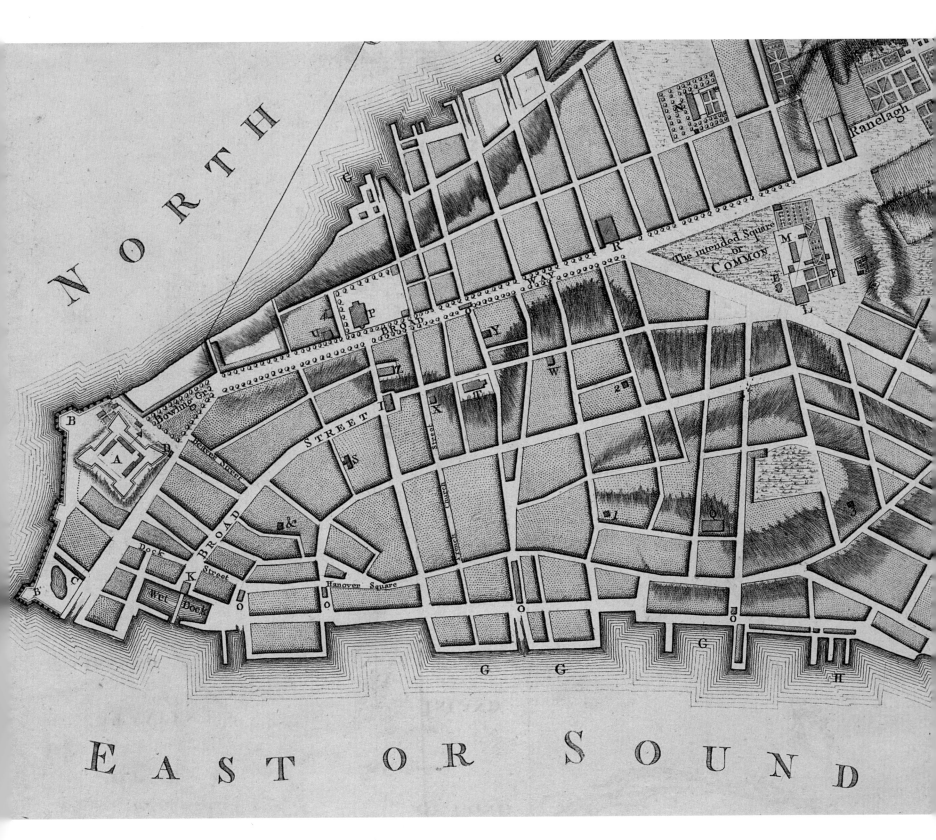

A Plan of the City of New-York, Detail #1: Lee had the cannon removed from the batteries (*B*) to the Common where the British barracks (*F*) had been vacated when the troops were shifted to Boston in 1775. The jail (*L*) would later house the ammunition laboratory, where cannon and musket cartridges were filled from the powder magazine (*E*) for distribution to the army. To prevent the British from capturing Fort George (*A*) at the foot of Broadway and using it as a battery to control the rest of the town, Lee tore down the southeastern wall, exposing the interior to American artillery.

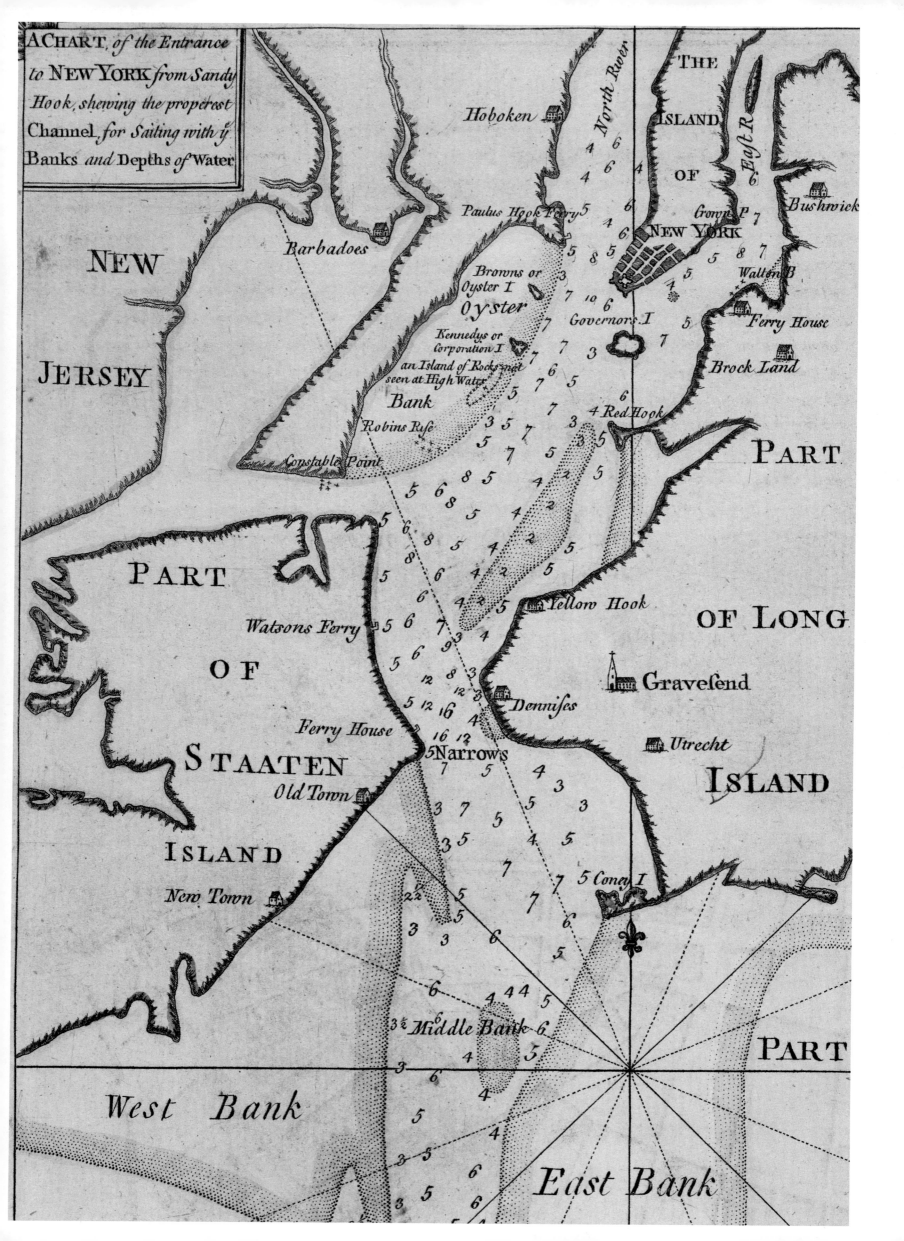

A CHART of the Entrance to NEW YORK from Sandy Hook, shewing the properest Channel for Sailing with ye Banks and Depths of Water

NEW

JERSEY

Barbadoes

Hoboken

North River

THE ISLAND OF

East R.

Bushwick

Paulus Hook Ferry

NEW YORK

Govrn P.

Walton B.

Browns or Oyster I.

Oyster

Kennedys or Corporation I.

an Island of Rocks not seen at High Water

Governors. I.

Ferry House

Brock Land

Bank

Red Hook

Robins Rise

PART

Constable Point

Yellow Hook

PART

OF

Watsons Ferry

OF LONG

Gravesend

Ferry House

Dennises

STAATEN

Utrecht

ISLAND

Narrows

Old Town

ISLAND

New Town

Coney I.

West Bank

Middle Bank

East Bank

PART

ABOVE: *A Map of the Province of New York, Detail #2:* The map shows the principal islands that define New York's waterways: Manhattan, Staten Island, and Long Island. There were only two entrances from the Atlantic for the British fleet, either from Long Island Sound through Hell Gate to the East River (top, right and center), or through the narrow channels between the sandbars next to Sandy Hook (bottom center). Hell Gate is the junction of the Sound and the East River, just east of Harlem. Both routes provided the Americans with opportunities to ambush British ships as they passed through in single file. (For the main map, see page 101.)

OPPOSITE: *A Plan of the City of New-York, Detail #2:* Lee informed Washington about the positions of British ships in the harbor in February 1776 by using small islands as reference points. "Nuttens Island" was an earlier name for Governors Island, shown directly south of Lower Manhattan. Lee refers to "Bedloes Island," labeled *Kennedys or Corporation I,* which is today's Liberty Island, directly west of Governors Island. The Narrows between Staten Island and Long Island was a ferry point, as indicated by the "Ferry House" and "Dennises" (Dennyse's Ferry).

driven from Boston by Washington's seizure of Dorchester Heights and Nook's Hill. (See ***A Plan of the City of New-York, Detail #2***, page 126. Western Long Island, today's Borough of Brooklyn, is labeled *Part of Long Island*, and Brooklyn, then a village, is marked *Brock Land*. The *Ferry House* is indicated at the East River shore, opposite New York City and Lower Manhattan.)

"What to do with the city, I own puzzles me," Lee told Washington. "It is so encircled with deep navigable water that whoever commands the sea must command the town."[7] For the British, the topography of New York and its environs presented an opportunity they had lacked in Boston: the ability to use their naval superiority to capture a water-bound city that provided access to the interior of the continent. For the same reason, New York posed a new challenge for the Americans: Unlike Boston, which they had besieged at its narrow neck, New York's waters offered the enemy multiple routes for invasion. While the British could have landed at various points around Boston Harbor, their troops would have had to proceed into the countryside without naval support, repeating the scenario of Lexington and Concord, when they retreated under fire. (The Charles and Mystic rivers were not deep enough for warships.) In New York, the waterways would allow the warships to follow the troops closely, covering their advance and retreat with massive firepower.

Would the British immediately try to capture New York City, at the southern tip of Manhattan, and if so, would they sail up the Hudson or East River—or both—to land their troops? Or would they first make an amphibious landing on western Long Island to capture the ground that commanded Lower Manhattan? Might they also put troops ashore in New Jersey after taking Staten Island? Ultimately, Washington would feel compelled to straddle two rivers, dispersing his troops along a sprawling defensive line from New Jersey to western Long Island.

During the early spring, Lee decided to prepare for urban combat. He could not hope to fend off the British navy, but he could fortify the city and try to fight for it from house to house, inflicting heavy casualties on the British once they landed their troops. "Tomorrow I shall begin to dismantle that part of the fort next to the town to prevent its being converted into a citadel," Lee told Washington. "I shall barrier the principal streets, and at least if I cannot make it a Continental garrison, it shall be a disputable field of battle."[8] Lee was assisted by an engineer, William Smith, and an artillery captain, Stephen Badlam, both sent from Cambridge. In addition to gun batteries facing the water on the southern end of Manhattan, they planned to put forts on the hills north of the city to create a line of defense against a British landing above the city.[9] (See ***A Plan of the City of New-York, Detail #1***, page 125.) Much of this work would be executed without Lee, since he soon received another assignment.

Brigadier General William Alexander, Lord Stirling.

On March 7 Congress dispatched Lee from New York to conduct the war in the South, where a British expeditionary force, led by General Henry Clinton with a sizable detachment from Boston, was bearing down on Charleston, South Carolina. In New York, William Alexander, known as Lord Stirling, took charge of fortifying the city. Washington urged him to "hinder the enemy from possessing the city or making a lodgment until the main body of this army can arrive." Washington seemed confident that if he could get there first, he could defeat the British. "New York is a post of infinite importance both to them and us," he told Governor Jonathan Trumbull of Connecticut, "and much depends on priority of possession."[10]

After the British left Boston Harbor on March 27, 1776, they retreated to Halifax, Nova Scotia, to regroup and prepare for a decisive blow against the American rebellion. While they received reinforcements in April and May, Washington completed the transfer of the Continental army from Cambridge to New York, arriving there himself on April 13. Initially his residence and headquarters were both in a town house on lower Broadway, near Bowling Green. However, when Martha Washington arrived on April 17, they settled into Abraham Mortier's mansion, about two miles north of the city near the Hudson shore, and Washington kept his headquarters in town.[11] (See ***A Plan of the City of New-York, Detail #3***.)

Montresor had made his map of New York City for General Gage in 1766, for military use, showing the "true form and course of the commanding grounds," inside and outside the city. This was exactly the kind of information Washington and Lee needed ten years later for placing fortifications around New York. On May 22, the General Orders included a list of completed forts, and they occupied some of the major hills shown on Montresor's map.[12] (See ***A Plan of the City of New-York, Detail #4***, page 130.)

"We have not been idle since I came here," Washington wrote to William Gordon on May 13. "Many capital works of defense are erected and others erecting. Ten or twelve days more will, I think, put us in a respectable posture for defending this city and the passage of the North River." Tempering his optimistic tone, Washington added that his force was "considerably reduced by the two brigades which have been sent to Canada, consisting of ten of our strongest regiments, under the command of Generals Sullivan and Thompson." (Sullivan would soon be supervising the retreat of the shattered Northern Army from St. Johns to Ticonderoga.) Washington also added that American efforts alone might not be enough to save the city: "No man has a more perfect reliance on the all-wise and powerful dispensations of the Supreme Being than I have, nor thinks his aid more necessary."[13]

If the defensive works in and around New York City failed to keep the British out of the Hudson, the Highlands forts, some forty miles upriver, would have to shut the river, while securing the roads and passes that connected New York City with Albany and points north by land. Washington had "great reason to fear that the fortifications in the Highlands are in a bad situation," and on May 21 he dispatched Lord Stirling to inspect the ongoing construction there.[14] (See *A Map of the Province of New York, Detail #3*, page 131.)

During the next few weeks Washington tried to anticipate where the British might attack—in New Jersey, in Manhattan, or on Long Island—and deployed his forces accordingly. As he had done in the waters around Boston, Lieutenant Colonel Benjamin Tupper now patrolled the New Jersey shore from Amboy to Sandy Hook with a sloop and some whaleboats.[15] If the British seized or burned the King's Bridge and the Free Bridge at the northern end of Manhattan, American forces would be completely cut off from the mainland. "I have been up to view the grounds about King's Bridge and find them to admit of several places well calculated for defense," Washington told Hancock, "and esteeming it a pass of the utmost importance have ordered works to be laid out."[16] (See *A Map of the Province of New York, Detail #2*, page 127)

A Plan of the City of New-York, Detail #3: Washington's headquarters was in William Smith's town house at the foot of Broadway near Bowling Green, just north of Fort George. After Martha joined him, their residence was at Abraham Mortier's mansion about two miles north of the city on the Hudson, just south of the village of Greenwich. Oliver DeLancey, a wealthy Loyalist, owned one of the estates north of Greenwich. The obelisk east of Greenwich honored General James Wolfe, who died capturing Quebec from the French in 1759. The estate north of Mortier's belonged to William Bayard.

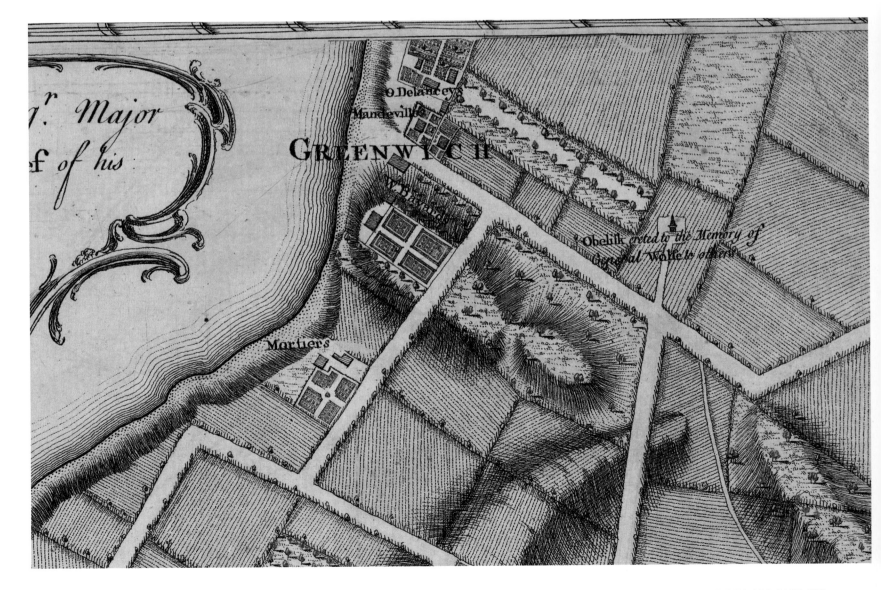

OPPOSITE: *A Plan of the City of New-York, Detail #4:* Lispenard's (top left), Bayard's (center), and Jones's (bottom right) were hills that formed a natural line of defense, and Washington enhanced them with redoubts and trenches. At Lispenard's the forts were south of the hill on the shore at Harrison's Brewery. Across the island, on the hill above Rutgers's farm, a redoubt sealed off the eastern end of the defensive line. Near the *Jews Burying Ground* (lower left), another redoubt provided a fallback position. Another battery was placed on an East River wharf directly below the Jewish cemetery.

ABOVE: *A Map of the Province of New York, Detail #3:* The river zigzags as it cuts a gorge through the Highlands, the cluster of hills north of Haverstraw Bay. The bends and promontories offered strong defensive positions that Washington used as a fortress throughout the war. Peekskill was at the mouth of Peeks Creek, which flowed into the Hudson from the east, between Anthony's Nose and Verplanck's Neck. Fort Montgomery was across the river, north of Popolopen Creek (*Coplops Kill*), with Fort Clinton south of the creek. Further north, West Point protruded into the river just below Butter Hill and across from Constitution Island.

ABOVE: General William Howe.

ABOVE, RIGHT: *A Map of the Province of New York, Detail #4:* In July Livingston reported to Washington: "Montauk Point or Neck, about eighteen miles in length and two in breadth, contains sixteen hundred head of cattle, five hundred horses, and ten thousand sheep. Should the communication be cut off between this Neck and the country, it would be a fine supply for our enemies . . . P.S. One of the companies is stationed on Montauk Point, another on Shelter Island about twenty miles from Montauk, another at Oyster Pond Point about seven miles from Shelter Island and twenty-four miles from Montauk."

Hoping to stop British ships from sailing up the Hudson, in June the Americans also began work on Fort Washington in northern Manhattan directly across the river from Fort Lee. Sunken obstructions in the Hudson (where the George Washington Bridge spans the river today) were supposed to stop or at least slow the British ships, exposing them to the cross fire from the two forts.[17]

The American defenses would soon be put to the test. General William Howe, sailing from Halifax aboard his flagship *Greyhound,* arrived at Sandy Hook on June 28. On that same day, General Clinton's mission to capture Charleston, South Carolina, for which he had departed Boston five months earlier, finally ended in failure, as the Americans, assisted by Charles Lee, repulsed the British fleet at the mouth of that harbor.

By the end of June Howe had been joined at Sandy Hook by 130 ships, the largest fleet ever seen in North America. To feed this armada, Governor Trumbull told Washington, Howe stationed several ships "between Montauk Point and Block Island to intercept the trade from the Sound," and they proceeded to capture numerous vessels laden with provisions.[18] Lieutenant Colonel Henry Beekman Livingston was on eastern Long Island, protecting the livestock from British landing parties. (See *A Map of the Province of New York, Detail #4.*)

Washington expected "that all soldiers who are entrusted with the defense of any work will behave with great coolness and bravery and will be particularly careful not to throw away their fire," his orders declared. The troops should load their muskets like shotguns, "with one musket ball and four or eight buckshot," as one such volley at close range, he predicted, would stop the British troops in their tracks. Preparing to shift troops to wherever they might be needed, Washington also gave orders to gather boats so New Jersey militiamen could be brought across the Hudson to defend Manhattan.[20] (See *A Plan of the City of New-York, Detail #2,* page 126. The ferries at Hoboken and at Paulus Hook—today's Jersey City— are at the top, center.)

On July 2, 1776, the day that Congress approved the Declaration of Independence, part of Howe's fleet moved up through the Narrows and began landing his army on Staten Island.[21] Expecting the British to attack immediately, Washington called upon his troops to stand firm. "The fate of unborn millions will now depend, under God, on the courage and conduct of this army. Our cruel and unrelenting enemy leaves us no choice but a brave resistance, or the most abject submission. This is all we can expect. We have therefore to resolve to conquer or die."[22] A week later, the British had not attacked, and Washington had the Declaration of Independence read on the Common. The cheering crowd mingled with some of the soldiers and marched down Broadway to Bowling Green, where they toppled the gilded equestrian statue of King George III, sending off the two tons of lead to be melted down for musket balls. (See *A Plan of the City of New-York, Detail #1,* page 125.)

Tearing down the statue of George III in New York City during the Revolutionary War.

Washington told John Hancock that he would ask Congress to send the Continental regiments in Massachusetts down to New York since "it now seems beyond question and clear to demonstration that the enemy mean to direct their operations and bend their most vigorous efforts against this colony, and will attempt to unite their two armies, that under General Burgoyne" coming down from Canada "and the one arrived here."[23]

From Connecticut, Governor Trumbull wrote that he was mustering several militia units to reinforce Washington, and in the meantime was sending ahead three cavalry regiments.[24] However, Washington would end up dismissing these horsemen a few days after they arrived because they refused to serve dismounted and he had barely enough forage to feed the army's draft and artillery horses. Moreover, Washington did not envision any role for cavalry in the coming battle.[25]

News that General Howe's brother, Admiral Richard Howe, was on his way from England with reinforcements prompted Washington to consider striking a blow before the British force reached full strength. "At a Council of War held at Head Quarters July 12, 1776 . . . The General proposed to the consideration of the board a plan of descent upon Staten Island in different places so as to form a general attack upon the enemy's quarters." The plan was apparently presented in writing with an accompanying map showing the routes and points of attack marked with an *X*, a pricked line, and the letters *A* through *G*. The map has been lost but is described in an undated document, in Lord Stirling's handwriting, which was probably the plan presented at the meeting.

The raid was to employ six detachments totaling some 3,500 men. (See *A Map of the Province of New York, Detail #2*, page 127.) One unit was to come from Long Island and strike below the Narrows; a second to attack the British camp opposite Amboy, New Jersey; a third to gather near Woodbridge and cross over to Richmond Town at the center of Staten Island; a fourth to attack from below Elizabethtown Point crossing to the northwest corner of the island; a fifth from Newark Bay to land on the north shore of Staten Island near Shooter's Island (shown but not labeled); and a sixth to attack the British guards at Constable Hook, the southeast corner of Bergen Point, north of Staten Island, opposite the Dutch Church. The attack was to include bombardments of the Staten Island shore to protect the boats collected to evacuate the troops after the raid. At the same time, fire rafts and fire ships were to be "towed down so as to fall in with the head of the fleet."[26]

The generals present unanimously voted down the risky idea. Attacking the enemy instead of waiting to be attacked was characteristic of Washington's thinking: He had urged it at Boston and was voted down in similar fashion. In New York the consequences of inaction would be less favorable: A raid against Howe's ten thousand troops—while they were scattered in camps across Staten Island and could be defeated piecemeal—was the Americans' only hope for disrupting the British offensive at New York. But the success of such a raid was hardly guaranteed. And Lord Howe's arrival with more troops on that same day, July 12, made the success of a raid more unlikely.

Moreover, the British were beginning to go on the offensive, probing the American defenses. That same day, two British warships, the *Phoenix* and the *Rose*, sailed up the Hudson, sustaining only minor damage from American gun batteries at Red Hook, Lower Manhattan, and Mount Washington. The ships anchored in the Tappan Sea, a wide stretch of the river that enabled them to elude American fire from both shores. (See ***A Map of the Province of New York, Detail #3***, page 131.) It was narrow enough, however, that any American vessel attempting to sail northward to resupply the army in Canada

The British warships *Phoenix* and *Rose* sail up the Hudson River, July 12, 1776.

would fall prey to these two powerful warships. Any supplies or troops would now have to be sent slowly and laboriously to Albany or Lake George by land. "I was of the opinion it would be much easier for the troops bound from Boston to the Northward to proceed this way for the benefit of water carriage," Washington wrote to General Ward. "This being entirely cut off by the ships up Hudson's River, you will speed their march by the nearest and most convenient route."[27]

Washington told Hancock that the British, having cut off the water route, might also have troops on board "to seize on the narrow passes on both sides of the river, giving almost the only land communication with Albany and of consequence with our northern army." Washington called for the militia from Albany County and from western Connecticut to converge immediately on these passes and secure them, "particularly the post where the road runs over Anthony's Nose."[28] (See *A Map of the Province of New York, Detail #3*, page 131.)

Relaying the news to Colonel Adam Stephen that British ships in the Tappan Sea had "cut off the water communication with Albany and our army on the lakes entirely," Washington assured him that he "did not let the anniversary of the 3rd and 9th [of July] pass off without a grateful remembrance of the escape we had at the Meadows and on the banks of Monongahela." In recalling the surrender at Fort Necessity in 1754 and Braddock's defeat a year later, Washington hoped "the same providence that protected us upon those occasions" would "continue his mercies, and make us happy instruments in restoring peace and liberty to this once favored and now distressed country."[29]

If these early defeats were any indication, Washington was fortunate already: His war council had vetoed his plans to attack the British in Boston and then on Staten Island—plans that might easily have gone awry. His attack on Jumonville's party in 1754 had led to reprisal by a vastly superior French force; and his advice to Braddock that the forward division race ahead contributed to its weakness when it collided with the French and Indian column. His inclination to strike the first blow promised great victories, but the potential for disaster was equally great.

And Washington was fully aware that timing was everything. He had continued to plot a raid on Staten Island after being voted down on the 12th, but by late July the opportunity to go on the offensive had clearly been lost. "Our situation at present," he told his brother John Augustine, "both with respect to men and other matters, is such as not to make it advisable to attempt anything against them, surrounded as they are by water and covered with ships, lest a miscarriage should be productive of unhappy and fatal consequences." Washington found it "provoking nevertheless to have them so near" without being able to attack.[30]

Nonetheless, Washington did plan to trap and attack the ships that had sailed up to the Tappan Sea. "I am preparing some obstructions to the channel nearly opposite the works at the upper end of [Manhattan]," he told Hancock on July 27. "When all things are ready, I intend to try, if it shall seem practicable, to destroy the ships and tenders above." On August 2, Washington received a report that the British ships had dropped down from Haverstraw Bay to a position between Teller's Point and Verdritige Hook, in the Tappan Sea. (See *A Map of the Province of New York, Detail #3*, page 131. The words *Verdritige Hook* follow the curve of the west bank of the Hudson, and *Tellers or Sarak Point* is indicated on the opposite shore.) The following day, the Americans attacked the *Phoenix* and *Rose* with three schooners and four row galleys.[31]

Lieutenant Colonel Benjamin Tupper reported to Washington about the two-hour engagement, in which both sides suffered casualties and damage to their vessels from the constant firing of cannon. The Americans retreated to Dobbs Ferry and were debating whether or not to drop down to Spuyten Duyvil Creek.* "We wish to give them another drubbing," Tupper wrote. "We saw many splinters drifting down." On August 4, the obstructions Washington had mentioned—"hulks and chevaux de frise"—were towed from the East River up the Hudson to the shore below Fort Washington "and will be sunk as soon as possible," he told Hancock. A second American attack, on August 16, using fire vessels, failed to ignite and destroy the *Phoenix* and *Rose*, but prompted them to sail back down the river and return to the safety of the fleet two days later, unhampered by the sunken obstructions between Fort Washington and Fort Lee.[32]

By the middle of August the Howes commanded the largest expeditionary force the British had ever deployed—427 vessels carrying twenty-four thousand ground troops and ten thousand sailors—which rivaled the population of Philadelphia, the largest city in America. Washington made a list of all his troops and their locations in addition to Lower Manhattan—Long Island, Governors Island, Paulus Hook, Red Hook, Horn's Hook, Fort Washington, and Kingsbridge—and came to a total of some seventeen thousand troops but only ten thousand fit for duty.[33] Outnumbered more than three to one, he speculated in a letter to Charles Lee about the various possible places "where the point of attack will be." Most of the intelligence suggested that "part of the enemy's fleet and army will go into the [East River and Long Island Sound], whilst another part of it runs up the [Hudson] River, thereby cutting off all communication by water with this place, whilst their troops form a chain across the Neck, and stop all intercourse with Connecticut by land. Others think they will not leave an army in their rear, whilst they have the country in their front, getting by that means between two fires."[34]

* Spuyten Duyvil Creek connects the Harlem River to the Hudson at the northern end of Manhattan.

ABOVE: British landing craft approaching Gravesend
Bay in Brooklyn, August 22, 1776.

RIGHT: Americans retreating across the Gowanus
Canal, August 27, 1776.

In an echo of his tactics at Bunker Hill, Howe decided to strike the rebels head-on and with a flanking maneuver, instead of trapping them on Manhattan by an extended encirclement: He would take Brooklyn Heights first, without sending a separate force up the Hudson to Kingsbridge. The British completed their troop buildup and on August 22 landed fifteen thousand troops on western Long Island at Gravesend Bay, just below the Narrows. By the 26th they had brought over five thousand more troops and were ready to strike.

To take Brooklyn Heights, however, Howe's force would first have to cross Gowanus Heights, a wooded ridge running east-west across Long Island, where Washington had stationed a total of 3,300 men (facing southward) to ambush the British at four passes. (See *A Map of the Province of New York, Detail #2*, page 127. The ridge is not shown; its western end was in the area filled by the word *KINGS*. The locations of the passes can be identified by the roads that went through them. From west to east: The shore road led to the Martense Lane Pass; the road from the village of Flatbush went through the Flatbush Pass; on the road south of the village of Bedford was the Bedford Pass; and four miles to the east, near the village of Jamaica, stood the Jamaica Pass.) That night the British engaged the Americans' attention at the two westernmost passes through the ridge while a third column marched quietly through the Jamaica Pass to the east, before taking the road westward to Bedford.

At 9:00 A.M. on August 27, the Battle of Brooklyn—the largest battle of the American Revolution and the first battle fought by the newly independent United States—began when the British fired two signal guns at Bedford, behind the ridge, and closed in on the Americans from all sides. The British killed or wounded some two hundred Americans and took eight hundred prisoners as they drove the defenders from the ridge. The defeat was relieved only by the heroic action of the Americans on the right wing, including Lord Stirling and the Marylanders, who held off the British at the Vechte House, enabling hundreds of Americans to escape across Gowanus Creek to the relative safety of Brooklyn Heights.

There is no mention of the Jamaica Pass in Washington's papers and no indication that he had a detailed map of western Long Island at the time of the battle. He did give an order that the British should be prevented, at all costs, from crossing the ridge. He also talked about the woods on the American right wing as a potential gap in the line and ordered that riflemen be posted there. Having left the details of the terrain largely to General Nathanael Greene, however, Washington was at a disadvantage when Greene fell ill on August 15. General Israel Putnam became overall commander on Long Island, with General John Sullivan in charge of the troops on Gowanus Heights. Cavalrymen from Connecticut, who might have provided reconnaissance on the left wing, at Jamaica, had been sent home by Washington because he did not see a role for them in the upcoming battle, and the army lacked the forage to feed their horses. Washington conceded, even before the battle, that he and his generals all lacked the "experience to move upon a large scale."[35]

However, Washington proved to be a master of the strategic retreat. Howe decided not to storm the American

General Washington guiding the retreat, August 29–30, 1776.

lines on Brooklyn Heights, and two days after the battle, on August 29–30, Washington evacuated all of his troops across the East River to Manhattan under the cover of night and early morning fog. The pattern was set for the campaign in and around New York City: The British lunged at the Americans with a series of amphibious landings, belatedly tried to encircle them, and ultimately saw them slip from their grasp.

Two weeks after the battle on Long Island, at the request of Lord Howe, three Americans—John Adams, Benjamin Franklin, and Edward Rutledge—sat down with him for a peace conference on Staten Island. Howe spoke of his slain brother's memory and the Howes' feelings of friendship for the Americans. The Americans were unwilling to

The peace conference on Staten Island, September 11, 1776.

give up their independence and return to the royal fold, so the negotiations quickly came to an end. The combination of overwhelming military force and diplomacy suggested that the Howes hoped to cow the Americans into submission instead of crushing them completely on the battlefield. Indeed, the Howes' failure to follow up each offensive with a decisive blow fueled speculation on both sides about their motives and competence. As General Israel Putnam remarked of General Howe, "He's either our friend or he's no general."[36]

On September 15, the British moved their landing craft into Newtown Creek (today the border between Brooklyn and Queens) while they pounded the Manhattan shore directly across from it at Kips Bay with broadsides from four battleships. (See *A Plan of the City of New-York, Detail #2*, page 126. Newtown Creek is the indentation in the Brooklyn-Queens shoreline just north of Bushwick. Opposite the mouth of the creek, the two indentations in

the Manhattan shore indicate Turtle Bay, now the United Nations complex, and Kips Bay, at today's East 34th Street.) After an hour-long bombardment from the battleships, British and Hessian troops came ashore at Kips Bay.

The British once again put the Americans to flight and captured a key piece of terrain, but failed to surround the American army. Instead of pressing westward to the Hudson shore, to cut off New York City to the south, the British generals took tea with Mary Murray at her nearby mansion (Inclenberg) and waited for the last troops to arrive at Kips Bay. Meanwhile, some 3,500 American soldiers escaped from the city up the west side of the island, completing the American retreat to the rocky plateau of Harlem Heights (See *Manhattan, September 1776*.)

By the following day the British were in possession of New York and much of Manhattan, but had lost the Battle of Harlem Heights—more symbolic than strategic—in which the Americans drove them from a buckwheat field (today's Barnard College campus). A week later, a quarter of the city mysteriously burned down, depriving the British of much needed housing stock as the fall and winter approached.

In a third attempt to cut off Washington's forces, the British skillfully navigated Hell Gate on October 12 to land four thousand troops at Throg's Neck. The peninsula was an island at high tide and twenty-five American riflemen kept the British from crossing the plank bridges across the flooded creek. A week later the British made a successful landing further north in Westchester County, at Pelham Bay. (See *A Map of the Province of New York, Detail #2*, page 127. In the upper right, Throg's Neck is labeled *Frogs Point*. Pelham Bay, not labeled, is directly to the north, just east of the town of Eastchester.) However, as their column marched inland, it was ambushed by an American detachment, which delayed its progress long enough for Washington to retreat from northern Manhattan to White Plains. Washington's column moved north with the Bronx River on the right as protection against a British attack from the east. (See *A Map of the Province of New York, Detail #5*.)

After defeating the Americans at White Plains on October 28, but again failing to cut them off, Howe finally gave up the chase and moved west to Dobbs Ferry on the Hudson, before heading back toward Manhattan. Despite the looming danger of Howe's movement southward, Washington agreed on November 8 to follow Greene's suggestion of leaving the 2,800 men at Fort Washington. Greene argued that the fort would help keep British ships out of the Hudson and that the garrison could be evacuated across the river if the British attacked. Washington countered that the post was now in enemy territory and had not served its purpose, but he gave in against his better judgment.

At the same time, Washington ordered Greene to evacuate any surplus provisions and supplies from Fort

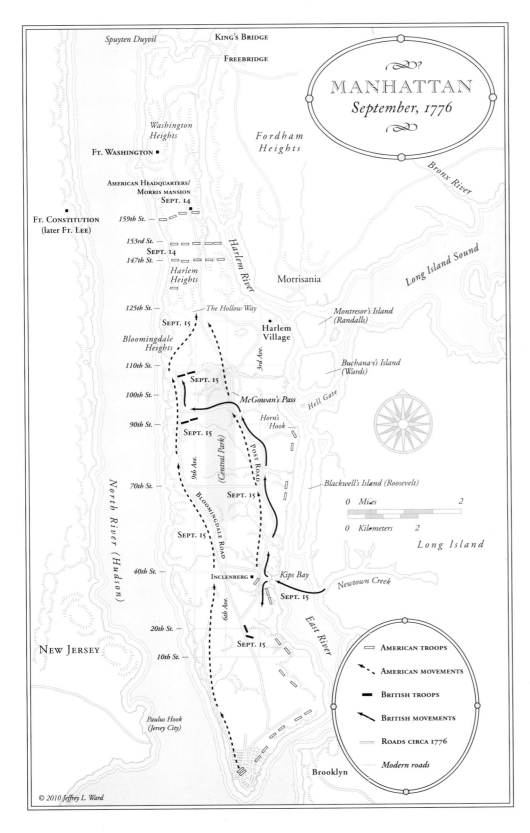

ABOVE: *A Map of the Province of New York, Detail #5:* As the British landed in Westchester County in October, Washington retreated from northern Manhattan to White Plains, keeping his column west of the Bronx River (*Brunx's River or Kill*) in order to fend off an attack. White Plains, not indicated, would be northeast of Philipsburg and southwest of Byram Pond.

Lee and prepare for a British attack. Expecting Howe to send part of his army into New Jersey and across to Pennsylvania, Washington also started sending reinforcements to block his advance. The Americans had been beaten in New York, but they had also humiliated Howe by their many escapes; Washington believed Howe needed to capture Philadelphia before year's end in order to salvage his reputation.[37]

Washington had pulled his forces back into the steep hills of North White Plains during and after the battle, and he sent Putnam's division up to Peekskill, where the troops crossed the Hudson at King's Ferry over the course of three days. (See *A Map of the Province of New York, Detail #3*, page 131. King's Ferry, center, ran between Verplanck's Neck and Stony Point, labeled *Stone Point*, slightly to the south.)

While the troops were crossing, Washington arrived at Peekskill on November 10, his first visit to the Hudson Highlands. The following day he toured Fort Montgomery and the other American works, which were in varying states of development. With several generals he went as far north as Constitution Island opposite West Point. The Americans had not planned a fort at West Point, but Washington could see that it was the most commanding post in the area and should be fortified. (See *A Map of the Province of New York, Detail #3*, page 131.)

Uncertain about Howe's plans, Washington left one division, under General William Heath, to continue work on the forts and defend the passes in the Highlands. Heath recalled riding on horseback with Washington early in the morning on November 12 to reconnoiter "the gorge of the Highlands, on both sides of the river." Washington ordered Heath to hurry on with the fortifications since the British were likely to attack and since it would be impossible to do "any spade work after the frost sets in." Washington then crossed the river and headed south to New Jersey.[38]

Washington arrived at Fort Lee the following day, and on November 16 he crossed the Hudson with several generals to inspect the disposition of troops around Fort Washington. They returned to Fort Lee apprehensive but satisfied, not knowing they had barely escaped the British onslaught that would capture the fort later that day. The 2,800 American prisoners from the fort were packed off to jails in the city and prison ships floating in Wallabout Bay, where as many as 11,000 inmates perished during the war. (See *A Plan of the City of New-York, Detail #2*, page 126. Wallabout Bay is indicated on the Brooklyn shore northeast of the ferry house.)

With a rare show of follow-through, Howe dispatched six thousand troops under General Charles Cornwallis across the Hudson on November 20. Hastily abandoning Fort Lee, the Americans headed west across the Hackensack River and regrouped at the town of Hackensack. Keenly aware of the landscape, Washington wanted to avoid being trapped between two rivers. The British apparently wanted "to enclose the whole of our troops and stores that lay between the [Hudson] and Hackensack Rivers, which form a very narrow neck of land," Washington told Hancock. "Our present situation between the Hackensack and Passaic Rivers being exactly similar to our late one . . . we are taking measures to retire over the waters of the latter."

With only 3,500 troops on this side of the Hudson, Washington again went west, across the Passaic River to Acquackanonk (today's Passaic), before turning south and arriving at Newark on the 22nd, his troops "much broken and dispirited."[39] (See *A Map of the Province of New York, Detail #2*, page 127. At the top left, the Hackensack and Passaic rivers flow into Newark Bay. The town of "Agquakenich or Acquakeneunk," today's Passaic, is shown eight miles west of Hackensack.)

Less than a week later, Washington was on the move again, barely escaping Cornwallis, "whose advanced guards were entering the town by the time our rear got out."[40] Leading his troops southward through Elizabethtown and Amboy to Brunswick on the far side of the Raritan River, he arrived there on November 30. (See *A Map of the Province of New York, Detail #2*, page 127. The *Rareton River* is on the lower left.)

The following day, Washington's force shrank by half when the enlistments of nearly two thousand New Jersey militiamen expired and they left for home. Even worse, Washington lamented, "Although most of the Pennsylvanians are enlisted till the first of January, I am informed that they are deserting in great numbers."[41] As the situation grew grim, Washington calculated that

Lieutenant General Charles Cornwallis's troops scaling the New Jersey Palisades, November 20, 1776.

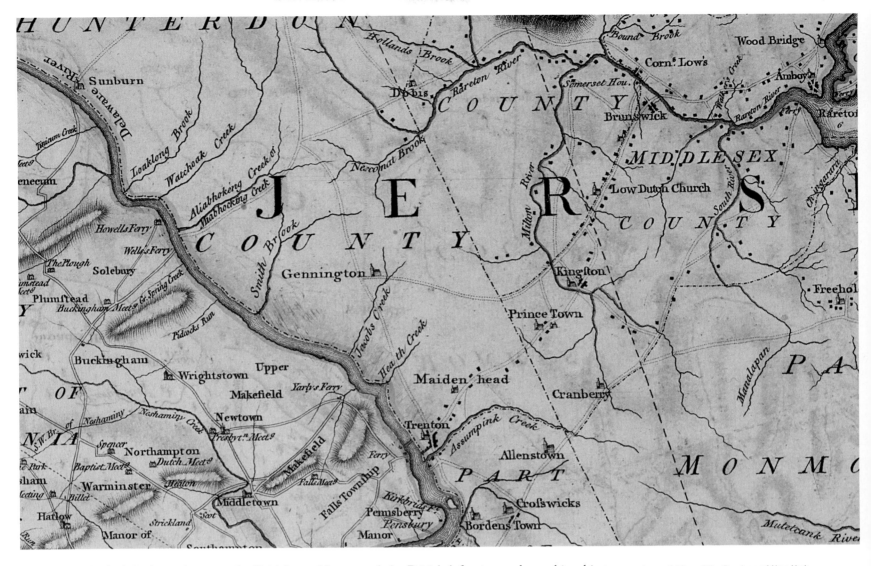

the worse it looked for him, the more the British would become overconfident. If they attempted to capture Philadelphia by the end of the year, he wrote presciently to Charles Lee, "there is a great probability that they will pay dearly for it and I shall continue to retreat before them so as to lull them into security."[42]

Washington continued southward through Princeton and Trenton—just hours ahead of Cornwallis's column—and crossed the Delaware River into Pennsylvania on December 8. (See *A Map of the Province of New York, Detail #6*.) Howe decided not to press on to Philadelphia that winter and instead set up a series of outposts, garrisoned by Hessian soldiers, stretching from Hackensack to Trenton. Before dawn on December 26, while the Hessians at Trenton were sleeping off their Christmas reveling, Washington brought his troops back across the Delaware and attacked during a snowstorm. Within forty-five minutes, the Americans had captured almost a thousand Hessians and suffered only a handful of casualties. Washington had struck a crucial blow that revived the American cause, just when the army seemed on the verge of collapse.

After taking the prisoners back across the Delaware, Washington embarked his forces for New Jersey again on December 30, and this time dug in on the south side of Assunpink Creek, below Trenton. Cornwallis arrived in Trenton, leading eight thousand troops, to finish off the Americans on the evening of January 2, 1777. When he postponed his attack until the following morning, Washington kept his campfires burning while slipping around the British left wing and marching his troops to Princeton. There the Americans defeated Cornwallis's rear guard and took some 350 prisoners. Washington had hoped to attack the British at Brunswick as well, but his men were in no shape to continue fighting: Many were shoeless and were leaving bloody tracks in the snow. Having ended the campaign of 1776 on a triumphant note, Washington took his army north to the hills around Morristown to settle in for the winter. (See *A Map of the Province of New York, Detail #7*, page 142.)

The Continental army suffered terribly from hunger and cold that winter, but Washington kept their condition and small numbers—fewer than five thousand men—a secret from the British and sent out disinformation exaggerating his strength. He also sent out detachments to ambush British foraging parties, thus supplying his own troops and keeping the British on edge. Only a day's march away, Cornwallis might have finished off the Americans, but instead stayed close to New York with his ten thousand well-furnished troops. The city provided comfortable quarters for the British commanders and a full calendar of lavish parties.

With the arrival of spring, the British resumed the military campaign, driving the Americans from their outpost at Bound Brook on April 13, 1777. The British let the Americans reoccupy the position the same evening, but Washington decided it was too vulnerable. Six weeks later, he evacuated the post and moved it to Middle Brook, well protected on a southern ridge of the Watchung

A Map of the Province of New York, Detail #6: South of Brunswick (upper right), the road forked to the left toward *Prince Town* and Trenton (bottom center).

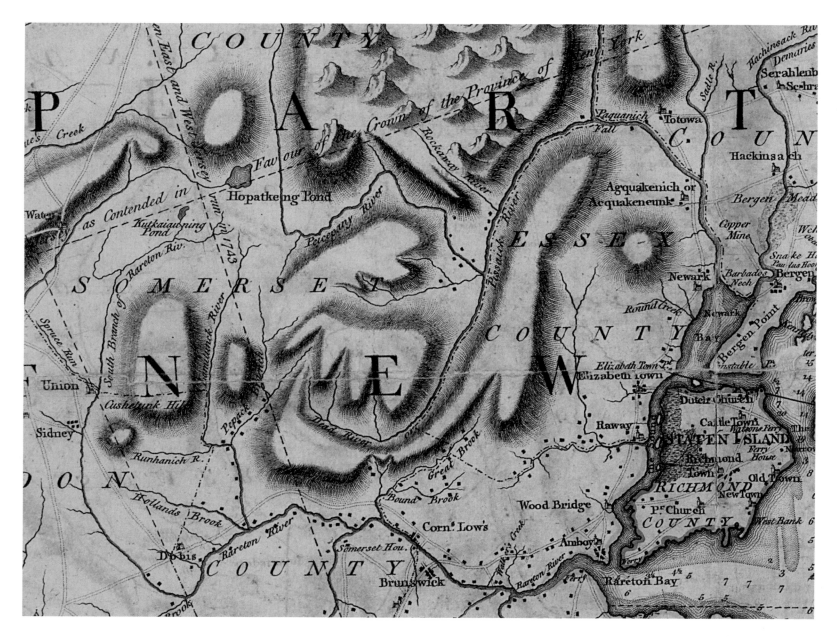

Mountains, directly north of Bound Brook. He also moved his main encampment there from Morristown so he could have a better view of British movements from the top of the mountains across the plain between Amboy and Brunswick. (See *A Map of the Province of New York, Detail #7*. Middle Brook, not named on the map, is near today's Martinsville.)

Washington's vigilance deterred Howe from crossing New Jersey in June, when he finally decided to capture Philadelphia. Instead, Howe went by water, which took longer and ensured that he would not return quickly enough to rendezvous at Albany with General John Burgoyne, who was descending from Canada to capture the Hudson River corridor. Howe's failure to meet Burgoyne would unravel the British grand strategy of dividing the colonies along the Hudson. Nor did Burgoyne get the help he expected from General Barry St. Leger, who was supposed to accomplish a third thrust of the plan. In addition to the armies going down and up the Hudson, St. Leger's army was to press from the west, through the Mohawk River Valley, and meet the others at Albany, rousing Loyalists and Indian allies along the way.

Burgoyne's expedition set off from St. Johns on June 13, 1777, a flotilla sailing south on Lake Champlain carrying some eight thousand troops and accompanied by roughly five hundred Indians in canoes. Burgoyne's target, at the southern end of the lake, was Fort Ticonderoga, defended by twenty-five hundred Americans under Major General Arthur St. Clair.

General Howe, meanwhile, had gathered flatboats and troops at Amboy and Brunswick, convincing Washington that he had "dropped all thoughts of an expedition up the North River" and was preparing to head west and cross the Delaware River. Washington left some troops to defend the Hudson Highlands but started sending most of the army toward the Delaware, to defend Philadelphia. However, by July 1, Howe had evacuated New Jersey and put his force onto ships, leading Washington to warn General George Clinton in the Highlands that "there can be little room to doubt that General Howe will cooperate with the Northern Army and make a sudden descent on Peekskill." From St. Clair's reports, Washington knew Burgoyne was approaching Ticonderoga and would soon attack.[43]

Proceeding slowly but skillfully, Burgoyne's forces landed a few miles north of the fort on July 1. Four days later Burgoyne sent his engineers and artillerists to Mount Defiance, the densely wooded elevation south and west of the fort, where they hacked a road to the summit. Shocked that the British had been able to drag cannon to that forbidding height and now commanded all the terrain below, St. Clair and his officers voted to evacuate the fort. That night, four hundred Americans escaped in boats up the extension of Lake Champlain, and the rest fled on foot along the road to Hubbardton and Castleton. (See *A Map of the Province of New York, Detail #1*, page 102, and *Detail #8*.) Attacked by the pursuing British at Hubbardton, the Americans dispersed and regrouped at Manchester. Writing to Schuyler on July 15, Washington expressed his "chagrin and surprise" that the fort had been abandoned to the enemy. He was relieved that St. Clair's force had not been captured, but utterly baffled that it had disappeared and had not been heard from since the evacuation.[44]

Equally baffling was Howe's behavior. His conduct, Washington told Schuyler a week later, was "puzzling and embarrassing beyond measure. So are the informations which I get. At one time the ships are standing off towards the North River. In a little while they are going up the [East River], and in an hour after they are going out of the Hook." Washington was at Ramapo on July 24, when he finally received word that the fleet carrying Howe's army had sailed from Sandy Hook. Guarding against a possible feint toward Philadelphia and a sudden return to New York, Washington ordered Stirling's unit, Morgan's, and the others with them to stop at Trenton if they had not yet crossed the Delaware or at Bristol if they had and to be ready to go forward to Philadelphia or come back to the Hudson.[45]

Burgoyne's offensive appeared to be making progress, but he had blundered in pursuing the Americans along Lake Champlain's southern extension instead of embarking his entire force at Ticonderoga and floating it to the southern end of Lake George, connected to the Hudson by a wagon road leading southeast to Fort Edward. (See *A Map of the Province of New York, Detail #8*, bottom center.) He went from Lake Champlain to Wood Creek to Fort Ann, and had to spend almost a month clearing a road to Fort Edward. Washington sized up the situation accurately when he told Schuyler that in addition to cutting a road, "the encumbrance they must feel in their baggage, stores, etc. will inevitably retard their march a considerable time."[46]

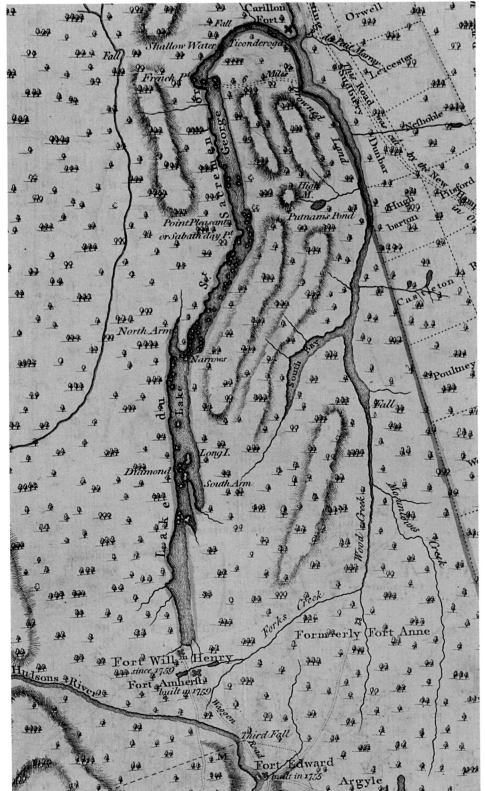

ABOVE: *A Map of the Province of New York, Detail #8:* Fort Ticonderoga (top center) is marked with a red *X* and labeled *Carillon Fort.* South of the fort, *Ticonderoga* is written on the site of Mount Defiance. Most of the Americans fled across a floating bridge to the point south and east of the fort and continued on foot toward Hubbardton (*Hugh barton*) and Castleton (just east of Lake Champlain's southern extension). The lake's extension, by the left fork, became Wood Creek, which led, by another left fork, to Fort Ann.

OPPOSITE, TOP: *A Map of the Province of New York, Detail #7:* In the winter of 1776–77, Washington encamped at Morristown (not labeled), nestled in the mountains, about fifteen miles southeast of *Hopatkeng Pond* (today's Lake Hopatcong) and just west of the Passaic River. The fishhook-shaped ridge on the eastern edge of the mountainous area—along the Passaic and Ramapo rivers—is part of the Watchung Mountains. Washington kept an outpost at Bound Brook, just south of the mountains and north of Brunswick, from which he could monitor the movements of the British, in case they marched toward Philadelphia.

OPPOSITE, BOTTOM: General John Burgoyne.

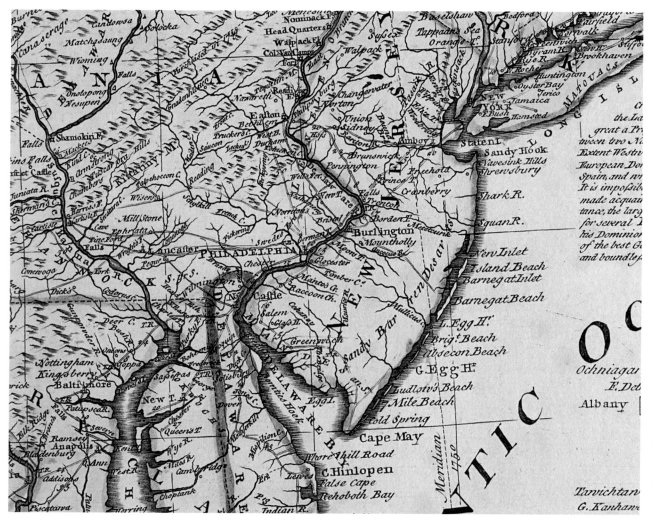

LEFT: *A General Map of the Middle British Colonies, Detail #9:* When the British fleet arrived at Delaware Bay (bottom center), Washington assumed Howe would sail up the Delaware River to capture Philadelphia (center).

OPPOSITE, TOP: *A General Map of the Middle British Colonies, Detail #10:* St. Leger's invasion route from Lake Ontario (upper left) to the Mohawk River (center) was supposed to bring him to the Hudson at Albany (lower right) to join forces with Burgoyne.

OPPOSITE, BOTTOM: *A Map of the Province of New York, Detail #9:* Washington urged Schuyler to establish a post near the falls east of *German Flatts* (left center) to maintain contact between Fort Stanwix (today's Rome, New York, off the map to the west) and his headquarters at *Still Water* on the west bank of the Hudson about twenty miles north of the Mohawk River (right center).

As Schuyler grew more alarmed by Burgoyne's approach, Washington reassured him, predicting that the expedition "will meet sooner or later an effectual check" and that "the success he has had will precipitate his ruin." Burgoyne would have to leave detachments in forts to protect his rear and his line of supply and communication to Canada, Washington wrote. His main force would grow smaller as he went, and the Americans could attack the detachments. Washington agreed with Schuyler about the "propriety of having a body of men stationed somewhere about the [New Hampshire] Grants," since this "would keep him in continual anxiety for his rear and oblige him to leave the posts behind him much stronger than he would otherwise do." (See *A Map of the Province of New York, Detail #8*, page 143, upper right. The New Hampshire Grants were parcels of land granted to individuals by that state that were also claimed by New York. The disputed area ultimately became the state of Vermont.)[47]

By July 30, Washington had arrived at Howell's Ferry on the Delaware, but had left Sullivan at Morristown, in case Howe came back to New York. (See *A Map of the Province of New York, Detail #6*, page 141, left, center, for Howell's Ferry.) He told Gates that "General Howe's, in a manner, abandoning General Burgoyne is so unaccountable a matter, that till I am fully assured it is so, I cannot help casting my eyes continually behind me." The following day Washington learned definitively that "the enemy's fleet, consisting of 228 sail," had arrived at Delaware Bay. Howe would now "make a vigorous push to

possess Philadelphia," Washington told Trumbull, "and we should collect all the force we can to oppose him."[48] (See *A General Map of the Middle British Colonies, Detail #9*.)

Some two hundred miles to the west of Burgoyne's army, St. Leger had landed sixteen hundred men, half of them Indians, at Oswego on Lake Ontario on July 25 and started marching toward the Mohawk River by way of the Oswego River, Oneida Lake, and Wood Creek. Fort Stanwix stood at the portage between Wood Creek and the Mohawk River and was garrisoned by 750 Continental troops. Warned of St. Leger's expedition two weeks earlier, Schuyler had dispatched troops to rebuild and resupply the fort (which dated from the French and Indian War). Washington had urged him to first establish a post downstream (further east) near "the Falls below the German Flatts, to secure our communication with that garrison" lest the "savages . . . intercept all supplies of men and provisions going thither."[49] With his usual courtesy, Washington offered this as merely a suggestion, saying Schuyler was "much better acquainted with that country than I." Nonetheless, the commander in chief had clearly been studying his maps. (See *A General Map of the Middle British Colonies, Detail #10*, and *A Map of the Province of New York, Detail #9*.)

St. Leger's force laid siege to Fort Stanwix on August 3, and the following day, Colonel Nicholas Herkimer mustered eight hundred militiamen at Fort Dayton, near German Flats, to expel the British. On the morning of

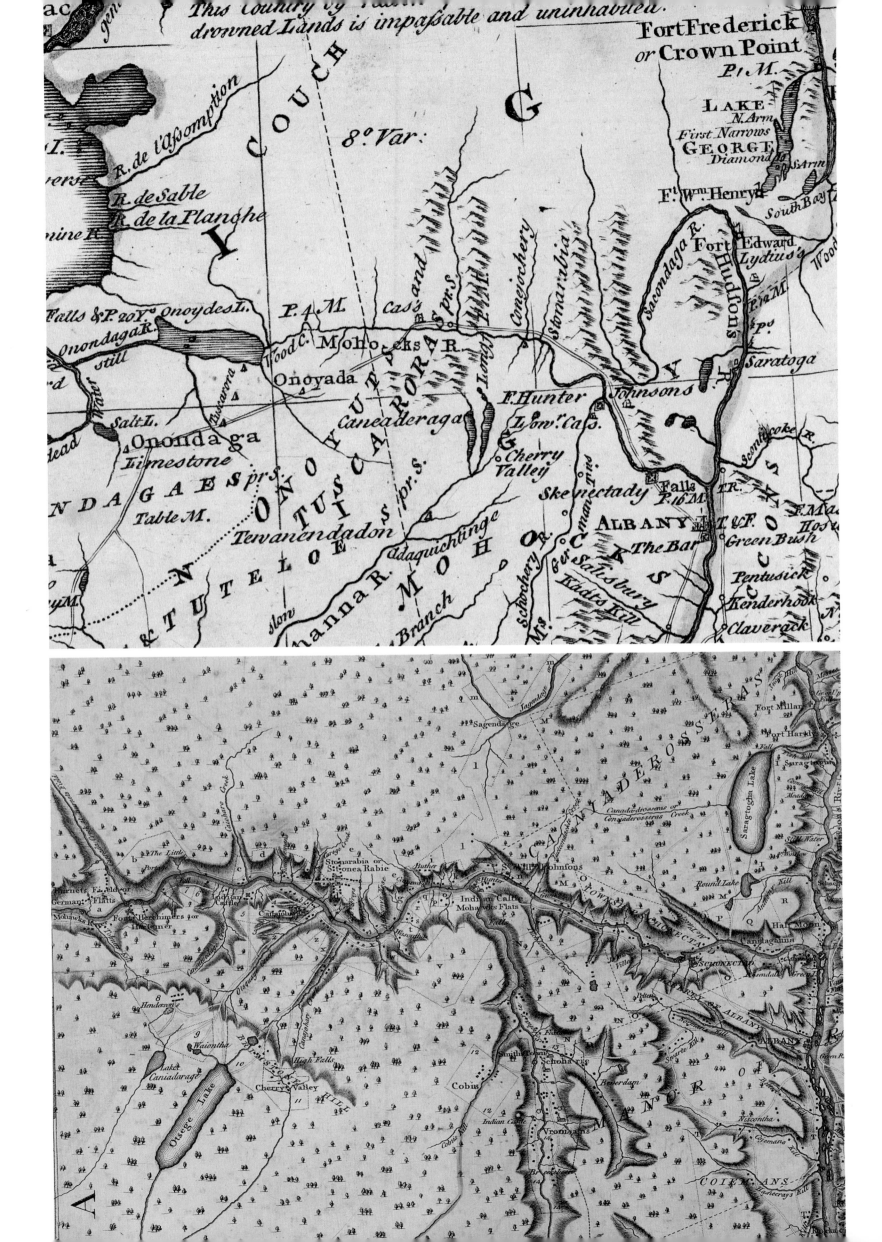

August 6, Herkimer's column was six miles from the fort, at Oriskany, when it was ambushed by four hundred Indians and Loyalists sent by St. Leger. In fierce fighting, the militiamen suffered heavy losses, and ultimately turned back without reaching the fort. However, Schuyler sent a relief column of nine hundred Continentals under Benedict Arnold.

Washington was "pleased" with "matters upon the Mohawk River," he wrote to Schuyler from Pennsylvania. "If the militia keep up their spirits after their late severe skirmish, I am confident they will, with the assistance of the reinforcement under General Arnold, be enabled to raise the siege." In the end, rumors of Arnold's column, exaggerating the number of troops, were enough to prompt the departure of St. Leger's Indian allies and force the British to retreat from the Mohawk Valley. Washington was no longer concerned about an invasion from "that quarter in this campaign."[50]

The departure of Arnold's column from the Hudson to the Mohawk left Schuyler with only 3,600 troops at Stillwater to face Burgoyne, who had arrived at Fort Edward, twenty-five miles to the north, with more than twice that number on July 29. However, General John Stark, a former Continental army officer from New Hampshire, had assembled a force of 1,500 men to defend the Connecticut River Valley and had just joined General Benjamin Lincoln at Bennington; militia units from Massachusetts were also arriving there. Writing to

Governor George Clinton of New York, Washington urged that they attack Burgoyne's flanks and rear, keeping him anxious and making him dilute his force with detachments.[51]

Burgoyne played into the Americans' hands when he allowed Lieutenant Colonel Friedrich Baum to go on a foraging expedition eastward into the New Hampshire Grants in search of horses for his three hundred Brunswick dragoons. Leading a column of eight hundred men, including Loyalists and Native Americans, Baum left Fort Miller on August 11. Ten miles east of Saratoga, at Sancoick's Mill, they were fired on briefly by two hundred American woodsmen behind trees and stone walls.

RIGHT: General John Stark.

BELOW: *A Map of the Province of New York, Detail #10: Fort Millar* (upper left) should be on the east side of the Hudson. From the fort, Baum's column headed south and east toward *Wallomsack Creek* and Bennington (lower right).

Pressing on, Baum's column marched into the Walloomsac River Valley on August 14. There, four miles northeast of Bennington, he was confronted by Stark's troops, who thrashed the Germans in battle two days later. Burgoyne sent reinforcements, but the arrival of three hundred Americans from Manchester (the remnant from Ticonderoga that had dispersed at Hubbardton) secured the victory. Burgoyne lost two hundred killed and seven hundred captured or missing. Reporting the triumph to the army in General Orders, Washington wrote that the Americans "pushed the enemy from one work to another, thrown up on advantageous ground, and from different posts, with spirit and fortitude, until they gained a complete victory." As Washington had predicted, the defeat of each detachment shrank Burgoyne's force and swelled the American ranks with new recruits. After Bennington, Burgoyne wrote to London that the New Hampshire Grants "hangs like a gathering storm upon my left." (See *A Map of the Province of New York, Detail #10*.)

Starting out with 8,500 men, losing the 1,600 who retreated with St. Leger, and another 900 at Bennington, Burgoyne marched his 6,000 remaining troops across a bridge of boats to the west side of the Hudson just below the town of Saratoga on September 14. Blocking his path down the river to Albany was General Horatio Gates, who had just replaced Schuyler as head of the Continental army's Northern Department and had staked out a strong position on Bemis Heights, two miles north of Stillwater. (See *A Map of the Province of New York, Detail #10*. The battlefield lay between *Still Water* to the south, *Saragtogha* to the north, *Saragtogha Lake* to the west, and the Hudson to the east. The fighting took place on the heights indicated by saw-toothed shading along the river valley.) Gates had 7,000 men, including Arnold and his relief column, back from Fort Stanwix, and new recruits were flooding in every day, spurred by reports of atrocities committed by Burgoyne's Indian allies, particularly the murder and scalping of Jane McCrea on her way to join her fiancé, a Loyalist officer in Burgoyne's camp.

On September 19, 1777, the two armies clashed at Freeman's Farm, just north of Bemis Heights, and the British suffered six hundred casualties, twice as many as the Americans, including many officers who had been targeted by American riflemen firing from the woods. At his camp in Pennsylvania, Washington ordered a parade, a gill of rum per man, and a thirteen-gun salute. If the fighting continued in this vein, he wrote Hancock, "I think we may count upon the total ruin of Burgoyne." Nonetheless, the British had managed to hold their ground, and planned to press forward against Gates's position to the south. However, Burgoyne decided to postpone his advance when he received an encouraging message from General Clinton in New York City, who proposed to come up the Hudson with part of his force.[53]

When Howe had embarked for Philadelphia in late July, he left Clinton to defend New York while assisting Burgoyne if possible. On October 3, Clinton embarked three thousand troops and sailed them forty miles up the Hudson from Manhattan to the Highlands. Washington warned Governor William Livingston of New Jersey that if Clinton seized the Highlands passes, he would probably capture the American forts as well. "This would open the navigation of the river and enable the enemy with facility to throw their force into Albany, get into the rear of General Gates, and oblige him to retreat or put him between two fires."[54]

Landing a thousand men at Verplanck's Point two days later, Clinton convinced General Israel Putnam at Peekskill that he was the sole target of a massive assault, causing him to retreat inland with his fifteen hundred men. Clinton could now proceed against Fort Clinton and Fort Montgomery across the river—which were deprived of reinforcements from Putnam. Landing his remaining two thousand troops to the west side of the river at Stony Point, Clinton marched them north and captured Fort Clinton and Fort Montgomery. The British general's American cousins, Brigadier General James Clinton and his younger brother Major General (and governor of New York) George Clinton, who were in charge of the forts, escaped with about half of their force after heavy fighting. The British also cleared away the chain blocking the

ABOVE: General Henry Clinton.

ABOVE, LEFT: General Horatio Gates.

river between Fort Montgomery and Anthony's Nose to seize the squadron of American ships anchored to the north, most of which the Americans burned to keep them out of British hands. On October 7, the garrison at Fort Constitution, on the island opposite West Point, fled as the British approached. Clinton had stormed the Highlands and opened the river, but he was not prepared to sail north—more than a hundred miles—to relieve Burgoyne, who was running out of time. Unwilling to leave his base at New York City exposed any longer, Clinton abandoned the forts soon after capturing them. (See *A Map of the Province of New York, Detail #3*, page 131.)

With his provisions running low and his line of communication to Canada threatened, Burgoyne pressed forward, attacking Gates's fortified position on Bemis Heights on October 7. The Americans, now eleven thousand strong, forced the British back to Freeman's Farm and inflicted another six hundred casualties. Arnold was instrumental in the victory, as he had been in the previous battle. Burgoyne's force, its fighting spirit broken, retreated north toward the town of Saratoga. A week later

Washington celebrated the victory in his General Orders, and exhorted his own troops to emulate the shining example of the Northern Army.[55]

After receiving reinforcements from Rhode Island, Clinton finally sent two thousand troops, under General John Vaughan, in galleys up the Hudson with orders to assist Burgoyne. They made it halfway to Albany, stopping to burn Kingston, the seat of New York's newly created state government, on October 15, and every building on the estate of Chancellor Robert Livingston, before they were intercepted by Continental troops under Putnam and Parsons. (See *A Map of the Province of New York, Detail #11*.) Washington predicted to Governor Clinton that "Sir Henry Clinton will not advance much farther up the river upon hearing of Burgoyne's defeat and retreat." Indeed, Vaughan embarked his troops and headed back to New York City when even worse news reached him: On October 14, Burgoyne had surrendered to Gates at Saratoga. The final terms were signed three days later, an American victory that would prove to be the turning point of the war. Washington used the word "God" sparingly but often spoke of "Providence" coming to the aid of the American cause. Now he was ecstatic, telling his troops: "Let every face brighten, and every heart expand with grateful praise to the supreme disposer of all events, who has granted us this signal success."[56]

While Gates reaped much of the glory for the victory at Saratoga, Washington had, indirectly, contributed to the demise of the British effort on the Hudson. Since September, he had been fighting a series of battles around Philadelphia, first to protect it from Howe's advance, and later to besiege his forces once they had taken the city. Howe's calls for reinforcements from New York ensured that Clinton's and Vaughan's efforts to rescue Burgoyne would be cut short.

On July 29, 1777 (the day Burgoyne had arrived at Fort Edward), Howe had arrived at Delaware Bay. However, reports of American fire rafts in the Delaware River prompted him to set sail again, leaving Washington once more to guess his destination. Finally, on August 25, after more than a month on board their ships, the British disembarked at the northern end of Chesapeake Bay and began marching north to seize Philadelphia.[57] (See *A General Map of the Middle British Colonies, Detail #11*.)

Washington, who had moved his forces down from Wilmington, Delaware, to White Clay Creek, sent troops out to harass the advancing British column, with orders to "give them as much trouble as you possibly can."[58] On September 3, at Cooch's Bridge on Christiana Creek, "the enemy came out with considerable force and three pieces of artillery, against our light advanced corps, and after some pretty smart skirmishing obliged [our troops] to retreat, being far inferior to them in number and without cannon," Washington reported to Congress.[59] It was the

A Map of the Province of New York, Detail #11: Kingston, on the west bank of the Hudson (left center), was the seat of New York State's first government in 1777 when it was burned by the British. Also burned was the estate of Chancellor Robert Livingston, marked as *Livingston's* on the east bank of the river (top center). It was also known as Clermont. The estate was part of the family's vast landholdings along the Hudson, the *MANOR OF LIVINGSTON* (upper right).

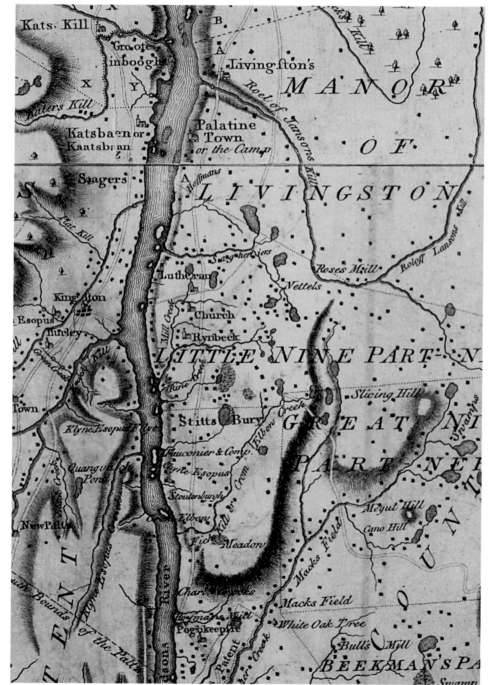

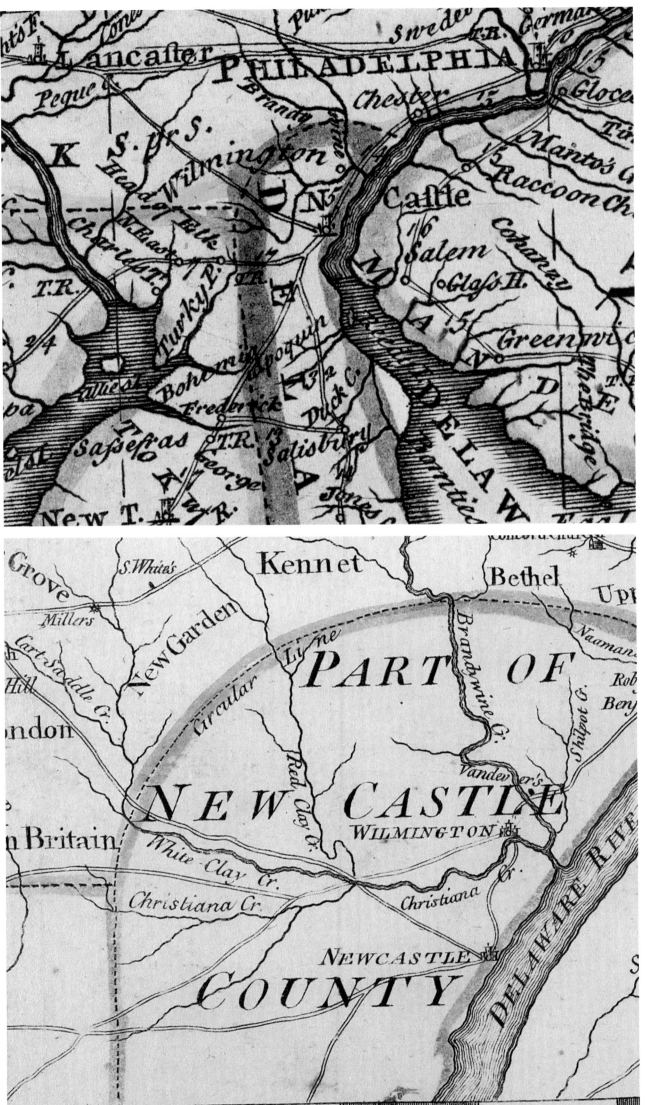

A General Map of the Middle British Colonies, Detail #11: At the end of July 1777 Howe arrived at Delaware Bay, but reports of American fire rafts in the Delaware River sent him southward to Chesapeake Bay. Landing at the northern end of the bay in the northeast corner of Maryland on August 25, he marched his army north from Head of Elk (left center) to capture Philadelphia.

A Map of Pennsylvania, Detail #4: When Howe landed at the northern end of Chesapeake Bay and marched his troops north toward Philadelphia, they clashed with American troops at Cooch's Bridge on Christiana Creek on September 3, driving them back to Washington's main encampment on White Clay Creek, four miles to the north. Christiana Creek and White Clay Creek (center) are primarily in Delaware, just east of the Elk River, and flow toward the Delaware River, feeding into it southeast of Wilmington.

largest engagement of the war in Delaware, and one of the first in which the Americans flew their new flag, the Stars and Stripes.[60] (See *A Map of Pennsylvania, Detail #4*, page 149.)

A week later, Washington told Congress that the British "only meant to amuse us in front, while their real intent was to march by our right and by suddenly passing the Brandywine and gaining the heights on the north side of that river, get between us and Philadelphia and cut us off from that city." To counter Howe's plan, Washington marched the army to "the high grounds near Chad's Ford," and on September 11 the two armies faced each other across Brandywine Creek, the Americans on the north bank and the British to the south.[61]

"Unfortunately, the intelligence received of the enemy's advancing up the Brandywine and crossing at a ford about six miles above us, was uncertain and contradictory," Washington told Congress. Trying to preserve his strength at Chad's Ford and doubting the reports of a British flanking maneuver, Washington did not send enough men fast enough to his right wing, where Howe's forces seized the high ground. Howe then hesitated, enabling the Americans to turn and face him. Once Howe attacked, General Wilhelm von Knyphausen could hear the sounds of battle and charged forward across the creek at Chad's Ford. Pressed on two fronts, the Americans were "obliged to leave the enemy masters of the field," Washington wrote.[62] (See *A Map of Pennsylvania, Detail #5*.)

Despite Washington's suspicion of the British plan, the battle had unfolded much like the Battle of Brooklyn a year earlier, with similar casualties: almost a thousand Americans killed, wounded, or captured. Once again, however, Howe had paused at a crucial moment and failed to crush Washington's forces, allowing most to escape instead. Supervising the retreat to Chester and beyond, Washington commanded that the troops "march on in good order through Derby to the bridge over Schuylkill, cross it, and proceed up to their former ground near the falls of Schuylkill, and Germantown, and there pitch their tents."[63] (See *A Map of Pennsylvania, Detail #5*, lower left to upper right.)

Twenty miles to the west, Howe was moving northward, heading for the fords on the Schuylkill near Valley Forge. Washington was adamant that the British not cross the Schuylkill and take Philadelphia, so he placed the army in Howe's path a few miles south of the river, near White Horse Tavern. The Battle of the Clouds erupted on September 16, so named because Howe was on the point of smashing the Americans from two sides when a heavy rainstorm disrupted the battle. Washington retreated north to Yellow Springs and then west to Warwick Forge. Heading northeast, Howe captured the American supply depot at Valley Forge. Instead of proceeding across the Schuylkill, however, Howe dispatched Major General Charles Grey to raid Brigadier General Anthony Wayne's

camp nearby at Paoli. Wayne was assigned to attack the British baggage train, but instead lost fifty-three killed and one hundred wounded in Grey's silent, surprise attack with bayonets before dawn on September 21.[64]

Howe's delay for the Paoli "Massacre" gave Washington time to cross the Schuylkill further north, at Parker's Ford, and move south to challenge the British when they crossed the river. However, "the enemy extended themselves up the river as if they meant to turn our right," Washington recalled, and he moved the army north to face them. Then, by "countermarching in the night," Howe "crossed some miles below us, the river being fordable in almost every part." (See *A Map of Pennsylvania, Detail #6*.) Howe's evasive maneuvers had given him a clear path to Philadelphia, and he marched the army into the city on September 26. Washington had been caught flatfooted, but his barefoot army could only be pushed so far: "Here I must remark that our distress for want of shoes is almost beyond conception," Washington wrote to fellow Virginian Thomas Nelson, "and that from this circumstance our operations and pursuit have been impracticable."[65]

Nonetheless, Washington rallied his troops for an attack on the British encampment north of Philadelphia, at Germantown. Washington's ambitious battle plan called for four columns of troops to proceed simultaneously and converge on the British, trapping them against the Delaware River. The attack began well enough, on the morning of October 4, driving in the British outposts, but in the predawn darkness and continuing fog, the American columns on the left and right never entered the fray, and the two at the center collided and fired on each other. The retreating British turned and counterattacked, driving the Americans back ten miles. The Americans had lost more than a thousand men killed, wounded, and captured—twice as many as the British—but American morale rose because the Continental troops at the center had performed well, forcing the British to retreat during the first phase of the battle. (See *A Map of Pennsylvania, Detail #7*, page 152.)

Washington now attempted to besiege the British in Philadelphia by cutting off supplies by land and water. He blocked the roads to the city and occupied two forts in the Delaware that could stop ships arriving from the Atlantic: Fort Mifflin on Mud Island and Fort Mercer on the New Jersey shore. Howe pulled back from Germantown so that his defensive line just north of Philadelphia was anchored by the Schuylkill on the west and the Delaware on the east, and required fewer troops. South of the city, he had the army build a bridge to Province Island, erect batteries there and on Carpenter's Island, and start bombarding Fort Mifflin. (See *A Map of Pennsylvania, Detail #8*, page 152.)

On October 21 Howe dispatched two thousand Hessians by land and two warships to capture Fort Mercer, but they were repulsed with heavy losses. Philadelphians were now on the verge of starvation. By November 10,

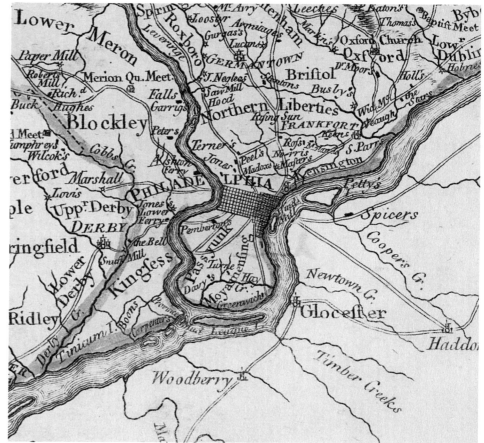

however, the British had completed a number of floating batteries in addition to those on Province Island, and after a weeklong bombardment they forced the Americans out of Fort Mifflin. A few days later, the garrison of four hundred Americans abandoned Fort Mercer as well when Cornwallis approached with a force of five thousand troops, which included reinforcements from New York. Washington kept the army at Whitemarsh, hoping to engage the British and lift American spirits before the end of the campaign. A brief skirmish in early December did not have the desired effect, and when Howe pulled back toward Philadelphia, Washington moved the army to winter quarters at Valley Forge. (See *A Map of Pennsylvania, Detail #6*, page 150, right, center.)

The army arrived at Valley Forge on December 19 and the exhausted men, lacking adequate food, clothing, and blankets, had to improvise shelter for themselves until they could build log huts. And these were the fortunate troops who were not sick or wounded. "For some days past there has been little less than a famine in the camp," Washington wrote to Governor George Clinton in the middle of February. "Naked and starving as they are, we cannot enough admire the incomparable patience and fidelity of the soldiery."[66] Despite the hardships, the army drilled regularly with Baron von Steuben, becoming more professional, particularly at marching and maneuvering. The spring also brought a formal alliance with France, resulting from increased confidence in American prospects after the victory at Saratoga, and the French navy neutralized Britain's sea power.

William Howe was recalled to London and replaced by his second in command, Henry Clinton, who took the army back to New York City overland, through New Jersey. Washington now had an opportunity to strike at the British army in the open, which he exploited at the Battle of Monmouth on June 28, 1778.[67] After the advance corps under Charles Lee retreated, Washington berated him and rallied the army, which stood its ground in a pitched battle, prompting the British to withdraw that night. Washington praised his men for their victory "over the flower of the British troops." (See *A Map of the Province of New York, Detail #12*.)[68]

Baron Friedrich Wilhelm von Steuben.

As Washington headed north through New Jersey to visit the works under construction at West Point, a French fleet commanded by the comte d'Estaing arrived off Sandy Hook. Washington was eager to coordinate a joint attack with the French to take New York City back from the British. Washington crossed the Hudson at King's Ferry, established his headquarters at White Plains, and promised d'Estaing he would descend through Westchester County to threaten the British by land. However, by July 22, it was clear that d'Estaing's massive warships would not be able to cross "the shallow entrance at Sandy Hook" to take on the British navy, Washington explained to Sullivan, so the allies agreed to shift their operations and make Newport, Rhode Island, their next target instead. Sullivan was at Providence with a thousand Continental troops; with New England militia and units under the marquis de Lafayette and Greene, he eventually had ten thousand troops to work with the French fleet.[69]

Washington sent Lieutenant Colonel John Laurens to act as liaison between Sullivan and d'Estaing, and on August 4 Laurens reported to Washington about the plan of attack. Sullivan had informed d'Estaing of the "three entrances to Rhode Island," namely, the two channels on the east and west sides of the main island and a third on the west side of Conanicut Island. Sullivan proposed that the French fleet sail into the central channel and trap the British in Newport Harbor, while detaching ships up the other two channels to clear them of enemy vessels and support the American troops marching down from Bristol and Tiverton, on the mainland. (See *A Map of . . . New England, Detail #2*,

OPPOSITE, LEFT: *A Map of Pennsylvania, Detail #7:* The Americans in the center, on the Germantown Road, drove the British from their forward post at Mount Airy (lower center) and continued southward. The Americans on the left halted near Armitage's Tavern and never got into the battle; neither did the column on the extreme right, which had marched along the Schuylkill and stopped at Wissahickon Creek, lower left. (The creek is labeled further north, above Whitemarsh, top left). After the two columns in the center collided and fired on each other, the British turned and counterattacked, pursuing the retreating Americans to Whitemarsh.

OPPOSITE, RIGHT: *A Map of Pennsylvania, Detail #8:* After the Battle of Germantown, Washington tried to cut off all supplies to Philadelphia by controlling the roads as well as the forts on the Delaware River below the city. Fort Mifflin was on Mud Island, across from Province Island, at the mouth of the Schuylkill (lower center). Fort Mercer was on the New Jersey shore south of Timber Creeks and north of Woodbury.

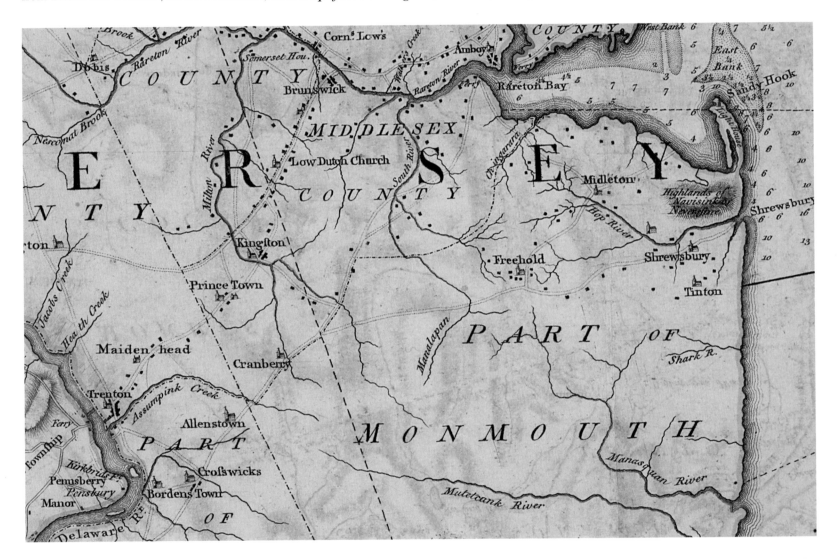

page 156.) Sullivan's forces would then bypass the British forts on the northern end of Rhode Island and attack those around Newport as quickly as possible. At the same time, d'Estaing should knock out the batteries defending the harbor, bombard the town, and land troops to cooperate with the Americans.[70]

The Americans landed on Rhode Island on August 9, but the arrival of British ships from New York unhinged the allied expedition. D'Estaing drove away the British squadron, but during the chase both fleets were caught in a storm and badly damaged. Returning to Newport on August 20, d'Estaing informed Sullivan that he was going to Boston for repairs and would not join in the attack. This prompted the militia to leave, cutting Sullivan's force in half, and emboldened the British to take the offensive, driving the Americans back to the northern end of Rhode Island, where they made a fighting retreat to Tiverton on the night of August 30.[71]

ABOVE: *A Map of the Province of New York, Detail #12:* A week after evacuating Philadelphia on June 18, 1778, Clinton's column arrived at Allentown (lower left) on its way to Freehold, Middleton, and the shore (west of Sandy Hook), where the navy would bring the troops up to Manhattan. Washington had moved east from Valley Forge and crossed the Delaware at Howell's Ferry, determined to engage Clinton's forces. Washington reached Kingston on June 26 and Cranbury on the 27th. (Cranbury is further east than indicated on the map.) The Battle of Monmouth took place between Freehold and the northern end of the Manasquan River (center right).

Despite Burgoyne's defeat, the British continued to wage war against the western frontiers of New York, Pennsylvania, and Virginia, with forces consisting mostly of Iroquois warriors aided by Loyalists displaced from the Mohawk Valley, led by Sir John Johnson, Colonel John Butler and his son Walter, and the Mohawk leader Captain Joseph Brant.[72] On July 3, 1778, John Butler and his forces raided the Wyoming Valley in Pennsylvania and defeated the Whig militia, taking many scalps and no prisoners. In September, the settlers around German Flats, New York, on the Mohawk River were attacked by Brant (based at Unadilla to the south), who put their homes and crops to the torch. The spiral of violence continued on October 8 when Whig forces destroyed Unadilla. Cherry Valley was next, attacked by Brant and Walter Butler in November. Reports of British, Loyalist, and Indian atrocities fueled a clamor for revenge.[73] (See *A General Map of the Middle British Colonies, Detail #1*, page 34. From Fort Niagara, upper left, the British organized attacks on Wyoming, bottom center, between the western and eastern branches of the Susquehanna River; Cherry Valley, upper right, northwest of Albany; and German Flats, not shown, on the Mohawk River.)

While pressure mounted for the United States to respond—and the devastation of farms and the massacre of the inhabitants took its toll on the Continental army's provisions as well as manpower—Washington knew, especially from his experience in Virginia during the French and Indian War, that he could not hope to protect the entire frontier, hundreds of miles long, with the few troops he could spare from the Northeast. Nor did he have the resources to launch another invasion of Canada, as Lafayette proposed, to disrupt the raids at their source.

While Congress applauded Lafayette's idea, Washington warned that such an invasion, employing a French fleet up the St. Lawrence to capture Quebec, risked a French takeover of Canada that would put the United States back in the vulnerable position of the British colonies before victory in the French and Indian War—under the threat of French harassment and domination from the north and west, as well as from the south at New Orleans. While the French were now an ally, Washington wrote, "hatred of England may carry some into an excess of confidence in France, especially when motives of gratitude are thrown into the scale." Unwittingly, Washington was accurately predicting the challenges he would face as president almost two decades later.[74]

In early November, d'Estaing took his fleet from Boston to the West Indies, without notifying Washington. A British squadron from New York also headed there and captured St. Lucia, while another detachment reinforced West Florida. Having reached a stalemate in the land war in North America, the British were redirecting their forces to face the new French threat and contest the valuable sugar islands. However, the British also left Newport and New York City strongly garrisoned. To remain within striking distance of New York, and prevent British forays, Washington settled his troops into winter quarters in a line of outposts straddling the Hudson from Danbury, Connecticut, in the east to Middlebrook and Elizabeth in New Jersey to the west. Washington's strategy for 1779 was to conserve his shrinking army by remaining on the defensive until the country's finances improved and Congress could strengthen his hand with more men, provisions, and supplies.

Barring the arrival of French land forces, the only offensive Washington planned was against the Iroquois.[75] As the British-backed frontier raids continued through the fall and winter of 1778, Congress resolved in February 1779 that Washington had to strike a decisive blow against the hostile Iroquois tribes. He would have liked to take the fort at Niagara but instead decided on a scorched-earth campaign against the Iroquois towns in northern New

York, focusing on the Senecas. Washington requested new sketch maps of the area, combed through explorers' diaries, and sent scouts to examine trails on the frontier.[76]

"Sir: The expedition you are appointed to command is to be directed against the hostile tribes of the Six Nations of Indians, with their associates and adherents," Washington wrote to Major General John Sullivan on May 31, 1779, ordering him to be thorough and remorseless in his mission. "The immediate objects are the total destruction and devastation of their settlements and the capture of as many prisoners of every age and sex as possible."

Sullivan was to assemble the main body of troops at Wyoming and move north to establish a base at Tioga, New York, "taking from that place the most direct and practicable route into the heart of the Indian settlements," Washington wrote. (See *A General Map of the Middle British Colonies, Detail #1*, page 34. Tioga, New York, not shown, was at the confluence of the Susquehanna and Chemung rivers; the latter is labeled *Cayuga Branch*. Northwest of Tioga along the Chemung River were the villages of Chemung and Newtown and the Seneca settlement of Catherine's Town, not shown.)

Washington ordered Sullivan to "establish such intermediate posts as you think necessary for the security of your communication and convoys," and leave men to defend the posts while diminishing his operating force as little as possible. Washington was clearly avoiding the mistakes of the Braddock expedition, and urged Sullivan "to guard against surprises, from an adversary so secret, desultory, and rapid as the Indians."

General James Clinton was ordered to gather his brigade at Canajoharie on the Mohawk River, and then follow Sullivan's orders "either to form a junction with the main body on the Susquehanna by way of Otsego, or to proceed up the Mohawk River and cooperate in the best manner circumstances will permit." If Clinton moved up the Mohawk, Washington told Sullivan, he had to beware of the British sending troops "from Oswegatchie and Niagara to Oswego without his knowledge, and for this purpose he should keep trusty spies at those three places."

Once Sullivan had penetrated the Iroquois country, he was to send detachments to burn crops and villages "in the most effectual manner, that the country may not be merely *overrun* but *destroyed*." Washington had also ordered Colonel Daniel Brodhead, the commander at Fort Pitt, to lead a smaller force up to the head of the Allegheny River and attack the Iroquois villages there, creating a distraction and then reinforcing Sullivan if possible.[77]

After two months of preparation, moving supplies north from Sunbury and west from Easton to Wyoming, Sullivan's expedition set off on July 31. He arrived at Tioga ten days later and was joined by Clinton's brigade on August 22, giving them a total of some four thousand troops. A week later, after destroying the village of Chemung, they fought a pitched battle against Butler's and Brant's forces at Newtown and drove them off. Sullivan's campaign had just begun.

(See *A General Map of the Middle British Colonies, Detail #1*, page 34. After destroying Catherine's Town, Sullivan continued to the northwest to the Little Seneca River, upper left, and torched the Seneca town of Genesee, not shown, before heading east through the Finger Lakes region, burning more fields and villages, including those of the Cayugas on Cayuga Lake, center. Further east, a detachment burned the town of Lower Mohawk Castle, not shown, on its way to Albany. The town of Onondaga, the site of the central council fire of the Six Nations, upper right, southeast of Oswego, had already been destroyed in April 1778 by U.S. forces deployed from Fort Stanwix, on the Mohawk River.)[78]

"Our loss was trifling," Washington told the marquis de Lafayette on September 12, after receiving a letter from Sullivan. The expedition had lost fewer than one hundred men killed and wounded, "although he had advanced to and destroyed fourteen towns, large and most flourishing crops of corn . . . etc.," Washington wrote. "He was proceeding in his plan of chastisement and will convince them, it is to be hoped, of two things: first, that their cruelties are not to pass with impunity; and secondly that they have been instigated to arms, and acts of barbarism by a nation which is unable to protect them and of consequence has left them to that correction which is due to their villainy."

Washington counted Sullivan's progress among "our little successes," he told Lafayette. In June the British had been forced to retreat after demanding the surrender of Charleston, South Carolina. This was followed in July by "the storming of Stony Point" by Anthony Wayne, and in August by Henry "Light-Horse Harry" Lee's "surprise of Paulus Hook (within cannon shot of the City of New York) and capture of the garrisons, the first amounting to six hundred men, the other to two hundred."

The bad news of the summer, Washington reported to Lafayette, was the humiliating defeat of an expedition from Boston to Penobscot, Maine, sent to expel some eight hundred British troops who had descended from Halifax and established a post "as is supposed for the purpose of getting masts and spars for their shipping." When hemmed in by a British squadron, the Massachusetts militiamen ended up burning their own vessels and fleeing by land. "This and the conflagration of Fairfield, Norwalk, and New Haven [Connecticut] by the intrepid and magnanimous [William] Tryon who in defiance of all the opposition that could be given by the women and children inhabitants of these towns performed this notable exploit with 2,000 brave and generous Britons adding thereby fresh luster to their arms and dignity to their king."

Looking ahead and hoping to gain some clue as to the next move of the British, Washington mentioned to Lafayette that "Admiral [Marriot] Arbuthnot with about 3 or 4,000 troops are arrived at New York, and will, it is to

Admiral, comte d'Estaing.

be presumed, afford Sir Henry Clinton an opportunity of displaying his intentions, or orders."[79]

Without a regular army, Butler and Brant could do little more than harass Sullivan's enormous column as it burned Newtown and moved deeper into Iroquois territory. Throughout September, Sullivan's forces burned at least forty villages and 160,000 bushels of corn across the whole expanse of Iroquoia, from the Senecas in the west to the Cayugas in the center, and the Mohawks in the east. The main body of troops returned to Tioga on September 30, razed the fort, and ended the expedition back at Wyoming a week later.[80]

"By this time I expect General Sullivan will have completed the entire destruction of the whole settlements of the Six Nations, excepting those of the Oneidas and such other friendly towns as have merited a different treatment," Washington wrote to John Laurens at the end of September. "By my last advices [of September 9] he had penetrated beyond their middle settlements, had burnt between 15 and 20 Towns, destroyed all their crops, and was advancing to their exterior villages. The Indians, men, women, and children, flying before him to Niagara (distant more than 100 miles) in the utmost consternation, distress, and confusion with the Butlers, Brandt, &ca. at their head."[81]

In mentioning women and children, Washington clearly did not equate Sullivan's expedition with the ravaging of the Connecticut coast by the British, which he so despised, because he saw the destruction of Iroquoia as just retribution for British and Indian frontier raids. The burning of fields, crops, and villages succeeded at burdening the British administration in Canada with a massive demand for food and shelter. The suffering and death toll were increased by the harsh winter of 1779–80, and more than five thousand Iroquois refugees appeared at Fort Niagara. While the Sullivan expedition did not stop the Iroquois from siding with the British or from attacking frontier settlements, it dealt a decisive blow to Iroquois military power and political influence, which was at its height in the century before the war. If it accomplished nothing else, the expedition set the stage for the westward expansion of the United States right after the war and during Washington's presidency, through one-sided treaties imposed on the Indians, coupled with more military campaigns.[82]

A Map of . . . New England, Detail #2: Laurens enclosed a map for Washington (no longer among his papers) "which may be useful in illustrating the proposed plan of operations." In every locale Washington sought detailed maps that could provide more information than the more general published maps in his collection. Nonetheless, this map of New England from the Yale atlas adequately illustrates the basic configuration of land and water in Rhode Island. The French, arriving from Sandy Hook, were met by American pilots at Point Judith (bottom left) and guided toward Newport.

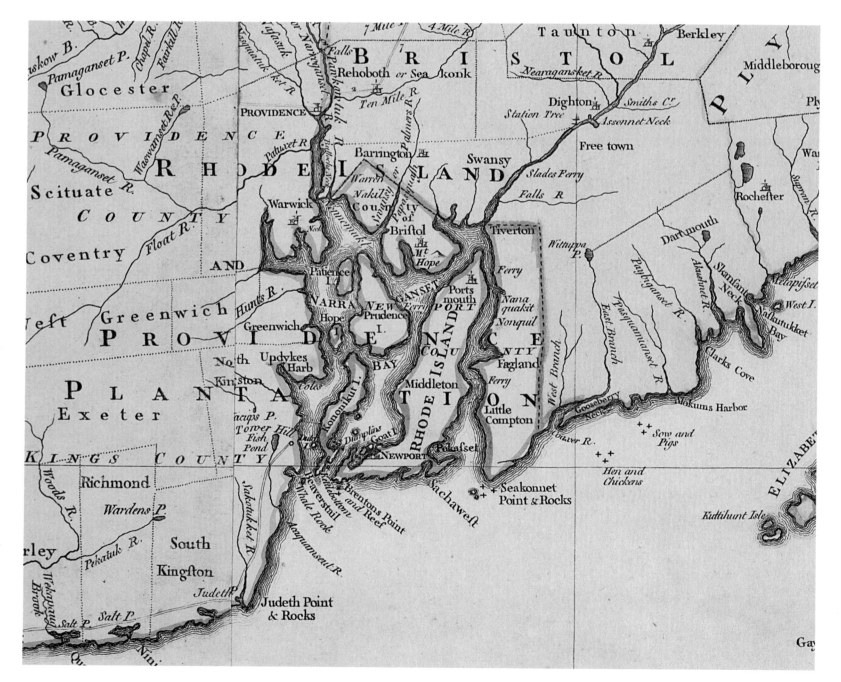

General John Sullivan.

Even more effective than Sullivan's expedition in staking the claim of the United States to the western territories were the exploits of George Rogers Clark, a twenty-five-year-old colonel in the Virginia Militia. In the summer of 1778, Clark had led 175 volunteers on a 900-mile expedition down the Ohio River from Pittsburgh to the mouth of the Tennessee River, then trekked another 125 miles north to capture the British post of Kaskaskia, on the east bank of the Mississippi, which they took by surprise on July 4, 1773, the second anniversary of American independence. Five days later, Clark captured Cahokia, to the north, and dispatched some of his men east to the Wabash River, where they took Vincennes. (See *A General Map of the Middle British Colonies, Detail #3*, page 40. On the lower left of this map, Kaskaskia is labeled *Kuskuskes*, and the Cahokia River is labeled but the post is not. The Wabash is shown at the bottom center, but Vincennes is not indicated. Detroit is shown just north of Lake Erie, right center.)

A British expedition from Detroit had recaptured Vincennes in December 1778, provoking Clark to march his men through the snow and cold and storm the fort in February 1779, when he captured the British lieutenant governor of Canada along with the entire garrison. Washington praised Clark's astonishing string of victories in a letter to Thomas Jefferson in July. "I hope these successes will be followed by very happy consequences," he wrote. "If Colonel Clark could by any means gain possession of Detroit, it would in all probability effectually secure the friendship or at least the neutrality of most of the western Indians."[83]*

As the Iroquois migrated northward to Canada and many white Loyalists went with them in the final months of 1779—and clashes across the globe with France and Spain drained Britain's resources—Lord George Germain, the British secretary of state in charge of the war in America, became all the more convinced that a strategy of tapping Loyalists in the South to fight the war was his best chance to save himself politically and put down the rebellion. The day after Christmas the waters around New York City were choked with ice as Sir Henry Clinton and his second in command, General Charles Cornwallis, set sail aboard their fleet of fourteen warships and ninety transports, carrying 8,500 troops for a second attempt to capture Charleston, South Carolina. New York remained strongly defended, however, with enhanced fortifications and 16,000 troops under General Knyphausen.

"The succession of tempestuous weather which immediately followed the departure of the fleet that sailed from New York the latter end of December we have been flattering ourselves will at least retard and disconcert their Southern operation," Washington told Benjamin Lincoln in February 1780. "We have yet had no distinct account of them; it will be fortunate indeed if they have been driven off and dispersed."[84]

* A hero of the Revolution, Clark would cause Washington much chagrin during his presidency by plotting a French-sponsored expedition to seize western territory that threatened to drag the country into war with Spain and England.

CHAPTER SIX

0   1   2   3   4   5   6

THE WAR IN THE

SOUTH

"We have everything to fear from the southward," Joseph Reed had warned Washington on March 15, 1776, while he was besieging Boston. "A cursed spirit of disaffection has appeared in the back parts of North and South Carolina which if not subdued before the forces arrive from England will prove a most formidable piece of business."[1] Reed's analysis was accurate as far as it went, but to some degree he was misled by the same myth that afflicted the British officials running the war from London: that by shifting the seat of war to the South they could tap a deep vein of Loyalist sentiment and have these "good Americans" do most of the fighting.[2]

It was true that the earliest settlers, the planters in the Tidewater areas along the coast, tended to be Whigs, while the second wave, who settled one hundred miles or more inland in the Piedmont (the foothills of the Appalachian Mountains), resented being taxed but not fairly represented by the colonial legislatures dominated by the Tidewater set. Ironically, these backcountry settlers tended to be Loyalists as a result. However, the picture was further complicated by a third swath of settlement, further west, in and over the Appalachian Mountains, consisting of Whig frontiersmen who resented British policies that protected Indian land and restricted westward expansion. (See *An Accurate Map of North and South Carolina*, pages 160–61.) As a result, a large component of the American Revolution in the South would be a savage civil war between Whigs and Loyalists. Militarily, misjudging the political makeup of the region would have disastrous consequences for the British. [3]

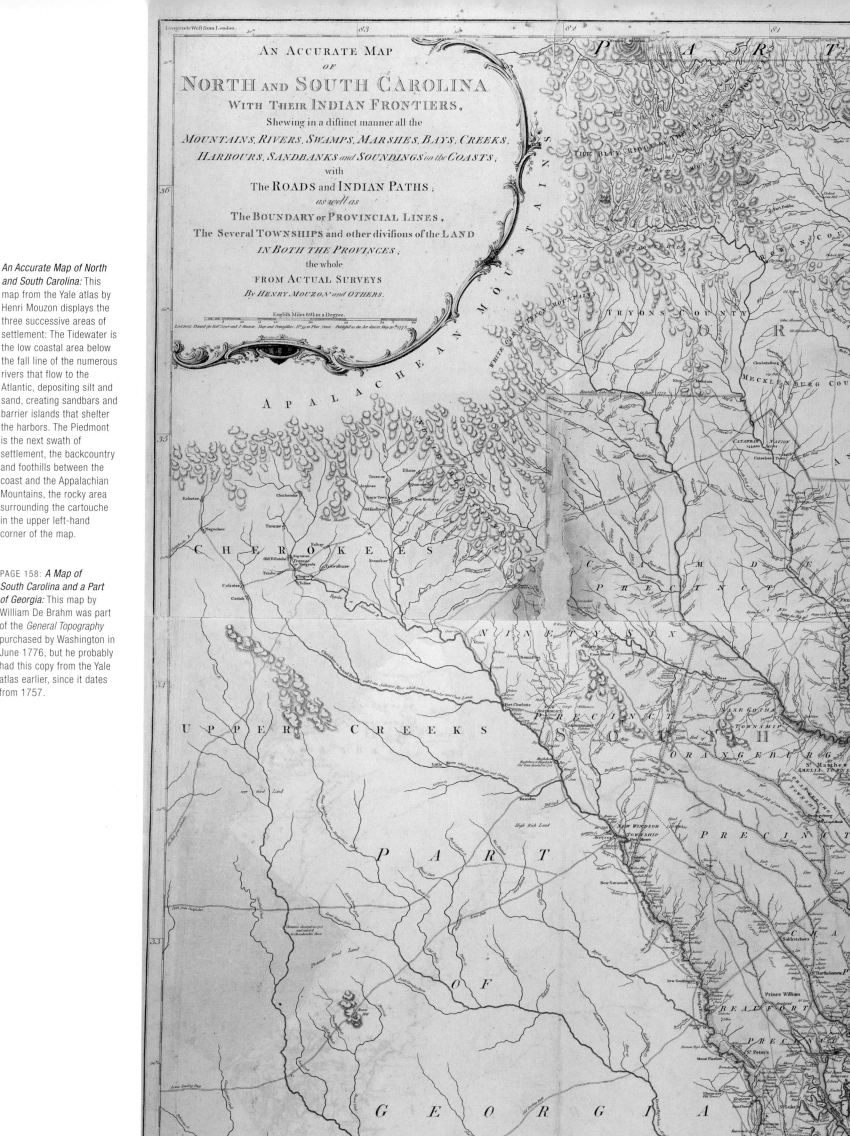

An Accurate Map of North and South Carolina: This map from the Yale atlas by Henri Mouzon displays the three successive areas of settlement: The Tidewater is the low coastal area below the fall line of the numerous rivers that flow to the Atlantic, depositing silt and sand, creating sandbars and barrier islands that shelter the harbors. The Piedmont is the next swath of settlement, the backcountry and foothills between the coast and the Appalachian Mountains, the rocky area surrounding the cartouche in the upper left-hand corner of the map.

PAGE 158: *A Map of South Carolina and a Part of Georgia:* This map by William De Brahm was part of the *General Topography* purchased by Washington in June 1776, but he probably had this copy from the Yale atlas earlier, since it dates from 1757.

A Map of South Carolina and a Part of Georgia, Detail #1: The map dramatically illustrates the vulnerability of Georgia to invasion by the British navy because of its porous coastline, penetrated by eight rivers, which created inlets and harbors to shelter ships from the Atlantic Ocean and coastal islands that provided staging areas for military operations.

Reed added that the Tory problem was even more worrisome "when connected with the hosts of Negroes in the lower part of the country," meaning that slaves would rebel, turning against their Whig masters to join the British. In November 1775, Virginia's royal governor, Lord Dunmore, had formed an "Ethiopian Regiment" by offering freedom to any slave who would desert his rebel owner and join the king's forces. In 1775–76, in his letters from Cambridge to Lund Washington, who was managing his property, Washington discussed the possibility of blockading the Potomac to thwart incursions by Dunmore and other British detachments.[4]

Warnings came not only from the Carolinas and Virginia but from Georgia, where the porous coastline, permeated by numerous rivers, was susceptible to invasion by the British navy. Lachlan McIntosh, a prominent plantation owner and colonel of Georgia's Continental battalion, wrote to Washington from Savannah on February 16, 1776: "Our province has a front along the sea coast of above one hundred miles, covered by a range of islands, divided from each other by eight rivers from the mainland, which makes as many good inlets and harbors, most of them capable of receiving any frigate, and as some say much larger ships." (See *A Map of South Carolina and a Part of Georgia*, page 158, and *Detail #1*.)

McIntosh argued that Georgia's immense production of rice and other provisions, along with its good harbors, made its defense a matter of interest to all the American colonies; if the British were allowed to take over, they would use the province as a source of supplies and a hub of their operations. "We are bounded [to the] south by the garrisoned province of East Florida who have . . . five hundred regulars in St. Augustine and a thousand more expected there daily from Europe. On the west of us is the province of West Florida, the numerous nations of the Creek, Choctaw, and Cherokee Indians, besides lesser tribes supposed to have at least ten thousand gunmen, brave, intrepid, and eager for war." (See *A General Map of North America, Detail #4.*)

By the Treaty of Paris in 1763, the defeated French king had turned over Louisiana and its capital, New Orleans, to his Bourbon cousin, the king of Spain; the victorious British, however, received all of Louisiana east of the Mississippi, which became part of a new colony, British West Florida. With Pensacola as its capital, West Florida included Mobile and other settlements on the Gulf of Mexico.[5]

McIntosh also described the imminent danger to Savannah, the capital. "Our metropolis is situated in the north corner of the province upon a bluff or sand hill thirty feet high or more above the water and fifteen miles up the River Savannah from the Inlet of Tybee, where five ships of war . . . besides tenders are now lying and two large transports having it is said above 300 men on board and expecting more in daily, with what design, whether for this

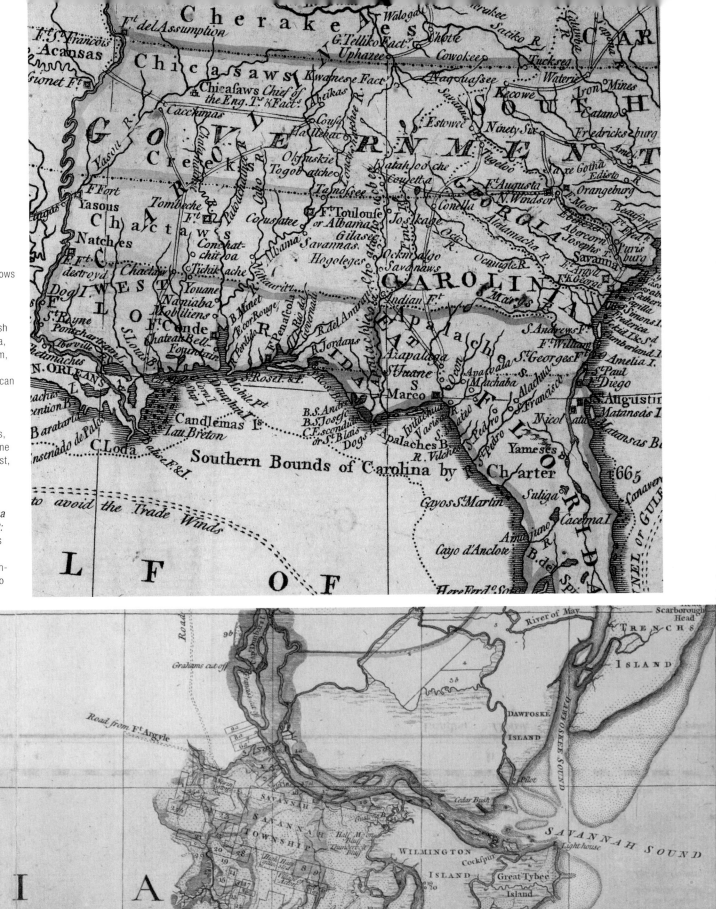

RIGHT: *A General Map of North America, Detail #4:* The map shows Georgia surrounded by hostile Indian tribes and by the British in East and West Florida. After the Revolution, when the Spanish controlled East and West Florida, they, like the British before them, incited the Indians against the expanding United States. American settlers were equally to blame, as they encroached on Indian land and raided their villages. Thus, as president in the 1790s, Washington would face this same set of problems in the Southwest, and maps of the region would continue to be crucial.

BELOW: *A Map of South Carolina and a Part of Georgia, Detail #2:* The city of Savannah, Georgia's capital, is located on the south side of the river, where its north-south course bends eastward to the ocean.

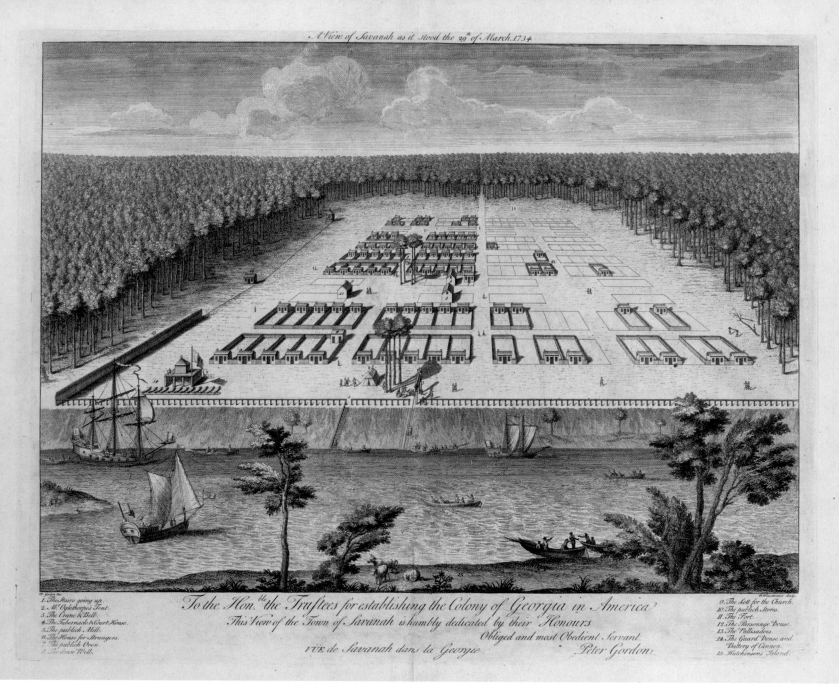

To the Hon.ble the Truftees for establishing the Colony of Georgia in America
This View of the Town of Savanah is humbly dedicated by their Honours
Obliged and most Obedient Servant:
VÜE de Savanah dans la Georgie.   Peter Gordon.

1. The Stairs going up.
2. M.r Oglethorpes Tent.
3. The Crane & Bell.
4. The Tabernacle & Court House.
5. The publick Mill.
6. The House for Strangers.
7. The publick Oven.
8. The draw Well.

9. The Sett for the Church.
10. The publick Stores.
11. The Fort.
12. The Parsonage House.
13. The Pallisadoes.
14. The Guard House and
     Battery of Cannon.
15. Hutchinsons Island.

ABOVE: *A View of Savannah:* This view, from the Yale atlas, is from more than forty years earlier. The city was less developed, but the layout and situation were the same. Note the thirty-foot-high riverbank.

OPPOSITE: *An Accurate Map of North and South Carolina, Detail #1:* The Loyalists assembled at Cross Creek, today's Fayetteville (upper left, just north of a swamp near the northwest branch of the Cape Fear River). As they marched southeast toward the coast at Brunswick, Whig troops removed the planks of Moore's Creek Bridge and lay in ambush. Moore's Creek (not shown) fed into the Black River about seven miles north of where it flowed into the Cape Fear River (seventeen miles northwest of Wilmington). The bridge was near the Black River about fifteen miles west of Bergaw Creek.

* McIntosh reported to Washington that on March 2–4, the British and Loyalists at Savannah had "done us great honor, by being the second province on the continent which they attacked, and were shamefully foiled."

colony only, or Carolina or both together, we are not yet informed." (See *A Map of South Carolina and a Part of Georgia, Detail #2*, page 163, and *A View of Savannah*.) Georgia had declared "a state of alarm" and was mustering the militia at Savannah "to oppose the landing of any troops."[6]

As tensions mounted in Georgia, the first battle of the American Revolution in the South took place in North Carolina on February 27, 1776. Authorized by the royal governor, Brigadier General Donald McDonald raised a force of fifteen hundred Loyalists from the Piedmont and marched them toward the coast, planning to meet General Henry Clinton's expedition at Brunswick. However, at Moore's Creek Bridge they clashed with a force of Tidewater Whigs under Colonel James Caswell. (See *An Accurate Map of North and South Carolina, Detail #1*.) As Joseph Reed relayed the news to Washington, the Loyalists were "totally defeated: above 30 left dead on the spot and a great number of prisoners taken." The Whigs had indeed killed or wounded fifty Loyalists and taken 850 prisoners. Reed, who had been warning Washington about "how troublesome and dangerous the back inhabitants of North Carolina were growing," was now overly optimistic. "The

whole Party is said to be so crushed and disappointed that nothing more is to be apprehended from them."[7*]

General Henry Clinton, with part of his expeditionary force—tasked with shoring up the royal governments in the South—had set out from Boston on January 20, 1776, stopped at New York and Hampton Roads, and belatedly arrived at Cape Fear, North Carolina, on March 12. However, Commodore Peter Parker's fleet, carrying eight regiments under General Charles Cornwallis, did not finish arriving from Ireland until the end of May, delaying the long-awaited attack on Charleston, South Carolina, until June 28.[8] This had given Charles Lee time to come down from New York in March to direct the fortification and defense of the city.

Lee reported to Washington that the British squadron "dropped their anchors about eleven in the forenoon at the distance of three or four hundred yards before the front battery" of the fort on Sullivan's Island "and immediately commenced the most furious fire that I ever heard or saw." From the island, Lee wrote, "we had no bridge finished of retreat or communication and the creek or cove which separates it from the continent is near a mile wide.

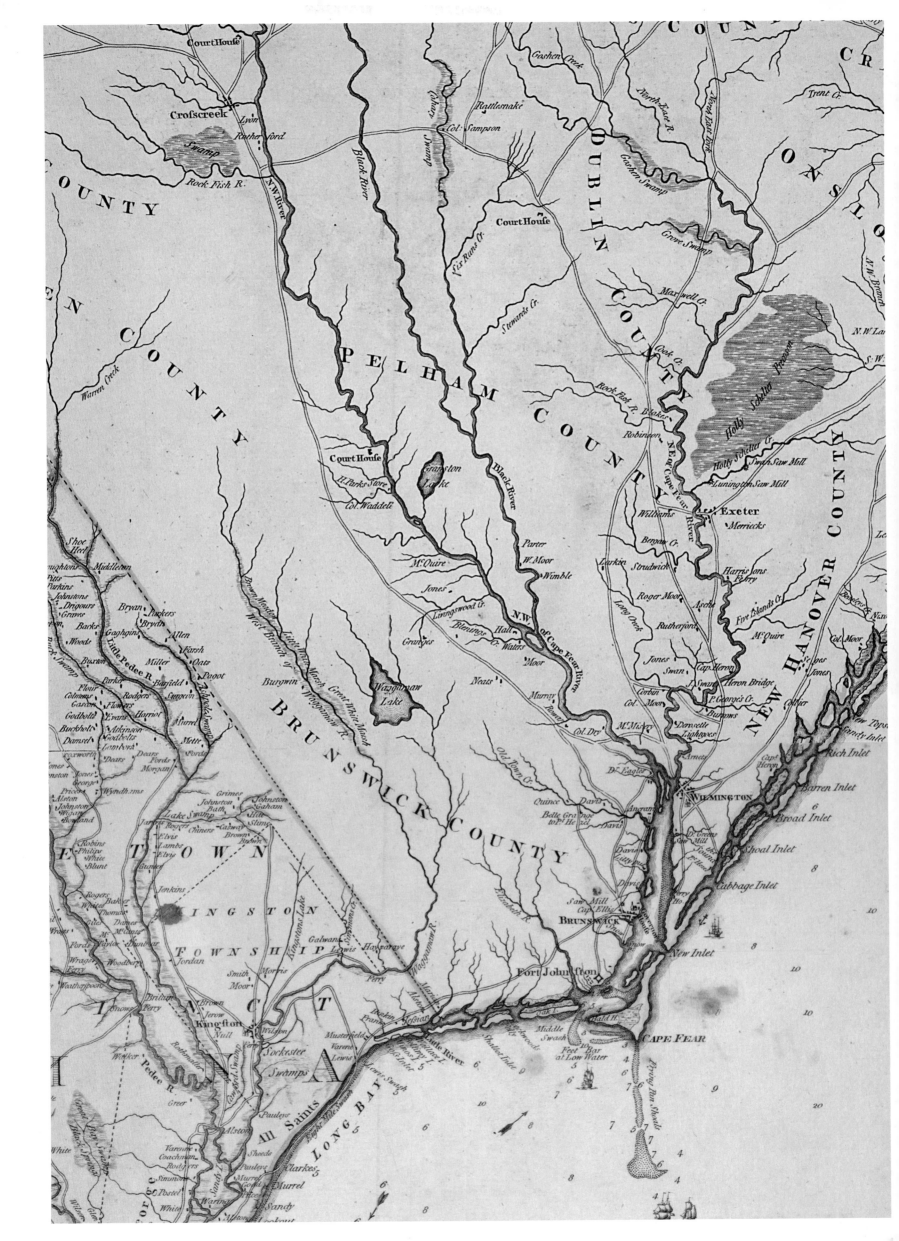

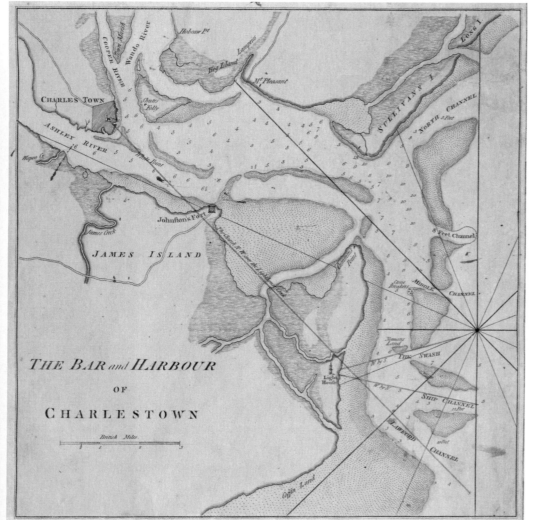

ABOVE: *An Accurate Map of North and South Carolina, Detail #2:* The sandbar stretching across the mouth of the harbor was divided by six channels, and the British squadron entered at the northernmost passage to attack the fort at the southern end of Sullivan's Island. The Americans refused to flee, and the two largest British ships ran aground on the long shoal in the gateway to the harbor, directly in front of the fort. After twelve hours of fighting, the battered squadron retreated beyond the bar and sailed to New York.

OPPOSITE: *An Accurate Map of North and South Carolina, Detail #3:* The Savannah River, between Augusta (top left) and Savannah (bottom right), would become both a major battlefront and a buffer between the American and British forces.

* Ternant had been a lieutenant in the French army when he resigned his commission and came to the United States with Baron von Steuben to offer his services to Congress. From April through September 1778, he had served as sub-inspector in Steuben's division, helping to train Continental troops. He would later be ambassador to the United States during part of Washington's presidency, from 1790 to 1793.

I had received likewise intelligence that their land troops intended at the same time to land and assault."[9]

To the dismay of the British, the walls of the fort, made of spongy palmetto logs, absorbed most of the twelve-hour bombardment, while North and South Carolina troops prevented Clinton's force from coming ashore at the other end of the island. The two largest warships ran aground on a shoal in the mouth of the harbor, becoming easy targets. (See *An Accurate Map of North and South Carolina, Detail #2.*)

Washington joyfully relayed the news in a letter a few weeks later, writing that "the enemy were obliged to sheer off with the loss of one frigate burnt, the two ships-of-the-line almost totally ruined and the frigates much shattered and the bomb-ketch unfit for further service until she can go into dock. They lost about 170 men killed besides a number wounded. During the whole action our men behaved with the greatest coolness and spirit and lost only ten killed and seventeen wounded, seven mortally." Colonel William Moultrie, whose leadership helped the Americans withstand the bombardment, was soon promoted to brigadier general and the fort was renamed in his honor.[10]

Clinton returned to New York aboard Parker's battered fleet to participate in the British landing in Brooklyn in August. During the next two and a half years, the contest in the North became the focus of the war. Then, in the fall of 1778, British strategy again involved the South—and Charleston was again a likely target. Washington wrote to Major General Benjamin Lincoln in October 1778, saying that "Congress have determined on measures for securing Charleston, in case the enemy should form an expedition against it, and have appointed you to command there."[11] To help instill the new professionalism gained at Valley Forge in the southern army, Congress also sent Lieutenant Colonel Jean-Baptiste de Ternant southward as inspector of the armies for Georgia and South Carolina.* At the end of November he wrote to Washington from the banks of the Ogeechee River in Georgia, giving him a geographical overview of the war in the southeastern states.

"My dear General . . . If you open your atlas you will see that the Savannah River forms the border between Georgia and South Carolina, and that on this river one finds the capital city and 150 miles further inland, Fort Augusta. The St. Marys River forms the line of demarcation on the enemy frontier" (the border between southeast Georgia and northeast Florida). "Between these two borders flow half a dozen rivers of considerable size . . . Since the beginning of the War of Independence, the Floridians have not ceased to make incursions into this state and annually to narrow its borders. Now they have annexed everything southwest of the Altamaha River."[12] (See *An Accurate Map of North and South Carolina, Detail #3.* See also *A General Map of North America, Detail #4,* page 163. On the right, center, the Altamaha

River is labeled *Alatamacha* and the St. Mary's River is slightly to the south.)

Ternant went on to describe the two-pronged invasion of southeastern Georgia in mid-November 1778 launched by General Augustine Prevost, the British commander at St. Augustine, in East Florida. Lieutenant Colonel Lewis Fuser marched up the coast, while Prevost's younger brother, Lieutenant Colonel James Marcus Prevost, proceeded to the interior, and they were to rendezvous at Sunbury, then the second largest port in Georgia, twenty-five miles southwest of Savannah. After seizing the American fort at Sunbury (later called Fort Morris), Fuser and Prevost were to wait for Lieutenant Colonel Archibald Campbell, dispatched by Clinton from New York City with three thousand troops, to march north and capture Savannah.

Fuser reached the fort, but Prevost never arrived. After a scorched-earth campaign around the town of Midway, ten miles west of the fort, he marched to the Ogeechee River, only fifteen miles from the capital, but, convinced by a false report that a large American force was at his rear, he suddenly retreated to Florida. Without a credible force to threaten the fort, Fuser retreated too, ending the nearly successful foray into Georgia.[13] (See ***A Map of South Carolina and a Part of Georgia, Detail #2***, page 163. The fort at Sunbury was on the southern shore of the Medway River, bottom center. The Ogeechee River, labeled *Hogohechie*, is ten miles north of Sunbury and fifteen miles south of Savannah.)

Lincoln, recently appointed by Congress to command the Southern Department, reported to Washington that the British "retreated over the Altamaha River," and "they plundered Negroes and cattle, etc. to a considerable amount. I am not able to learn whether they have left the state or not . . . There are some reasons to suppose they expected to act in conjunction with a body from New York."[14]

Lincoln had been directed by Congress to invade East Florida, and in mid-December Edward Rutledge noted the strategic value of St. Augustine in a letter to Washington. "The reduction of the place is certainly of importance to the more southern states, as it affords assistance to the Indians and a place of refuge to a banditti called the Florida Scout, who are committing continual depredations on the frontiers, and as they live by plunder, it is not to be supposed that they will cease their incursions till Augustine is our own." All plans for Lincoln's offensive were scrapped, however, when the British finally won a victory in the South, capturing Savannah on December 29.[15]

Lincoln reported to Washington that on the 25th he received word at Charleston "that the enemy had arrived with upwards of twenty ships at Tybee, near the mouth of the Savannah River, and in a harbor south of the river. The few troops at Charles-Town were immediately put in motion, and marched for Georgia." After leaving New York City and dropping down to Sandy Hook on November 7, Campbell with his three thousand troops had finally set sail for Georgia almost three weeks later, arriving off Tybee Island on December 23. On his way to Georgia, Lincoln received a message from Major General Robert Howe "informing that on the morning of the 29th the enemy landed in force a little below the town of Savannah" at Brewton Hill.

Even without the expected cooperation of Fuser and Prevost, Campbell outnumbered Howe's 850 Continentals and militia more than three to one. Howe ordered a retreat when Campbell maneuvered to surround them, but the British took almost five hundred prisoners as they captured Savannah. Howe took his remaining troops across the Savannah River and met up with Lincoln at Purrysburg, South Carolina, about twenty miles north of Savannah, where they regrouped, assembling a force of some fifteen hundred men.

"As soon as a body of men equal to covering the state of Georgia can be collected, we shall re-cross the Savannah," Lincoln told Washington. "It ought to be with a respectable force, for the communication with this state is frequently cut off by the Savannah's overflowing its banks, which renders the causeways impassible in boats or otherwise."

The British had opened their southern campaign in earnest, and the topography of the region would play a major role. Lincoln lamented to Washington that "the country abounds with navigable rivers, all of which the enemy command, and through which they can at any time fall in our rear." The Savannah River was rapidly becoming both the main battlefront and a buffer zone separating the two armies while they maneuvered for advantage before the next battle.[16] (See ***A Map of South Carolina and a Part of Georgia, Detail #3***.)

General Augustine Prevost arrived in Savannah from Florida with a thousand troops and sent Campbell up the Savannah River to recruit Loyalists. At Augusta he gained fourteen hundred volunteers. However, moving around the British left flank north of Augusta, the Americans won a small victory in the Georgia backcountry on February 14, 1779, at the Battle of Kettle Creek, when American militiamen tracked down and defeated an encampment of seven hundred Loyalists marching eastward to meet Campbell at Augusta. And when Lincoln assembled an American force of some twenty-five hundred men across the river from Augusta, Prevost ordered Campbell to retreat to Savannah.

"I congratulate you most cordially on Campbell's precipitate retreat from Fort Augusta," Washington wrote to Henry Laurens, a delegate to Congress from South Carolina, on March 20. "What was it owing to? It seems to have been a surprise even upon [Brigadier General Andrew] Williamson [of the Georgia Militia].

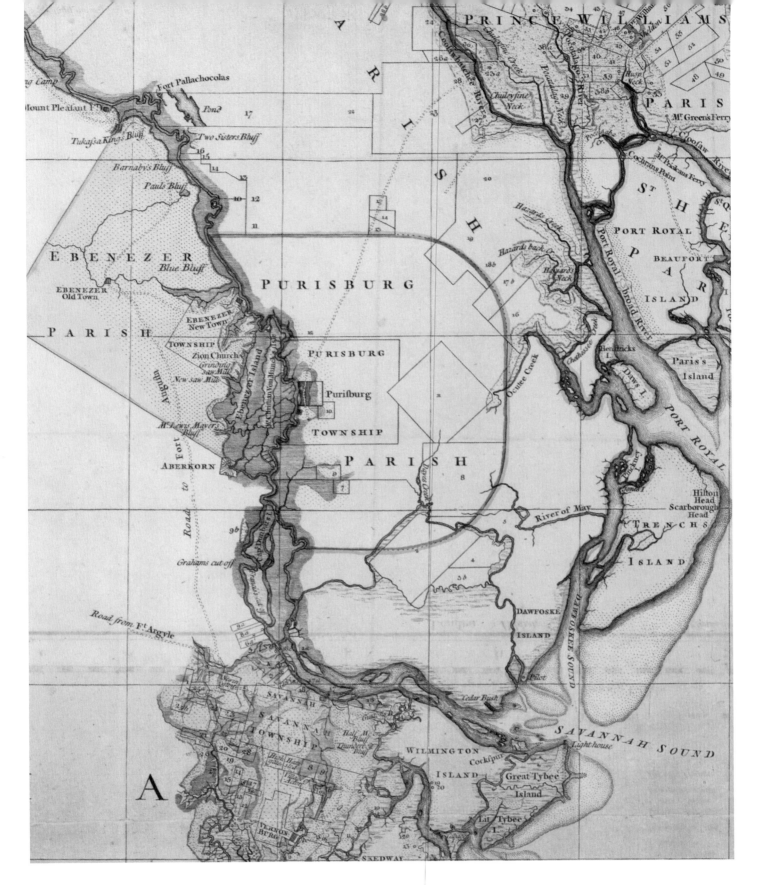

But I rejoice much more on account of his disappointed application to the Creek Indians. This I think is to be considered as a very important event, and may it not be the conjectural cause of his (Campbell's) hasty return? This latter circumstance cannot but be a fresh proof to the disaffected (in that country) that they are leaning upon a broken reed. Severe examples should, in my judgment, be made of those who were forgiven former offenses and [are] again in arms against us."

As Campbell moved his force down the west side of the Savannah River, James Marcus Prevost moved up to support him and launched a stunning surprise attack on the Americans at Brier Creek on March 3. With four hundred killed and wounded, the Americans were forced to

cede extensive territory to the British. [17] (See *An Accurate Map of North and South Carolina, Detail #3*, page 167. "Bryar Creek" is shown on the left, center, flowing southeast into the Savannah River. The battle took place in the area near the mouth of Brier Creek.)

"The relief of the southern states appears to me an object of the greatest magnitude and what may lead to still more important advantages," Washington wrote to Gouverneur Morris on May 8.* "I feel infinite anxiety on their account. Their internal weakness, disaffection, the want of energy, the general languor that has seized the people at large makes me apprehend the most serious consequences. It would seem too, as if the enemy meant to transfer the principal weight of the war that way . . .

A Map of South Carolina and a Part of Georgia, Detail #3: Campbell arrived off Great Tybee Island (lower right) just below the mouth of the Savannah River. After Campbell captured Savannah, the Americans retreated across the river to South Carolina and regrouped at Purrysburg (*Purisburg*, center) twenty miles to the north.

* Beginning in January 1778, Morris served as a delegate to Congress from New York but did not win reelection in 1779.

Charleston it is likely will feel the next stroke. This, if it succeeds, will leave the enemy [in] full possession of Georgia by obliging us to collect our forces for the defense of South Carolina and will consequently open new sources [of] men and supplies."[18]

Indeed, Prevost marched to Charleston in June 1779 and demanded the surrender of the city. The governor of South Carolina tried to strike a bargain: The state would remain neutral if the city were left alone. Prevost declined but had to withdraw since Lincoln's forces were bearing down on him. A rear guard skirmish ensued at Stono Ferry on June 19.[19] "We have accounts of a late attack made by you on the enemy at Stono, which did not end so happily as might have been wished," Washington wrote to Lincoln, "but we have some subsequent rumors of a more agreeable complexion . . . that a detachment sent by you from Charlestown had taken possession of James Island, the troops upon which had been drawn off to reinforce Prevost at the time of your attack, and that you were in a fair way of interrupting by the help of your galleys the communication of the enemy on the main with their shipping."[20] Correspondence traveled slowly, and two months later, Washington wrote: "The details you give me of your attack upon Stono Ferry are obliging and satisfactory . . . I have no doubt that the attempt had a good effect and at least accelerated the retreat of the enemy."[21] (See *A Map of South Carolina and a Part of Georgia, Detail #4*.)

The royal governor returned to Savannah on July 14, 1779, and Georgia became the only state to officially return to colonial status, but exempt from taxation. Washington was convinced the British would "make another and more vigorous effort to the Southward

A Map of South Carolina and a Part of Georgia, Detail #4: Lincoln speeded Prevost's retreat from Charleston (upper right) by engaging his rear guard at Stono Ferry (not shown), which connected Johns Island (center right) with the mainland near St. Paul's Church (center). James Island is shown on the right, center.

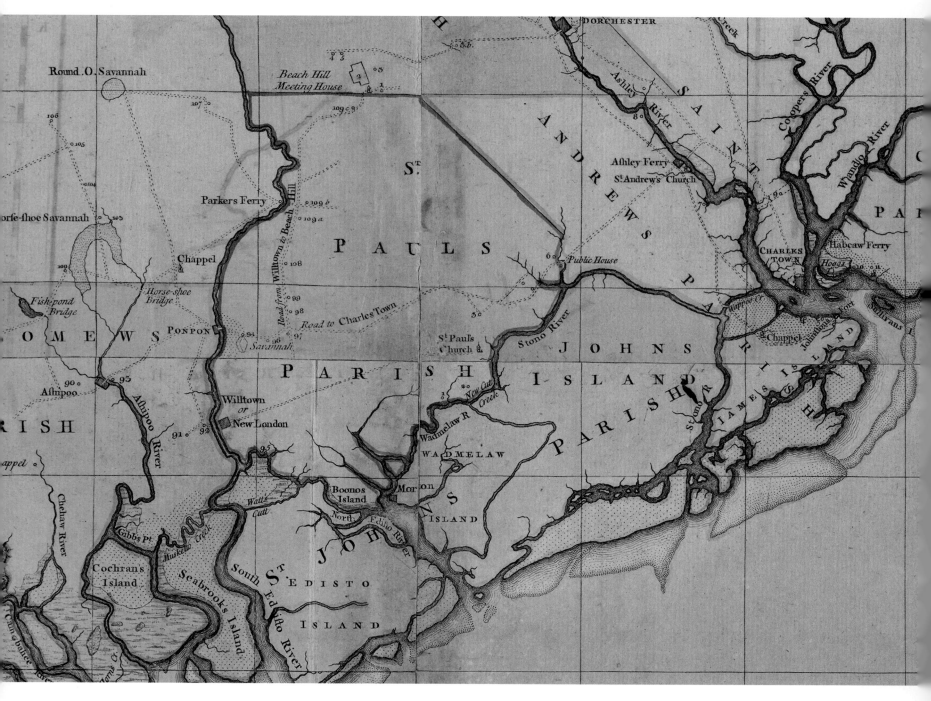

this campaign. They have very powerful motives to it. The full possession of Georgia and the acquisition of South Carolina would be a good counterpoise to their losses in the Islands . . . Southern operations appear to have been for some time past a favorite object in the British cabinet. The weakness of the southern states affords a strong temptation; the advantages are important and inviting, and even the desperate aspect of their affairs itself may inspire a spirit of enterprise."[22]

On October 1, 1779, Washington was delighted to inform Governor Clinton that he had news of "the arrival of Count d'Estaing on the Coast of Georgia" and of "his intention to attack the enemy on the 9th" at Savannah. D'Estaing had spent eight months fighting the British in the West Indies but had finally returned in force. "This agreeable news gives us hope [for] the effectual deliverance of the southern states," Washington wrote. But the joint operation would be a fiasco. On September 12, d'Estaing had landed 3,500 troops at Beaulieu's Plantation on the Vernon River eight miles south of the city, and they were joined a few days later by 1,500 Americans under Lincoln. (See *A Map of South Carolina and a Part of Georgia, Detail #2*, page 163. The Vernon River is shown at the center, directly south of Savannah.) When they demanded surrender, however, Prevost stalled long enough to pull in several detachments from outside Savannah and then refused to capitulate. On the 23rd, the allies began the laborious process of digging trenches and laying siege to the city. "Our batteries of 38 heavy pieces of cannon and 8 mortars would be in readiness to open on the 2nd or 3rd of October and there was every appearance of reducing the place in the course of five or six days," Washington enthused as word reached him at West Point.[23] Then came the bad news.

"It would appear that there was a necessity for the Count's returning to the West Indies, which made it impracticable to spend that time before the works of Savannah requisite to carry them by regular approach," Washington told Jonathan Trumbull. "This induced the allied arms to hazard the reduction of the place by assault." The British threat to the French sugar islands pressured the French to maintain a strong fleet in the West Indies. On October 9, the Americans and French tried and failed to storm the heavily fortified city and suffered 752 casualties. "The Count d'Estaing was slightly wounded in the leg and arm; and General Pulaski died a few days after of his wounds. The allied officers and men behaved with great bravery and spirit," Washington wrote.

While making clear that the decision to storm the works was driven by d'Estaing, Washington also asked that the information be kept private as long as possible, in order to contain potential damage to the alliance with France. "The disaster at Savannah puts matters at least on a delicate footing in the South," Washington remarked to Schuyler. "I do not know what we can do." With General Henry Clinton concentrating British forces in and around New York City, and with "all prospect of a cooperation with the French fleet ceasing," Washington hunkered down in the Hudson Highlands for the winter.[24]

To build on the British success at Savannah, Henry Clinton embarked a large force at New York at the end of December 1779 and sailed south to besiege Charleston, South Carolina. The fleet was beset by stormy weather, which prolonged the voyage, and left Washington to speculate as to its destination. He suspected the Carolinas were the target, but Clinton might also have been headed to Florida, where the Spanish were threatening British territory. Spain hoped to weaken or destroy the British Empire, its longtime rival, without encouraging rebellion in its own New World domains. Buying time to prepare themselves militarily, the Spanish had declared themselves neutral while selling supplies to the Americans covertly. When the Spanish finally declared war on England, in June 1779, they declined to recognize the United States as an independent nation.[25]

On February 27, 1780, Washington told Lincoln he had just received word from Don Juan de Miralles—a Cuban merchant who became the de facto Spanish ambassador to the United States—enclosing "accounts from the governor of Havana of the success of the Spaniards in the Floridas." In September, the Spanish had captured the forts at Manshac, Baton Rouge, and Natchez on the lower Mississippi River and were planning attacks on Mobile and Pensacola. All of these posts were in British West Florida. (See *Course of the Mississippi River, Detail,* page 172.) For Mobile and Pensacola, see the Gulf Coast on *A General Map of North America, Detail #4,* page 163.)

Washington hoped the Spanish challenge in the Floridas would draw the British away from their conquest of the southern states. Conversely, Miralles hoped Washington would create a diversion, attacking the British in Georgia to keep them from reinforcing their posts in the Floridas. Washington told Miralles he would coordinate with the Spanish, unless the British attacked the Carolinas, in which case Lincoln's forces would be tied down there.[26]

Not until the middle of April did Washington receive a letter from Lincoln (dated February 23) announcing "the arrival and progress of Sir Henry Clinton to Stono," the Stono River, just south of Charleston (where Lincoln had attacked Prevost's rear guard at the ferry in 1779). Determined not to repeat the failure of his attack in 1776, Clinton landed his troops at the North Edisto Inlet and marched to James Island, taking Fort Johnson and using the island as a staging area. He then moved to cut off the city by land in addition to attacking from the harbor.[27] (See *A Map of South Carolina and a Part of Georgia, Detail #4.* The North Edisto River is at the bottom center; James Island and Fort Johnson are on the right, center.)

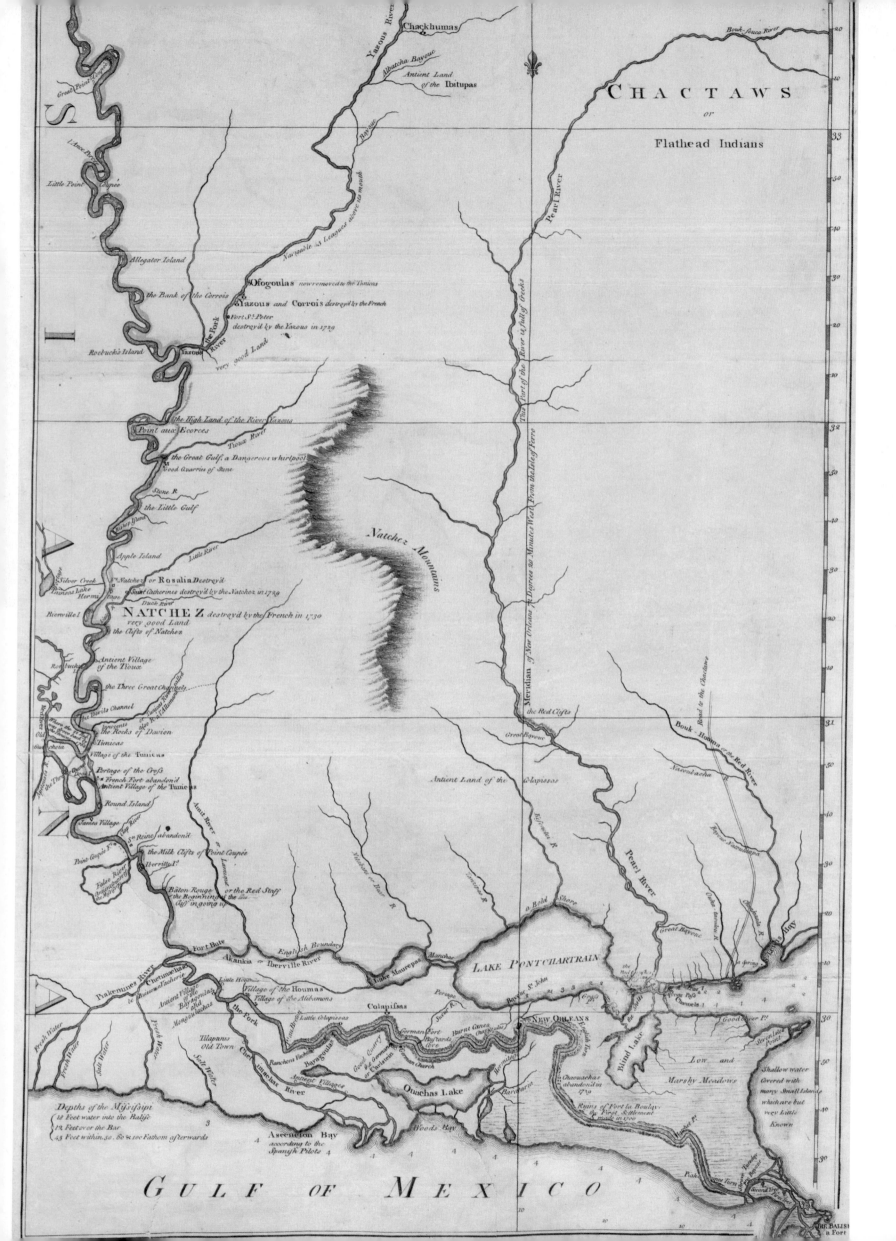

ABOVE: Charleston under siege, March 1780.

OPPOSITE: *Course of the Mississippi River, Detail:* British West Florida consisted of the east bank of the lower Mississippi River and the coast of the Gulf of Mexico west of the Florida peninsula. The Spanish captured Manshac, Baton Rouge, and Natchez. Manshac is on the lower Mississippi, just west of Lake Pontchartrain. Baton Rouge is west and north of Manshac, and Natchez is further north. New Orleans appears on the bend in the river directly below Lake Pontchartrain. The city came under Spanish control in 1763 and became an important source of supplies for the Americans during the Revolution.

* John Laurens, the son of Henry Laurens, had served as an aide to Washington before he was elected to the South Carolina House of Representatives. He was in Charleston during the siege.

"My apprehensions, after all, are principally for the harbor," Washington told Lincoln. "If this is secured, the operations against you must become critical and arduous." On the other hand, "If they succeed against Charleston, there is much reason to believe the southern states will become the principal theater of the war."[28] Ten days later Washington told John Laurens, "The impracticability of defending the bar, I fear, amounts to the loss of the town and garrison . . . Since your last to me I have received one from General Lincoln of the 24th of March, in which he informs me that the enemy had gotten a sixty-four gun ship with a number of other vessels over the bar and that it had been determined to abandon the project of disputing the passage by Sullivan's Island, and to draw up the frigates to the town and take out their cannon. This brings your affairs nearer to a dangerous crisis, and increases my apprehensions."[29]* (See *An Accurate Map of North and South Carolina, Detail #2*, page 166. Washington had clearly hoped for a repetition of 1776, when the British fleet was stopped at the mouth of the harbor.)

"I have letters from General Lincoln up to the 9th of April," Washington told Robert Howe on May 5. "The enemy had then broken ground upon the neck of Charleston, about 1100 yards from our works. General Woodford, with the Virginia troops [arrived on] the 7th, which gave great spirits to the garrison. The [British] ships passed Fort Moultrie with the loss of one transport, but the communication was still open with the country by the Cooper River, which communication General Lincoln hoped to preserve by obstructing the mouth of the river."[30]

An American cavalry unit under Brigadier General Isaac Huger "was surprised by the enemy and sustained the loss of 20 men and 30 horses," James Duane wrote to Washington on May 9, adding that "this success enabled the enemy to head Cooper River, and take post on the north side, and that it will eventually complete the blockade of the town."[31] (See *A Map of South Carolina and a Part of Georgia, Detail #4*, page 170. The Charleston peninsula, between the Ashley and Cooper rivers, is on the upper left.)

Charleston fell to the British on May 12, 1780, the Americans' worst defeat of the war. "This is a severe blow, but not such as will ruin us, if we exert ourselves virtuously and as we are able," Washington wrote to James Bowdoin several weeks later. "Something like it seems to have been necessary to rouse us from the more than thrice unaccountable state of security in which we were sunk. Heaven grant the blow may have this effect. If it should, the misfortune may prove a benefit and the means of saving us."[32]

After capturing Charleston, Clinton asserted British authority across South Carolina with a series of military outposts, which prompted many Americans to profess loyalty to the king. Clinton also offered to pardon all rebels who would lay down their arms, and most obeyed, suggesting that peace and stability would follow. However, on June 3, 1780, Clinton revised his initial proclamation and demanded that citizens prove their loyalty by taking "an active part in settling and securing His Majesty's government," in order to be pardoned. By forbidding Americans to remain quietly neutral, Clinton polarized the population and set the stage for civil war in the Carolinas. Rushing back to defend New York City against a possible attack by a French fleet, Clinton left Cornwallis in charge of the explosive situation.

Washington had received word from Lafayette a few weeks earlier and Clinton had learned through intelligence reports that the comte de Rochambeau, a lieutenant general leading six thousand troops, had set sail from Brest aboard a fleet of eight ships commanded by the chevalier de Ternay. After the failure of Franco-American cooperation under d'Estaing, a new phase of the alliance had begun. On July 10 Rochambeau and Ternay arrived at Newport and established themselves in the harbor, abandoned by Clinton in preparation for his southern campaign.

During the course of the summer, Loyalist and Whig partisans in the South fought some two dozen battles, marked by unbridled violence that cast aside the conventions of eighteenth-century warfare between regular troops. Loyalists took their cue from Colonel Banastre Tarleton and his saber-wielding cavalrymen, who had reportedly slaughtered more than 250 Continental troops, many of whom had already surrendered, at Waxhaws on May 29.* Led by Colonel Thomas Sumter, "the Carolina Gamecock," and General Francis Marion, "the Swamp Fox," among others, the Whigs took revenge. Expecting to find a silent majority of Loyalists, draw them out, and stifle the rebellion in the South, the British instead had pitted neighbor against neighbor in a bloody cycle of mutual recrimination and retribution.[33]

Washington was clearly frustrated that the Americans' conventional military force in the South had been swept away and replaced by scattered partisan warfare and that he had few resources to support these efforts. He wrote to Congress in August that "from all the accounts we receive from thence the affairs of the southern states seem to be so exceedingly disordered, and their resources so much exhausted, that whatever should be undertaken there, must chiefly depend on the means carried from hence. If these fail we shall be condemned to a disgraceful and fatal inactivity." He promised that "if any efforts of mine can enable us to act with vigor, either here or elsewhere, it certainly shall be done. But there is a complication of embarrassments that menace us on every side with disappointment."[34]

"The situation of America at this time is critical, the government without finances, its paper credit sunk," Washington told the comte de Guichen on September 12, 1780.† And the military picture was equally grim: Sir Henry Clinton controlled New York City and much of New York State; the Indians were harassing the western frontier; and to the south Cornwallis, with some eight thousand men, controlled Georgia and South Carolina, while a third state, North Carolina, was "by recent misfortunes at his mercy." Washington had learned from General Gates that on August 16, "attempting to penetrate and regain the state of South Carolina, he met with a total defeat near Camden, in which many of his troops have been cut off and the remainder dispersed, with the loss of all their cannon and baggage." (See **An Accurate Map of North and South Carolina, Detail #4,** page 176.)[35]

Making matters worse, a second division of French troops, expected at Newport, never departed from France because the British fleet had managed to blockade the port of Brest. The French fleet already at Newport was also immobilized by a powerful British squadron stationed nearby.[36] On September 15, 1780, Washington wrote to Congress that the aim in the South should be to assemble a force of five or six thousand regulars, not a large force of militia, and to use the regulars to contain the British, while waiting until the French arrived to finally expel the enemy.[37]

Another aspect of the war in the South was also brewing. At the end of September Washington made a shocking announcement. Writing to General William Heath from the Hudson Highlands, Washington revealed news "which will strike you with astonishment and indignation. Major General Arnold has gone to the enemy." Placed in charge of West Point at his own request as he recovered from an injury to his leg, Arnold had turned over the plans of the fort and other vital information to the British. Washington explained to Congress how Arnold, learning that his handler, Major John André, had been

General Francis Marion.

* The Americans lost 113 killed and 203 captured, all of the latter wounded, most of them severely. Only about 100 infantry and a few horsemen escaped. Tarleton claimed that his horse was shot out from under him just when the Americans sent in a flag of truce; he did not receive the flag, and his men fought on vengefully, thinking their leader had been killed.

† Guichen had recently arrived in the West Indies with a powerful fleet to replace d'Estaing, who had returned to France.

Colonel Banastre Tarleton.

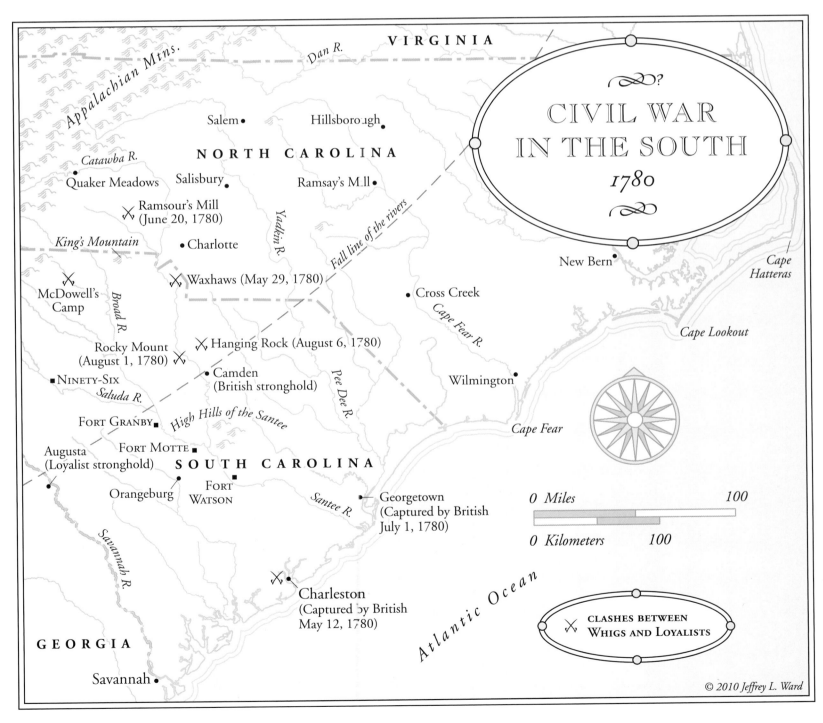

VIRGINIA

Dan R.

Appalachian Mtns.

CIVIL WAR IN THE SOUTH
1780

Salem •   Hillsborough •

NORTH CAROLINA

Catawba R.

Quaker Meadows •   Salisbury •   Ramsay's Mill •

✕ Ramsour's Mill
(June 20, 1780)

Yadkin R.

Fall line of the rivers

King's Mountain   • Charlotte

New Bern •   *Cape Hatteras*

✕ Waxhaws (May 29, 1780)

McDowell's
Camp

Broad R.

• Cross Creek

Cape Fear R.

Cape Lookout

✕ Hanging Rock (August 6, 1780)

Rocky Mount
(August 1, 1780) ✕

Pee Dee R.

• Camden
(British stronghold)

Wilmington •

■ NINETY-SIX

Saluda R.

High Hills of the Santee

FORT GRANBY ■

Augusta
(Loyalist stronghold)   FORT MOTTE ■

Cape Fear

SOUTH CAROLINA

Orangeburg •   FORT
WATSON

Santee R.   — Georgetown
(Captured by British
July 1, 1780)

0 *Miles*   100

0 *Kilometers*   100

✕ Charleston
(Captured by British
May 12, 1780)

Atlantic Ocean

GEORGIA

✕ CLASHES BETWEEN
WHIGS AND LOYALISTS

Savannah •

© 2010 Jeffrey L. Ward

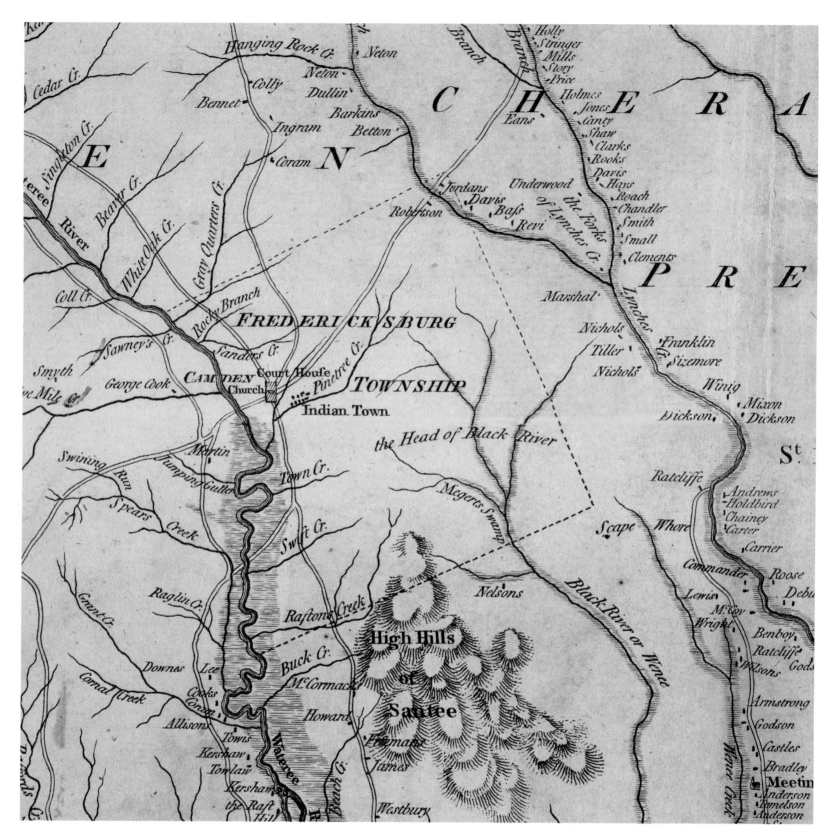

An Accurate Map of North and South Carolina, Detail #4: On August 16, 1780, Gates was defeated by the British five miles north of Camden, South Carolina. Camden is shown in the middle of the state, northwest of the High Hills of Santee. The battlefield straddled the road just north of Sanders Creek. After the battle, Cornwallis was rewarded by London with more autonomy. Following his own plans instead of Clinton's, Cornwallis would mismanage the southern theater of the war disastrously, leading some to observe that the victory at Camden cost the British the war.

LEFT: General Nathanael Greene.

OPPOSITE: *An Accurate Map of North and South Carolina, Detail #5:* Descending from the mountains before the battle, the frontiersmen rendezvoused at Quaker Meadows (top left corner.) King's Mountain (upper center) straddles the border between the Carolinas east of the Appalachians and west of Charlotte, labeled *Charlottesburg.*

BELOW: *An Accurate Map of North and South Carolina, Detail #6:* While Morgan moved south toward Ninety Six (top left to left center), Greene moved the rest of his army south and east to the Great Pee Dee River (right center) in the Cheraws Precinct. Dividing his force made it easier for each component to live off the land. Greene had maps made of the crossing points on the Catawba and Yadkin rivers (top center and upper right) to ensure that the smaller, more nimble American forces would be able to outmaneuver Cornwallis and his four thousand troops (*EAR,* 2:1076).

"[Major General Alexander] Leslie and his detachment having landed at Charleston, was marching to form a junction with Cornwallis," Washington reported to the comte de Rochambeau. Greene, who "had previously established a post on the south side of the Catawba near the forks of the Broad River to straiten the limits of the enemy and cover the upper country . . . had taken a new position . . . which gives him the command of a country more abundant in itself and less exhausted by military operations."[44]

Washington had tremendous confidence in Greene's abilities, followed his campaign closely, and expressed approval. "From the general idea I have been able to acquire of the country, by maps, as well as from the description you give of it, and its resources, your position at Cheraws, on the east side of the Pee Dee River seems to have been very judiciously chosen. The motives for detaching Brigadier General Morgan, and the objects given him in charge, appear also to be supported upon just military principles," namely, containing the enemy and preventing him from taking the offensive until American forces in the South could be built up.[45]

(See *An Accurate Map of North and South Carolina, Detail #5*, page 178.) In North Carolina the Catawba River flows east out of the Appalachians and turns south, descending between King's Mountain and Charlotte into South Carolina, upper right to right center. In order to contain the British to the south, Greene originally established a post just below the state boundary, southwest of the Catawba River and northeast of the forks of the Broad River, center. Greene also dispatched Morgan to threaten Ninety Six, bottom left corner. The settlement at Ninety Six was so named because it was on a path to Cherokee territory and was supposed to be ninety-six miles from their nearest village, Keowee. See also *An Accurate Map of North and South Carolina, Detail #6*, page 179.)

In late December 1780 and early January 1781, Benedict Arnold had sailed from New York to Virginia and made an "incursion to Richmond," Washington told Rochambeau. "He burnt there some public and private stores and buildings, a foundry and some other public works in the vicinity, and afterwards retired to Westover, where he first landed, five and twenty miles

from Richmond . . . Virginia, intersected as it is with large navigable rivers, is greatly exposed to those kinds of predatory expeditions. Nor is there any remedy against them but a naval superiority."[46] By making inroads in Virginia, the British threatened to isolate Greene to the south, cutting him off from reinforcement from the North. (See *A Map of . . . Virginia, Detail #6*.) Washington hoped a joint operation with the French against New York City would force Clinton to withdraw troops from the South, but this would take time. To provide immediate relief for Greene—and to capture Arnold—Washington dispatched the marquis de Lafayette southward with twelve hundred men.

Cornwallis meanwhile had stopped retreating and moved north again, positioning his army between Greene and Morgan, while dispatching Tarleton and his legion to protect Ninety Six against Morgan and destroy his detachment. After retreating to Cowpens, a crossroads near the North Carolina border, Morgan was reinforced by local militia, and he turned to face Tarleton's eleven hundred troops with a comparable force on January 17. Morgan avoided Gates's mistake at Camden of deploying the militia without Continentals directly behind them for support. Instead, he lured Tarleton into a trap by having the militia fire two volleys and then retreat: Advancing over the crest of a hill, the British were surprised by an American cavalry charge and a line of disciplined veterans, who blasted away at close range. A third defensive line and a reserve of cavalry clinched Morgan's victory, which cost Tarleton more than one hundred killed and eight hundred captured, two hundred of them wounded, and sent American morale soaring.[47] (See *An Accurate Map of North and South Carolina, Detail #5*, page 178. The battle at Cowpens took place in the area south and west of King's Mountain between the Pacolet and Broad rivers near Thicketty Creek, labeled *Thickelle*.)

"General Morgan's signal victory over Colonel Tarleton, with the flower of the British army, reflects the highest honor upon our arms," Washington told Congress, "and I hope will at least be attended with this advantage, that it will check the offensive operations of the enemy until General Greene shall have collected a much more

respectable force." However, Washington also worried that the battle would breed complacency in the South, and he urged a continued drive to "crush an enemy pretty severely shaken by the two successful strokes upon Ferguson and Tarleton."[48]

For the moment, however, Greene and Morgan could only retreat northward, since Cornwallis was positioned between them and had burned his own supply wagons to travel swiftly in furious pursuit of Morgan. "Our last advices from General Greene are of the 31st January," Washington told Lincoln. "Lord Cornwallis with 2,500 men entirely divested of baggage had made a push against General Morgan and was near recovering the prisoners taken upon the 17th January, but General Morgan got them off and they had crossed the Yadkin on their way to Virginia." Greene's and Morgan's forces rendezvoused at Guilford Court House in North Carolina on February 8. (See *An Accurate Map of North and South Carolina, Detail #7*.) "Lord Cornwallis was still advancing, and General Greene studiously avoiding an engagement," Washington wrote. "I am very anxious for the issue of this maneuver, which may be productive of the most important consequences."[49]

In March Washington was relieved to learn that Greene and Morgan had escaped into Virginia and put the Dan River between themselves and the British. Cornwallis had given up the chase and headed toward Hillsborough, North Carolina. Washington told Greene he was delighted "that you had saved all of your baggage, artillery, and stores notwithstanding the hot pursuit of the enemy and that you in turn were following them." The spectacle of Greene running Cornwallis ragged was "highly applauded by all ranks and reflects much honor on your military abilities."[50] Nonetheless, with Cornwallis retreating, Greene advancing, and the militia rallying to his side, Washington was apprehensive because he could not fathom Cornwallis's larger intentions. "The situation of things there and in Virginia is critical and big with important events," he told Schuyler. "God grant that they may be favorable to us."[51]

Ten days later, Washington wrote to Rochambeau, relaying the details of a battle fought between Greene and Cornwallis on March 15, 1781, at Guilford Court House. While "the enemy may have won the glory of maintaining the field of battle," Washington wrote, their five hundred casualties were almost twice those of the Americans. The dead detracted from Cornwallis's force, and the wounded would hamper "his future movements and operations." Greene had made clear to Washington before the battle that this was precisely his intention.[52]

At the same time, the middle of March, Lafayette had arrived in Virginia. He was supposed to cooperate with a French squadron from Newport, but a British squadron had driven it out of Chesapeake Bay. Clinton had sent General William Phillips from New York with 2,600 men, and he had looted Petersburg. On April 29 Lafayette arrived in Richmond, preventing Phillips from burning it too. "I hope the advance of the Marquis de la Fayette with the choice body of Continental troops under his command will check the progress of General Phillips," Washington told Governor Thomas Jefferson, assuring him that as soon as further dispatches arrived from the Court of France, the allies would be able to "settle a plan of campaign," and "every attention shall be paid to the relief of the southern states." [53]

Because published maps lacked local detail, and because letters could be exchanged no faster than men on horseback could travel on bad roads, Washington periodically lost direct contact with his generals in the South. In mid-May he asked the Baron von Steuben (who oversaw an encampment with Lafayette's supplies in Virginia) to forward

intelligence reports to Greene and Lafayette, because "my uncertainty of the position of either of them prevents my writing immediately to them."[54*]

Cornwallis's force was not only bloodied at Guilford Court House but had also run out of food, spurring him to march eastward to the Atlantic coast at Wilmington, North Carolina, where the British navy could bring him supplies. Greene headed south, forcing Cornwallis to choose between his drive northward and defending British-occupied areas in South Carolina and Georgia. Cornwallis made the conquest of Virginia his priority, and by May 20 had marched north and joined forces with Phillips at Petersburg. With British troop strength in Virginia now at seven thousand, Lafayette was heavily outnumbered. He decided to skirmish whenever possible and avoid a major battle, while retreating north to the Rapidan River to gather reinforcements. Unable to catch Lafayette, in early June Cornwallis dispatched Tarleton to raid Charlottesville, where he captured seven of the state's assemblymen and Governor Jefferson barely escaped.[55] (See *A Map of . . . Virginia, Detail #6*, page 181. Petersburg is on the lower left; the "Rapid Anne" is in the upper left; and Charlottesville, not shown, is northwest of Richmond in the foothills of the Blue Ridge Mountains.)

Cornwallis had entrusted the defense of South Carolina and Georgia to Lord Francis Rawdon, who commanded eight thousand troops—mostly in Loyalist units—spread out at small, far-flung outposts in those two states. "The project you had adopted of endeavoring to transfer the war [southward] has many favorable sides," Washington had told Greene on April 22. I am persuaded you have adopted it on sound principles."[56] Indeed, the strategy soon produced dramatic results.

On April 23, Fort Watson fell to General Francis Marion and Colonel Henry Lee, Washington told Rochambeau. Two days later, at Hobkirk's Hill, just north of Camden, Rawdon drove Greene's forces back a few miles but suffered greater losses than the Americans. The battle prompted Rawdon to begin evacuating Camden and consolidating his forces at Charleston. "If Lord Cornwallis does not march to the relief of his frontier posts in South Carolina," Washington predicted, "more of them will probably fall."[57]

On May 2, Washington wrote to Francisco Rendon, a Spanish agent, congratulating him on the recapture of Fort San Juan de Nicaragua, and expressing hope for "further and more important successes against the British at Pensacola." A week later, the British garrison at Pensacola surrendered to Louisiana governor Bernardo de Galvez after a prolonged siege, giving the Spanish control of West Florida. Washington had been eagerly awaiting this development for more than a year (since de Galvez had captured Mobile in March 1780), and now confirmation of the news and full details of the battle at Pensacola would take additional months to reach him.[58]

By mid-May, the Americans under Greene, Sumter, Marion, and Lee were rolling back the British occupation. Washington noted to Heath that "while Lord Cornwallis is playing this strange game in Virginia, General Greene is depriving him of all the posts he had occupied in South Carolina." These included Camden, Fort Motte, Fort Granby, and Orangeburg, Washington wrote. "At the same time, the posts of Augusta and Ninety Six were invested by General Pickens," and Greene was marching his army to Georgia to hasten their surrender.[59] (See *Civil War in the South*, page 175, and *An Accurate Map of North and South Carolina, Detail #8*.)

On May 6, Rochambeau's son and the comte de Barras had both arrived in Boston on the French frigate *Concorde*, without the promised second division of French troops, but with good news nonetheless. The younger Rochambeau announced that Admiral François Joseph Paul de Grasse was on his way from Brest to the West Indies with a substantial fleet, from which he had dispatched transports to Newport with six hundred troops.[†] De Grasse's main mission was ostensibly to collaborate with the Spanish in attacking Jamaica. However, de Barras carried a secret letter for Rochambeau saying that de Grasse would come to the coast of North America during the Caribbean hurricane season—July through October. Presumably to maintain secrecy against British spies and to postpone a commitment to the Americans, Rochambeau did not reveal the news to Washington immediately, but he proposed a conference to decide what their next steps should be under current conditions.

They met at Wethersfield, Connecticut, on May 22 and reviewed the overall strategic picture. Clinton in New York had 10,500 troops and strong defenses, against Washington's 3,500 troops in the Hudson Highlands. The 5,000 French troops and the small fleet at Newport, now commanded by de Barras, were shut in by a British squadron between Block Island and Point Judith.[**] Greene was in the Carolinas, while Lafayette moved south to confront Cornwallis near Williamsburg. And, as in 1776 and 1777, British forces were again moving south from Canada on Lake Champlain, poised to invade northern New York.[60]

Washington proposed that Rochambeau march his forces west from Newport and that together they attack northern Manhattan as a prelude to retaking New York City. This made more sense, he said, than trying to march more men southward and lose many along the way. Rochambeau argued that after five years of British occupation New York was impregnable by land, and that French ships were shut out by the bar at Sandy Hook. Nonetheless, Rochambeau agreed to join forces on the Hudson to see what might be attempted. Still withholding de Grasse's news, Rochambeau spoke hypothetically of getting more naval support from the West Indies. Washington agreed that this would provide more and better options, so the

OPPOSITE: *An Accurate Map of North and South Carolina, Detail #8:* On the Santee and Congaree rivers in South Carolina, in a line stretching from southeast to northwest, stood Fort Watson, Fort Motte, and Fort Granby (not shown), which occupied strategic points on the British line of communications to the interior. On the Santee, sixty miles northwest of Charleston (right center), Fort Watson was a link to the city (bottom right). Fort Motte served as a depot at the confluence of the Congaree and Wateree rivers (top center). Similarly, Fort Granby, on the south bank of the Congaree near the mouth of the Saluda River (upper left), was a vital post, as was Orangeburg (center).

* At the time of the Revolution, it could take almost a month for a letter from New England to reach the South, and mail going northward could take even longer. In late 1781, news of the battle at Eutaw Springs, in South Carolina, did not reach Congress in Philadelphia for five weeks. News traveled faster by water, but it still took eight days for orders from Clinton in New York City to reach Cornwallis, some three hundred miles away, in Virginia (*EAR*, 1:242).

† Distracted by developments in the Mediterranean, the British had neglected to blockade de Grasse, as they had failed to stop d'Estaing's departure from Toulon three years earlier.

** Barras had assumed command of the French squadron at Newport from the chevalier Destouches, who had replaced Ternay when he died in December 1780.

Comte de Rochambeau.

British had the fewest ships at the time. New York was the best place to attack "under present circumstances," he told Rochambeau, but if the allies were able "to secure a naval superiority, we may perhaps find others more practicable and equally advisable."[64]

In Georgia, Fort Augusta had fallen to the Americans on June 5, but in South Carolina, Ninety Six still held out, because Rawdon had marched to it with reinforcements. "Thus are our affairs in [the South] situated at this momentous crisis," Washington declared on June 14 in a letter to General Heath, "when the eyes of the whole world are upon us, when the weakness of the enemy's most important posts in every part, and the dispersed state of their troops invites us, and when our own circumstances impel us to make one great effort in conjunction with our generous allies to drive our foes entirely from the continent."[65]

While Greene was retaking the Carolinas, Lafayette was reinforced by Wayne and Campbell at the South Anna River. With five thousand troops, he marched south again, ready to take on Cornwallis. On June 26, American and British units skirmished near Cornwallis's camp at Williamsburg. However, Clinton was less concerned about the war in Virginia than he was about the planned Franco-American attack on New York—discovered in an intercepted letter—and ordered Cornwallis to send him three thousand men. These troops would have to be embarked at Portsmouth, so on July 4 Cornwallis began crossing the James River at Greenspring, near Jamestown.

Lafayette sent Wayne with five hundred men to attack the British rear during the crossing, expecting to catch them off guard. Instead, Cornwallis had sent his baggage across first, and Wayne's detachment suffered heavy casualties trying to retreat from an engagement with the main British force. Arriving at Portsmouth, Cornwallis received word from Clinton saying he no longer needed the reinforcements. Instead, he ordered Cornwallis to take his army and establish a naval base at a port with water deep enough for the largest British ships. While Cornwallis embarked his troops for Yorktown, Lafayette took Williamsburg, setting the stage for a final confrontation.[66] (See *A Map of . . . Virginia, Detail #7.*)

two commanders resolved to urge de Grasse to come to Sandy Hook.[61]

Ten days later Washington wrote Greene that the allies had "finally determined to make an attempt upon New York with its present garrison in preference to a southern operation." In addition to the lack of a clear French naval advantage, Washington wrote, other considerations included "the inevitable loss of men from so long a march, more especially in the approaching hot season, and the difficulty, I may say impossibility, of transporting the necessary baggage, artillery, and stores by land." From the attack on New York City, he hoped that "one of these consequences will follow: The enemy will be expelled from the most valuable position which they hold upon the Continent or they will be obliged to recall part of their force from the southward to defend it. Should this happen, you will be most essentially relieved by it."[62]

However, as Washington wrote this, the chevalier de La Luzerne, the French minister in America, was advising Rochambeau and Barras—and Rochambeau was advising de Grasse—that the Chesapeake would be a far better choice than New York. Rochambeau told Washington that he had submitted both plans to de Grasse, suggesting he attack the British naval force in the Chesapeake first and then come to New York, bringing more troops, along with hard money from the West Indies to finance continued French operations in America.[63]

Then, on June 13, Washington received confirmation of the momentous news already circulating unofficially in Congress. In a letter from de Grasse, forwarded by Rochambeau, Washington learned that the admiral had arrived safely in the West Indies with twenty-five ships and would bring them to North America in mid-July. Where he would arrive and how long he would stay remained to be seen. Washington became less fixated on New York and urged that de Grasse go wherever the

Hoping to relieve Lafayette by drawing British troops back from Virginia to defend New York, Washington urged Rochambeau to begin marching his troops westward from Newport across Connecticut for the joint attack on northern Manhattan, which he did during the first week of July. (See *A Map of . . . New England, Detail #3*, page 188.) On July 21, Washington wrote to de Grasse: "In full confidence that you will soon be upon this coast, I have the honor to inform you that the allied armies have formed a junction and taken a position about ten miles above the enemy's posts on the north end of York Island, their right at Dobb's Ferry on the North or Hudson's River, their left extending to a small river called the Bronx."[67] (See ***A Map of the Province of New York, Detail #5***, page 139. Dobbs Ferry, not shown, was at the southern end of the Tappan Sea, north of Wepperham.) Including militia, the allies had nine thousand troops, half French and half American. For the next few weeks, Washington and Rochambeau reconnoitered the British defenses on Manhattan, searching for vulnerable points to attack but finding none.

Finally, on August 14, a French frigate arrived at Newport with definitive news from de Grasse. "He was to leave St. Domingo the 3rd of this month with a fleet of between 25 and 29 sail of the line and a considerable body of land forces," Washington wrote to Lafayette the following day. "His destination is immediately for the Chesapeake." De Grasse wrote that he would stay on the North American coast until the middle of October if necessary, but no later. Washington ordered Lafayette to keep a lookout for de Grasse's arrival and to trap Cornwallis on the Yorktown peninsula until the allies arrived from the Hudson to

prevent his "sudden retreat through North Carolina." Calling on the northeastern states to fill their quotas for the Continental army, Washington declared that if the concentration of allied forces in Virginia came together as planned, it would provide "the fairest opportunity to reduce the whole British force in the South and to ruin their boasted expectations in that quarter."[68]

With no choice but to adopt the French plan for the Chesapeake, Washington reluctantly gave up his long-held ambition of taking back New York. Leaving Heath to defend the Hudson Highlands with 2,500 troops, Washington and Rochambeau began marching their 2,000 American and 4,500 French troops southward on August 21. They wrote to de Grasse, urging him to "send up to Elk River at the Head of Chesapeake Bay all your frigates, transports, and vessels proper for the conveyance of the French and American troops down the bay," since they expected to find few vessels at Baltimore and other ports along their route. They also asked de Grasse to watch for

A Map of . . . Virginia, Detail #7: Yorktown (center) is on the southern shore at the bend in the York River, across from Gloucester Point. Williamsburg is to the west (left center). Green Spring and Jamestown are south of Williamsburg on the James River. Portsmouth (not shown) is just west of Norfolk (bottom center).

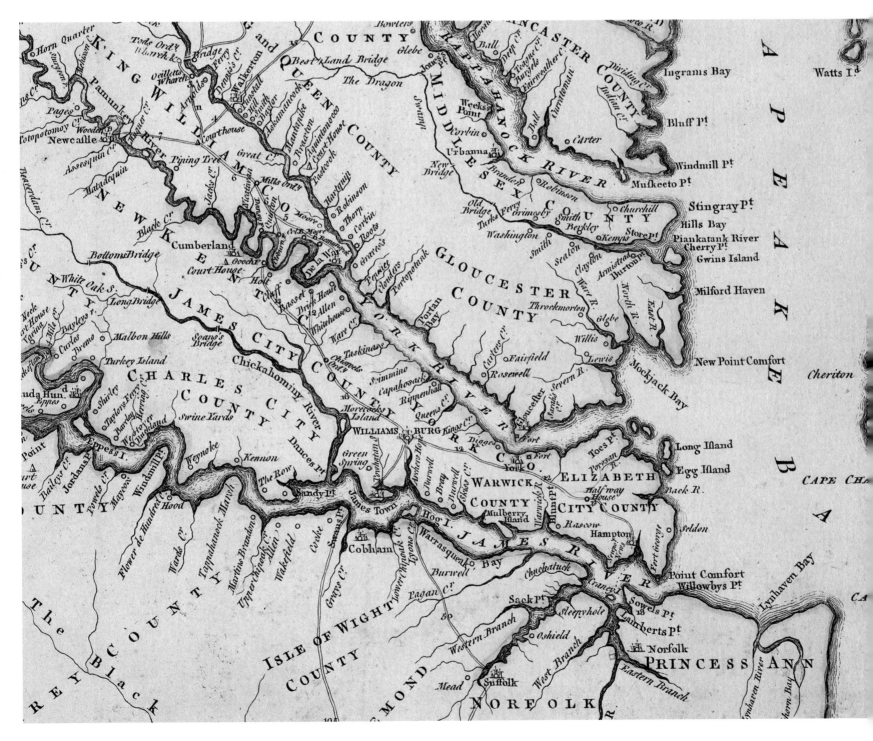

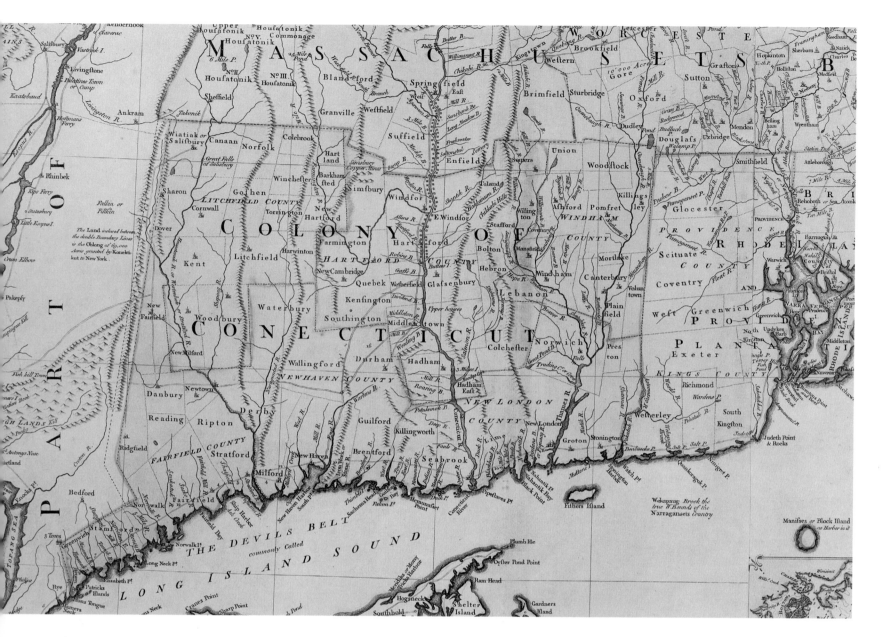

de Barras, who planned to bring his ships from Newport to the Chesapeake, bearing heavy siege artillery.[69]

Both armies had crossed the Hudson at King's Ferry by August 25, and proceeded in three parallel columns across New Jersey. To keep Clinton pinned down in New York they also launched a campaign of disinformation, announcing that a French fleet was expected hourly, and building bread ovens to convince British spies that they were digging in around the city. Washington also had two columns pause for a day, the Americans at Springfield and the French at Whippany, while the third feigned an attack on Staten Island, where the British were defensively massing troops. The delay in the march helped convince the British that the operation was against New York, enabled the rear to catch up, and allowed more time to gather boats at Trenton, a step Washington delayed as long as possible to avoid discovery of the allies' true plans.[70] Not until Washington's troops were passing through Philadelphia on September 2 did Clinton realize their destination and send a warning to Cornwallis.[71]

"I shall set out tomorrow for Head of Elk," Washington wrote to Greene from Philadelphia on September 4, "and shall expedite the movement of the troops, ordnance and stores as much as possible, that not a moment may be

lost, when the fortunate, long wished for period arrives." Washington explained to Greene that de Barras's squadron had sailed from Newport for the Chesapeake on August 24 to rendezvous with de Grasse's fleet coming up from the West Indies. Five days later, a British fleet of thirteen warships under Admiral Samuel Hood had arrived at Sandy Hook from the West Indies, joined forces with seven more ships under Admiral Thomas Graves, and sailed south, presumably for the Chesapeake. "Nothing has since been heard of either of the [French] fleets," Washington wrote. "From the circumstances related, you will readily conceive that the present time is as interesting and anxious a moment as I have ever experienced."[72]

The following day, September 5, Washington was delighted to learn of de Grasse's safe arrival in the Chesapeake with twenty-eight ships of the line. Washington planned to hurry the troops forward to Head of Elk, embark as many as possible on the available boats, and march the rest to Virginia by land. He told de Grasse that the troops coming by water would land at Jamestown and join forces with Lafayette. Still, there was no word of de Barras, and de Grasse's time limit on the Chesapeake operation made Washington uneasy. Arriving at Head of Elk on September 6, Washington struggled to assemble

A Map of . . . New England, Detail #3: Rochambeau's expeditionary force encamped in nine Connecticut towns on its march westward from Newport (right center) to meet Washington on the Hudson: Plainfield, Windham, Bolton, East Hartford, Farmington, Southington, Middlebury (not shown), Newtown, and Ridgefield. (Lebanon, just south of Windham, had hosted some two hundred and twenty hussars of the duke de Lauzun's Legion during the winter of 1780–81.) Crossing into New York, Rochambeau proceeded to Bedford, North Castle (today's Mount Kisco), and Philipsburg, on the Hudson (bottom left).

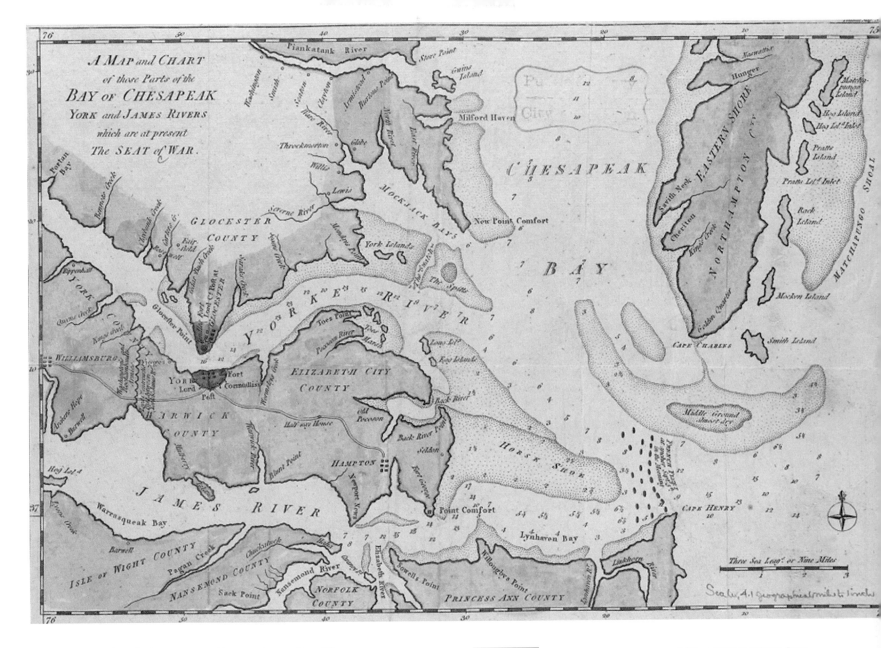

A MAP and CHART
of those Parts of the
BAY of CHESAPEAK
YORK and JAMES RIVERS
which are at present
The SEAT of WAR.

enough boats for all the men, artillery, and supplies: He sent out personal appeals to influential citizens in the Baltimore area, begging for assistance.[73]

For the moment, at least, Cornwallis appeared to be trapped. De Grasse had "occupied the intermediate space between Cape Henry and the Middle Grounds, which effectually secures the passage of the Bay and places them in the most perfect situation of defense," Washington told David Forman. (See *A Map and Chart of Those Parts of the Bay of Chesapeak, York and James Rivers Which Are at Present the Seat of War.*) "The Count immediately landed 3,000 men with orders to join the Marquis de Lafayette" at Williamsburg and prevent the retreat of Lord Cornwallis's force, which "occupies the towns of York and Gloucester in Virginia, situated on the south and north margin of York River, fortifying with increased industry." (See *A Map of . . . Virginia, Detail #7*, page 187)

While the allied forces closed in on Cornwallis in Virginia, the Carolinas and Georgia were falling into American hands: By August, Fort Ninety Six had surrendered, leaving only Wilmington, Savannah, and Charleston to the British—a reversal of all their gains in the previous eighteen months. Washington was also pleased to learn that Lord Rawdon was taken prisoner when de Grasse's fleet captured the packet on which he was sailing from Charleston to London.[74]

"I have not yet heard what is become of the British fleet commanded by Admiral Hood," which was last seen "a little to the south of Cape Henlopen" and heading north, Washington told Forman on September 7.[75] Hearing only that de Grasse had sailed out of the Chesapeake, Washington halted his troops at Head of Elk, fearing they might sail down the bay into the hands of the British navy. (See *A Map of . . . Virginia, Detail #8*, page 190, and *A General Map of North America, Detail #5*, page 191.) Not until he reached Lafayette's camp at Williamsburg a week later, on September 14 (after a stop at Mount Vernon, which he had not seen for six years), did Washington learn about the Battle of the Virginia Capes, fought on September 5. De Grasse, "who had put to sea on the 5th in pursuit of the British fleet, had returned to his former station at Cape Henry, having driven the British from the coast, taken two of their frigates, and effected a junction with the squadron of the Count de Barras," Washington reported happily to Congress. While De Grasse was engaging the British, de Barras, with the heavy siege guns, had slipped into the Chesapeake. De Grasse's return closed the trap on Cornwallis. The troops at Head of Elk were now ordered to proceed "with every dispatch possible."[76]

When he met with De Grasse aboard his flagship at Cape Henry on the 17th, Washington stressed the

A Map and Chart of Those Parts of the Bay of Chesapeak, York and James Rivers Which Are at Present the Seat of War: This British map was published in 1781, but after September 5, so Washington would not have used it in the Yorktown campaign. Nonetheless, he would have had similar nautical charts showing that the French fleet (lower right) needed to close only the mouth of the bay south of the Middle Ground, since the portion to the north was not navigable for large ships. (*A General Map of the Middle British Colonies* from the Yale atlas, published in 1775, does not show the Middle Ground, but it appears in the 1776 edition.)

importance of keeping the French fleet in the Chesapeake for as long as the siege might take. If the allies rushed to storm Yorktown because of a deadline for the fleet's departure, the result "must be bloody and precarious." (Washington undoubtedly had in mind the failed allied assault on Savannah in 1779.) Washington also asked that the French ships force their way into the York River and get past the enemy posts at Yorktown and Gloucester Point. By wresting control of the river upstream from Cornwallis, the allies would complete their encirclement of his positions. Moreover, they would be able to communicate efficiently with their units on the Gloucester side, and their vessels would be able to "draw the supplies of the country" along the entire length of the river. De Grasse told Washington he had to reconnoiter the area before making a decision.[77]

"Lord Cornwallis is incessantly at work on his fortifications, and is probably preparing to defend himself to the last extremity," Washington told Heath on the 23rd. "A little time will probably decide his fate. With the blessing of Heaven, I trust it will prove favorable to the interests of America." The following day, the last of the allied troops arrived from Head of Elk, and on the 28th, the army marched from Williamsburg to lay siege to Yorktown. Surprisingly, after token resistance "the enemy abandoned all their outposts . . . and retired to the town" on the night

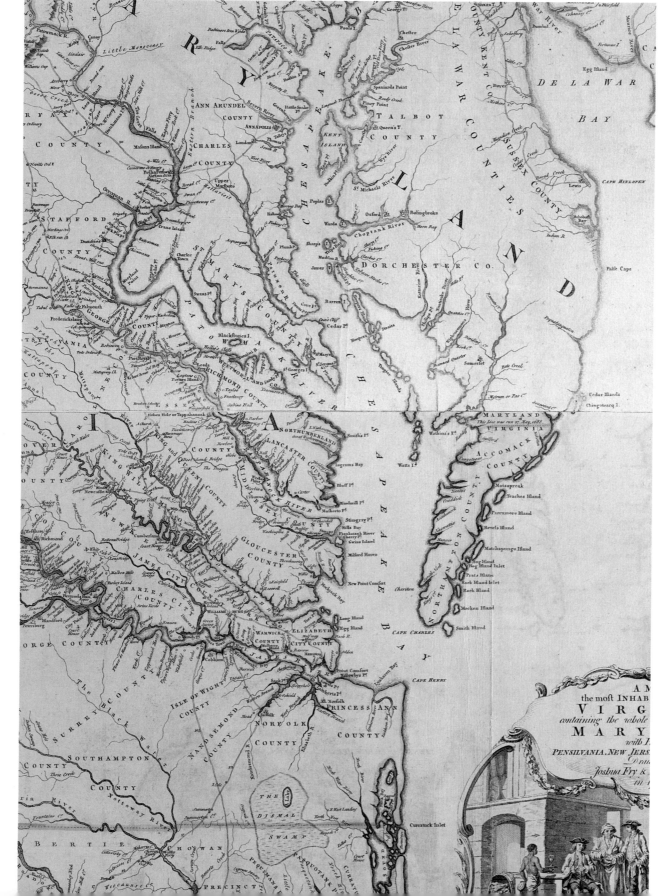

A Map of . . . Virginia, Detail #8: When British ships were spotted off Cape Henlopen (upper right, across from Cape May at the entrance to Delaware Bay) Washington halted his troops at Head of Elk (top center). After learning of the British victory in the Battle of the Virginia Capes, he rushed the troops forward on the last leg of their journey. The boats took the soldiers down the Chesapeake to Jamestown, southwest of Yorktown, on the James River (lower left).

of the 29th, Washington wrote to Heath. Suspecting that Cornwallis might be preparing to evacuate his army across the river and make an escape, Washington alerted the allied troops on the Gloucester side to block any such attempt. Meanwhile, he told Heath, "the heavy artillery will be brought up as soon as possible and the siege pushed with vigor."[78]

While Gloucester Point needed to be watched, Washington was more concerned that Cornwallis would escape up the York River. On October 1 Washington renewed his request that de Grasse station "two or three ships above the enemy's posts on York River." Because the British were not completely surrounded, their vessels commanded the river for twenty-five miles upstream from Yorktown and were capturing supplies en route to the allies' camp, effectively prolonging the siege. This situation, Washington wrote, also required the allies to assign seven or eight hundred men to protect Williamsburg and the ammunition depots in the army's rear, further weakening the offensive.

Without this rear guard, "the enemy might in the greatest security land above Queen's Creek to cover his left flank, and by a very short march effect the most destructive purposes." British control of the river above Yorktown also made it impossible for the allies to act in concert with their troops on the Gloucester side, "being obliged, in order to communicate with them, to make a circuit of near ninety miles." Most important, Washington stressed to de Grasse, "Lord Cornwallis has by the River York an outlet for his retreat." He could sail up the York and deposit his troops between the Pamunky and Mattapony rivers, which would protect their flanks. Then, by putting most of his troops on horseback and making "successive forced marches," he could "push his way, with a compact disciplined army, through a country whose population is too scattered to be collected for sudden opposition and make it impossible for us to overtake him."[79] (See *A Map of . . . Virginia, Detail #6*, page 181, where the Pamunkey and Mattapony rivers are labeled, center and top center; and *Detail #7*, page 187, which shows *Queens Creek* on the York River northeast of Williamsburg.)

A General Map of North America, Detail #5: French troops from Boston and Newport marched across Connecticut and through New York, New Jersey, Pennsylvania, Delaware, Maryland, and Virginia to reach the Yorktown peninsula, a journey of some six hundred miles (some soldiers going by boat from Head of Elk). Today the Washington-Rochambeau Revolutionary Route (W3R) is a National Historic Trail, marked by signs along the roads from Boston to Yorktown.

The surrender of General Cornwallis.

De Grasse was concerned about the British attacking his vessels with fire rafts in the confines of the York River, so he declined Washington's suggestion. Washington tactfully accepted the situation, saying, "It is mine to propose and Your Excellency's part to decide in naval affairs." Nonetheless, over the next two weeks, he continued to press de Grasse for ships upriver as the allies tightened their grip around Yorktown.[80] On October 6, Washington congratulated the army for Greene's thrashing of the British at Eutaw Springs in South Carolina on September 8, which further diminished their presence outside their remaining strongholds at Charleston, Savannah, and Wilmington. (See *An Accurate Map of North and South Carolina, Detail #8*, page 185. Eutaw Springs, not labeled, flowed into the Santee River at Nelson's Ferry, center, on the south side of the river directly south of the High Hills of Santee, where Greene rested his troops before and after the battle.)[81]

Between October 6 and 14, the allies dug two parallel trenches outside Yorktown, opened fire with their siege guns, and stormed two redoubts that helped complete their encirclement of Cornwallis.[82] On October 16, Washington told de Grasse that Cornwallis's only hope lay in a fleet from New York coming to his rescue. Since the French had thirty-six ships of the line guarding the Chesapeake, Washington was not overly concerned about this scenario. Nonetheless, if a fleet did arrive, he expected the British admiral to try drawing the French fleet into combat away from the mouth of the Chesapeake, while

sending transports "to the mouth of the Piankatank near Gwyn's Island, where the troops may be debarked at the distance of six leagues from Gloucester and march without obstacles of rivers, or any other impediments of consequence, to force our posts on that side, and relieve the garrison." Presumably the shallow draft of the transports would enable them to pass over the sandbars between Cape Charles and the Middle Ground, the long sandbar dividing the mouth of the Bay in half.[83] (See *A Map of . . . Virginia, Detail #7*, page 187. The Piankatank River and Gwyn's Island are near the top, center.)

Cornwallis, however, had despaired of help from the fleet, and that night attempted to ferry his forces across the river to Gloucester Point, in preparation for an escape to the north. His plan was thwarted after the first trip, not by the allies, but by a storm that tossed the boats in all directions. The next morning, October 17, the British raised a white flag, and the allied bombardment ceased. The British fleet at New York finally managed to get past the bar at Sandy Hook and sail south to rescue Cornwallis on the 19th, just as he was signing the surrender.

Despite the capture of Cornwallis's army of some eight thousand troops and sailors, the war was not over. The British had lost a quarter of their North American army, but they still had troops in Quebec, Montreal, Halifax, Penobscot, New York City, Wilmington, Charleston, and Savannah, as well as forts on the western frontiers. And they knew that French naval superiority would last only as long as de Grasse remained on the American coast. The day after the surrender ceremonies at Yorktown, Washington wrote to de Grasse asking him to support an allied assault on Charleston, or at least Wilmington. De Grasse said he could do neither, since his orders required him to return to the West Indies for joint operations with the Spanish. Fortunately for the allies, however, de Grasse was still in the Chesapeake on October 28th when the British fleet arrived from New York. The French fleet was clearly too strong, and the British returned to New York without attempting to rescue Cornwallis.

Fearing that the victory at Yorktown would lead to complacency, Washington urged Congress and the state governors to "keep a well-appointed, formidable army in the field, as long as the war shall continue."[84] He prepared to reinforce Greene in South Carolina with two thousand troops from Pennsylvania, Maryland, and Virginia, and sent the troops from the northeastern states back to the Hudson for future operations against the British in New York City. The capture of New York could end the war once and for all, but it depended on French cooperation. De Grasse sailed southward on November 5, promising to return the following spring or summer. American troops moved up Chesapeake Bay, retracing their course to Head of Elk, and Washington headed to Mount Vernon for a visit, while the French troops remained in Virginia under Rochambeau.

As American troops under General Arthur St. Clair marched south to reinforce Greene, the British saw that Wilmington, North Carolina, would be cut off, and on November 18 they withdrew the garrison to Charleston. Two days later, Washington left Mount Vernon for Philadelphia, where he remained for the winter, conferring with Congress and trying to prevent the victory at Yorktown from sinking the states into "supineness" and a false sense of security.[85]

Even as Washington remained cautious and pessimistic, the war was slowly beginning to wind down. In late February 1782 the House of Commons passed a resolution to suspend, unilaterally, all offensive military operations in America. Lord North's ministry soon fell from power and the opposition formed the new administration under the marquis of Rockingham, the man who had proposed the repeal of the Stamp Act in Parliament.

When news of these developments arrived in America at the beginning of April, Washington was back on the Hudson, establishing his headquarters at Newburgh, New York, just north of his previous post at New Windsor. (See *A Map of the Province of New York, Detail #3*, page 131.) He waited for the return of the French fleet and plotted small raids, while the British continued to fortify Manhattan.

As the fighting in North America reached a standstill, the West Indies had become the focal point of combat operations, and Washington followed developments there closely, sharing news with Rochambeau about the French capture of St. Kitts, which took an entire month, succeeding finally on February 11, 1782:

The news which your Excellency has received from St. Thomas's is true in part. The troops under the command of the Marquis de Bouillie escorted by the Fleet of Count de Grasse landed without opposition upon the Island of St. Kitts. The inhabitants capitulated, but the garrison retired to the strong post of Brimstone Hill, against which the Marquis was throwing up works. By a flag of truce, which arrived the day before yesterday from Antigua, we are informed that there has been an action off St. Kitts, between Count de Grasse and Admiral Hood. We have no particulars, but from the complexion of the *Antigua Gazette*, in which the affair is mentioned, we will hope that the Count was fortunate.[86]

(See *A General Map of North America, Detail #2*, page 31, right center. St. Kitts, northeast of Guadeloupe, is labeled *Charles Town* and *Basse Terre*, just north of Nevis. Antigua, directly north of Guadeloupe, is labeled *Antego*. St. Thomas, northeast of St. Kitts and east of *Porto Rico*, is followed by a *D* for Dutch.)

On May 28, Washington told Rochambeau that "our accounts of the action in the West Indies between the two fleets remain very uncertain and vague."[87] As Washington would learn a few days later, de Grasse had not been fortunate this time. On April 12, in a battle off Les Saints, just south of Guadeloupe, Admiral George Rodney had soundly defeated the French fleet and captured de Grasse, who accused his subordinates of abandoning him during the action. (See A *General Map of North America, Detail #2*, page 31, right center.)

While the defeat of the French fleet thwarted Washington's hopes for a joint operation against New York, it hastened the end of the war by facilitating the peace process. In London as a prisoner for ten days in August, de Grasse had several conversations with Lord Shelburne, who outlined British preconditions for peace negotiations.* Returning to Paris on parole, de Grasse reported the British position to the comte de Vergennes, enabling him to draw up his "Preliminary Articles of Peace." De Grasse then acted as liaison between Shelburne and the French government. Formal negotiations between the British and the Americans began in September 1782, when the Shelburne ministry effectively recognized the former colonies' independence by authorizing its representative in Paris to negotiate with the commissioners of the "13 United States."[88]

Washington remained wary of the British and kept the army intact, even as Congress failed to pay the troops and officers. He had remarked to Rochambeau that "the

Admiral, comte de Grasse.

* Rockingham had died in July, and Shelburne had formed a new ministry.

amusement of peace held out by our enemies has been much augmented by the arrival of Sir Guy Carleton in New York, who announces himself as commander in chief in America, with powers of conciliation to these states," gestures which Washington dismissed as "delusory and vain."[89] Washington had also moved the army down to Verplanck's Point at the end of August to curtail possible British forays from Manhattan. (See *A Map of the Province of New York, Detail #3*, page 131.)

In mid-September, Rochambeau's troops arrived from Virginia and crossed the Hudson at King's Ferry for a joyful reunion with the Americans at Verplanck's Point. The allies stayed there through September, as Carleton retrenched in New York City. Rochambeau's troops gradually left for Boston, departing from there for the West Indies at the end of October. In November Washington moved the army back north to winter quarters at Newburgh.

Washington wrote to his brother John Augustine in mid-January 1783 that "the army as usual is without pay and a great part of the soldiery without shirts; and the patience of them is equally threadbare. It seems to be a matter of small consequence to those at a distance."[90] On March 15, 1783, Washington spoke to a gathering of the army's officers at Newburgh and defused a plot to press the army's demands by threatening Congress and the state governments with the use of force. "Gentlemen, you will permit me to put on my spectacles," Washington said, as he strained to read from the paper in his hands, "for I have not only grown gray, but almost blind in the service of my country." This gentle reminder of Washington's own sacrifices and his solidarity with the officers had a powerful effect. "The good sense, the virtue, and patient forbearance of the army," he told his cousin Lund, "on this, as upon every other trying occasion which has happened to call them into action, has again triumphed and appeared with more luster than ever."[91]

A month later, on April 15, Congress ratified a preliminary treaty with the British. It had been signed in Paris several months earlier and with few changes would become the final treaty. On April 19, 1783, exactly eight years after the clashes at Lexington and Concord, Washington publicly proclaimed a cessation of hostilities. In early May, he met Carleton at Tappan, New York, "to make arrangements with him for delivery of the posts, Negroes, and other property belonging to citizens of the United States." Washington was convinced by the conversation "that the slaves which have absconded from their masters will never be restored to them," he told Governor Benjamin Harrison of Virginia.* During the course of the war the British had issued two proclamations promising freedom to slaves who would fight for the king. "Vast numbers of them are already gone to Nova Scotia," Washington told Harrison, "and the construction which [Carleton] puts upon the seventh article of the provisional treaty differs very widely from ours." Washington pressed the issue on

behalf of his fellow slaveholders, but had submitted no claims for his own escaped slaves.[92]

As for the posts in the Northwest, Washington assumed that the British would promptly transfer them to the United States as required by the treaty. In May Washington included detailed planning for these posts when he submitted to Congress a proposal for national defense entitled "Sentiments on a Peace Establishment."[93] He called for a permanent army after the war despite the abiding concern of many Americans that standing armies were a threat to republican government. In another effort to expand the power of the central government, Washington proposed a national militia, separate from those raised by the individual states, which would be under the authority of Congress and would have uniform standards for organization and training throughout the country. He also called for the establishment of military academies, arsenals, and factories to produce war materiel.

Washington framed these proposals in terms of the new nation's geography and borders. "First. A regular and standing force, for garrisoning West Point and such other posts upon our northern, western, and southern frontiers, as shall be deemed necessary to awe the Indians, protect our trade, prevent the encroachment of our neighbors of Canada and the Floridas, and guard us at least from surprises." Washington reassured Congress that the army would not have to be large—only some 2,600 troops—because "our distance from the European states in a great degree frees us from apprehension."

To those who might think this was too many troops, Washington warned that "the British force in Canada is now powerful, and, by report, will be increased; that the frontier is very extensive; that the tribes of Indians within our territory are numerous, soured, and jealous." According to the preliminary treaty, Washington noted, "half the waters, and the free navigation of the [Great] Lakes appertain to us, yet, in case of a rupture with Great Britain" communication with the northernmost American posts via lakes Erie and Ontario would be cut off, since the British were likely to maintain their naval superiority in that region. (See McMurray, *A Map of the United States, Detail #2*, page 209. The line passing through the middle of the lakes marks the northern border of the United States.)

Washington urged Congress to "open new or improve the present half-explored communications with Detroit and other posts on the Lakes, by the waters of the Susquehanna, Potomac, or James River to the Ohio, from whence, with short portages, several communications by water may be opened with Lake Erie." Establishing posts at key points on the Ohio River "would open several doors for the supply of the garrisons on the Lakes," Washington wrote. The Ohio forts would also be essential for supporting any posts that might be established on the Mississippi River, since the Ohio was the best route "to the Illinois settlements, and the whole country below on the

* Jefferson had left office in June 1781 and retired to Monticello. He was followed by three governors who served for short periods until Harrison took office in December and served through 1784.

Washington's headquarters at Newburgh, New York.

Mississippi, quite to our southern boundary," at the 31st parallel. (See McMurray, *A Map of the United States, Detail #4*, page 217, upper left to lower left.)

American posts should also be built "beyond Detroit, to the northward and westward, but a strong post on the Scioto, at the carrying place between it and the River Sandusky, which empties into Lake Erie, mentioned in Hutchins's description of that country, page 24, and more plainly pointed out by Evans's map, is indispensably necessary for the security of the present settlers." (See *A General Map of the Middle British Colonies, Detail #2*, page 35. The Scioto River, labeled *Siota*, flows into the Ohio at Lower Shawnee Town, lower left. The four-mile "carrying place" between the Scioto and Sandusky rivers is marked *Portage 4M*, upper left.)*

All of Washington's careful planning, however, was blocked in August by the British refusal to give up the Northwest posts. (See McMurray, *A Map of the United States, Detail #2*, pages 208–9.) Washington received word that the overtures of "the Baron Steuben, who was sent into Canada to make arrangements with General [Frederick] Haldimand for withdrawing the British forces from the posts within the territory of the United States," had been rebuffed.[94] The British had evacuated Savannah and Charleston, however, and were inundated by Loyalist refugees pouring into New York, where Carleton was still arranging for their evacuation in August. The first convoys sailed in October for Nova Scotia, Canada, and West Indies.

"With anxious expectations we have been upon the lookout, day after day these four months for the arrival of the definitive treaty of peace," Washington wrote to Lafayette on October 12. The treaty had been signed in Paris on September 3, 1783, but the news would not reach Congress until November 1. "In equal expectation have we been the last two [months] of the evacuation of New York by the British forces. On the happening of either of these events, I have placed my retirement to the walks of private life, and look forward to the epoch with heart felt satisfaction."

Washington could make no definite plans until he returned home and put his private affairs in order, he told Lafayette, but his dreams for the future were already formed in his mind, and they consisted of exploring the United States by making a grand circuit of all the territory that up to now he had seen only on maps:

> I have it in contemplation, however, to make a tour through all the eastern states, thence into Canada; thence up the St. Lawrence, and through the Lakes to Detroit; thence to lake Michigan by land or water; thence through the western country by the river Illinois, to the river Mississippi, and down the same to New Orleans; thence into Georgia by the way of Pensacola; and thence through the two Carolinas home. A great tour this, you will say, probably it may take place nowhere but in imagination, though it is my *wish* to begin it in the latter end of April of next year. If it should be realized, there would be nothing wanting to make it perfectly agreeable, but your company.[95]

* Washington correctly anticipated that the border posts in the Northwest would be a zone of contention with the British after the war. He also recommended establishing posts in the following locations, from east to west and north to south: the Penobscot or St. Croix River; the northern end of Lake Champlain; the Connecticut River near the 45th parallel; Ticonderoga; Niagara; Oswego; Fort Erie; Detroit; the straits between Lake Huron and Lake Superior; Fort Pitt; the mouth of the Scioto; the mouth of the Kentucky River; the mouth of the Ohio River; the heights at the mouth of the Illinois River; and on the frontiers of the Carolinas and Georgia.

CHAPTER SEVEN

0 1 2 3 4 5 6 7

AFTER THE REVOLUTION—UNITING

AN EXPANDING NATION

As he waited impatiently for news of the definitive peace treaty in October 1783, Washington told the comte de Chastellux he was anxious "to quit the walks of public life, and under the shadow of my own vine, and my own fig tree, to seek those enjoyments, and that relaxation, which a mind that has been constantly upon the stretch for more than eight years, stands so much in need of."[1] During this limbo before the formal end of the war, Washington got a start on the intended journey he had described to Lafayette. Washington told Chastellux about a three-week tour he had taken in July, visiting New York's northern and western frontiers.

(See *A General Map of the Middle British Colonies, Detail #10*, page 145. He went first to Lake George and to the fort at Crown Point on Lake Champlain, upper right. Returning to Schenectady, lower right, he traveled up the Mohawk River to Fort Stanwix—renamed Fort Schuyler, not labeled—just east of Wood Creek and Lake Oneida. At Wood Creek he turned south and east to the head of the East Branch of the Susquehanna and Lake Otsego, northwest of Schenectady and Cherry Valley. He then examined the portage northward to the Mohawk River at Canajoharie, labeled *Conejochery*.)

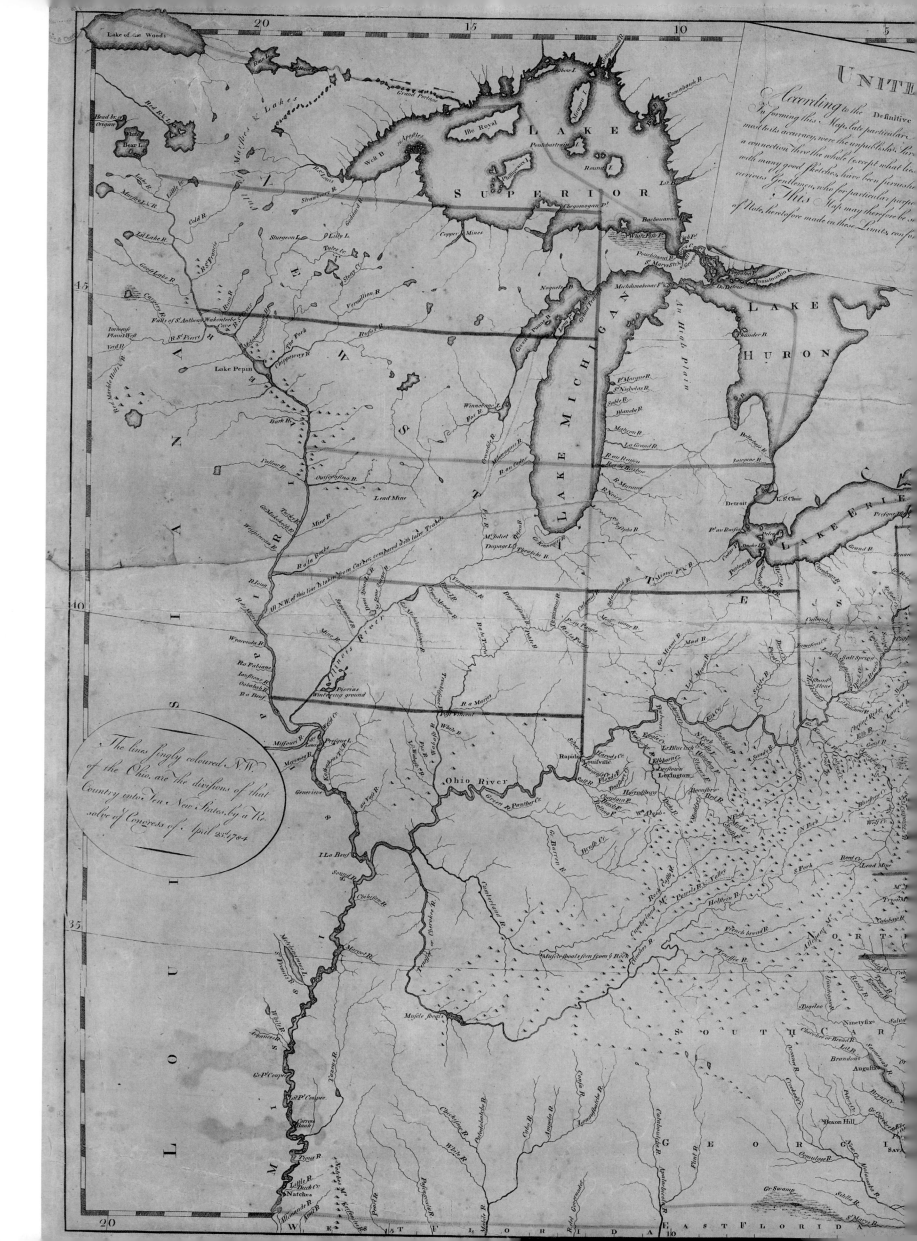

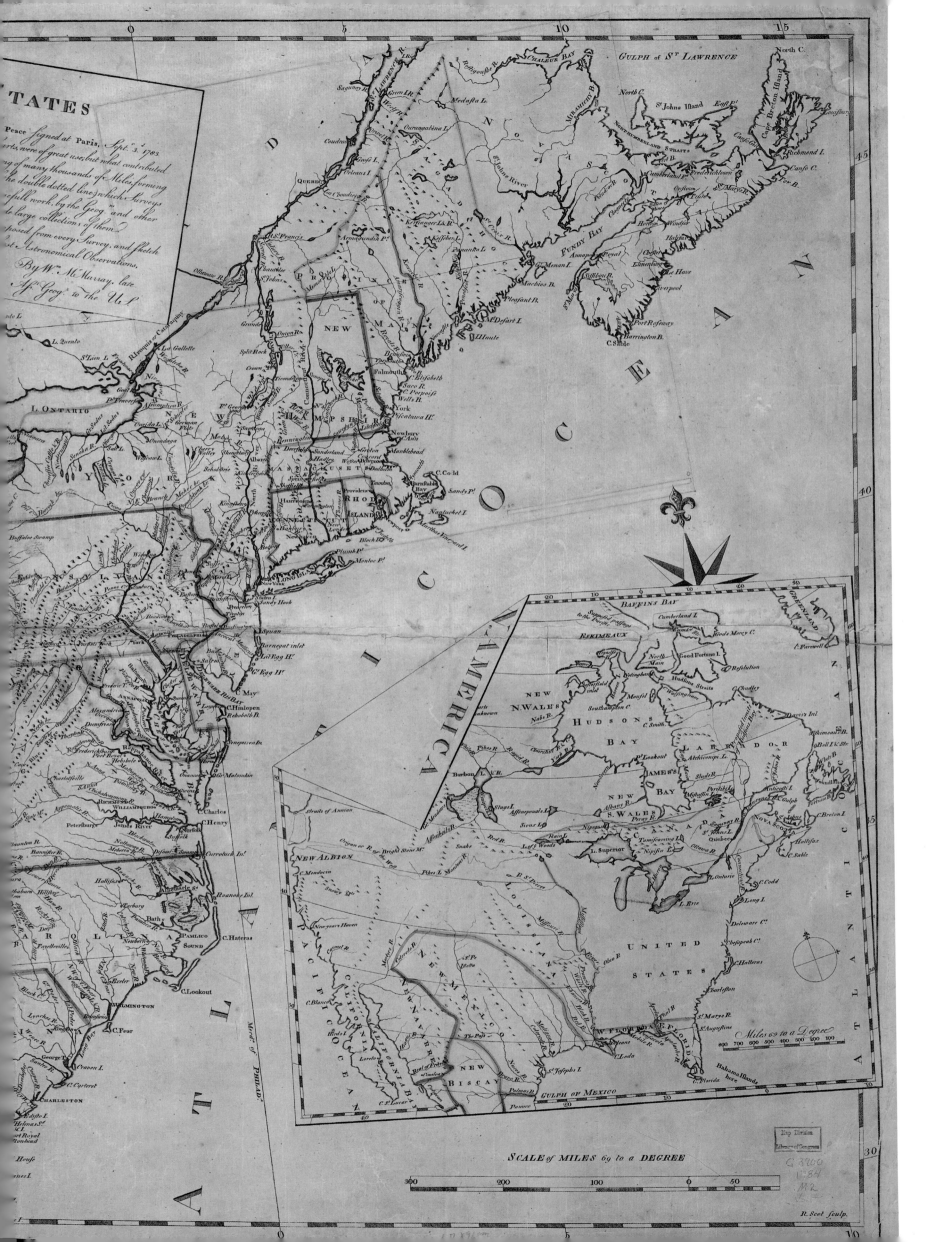

The journey along the Hudson and Mohawk river corridors—combined with Washington's lifelong habit of studying maps and reports—produced an epiphany. "Prompted by these actual observations, I could not help taking a more contemplative and extensive view of the vast inland navigation of these United States, from maps and the information of others; and could not but be struck with the immense diffusion and importance of it; and with the goodness of that Providence which has dealt her favors to us with so profuse a hand." The new nation was blessed with rivers that, made navigable, could physically and politically bind together its sprawling parts, east and west. "Would to God we may have wisdom enough to improve them. I shall not rest contented 'till I have explored the western country, and traversed those lines . . . which have given bounds to a new empire."[2*]

Washington had first thought of the West as a means of accumulating personal wealth and social status, then as a refuge if the Revolution failed. Aside from the fate of Native Americans, his views now became more public-spirited and expansive. He began to see the region as a national resource to be shared by all the states in order to strengthen the Union internally, while giving it imperial status on the world stage.[3]

As for Native Americans, Washington advised Congress to be firm but magnanimous with them. The Indians "should be informed, that after a contest of eight years for the sovereignty of this country Great Britain has ceded all the lands of the United States" set forth in the Provisional Treaty signed in September 1783.[4] (See McMurray, *A Map of the United States According to the Definitive Treaty*, pages 198–99, and *Detail #1*.)[5] The Indians should be reminded, Washington wrote, that despite "all the advice and admonition which could be given them at the commencement; and during the prosecution of the war" they "were determined to join their arms to those of Great Britain and to share their fortune; so, consequently, with a less generous people than Americans they would be made to share the same fate, and be compelled to retire along with them beyond the Lakes." However, the Americans preferred peace, Washington continued.

"As the country is large enough to contain us all, and as we are disposed to be kind to them and to partake of their trade, we will from these considerations and from motives of compassion, draw a veil over what is past and establish a boundary line between them and us beyond which we will *endeavor* to restrain our people from hunting or settling, and within which they shall not come," except for peaceful purposes. Washington's assurances were also deceptive. His real intention, as he would soon explain, was to take the Indians' land, but to do it gradually—by treaty and by purchase—in order to avoid the far higher costs of waging war on the frontier. The Indians "will ever retreat as our settlements advance upon them," Washington wrote, "and they will be as ready to sell, as we are to buy."[6]

He believed, in any event, that gradual expansion was in the best interests of the United States. Allowing "a wide extended country to be overrun with land jobbers, speculators, and monopolists or even with scattered settlers," he wrote, would merely reward the greedy few, while undermining law and order and the support for government that would be fostered by compact settlements. Relations with the Indians should be considered together with the formation of new states in the Northwest, he told Congress, and he had specific suggestions for laying out their borders.

In 1783, Washington suggested to Congress the borders for what would become the states of Ohio and Michigan:

> From the best information and maps of that country, it would appear that from the mouth of the Great Miami River, which empties into the Ohio, to its confluence with the Mad River, thence by a line to the Miami Fort and Village on the other Miami River, which empties into Lake Erie, and thence by a line to include the settlement of Detroit, would with Lake Erie to the northward, Pennsylvania to the eastward and the Ohio to the southward, form a government sufficiently extensive to fulfill all the public engagements, and to receive moreover a large population [of] emigrants . . . Was it not for the purpose of comprehending the settlement of Detroit within the jurisdiction of the new government, a more compact and

PAGES 198–99: McMurray, *A Map of the United States According to the Definitive Treaty:* The Treaty of Paris was negotiated using the enormous, definitive map of eastern North America by John Mitchell, entitled *A Map of the British Colonies in North America* (1775), which measured approximately 6$\frac{1}{2}$ x 4$\frac{1}{2}$ feet. Washington owned a copy of this map by William McMurray, which showed the terms of the treaty at a more manageable size of about 3 x 2 feet.

* In 1825, the Erie Canal, running through the Mohawk River Valley, would connect the Hudson River with the Great Lakes.

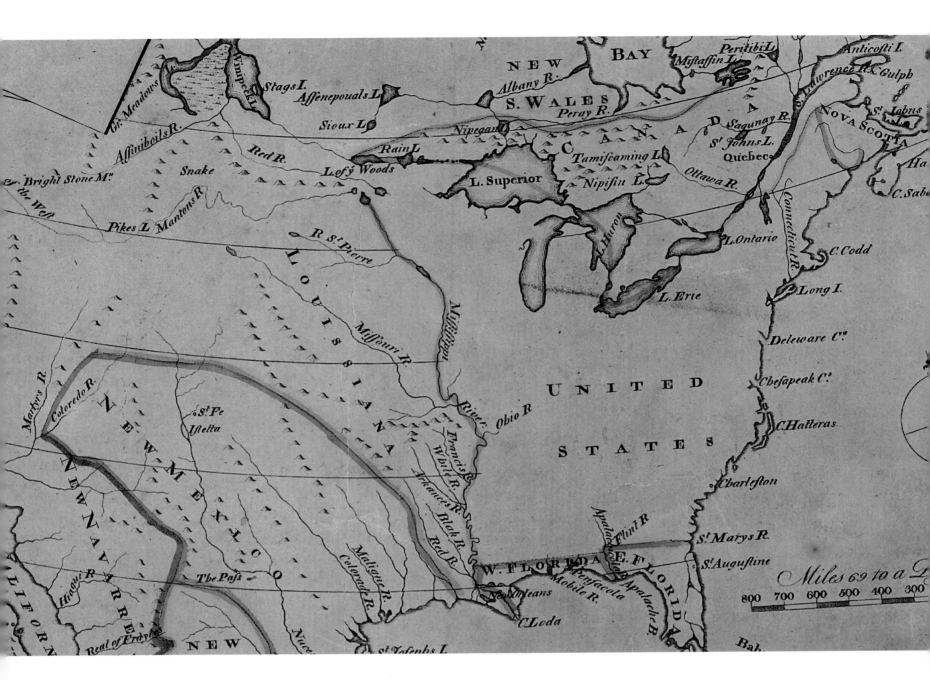

McMurray, *A Map of the United States, Detail #1:* This inset from the lower right side of the map shows that the United States was to extend from the Great Lakes in the north to the 31st parallel to the south, and from the Atlantic coast in the east to the Mississippi River to the west. The British kept Canada, while Spain acquired East and West Florida and Louisiana west of the Mississippi.

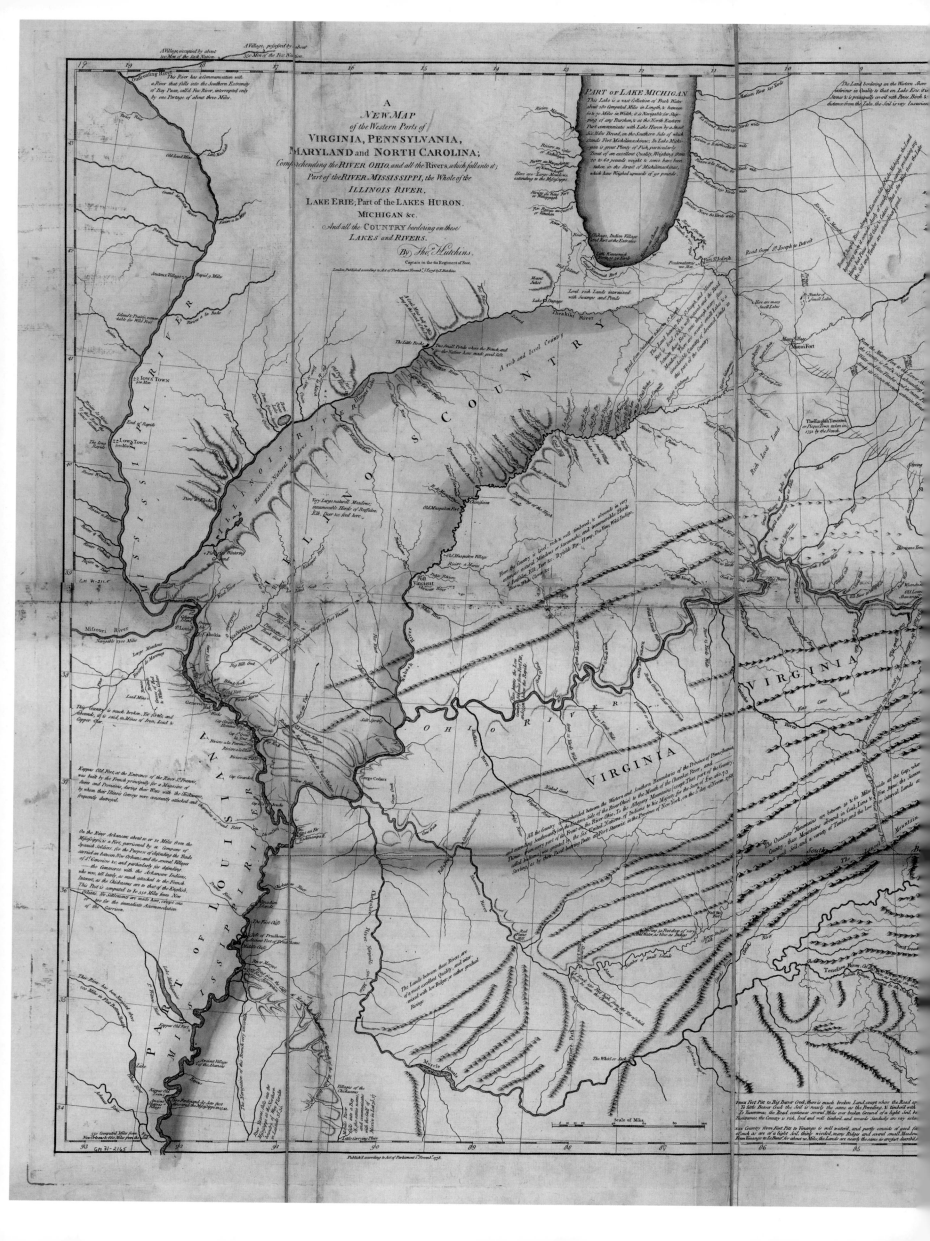

A
NEW MAP
of the Western Parts of
VIRGINIA, PENNSYLVANIA,
MARYLAND and NORTH CAROLINA;
Comprehending the RIVER OHIO, and all the Rivers, which fall into it;
Part of the RIVER MISSISSIPPI, the Whole of the
ILLINOIS RIVER,
LAKE ERIE; Part of the LAKES HURON,
MICHIGAN &c.
And all the COUNTRY bordering on these
LAKES and RIVERS.
By Thos Hutchins.
Captain in the 60 Regiment of Foot.

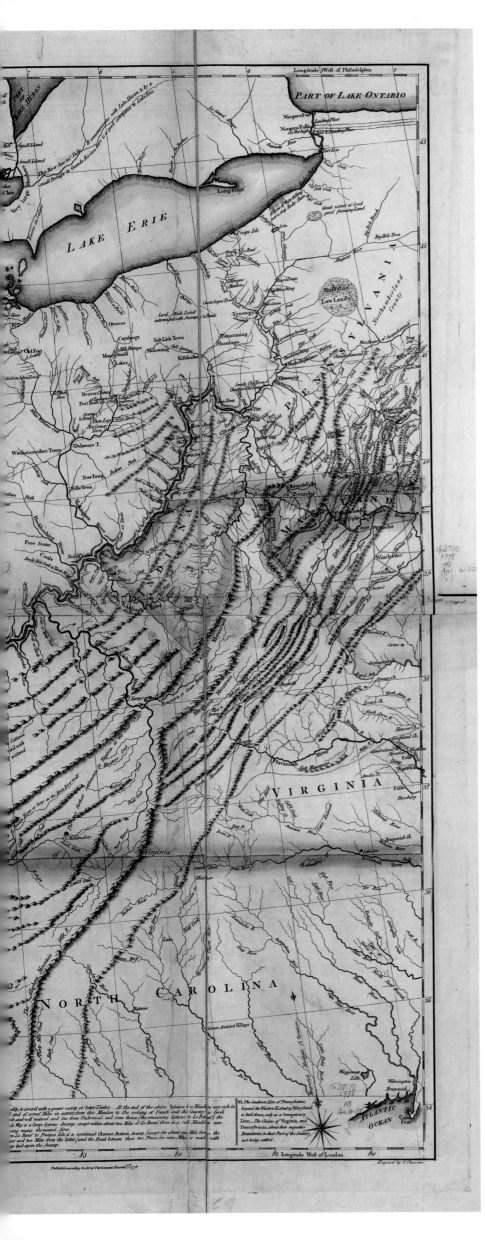

Hutchins, *A New Map of the Western Parts of Virginia, Pennsylvania, Maryland and North Carolina:* Washington considered the Evans map *A General Map of the Middle British Colonies* to be amazingly accurate for its time (1755) but superseded by the work of Thomas Hutchins in 1778. After the Revolution, Washington referred to this map by Hutchins when discussing the West.

better-shaped district for a state would be for the line to proceed from the Miami Fort and Village along the River of that name to Lake Erie, leaving in that case the settlement of Detroit, and all the territory north of the Rivers Miami and St. Josephs between the Lakes Erie, St. Clair, Huron, and Michigan to form, hereafter, another state equally large, compact, and water-bounded.

(See Hutchins, *A New Map of the Western Parts of Virginia, Pennsylvania, Maryland and North Carolina*, pages 202–3, and *Detail #1*.) For the outline of the second state (Michigan), see McMurray, *A Map of the United States, Detail #1*, page 201, upper center.[7]

With the arrival of the definitive treaty came the British evacuation of New York City on November 25, 1783. There, at Fraunces Tavern, Washington said farewell to his officers in early December. On December 23 he resigned his commission at Annapolis, relinquishing power and displaying the subordination of military to civil authority that would mark the new republic. By Christmas he was finally back at Mount Vernon. Retirement would not be entirely carefree, however, because of money problems. He always believed the sale or lease of his western lands would make up for the financial setbacks inflicted by the war and the money he had put into Mount Vernon. He predicted that a flood of immigrants to the frontier would drive up the price of land.[8]

To profit from his holdings, he would first have to determine what they were and assert his ownership. Some of his papers were lost, and the rest in such disarray, "occasioned by frequent hasty removals of them out of the way of the enemy," that on February 1, 1784, he appealed for help to Thomas Lewis, the surveyor of Augusta County. "Sir: After an absence of almost nine years, and nearly a total suspension of all my private concerns, I am at length set down at home; and am endeavoring to recover my business from the confusion into which it has run during that period." He requested information about "the lands which I am entitled to in my own right, and by purchase under the Royal Proclamation in 1763, (west of the mountains)."[9] The king's instructions had forbidden the patenting of any land in the West, except for tracts given as a bounty for military service.[10]

Washington was focused on his neglected private concerns when Thomas Jefferson wrote to him in March 1784, recalling his attention to the ambitious project—interrupted by the war—of improving the navigation of the Potomac River and making it the great commercial artery connecting the East to the West. Commerce was a "modern source of wealth and power" for the new nation and must be encouraged, Jefferson wrote. The Mississippi, Hudson, and Potomac rivers were in competition to bring in trade from the West, he noted, but the first was not an option. Flour, lumber, and other heavy goods were floated on rafts down the Mississippi, but the upstream voyage was so "difficult and tedious" that the river was unlikely to be a route for European imports. (American traders, in fact, would return upriver by land after selling their rafts at New Orleans.)

The remaining exports from the upper Mississippi, the Great Lakes, and the Ohio country would be shipped east either by the Hudson or the Potomac, and the latter was by far the better, shorter route, with fewer portages, Jefferson asserted. (See Hutchins, *A New Map, Detail #2*, page 207.)[11] "Nature then has declared in favor of the Potomac," Jefferson wrote, "and through that channel

George Washington resigning his commission at Annapolis, December 23, 1783.

Thomas Jefferson, governor of Virginia, by Charles Willson Peale.

OPPOSITE: Hutchins, *A New Map, Detail #1:* The borders Washington described for the first proposed state (Ohio) extend from the lower left of this view to the top center, across to the right side, down to the bottom, and back to the lower left.

offers to pour into our lap the whole commerce of the western world."

Washington replied that "my opinion coincides perfectly with yours respecting the practicability of an easy and short communication between the waters of the Ohio and Potomac" and "the preference it has over all others," but he was pessimistic about the Maryland and Virginia legislatures' ability or desire to impose a new tax for the project on a skeptical public—funds that would be needed to build canals and clear rocks and other obstructions from the river. Moreover, Washington's reputation as a disinterested leader of all Americans needed to be preserved and his influence used only for truly vital national issues—as the struggle to ratify the Constitution would show, just a few years later.[12] "I am not so disinterested in this matter as you are," Washington told Jefferson, who did not own any western land and did not plan to buy any, "but I am made very happy to find [that] a man of discernment and liberality (who has no particular interest in the plan) thinks as I do, who have lands in that country, the value of which would be enhanced by the adoption of such a scheme."[13]

Jefferson's letter had clearly reignited Washington's passion for the project, despite the physical obstacles and the problem of self-interest. "More than ten years ago, I was struck with the importance of it," Washington wrote, and he recalled how he had lobbied for the bill allowing a private company to make the Potomac navigable "from the tidewater to Wills Creek (about 150 miles.)" That plan was in motion when Washington set off for Cambridge in 1775, but was then derailed by opposition from Marylanders, including Baltimore merchants, who feared that the flow of trade would be diverted from them to Virginia. The interruption of the war had stalled the project further, but Washington was now eager to restart it before New York won the competition by linking the Hudson and the Great Lakes, he told Jefferson. "I know the Yorkers will delay no time to remove every obstacle" along their chosen route, he continued, "so soon as the posts at Oswego and Niagara are surrendered."[14] However, getting the British to comply with the Treaty of Paris and relinquish the seven northern posts they retained on American soil would take more than a decade. (See McMurray, *A Map of the United States, Detail #2*, pages 208–9.)

Despite the letter from Jefferson, for much of 1784 Washington remained focused on his private business, attempting to confirm his legal title to his Ohio lands. And he explored ways to make the land profitable, advertising for tenants in America and seeking possible settlers from Europe.[15] On September 1, accompanied by his old friend and comrade-in-arms Dr. James Craik and some servants, Washington set off on a month-long journey on horseback to the Ohio Valley to visit his properties. Craik, who had served as a physician and surgeon in

Dr. James Craik.

the Continental army, also had tracts of western land, near Washington's, that required attention. At Berkeley Springs (since 1776 the town of Bath) they were joined by Washington's nephew Bushrod and Craik's son William.[16] (See the "Medicinal Spring" on the upper right on *A Map of . . . Virginia, Detail #4*, page 29.)

Now Washington began to pursue his private and public goals in tandem, noting in his diary that "one object of my journey being to obtain information of the nearest and best communication between the eastern and western waters and to facilitate . . . the inland navigation of the Potomac, I conversed a good deal with General Morgan on this subject." Daniel Morgan, the Revolutionary War hero, "and many other gentlemen" who lived in the area came to see Washington when he stopped at the home of his brother Charles Washington in the Shenandoah Valley to collect back rent from his Berkeley County tenants that had accumulated during the war.[17]

Studying maps, Washington tried to determine the best route for a road between the headwaters of the Potomac and one of the rivers that would link it to the Ohio.[18] He questioned the frontiersmen and settlers who came out to greet him about the links between the Potomac and the Ohio, and also between the Ohio and the Great Lakes—which streams were navigable and where it was necessary to portage.[19] Washington became convinced that the Monongahela and Youghiogheny rivers "afford *much* the shortest routes from the Lakes to the tidewater of the Atlantic" but they were not under Virginia's control, he noted in his diary. Both rivers crossed into Pennsylvania—the Monongahela from two miles above the fork of the Cheat River down to the Forks of the Ohio, and the Youghiogheny, which began in Maryland but flowed through Pennsylvania to the Monongahela—leading to political complications: Philadelphia would not

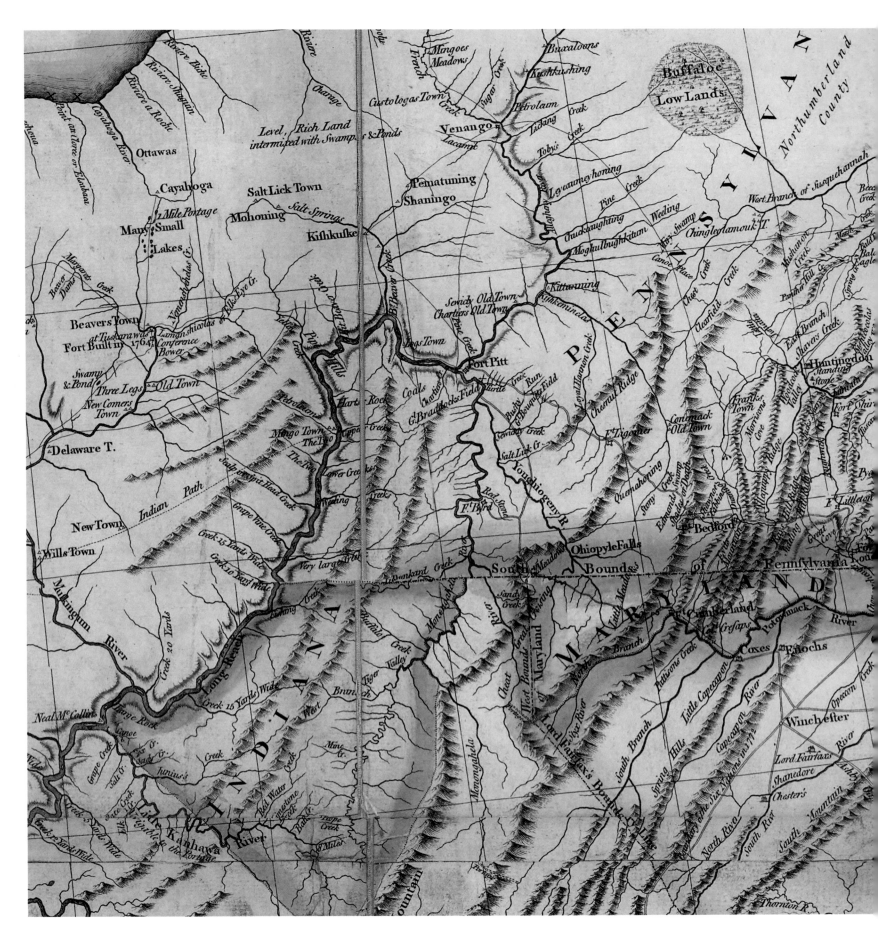

Hutchins, *A New Map, Detail #2:* Assuming western exports were brought to the southern shore of Lake Erie, Jefferson argued, the shortest route to the eastern seaboard was up the Cuyahoga River (*Cayahoga*, upper left corner), east to the West Branch of Beaver Creek (upper left), and then up the Ohio and Youghiogheny rivers, or the Monongahela and the Cheat (upper left to bottom center), to reach the South Branch of the Potomac, Alexandria, and the rest of the Atlantic coast and Europe.

Chegomogan Pt

Bachouanan B

White Fish Pt

Oak Pt

Pouchitaoui R.

St Marys Str. Falls

St Georges

Gros C.

St Joseph

L Ellaton Pt

Maniatoualin I.

Du Detour

Noquets B.

Michilimakinac Ft & St

LAKE

Puans B.

Long Pt

Grand Travase

An High Plain

Thunder B.

HURON

MICHIGAN

Pt Marque R.

St Nicholas R.

Sable R.

Blanche R.

Saguinam B.

Maticou R.

Bellechati R.

La Grand R.

R. au Raison

Sawpine R.

R. au la Barbue

R. Murame

R. Noire

L. St Clair

Detroit

Cr. Kennomic R.

St Josephs R.

Pt au Raison

Presque Il.

LAKE ERIE

Delee P.

kiki R.

Cedar P.

Smoke I.

Grand R.

Venango

Portage R.

Huron R.

Cavahoga R.

Gr. Beaver Cr.

maws R.

Calumet R.

Salamanie R.

Miami Ft & R.

T

E

S

Kellota Cr.

of Note, heretofore made in these Limits, confor

Map may therefore be sai

McMurray, *A Map of the United States, Detail #2:* From west to east, the seven posts were Michilimakinac (top left), Detroit, Miami (bottom left corner), Niagara (center), Oswego, Oswegatchi (not shown, below La Gallette at the Wegatche River), and Point au Fer (not shown, on the western shore of Lake Champlain just below the border). The line through the lakes clearly indicates that all seven were in the United States. (For Oswegatchi and Point au Fer, see *A General Map of the Middle British Colonies, Detail #6*, page 58.)

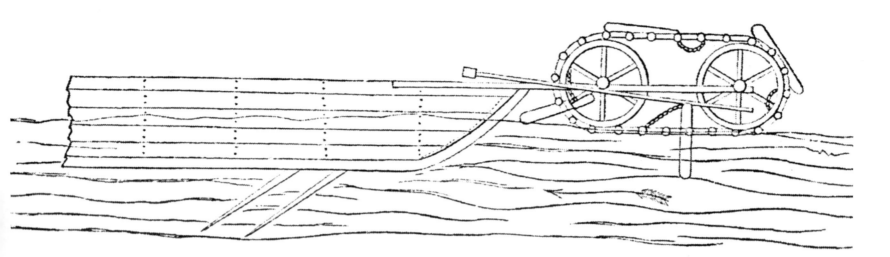

James Rumsey's mechanical boat.

want trade diverted from the state's western parts to Virginia and would therefore oppose such a route. (See Hutchins, *A New Map, Detail #2*, page 207.)[20]

One option was to piece together an alternate route avoiding Pennsylvania by going south on the Monongahela (instead of north) to the Little Kanawha River, which flows into the Ohio. At Bath, Washington spoke with Colonel Normand Bruce, who said "he had traveled from the North Branch of the Potomac to the waters of the Youghiogheny and Monongahela." It turned out that most of Bruce's information was secondhand, so Washington proposed that they each explore part of the alternate route. Bruce was to investigate a route across Laurel Hill from the North Branch of the Potomac to the Cheat River via Sandy Creek. (See Hutchins, *A New Map, Detail #2*, page 207, center.) Washington planned to inspect his lands on the Ohio, and on the way back move up the Little Kanawha and portage to Tenmile Creek, a tributary of the West Branch River, leading down the Monongahela. Another portage, from the Monongahela to the Cheat at Sandy Creek, would complete the route. (See Hutchins, *A New Map, Detail #2*, page 207, lower left to center. Tenmile Creek is not shown.)[21]

Another option was to break western Pennsylvania off from the rest of the state. Washington was so fixated on creating an east-west route that he even favored the separatist movement that was brewing in western Pennsylvania (ironic given that during his presidency he would staunchly oppose separatists in Kentucky and the Southwest and suppress the Whiskey Rebellion in western Pennsylvania). He noted that while Philadelphia might oppose the route, "any attempt by that government to restrain it . . . would cause a separation of their territory, there being sensible men among them who have it in contemplation at this moment."[22]

At Bath, Washington was delighted by a private demonstration of James Rumsey's model for a mechanical boat that could paddle upstream. The invention seemed to accomplish what Washington had deemed virtually impossible and promised to overcome difficult portions of the route connecting the Potomac to the West. Washington was convinced that "it might be turned to the greatest possible utility in inland navigation and in rapid currents that are shallow." The water would have to be shallow, because a paddle wheel, turned by the current, was to operate two poles extending down to the riverbed, enabling the boat to "walk" upstream. The full-size prototype later proved unsuccessful, and Rumsey moved on to developing a steamboat.[23]

Proceeding to Old Town, Washington stayed at Colonel Cresap's as he had on his first trip to the frontier in 1748. Cresap was by then about ninety years old and blind, but otherwise in good health. (See *A Map of . . . Virginia, Detail #4*, page 29, upper left.) Following what had been Braddock's Road, Washington departed from the ruins of Fort Cumberland—abandoned for the previous twenty years—and proceeded to Great Meadows to inspect his property there, some 234 acres purchased in 1770 that included most of the Meadows and the site of Fort Necessity, which he hoped to lease as a good place for a tavern.[24] (See *A Map of Pennsylvania, Detail #1*, page 38.)

"In passing over the mountains," Washington noted, "I met numbers of persons and pack horses . . . from most of whom I made enquiries of the nature of the country between the Little Kanawha and Tenmile Creek (which had been represented as a short and easy portage) and to my surprise found the accounts which had been given were so far from the truth that numbers with whom I conversed assured me that the distance between was very considerable," and "that Tenmile Creek was not navigable even for canoes more than a mile from its mouth." As for connecting the Cheat River with the North Branch of the Potomac, the country between them, everyone seemed to agree, was "rough and a good way not to be found." (See Hutchins, *A New Map, Detail #2*, page 207, bottom left and bottom center.)

The settlers also reported to Washington about "the late murders and general dissatisfaction of the Indians," sparked by white pioneers' attempts to settle on land north and west of the Ohio River—which the Native Americans claimed as their own. "Our delay to hold a treaty with them," Washington noted, also made the Native Americans suspicious that more white expansion was imminent. He began to think it would be unwise to proceed to his lands on the Kanawha River, but he delayed a decision until hearing more reports.[25]

On September 12, Washington reached the first piece of land he had claimed west of the Appalachian Mountains: a 1,644-acre tract of bottomland along the west bank of the Youghiogheny River, some thirty-five miles southeast of Fort Pitt (today's Perryopolis, Pennsylvania) that William Crawford had surveyed for him in 1768. (See *A Map of Pennsylvania, Detail #1*, page 38, left center, northeast of Red Stone Creek along Mill Run.) For the previous decade, Washington had owned the land, known as Washington's Bottom, "in co-partnership" with Gilbert Simpson Jr., who signed on as the resident manager in 1773. Simpson had made some modest improvements and found a few tenants to settle parts of the property, but Washington never saw any income from it.

Tired of Simpson's endless complaints and crafty excuses, Washington had come to dissolve the partnership, sell off his own share of the slaves, livestock, and supplies, and lease Simpson's six-hundred-acre farm to the highest bidder.[26] Curious settlers came from all around to the auction Washington had advertised for the 15th, but they were cash-poor and bought little. With the shortage of hard money in the region, Washington ended up leasing the farm and slaves back to Gilbert Simpson at an annual rent of five hundred bushels of wheat. Determined to get his land under proper management, Washington imposed stricter leases on the other tenants at Washington's Bottom and appointed an agent, Major Thomas Freeman, "to superintend my business over the mountains."[27]

At Simpson's farm Washington received a visit from the commander at Fort Pitt, who confirmed recent reports of Native American attacks and convinced him not to visit his property on the Kanawha River. On the 18th he set out for his land on Miller's Run, a branch of Chartiers Creek, southwest of Fort Pitt (a few miles south of today's Carnegie, Pennsylvania). The settlers who occupied Washington's 2,813 acres asserted their right to the land, but offered to buy it at a moderate price to avoid a legal battle. Negotiations broke down, and Washington left, determined to take the settlers to court and evict them.[28] (See *A Map of Pennsylvania, Detail #3*, page 55.)

Instead of proceeding down the Ohio to the Kanawha River, Washington left his baggage with the Craiks and set off with Bushrod and a guide southward to the Cheat River, which seemed to be the solution to the great problem of connecting the Potomac to the West.[29] Despite the discouraging reports from settlers, Washington calculated that from the Cheat the portage to the North Branch of the Potomac would be a mere ten miles. (See Hutchins, *A New Map, Detail #2*, page 207, bottom center. The pair of dotted lines connecting the rivers is labeled *Portage*.)

On September 23, Washington arrived at the confluence of the Cheat and Monongahela rivers (just north of today's Morgantown, West Virginia). He had hoped to keep moving south, up the Cheat to its source, but was discouraged by reports that the river "where it runs through the Laurel Hill is . . . so incommoded with large rock stones, rapid and dashing water from one rock to another as to become impassible," and that there was no room for a canal next to the river between the hills. (See Hutchins, *A New Map, Detail #2*, page 207. The ridge at the bottom center, just east of the Monongahela, is Laurel Hill. The Cheat crosses the ridge south of Sandy Creek.) Washington decided instead to investigate the route between the Cheat and the Potomac via Sandy Creek that he had asked Normand Bruce to map when they met at Bath.

About seven miles upstream from the mouth of the Cheat, Washington and his nephew crossed the river at Ice's Ferry. Taking a rocky trail for fifteen miles across Laurel Hill, Washington reached the ford of Sandy Creek on the other side. Laurel Hill was not terribly steep, he noted, but the deep, rocky soil would make it difficult to build good roads. And the creek, he was forced to acknowledge, "has a fall within a few miles of its mouth of forty feet, and being rapid besides, affords no navigation at all." (For Sandy Creek, see Hutchins, *A New Map, Detail #2*, page 207, center.) Traveling almost twenty more miles, Washington noted that the last half was through "a deep rich soil in some places, and a very rocky one in others, with steep hills and what is called the Briery Mountain" which was "intolerable" to cross.

Coming to a clearing at the headwaters of the Youghiogheny River, far from any human habitation, Washington wrote that "I lodged this night with no other shelter or cover than my cloak, and was unlucky enough to have a heavy shower of rain." Setting out at dawn the next morning in a steady downpour, Washington's party pushed on for ten more miles to the nearest dwelling, where "we could get nothing for our horses and only boiled corn for ourselves." Heading east toward the North Branch of the Potomac, Washington gathered more information from the few local inhabitants as he evaluated the existing roads and the potential for building new ones. By September 27 Washington was back on familiar terrain at Patterson's Creek, southeast of Fort Cumberland, near Colonel Cresap's.

However, he decided to take a circuitous route back to Mount Vernon, and did not reach home until sundown on October 4, "having traveled on the same horses since the first day of September by the computed distances 680 miles." He was disappointed that he had been unable to visit his lands on the Ohio and Great Kanawha, "and to take measures for rescuing them from the hands of land jobbers and speculators—who I had been informed regardless of my legal and equitable rights, patents, &ca., had enclosed them within other surveys and were offering them for sale at Philadelphia and Europe." However, he was undeterred in his quest to connect Virginia to the Ohio country, despite the obstacles he had encountered at every turn—both by report and direct observation. "The more the navigation of the Potomac is investigated and duly considered," he declared in his diary, "the greater the advantages arising from them appear."

After he returned home in October, Washington devoted himself in the fall and early winter of 1784–85 to an almost solo campaign for a Potomac company. On October 10 he wrote to Governor Benjamin Harrison of Virginia and cited Evans's and Hutchins's maps of the middle colonies to back up his assertion that the Potomac would be the "shortest, easiest, and least expensive" route to the West. "Nor am I singular in this opinion. Evans, in his map and analysis of the middle colonies which (considering the early period at which they were given to the public) are done with amazing exactness, and Hutchins since, in his topographical description of the western country (a good part of which is from actual surveys), are decidedly of the same sentiments." Anyone who had studied the matter agreed, Washington wrote. To further bolster his argument, Washington enclosed a table of distances.[30]

The commercial advantages of opening the way to the West were evident, Washington wrote, but "there is a political consideration for so doing which is of still greater importance." Washington's quest was no longer just personal and local but rather in the national interest. American independence had changed his perspective. "I need not remark to you Sir that the flanks and rear of the United States are possessed by other powers—and formidable ones too; nor how necessary it is to apply the cement of interest to bind all parts of the Union together by indissoluble bonds—especially that part of it which lies immediately west of us."

For now, the Spanish had closed the Mississippi to American commerce, and the British, still hostile, were holding on to the forts along the Canadian border. However, if westerners could not get their goods to market in the East, and if the Spanish to the south and the British to the north "instead of throwing stumbling blocks in their way as they do now, should hold out lures for their trade and alliance," westerners would break away from the United States, Washington predicted, especially since many of them were recent immigrants, "foreigners who will have no particular predilection towards us." These settlers, Washington told Harrison, "stand as it were upon a pivot—the touch of a feather would turn them any way."[31]

Over the next two months, Washington realized that it would be too difficult to get public money for improving inland navigation via the Potomac, so he convinced the assemblies of both Virginia and Maryland to consider a bill authorizing a Potomac River company composed of private investors. Then, in mid-December, he turned his attention to the national legislature. Washington wrote to Richard Henry Lee, chairman of the Confederation Congress, that he hoped funds would be forthcoming to "have the western waters well explored, the navigation of them fully ascertained, accurately laid down, and a complete and perfect map made of the country."

Washington urged Congress to map the Northwest "at least as far westerly as the Miamis, running into the Ohio and Lake Erie, and to see how the waters of these communicate with the St. Joseph River, which empties into Lake Michigan, and with the Wabash . . . Miami Village in Hutchins's map, if it and the waters are laid down with accuracy, points to a very important post for the Union." (See Hutchins, *A New Map, Detail #3*.)

The expense of this exploration and mapping would be minimal, Washington told Lee, and "the advantages would be unbounded." Once the abundant natural resources of the area were discovered, the federal government could sell the land at a good price to raise revenue for the Union. Washington further suggested that the mines, minerals, and salt springs be reserved for special sale, so that the public rather than a few individuals would benefit. It would penalize the speculators who were now causing conflict with the Indians by "roaming over the country marking and surveying the valuable spots" in defiance of the law. All of this must be worked out soon, Washington warned. "The spirit of emigration is great. People have got impatient. And though you cannot stop the road, it is yet in your power to mark the way. A little while, and you will not be able to do either."[32]

While Washington lobbied for inland navigation to and from the West, Congress was busy wringing concessions of land from the Iroquois in the Treaty of Fort Stanwix, concluded on October 22, 1784. "I have the pleasure of enclosing you a copy of the treaty lately concluded with the Six Nations, in which the carrying place and the fort of Niagara, together with a competent district round Oswego are secured to the U.S.," one of the negotiators,

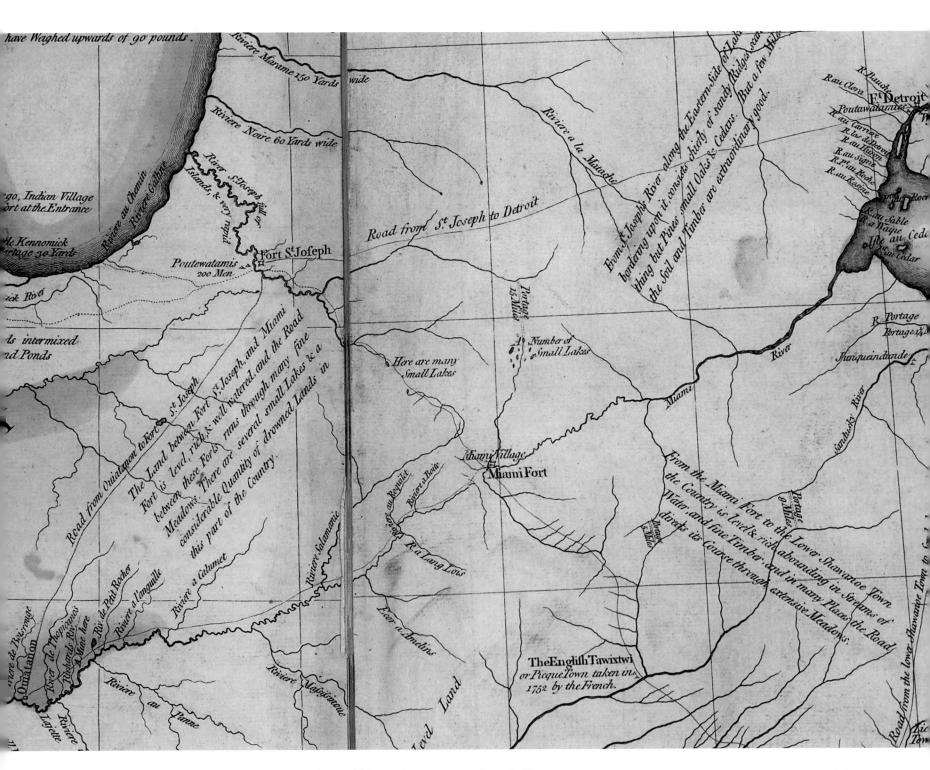

Hutchins, *A New Map, Detail #3:* Indeed, Miami Village (center, today's Fort Wayne, Indiana) was strategically located, like a crossroads, near the headwaters of four key rivers and was an important point on the route between the Great Lakes and the Mississippi. Miami Village would be the target of three military campaigns against the Northwest Indians launched by Washington as president. (Miami Fort, center, is located incorrectly. It should be below the rapids, near the mouth of the river. See Bradley, *A Map of the United States, Detail #2*, page 239, where it is labeled *British Garrison*.)

Arthur Lee, wrote to Washington on November 19.[33] Lee, who was proceeding via Fort Pitt to Cuyahoga, hoped to have a second treaty, with the Northwest tribes, "by the middle of next month, so that the laying off of that country" into parcels for sale "may commence in the spring."[34] Washington told Richard Henry Lee (Arthur Lee's brother) that "if the western tribes are as well disposed to treat with us as the Six Nations have been; and will cede a competent district of land northwest of the Ohio to answer our present purposes, it will be a circumstance as unexpected as pleasing to me."[35] The second treaty, with the Wyandot, Delaware, Chippewa, and Ottawa nations, was agreed to at Fort McIntosh (on Beaver Creek roughly thirty miles down the Ohio from Fort Pitt) on January 21, 1785.[36]

Hugh Williamson, a delegate to Congress from North Carolina, told Washington that the Native Americans "have reserved a quadrangular piece of land" south of Lake Erie. (See Hutchins, *A New Map, Detail #1*, page 204.) Williamson described the area as "Beginning at the mouth of the Cayahoga thence up the river to the portage to the Tuscarawas Branch of the Muskingum, then down that branch to the forks above Fort Lawrence, then west to the portage of Big Miami which runs into the Ohio, then along the portage to the Great Miami or Omai, thence down to its mouth, thence along the south shore of Lake Erie to the mouth of Cayahoga." (Fort Lawrence is labeled *Fort*

Built in 1764; Williamson reversed the names of the two Miami rivers: The first one mentioned should have been the Great Miami, and the second simply the Miami.)[37]

On February 14, Richard Henry Lee enclosed a copy of the treaty in a letter to Washington. Lee noted that the Shawnees had refused to be part of the treaty, but he hoped the Wyandots would keep them in line. "Another treaty will be held with the more southern Indians in the spring or first of the summer," Lee continued. "The policy seems to be a good one, of enclosing as it were, the Indian nations within our acknowledged territory. It will probably tend to civilize them sooner, and by preventing intrigues with them, render them more certainly our friends."[38]

In March, Washington told Arthur Lee he was "pleased to find that the Indians have yielded so much. From the temper I heard they were in, I apprehended less compliance on their part."[39] Had they not been compliant, Washington clearly intended to crush them by force, which included pitting other tribes against them. To Richard Henry Lee, Washington observed that "the Shawnees are pretty numerous, and among the most warlike of the Ohio Indians, but if the subscribing Indians mean to keep good faith, and a treaty should be favorably negotiated with the more southerly Indians, their spirit must yield, or they might easily be extirpated."[40]*

The Maryland and Virginia assemblies had authorized a new Potomac Company by January 1785 with Washington as its president. The bill also supported improvement of the James River, but with public funds.

(See McMurray, *A Map of the United States, Detail #3*.) In August Washington and the directors of the Potomac Company went up the river and clambered into canoes to inspect Seneca Falls and Great Falls. They were accompanied by James Rumsey, the inventor Washington had met at Bath and recommended for his position as manager of the company's operations.

With stubborn optimism, Washington asserted in his diary that "the water through these falls is of sufficient depth for good navigation, and as formidable as I had conceived them to be, but by no means impracticable. The principal difficulties lie in rocks which occasion a crooked passage. These, once removed renders the passage safe without the aid of locks" to raise and lower boats, Washington concluded, and the river could be cleared within the proposed budget. After making a similar judgment about Shenandoah Falls, further up the river at Harpers Ferry, Washington and the directors instructed Rumsey to hire as many workers as he needed. After spending some time watching the laborers at their various tasks, blasting and removing rocks, Washington returned home satisfied "after an absence from it of ten days."[41]

In South Carolina, leaders of the Revolutionary generation were pursuing similar projects. William Moultrie wrote to Washington that "a number of gentlemen of this state have entered into an association which is sanctioned by the legislature to open an inland navigation by a communication from the Santee to the Cooper River, the distance across being about twenty miles. We intend

McMurray, *A Map of the United States, Detail #3:* Improvement of the James River (right center) was to connect it with the Ohio River (upper left) via the Great Kanawha River (upper left), New River (center left), and Fluvanna River (center right).

* As Richard Henry Lee had suggested, the Treaty with the Cherokee (Treaty of Hopewell), concluded at Hopewell, South Carolina, in 1785, enclosed the southern Indians within a specified area of the United States.

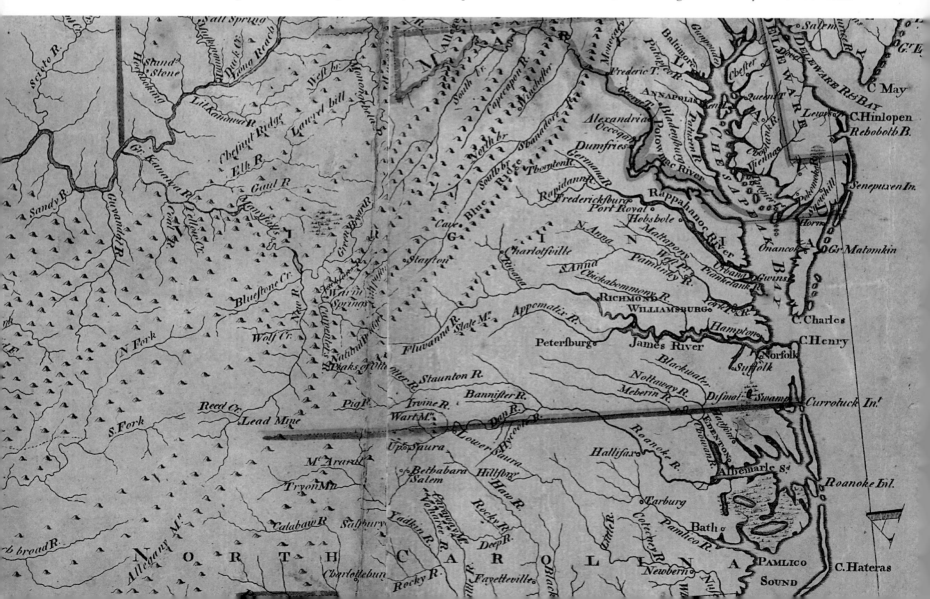

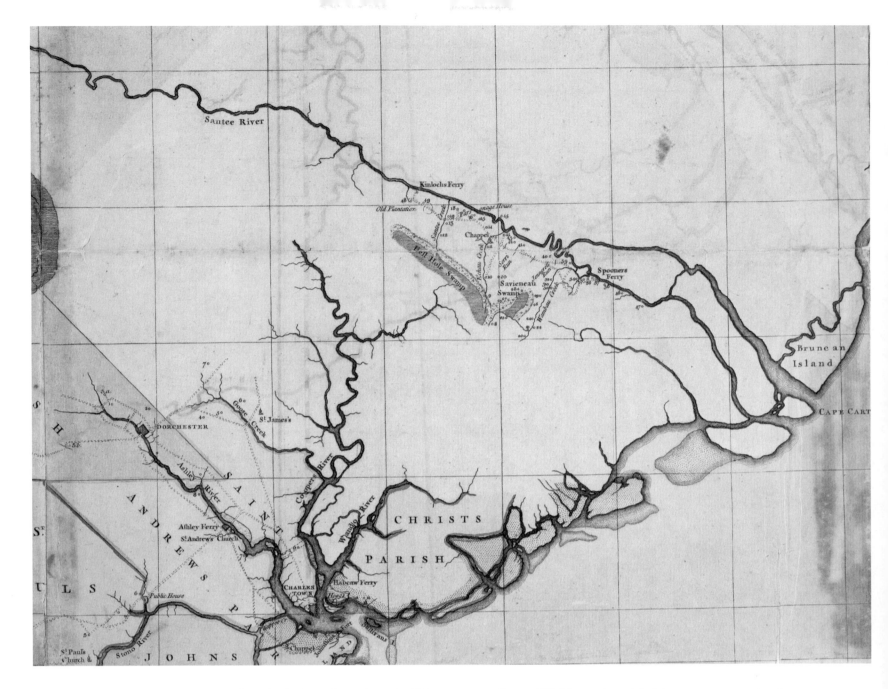

A Map of South Carolina and a Part of Georgia, Detail #5: South Carolina's legislature chartered the Santee Canal Company in 1786, but construction of the twenty-two-mile canal between the Santee and Cooper rivers did not begin until 1793 and was not completed until 1800. From Charleston in the lower left, the Cooper River extends directly northward (while the Ashley flows from the north-west). The canal was built at the large fork in the Cooper (today's Lake Moultrie), directly west of the Hell Hole Swamp, to connect the Cooper and Santee rivers.

it to be done by locks and canals, and will be a means of shortening the present navigation at least 150 miles." (See *A Map of South Carolina and a Part of Georgia, Detail #5*.) Among the directors were John and Edward Rutledge, General Thomas Sumter, and General Francis Marion.

Washington agreed to help Moultrie contact James Brindley, the engineer working for the Susquehanna Company on Pennsylvania's canal project. "It gives me pleasure to find a spirit for inland navigation prevailing so generally," Washington told Moultrie. "No country is more capable of improvements in this way than our own—none which will be more benefited by them."[42]

In writing to Lafayette, Washington described the Potomac project in biblical terms. "I wish to see the sons and daughters of the world in peace and busily employed in the more agreeable amusement of fulfilling the first and great commandment, *Increase and Multiply*: as an encouragement to which we have opened the fertile plains of the Ohio to the poor, the needy and the oppressed of the Earth; anyone therefore who is heavy laden, or who wants land to cultivate, may repair thither and abound, as in the Land of Promise, with milk and honey: The ways are preparing, and the roads will be made easy, thro' the channels of the Potomac and James rivers."[43]

Washington's social vision was conservative, however, and he expected to profit—through long-term leases of his land—by extending the traditional hierarchy of the tenant-landlord system to the West, rather than encouraging numerous independent farms. This was not Jefferson's vision of freeholders—an agricultural republic of small family farms whose owners' economic self-sufficiency would ensure their political independence, their freedom to vote without fear of intimidation by an oligarchy of wealthy planters.[44] Ultimately, Washington would prove to have the more radical vision of human freedom and equality, however, as Jefferson made excuses for perpetuating chattel slavery at Monticello, and Washington took action by freeing his slaves, even giving directions for the young to be educated.[45]

In addition to lobbying for inland navigation, Washington had advised Congress on the Land Ordinance of 1785, which was passed on May 20, dividing the land in the Northwest Territory into townships, to be subdivided into lots of 640 acres for sale, with one seventh of the region reserved for veterans of the Continental army.[46] The settlers would need protection, and Henry Knox, Washington's former artillery chief and the newly appointed secretary of war, had a federal force of only seven hundred men. Knox asked Washington for advice on how to deploy them. Washington replied that British intentions left much uncertainty in the Northwest, but he ventured some advice.

Washington recommended only one hundred men at Fort Pitt, Fort McIntosh, or the mouth of Big Beaver Creek, with one of those forts serving as a supply depot for all the rest. (See Hutchins, *A New Map, Detail #1*, page 204, right center for Beaver Creek. Two hundred men should be posted on the Cuyahoga River, with a detachment at the portage to Big Beaver Creek, since this was the likely route for transporting much of the "fur and peltry of the Lakes" once the British ceded the northwestern posts. (See *Detail #1*, right center.) "The spot marked Miami Village and Fort in Hutchins's map, I have always considered as of importance, being a central point between Lake Erie, Lake Michigan, and the Ohio River, communicating with each by water," Washington told Knox, and it should have two hundred men. (See *Detail #1*, left center.) Another 150 men should go to "the Falls of the Ohio, or some more convenient spot for the lower settlements." The Falls are just west of the mouth of the Great Miami River. (See *Detail #1*, bottom left.) The last fifty men should be sent to "the conflux of the Great Kanawha and Ohio for security of the river—protection of trade, and covering immigrants." (See *Detail #1*, bottom right.)[47]

Josiah Harmar had been appointed lieutenant colonel of the seven hundred troops in 1784 and would become a brigadier general three years later. Construction of Fort Harmar, his headquarters at the mouth of the Muskingum River, would begin in the fall of 1785. Eventually, his forces would be deployed as far west as the Wabash River. (See Bradley, *A Map of the United States, Detail #1*.)[48]

Bradley, *A Map of the United States, Detail #1:* Washington owned a copy of this map by Abraham Bradley, published in 1796, only a year after conquest of the area by the United States was completed. Retrospectively, it shows the locations in the Northwest Territory relevant to Washington in the late 1780s and the 1790s. Fort Harmar was built in the fall of 1785 at the mouth of the Muskingum River (right center). Josiah Harmar's troops were later deployed as far west as the Wabash River (left).

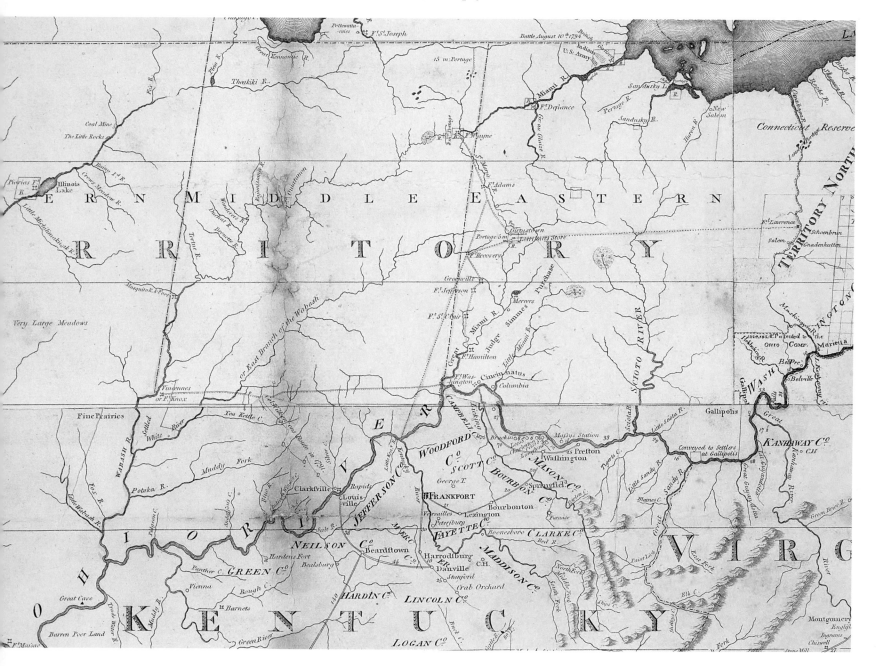

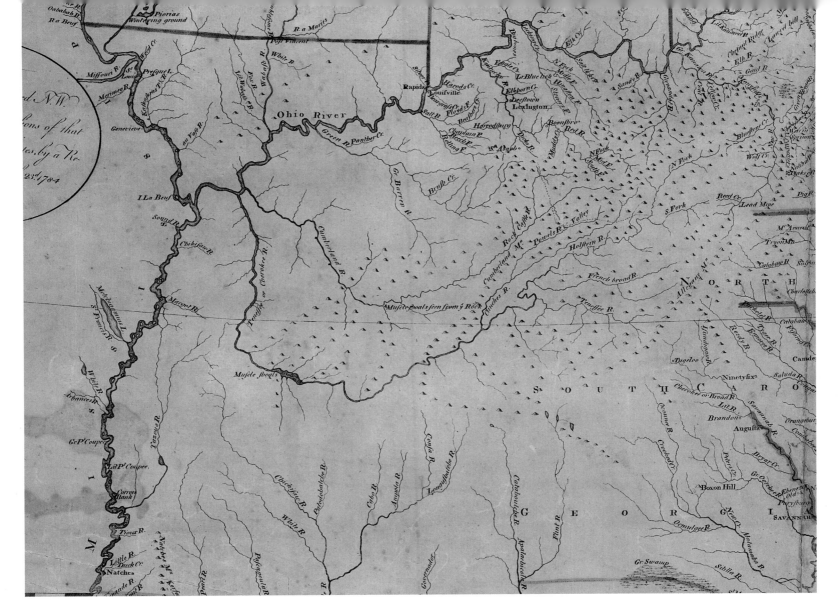

There was hope for progress on outstanding issues with the British because John Adams had arrived in London as the American ambassador, Richard Henry Lee told Washington in July 1785. However, Adams soon found the British hostile and intransigent, and conflict continued to fester regarding American grievances—the closing of British markets to American trade, the British presence in the Northwest, compensation owed for American slaves evacuated at the end of the war—and British complaints about American violations of the Treaty of Paris, including nonpayment of Americans' prewar debts to British merchants.[49]

Tensions mounted in the Southwest that summer too, the governor of Georgia reporting a clash between settlers and Spanish troops at Fort Natchez, with deaths on both sides.[50] In the treaty ending the Revolutionary War, England had agreed to make the 31st parallel the southwestern border of the United States. However, in a separate treaty, Britain gave Spain West Florida, with its northern border more than one hundred miles above the 31st parallel at 32° 28° where the Yazoo River flowed into the Mississippi. With a fort at Natchez, the Spanish retained control of the disputed territory—the Yazoo Strip—stretching from the Mississippi in the west to the Chattahoochee River in the east. The Spanish also asserted a right to territory once held by the British as far north as the Tennessee River and even the Ohio. (See McMurray, *A Map of the United States, Detail #4*.)[51]

Not only had Spain closed the Mississippi in 1784, but in Louisiana and the Floridas, Spanish officials courted the Native Americans—the Creeks, Cherokees, Chickasaws, and Choctaws—and stoked their hostility to American pioneers in Kentucky, the Tennessee country, and the Piedmont plain of Georgia in order to strangle western settlement and check the expansion of the United States. (See *A General Map of North America, Detail #4*, page 163. The Native American tribes are indicated on the left, between the Mississippi on the west and the southern states to the east.)[52]

Lee told Washington that Congress, hoping to defuse the conflict, had commissioned John Jay to open negotiations with Don Diego de Gardoqui, the Spanish

McMurray, *A Map of the United States, Detail #4*: The Spanish fort at Natchez (bottom left) dominated the Yazoo Strip, which extended from the lower Mississippi (bottom left) to the Chattahoochee (*Catahoulche R.*, bottom center) and as far north at the mouth of the Yazoo River (*Yazous R.*, lower left). The Spanish also claimed lands as far north as the Ohio and Tennessee rivers (top and center).

ambassador, "concerning navigation of Mississippi, boundary, commerce, etc."[53] Washington, while eager to regain the Northwest posts from the British, was in no rush to open the Mississippi, he told Lee. "However singular the opinion may be, I cannot divest myself of it, that the navigation of the Mississippi, at this time, ought to be no object with us. On the contrary, till we have a little time allowed to open and make easy the ways between the Atlantic states and the western territory, the obstructions had better remain."[54]

As Washington knew, there were speculators and settlers who would not be willing to wait. At the same time, the mixed-race chief of the Creeks, Alexander McGillivray, had allied himself with the governor of Spanish Louisiana, Estéban Miró, and with the Choctaws and Chickasaws, to wage war on the southern border of the United States. However, the border warfare was provoked by both sides. American land speculators encroached on the hunting grounds of the Native Americans, and pioneers made merciless raids on their villages.

William Blount had launched the Muscle Shoals Company in 1784 to settle whites on Cherokee land at the Great Bend of the Tennessee River. James Robertson planned to put settlers at Chickasaw Bluffs on the Mississippi. (See McMurray, *A Map of the United States, Detail #4*, page 217. Muscle Shoals is shown, left center, where the Tennessee River widens and is studded with rocks. Chickasaw Bluffs, northwest of Muscle Shoals on the Mississippi River below the Margot River, left center, is not labeled. The Georgia legislature unilaterally announced that it would authorize speculators to take pieces of the Yazoo Strip.[55] James Wilkinson and disaffected fellow Kentuckians would even be prepared to abandon the United States after Congress failed to grant them statehood in 1788: In exchange for trading privileges from Miró, they plotted to break away and submit their portion of the West to Spanish sovereignty.[56]

Washington did not regard himself as a speculator, but when a proper offer came, he was willing to sell all of his land in the West. Henry Charton, described as "a French gentleman," visited Washington at Mount Vernon on March 18, 1786. Along with two partners, Albert Gallatin and Savary de Coulon, he proposed to buy land and settle immigrants on the Ohio River. Washington had advertised his Ohio tracts for rent two years earlier, and had not intended to sell because "I well knew they would rise more in value than the purchase money would accumulate by interest." However, as he had no children of his own and "wished to live easy, and to spend the remainder of my days with as little trouble as possible," he would reconsider "if a good price could be obtained."

In May he wrote to Charton, declaring the land to be the finest anywhere and describing its abundant "natural advantages." As for the location of the seven parcels, totaling 32,373 acres, "none can be more advantageous"

OPPOSITE: George Washington's hand-drawn map showing three tracts of his land on the Ohio River.

he wrote, "for lying about midway between the upper and lower settlements on the Ohio, the trade must pass by the land, whilst the occupants of it, equally convenient to both, might embrace the inland navigation of either the Potomac or James River as soon as they are made to communicate with the western waters, which no doubt will be soon effected as both works have commenced." (See McMurray, *A Map of the United States, Detail #3*, page 214, upper left. With the Kanawha extending southeastward toward Virginia, and the Ohio northeastward to Pennsylvania, Washington envisioned a major commercial hub here, at today's Point Pleasant, West Virginia.) For these lands of "superior value" he would accept no less than the princely sum of "thirty thousand English guineas (of the proper weight) or other specie current in this country at an equivalent value."[57]

Washington was energetic not only in praising his own lands for sale, but in burnishing the reputation of the nation as a whole. The dim view of the United States purveyed by British newspapers since the end of the war was unfortunately bolstered by the weakness of Congress and the failure of some states to send representatives to Philadelphia, Washington lamented. "In a word it hurts us," he told William Grayson, a delegate to Congress from Virginia. "Our character as a nation is dwindling, and what it must come to if a change should not soon take place, our enemies have foretold."[58] To counter the negative picture put forth by the British, Washington described to La Luzerne in glowing terms all the progress Americans had made. Congress would soon have greater powers he wrote, and the state governments were "daily acquiring strength":

The laws have their fullest energy; justice is well administered. Robbery, violence, or murder is not heard of from New Hampshire to Georgia. The people at large (as far as I can learn) are more industrious than they were before the war. Economy begins, partly from necessity and partly from choice and habit, to prevail. The seeds of population are scattered over an immense tract of western country. In the old states which were the theaters of hostility, it is wonderful to see how soon the ravages of war are repaired. Houses are rebuilt, fields enclosed, stocks of cattle which were destroyed are replaced, and many a desolated territory assumes again the cheerful appearance of cultivation. In many places the vestiges of conflagration and ruin are hardly to be traced. The arts of peace, such as the clearing of rivers, building of bridges, establishing conveniences for traveling, etc. are assiduously promoted. In short, the foundation of a great empire is laid, and I please myself with a persuasion that Providence will not leave its work imperfect.[59]

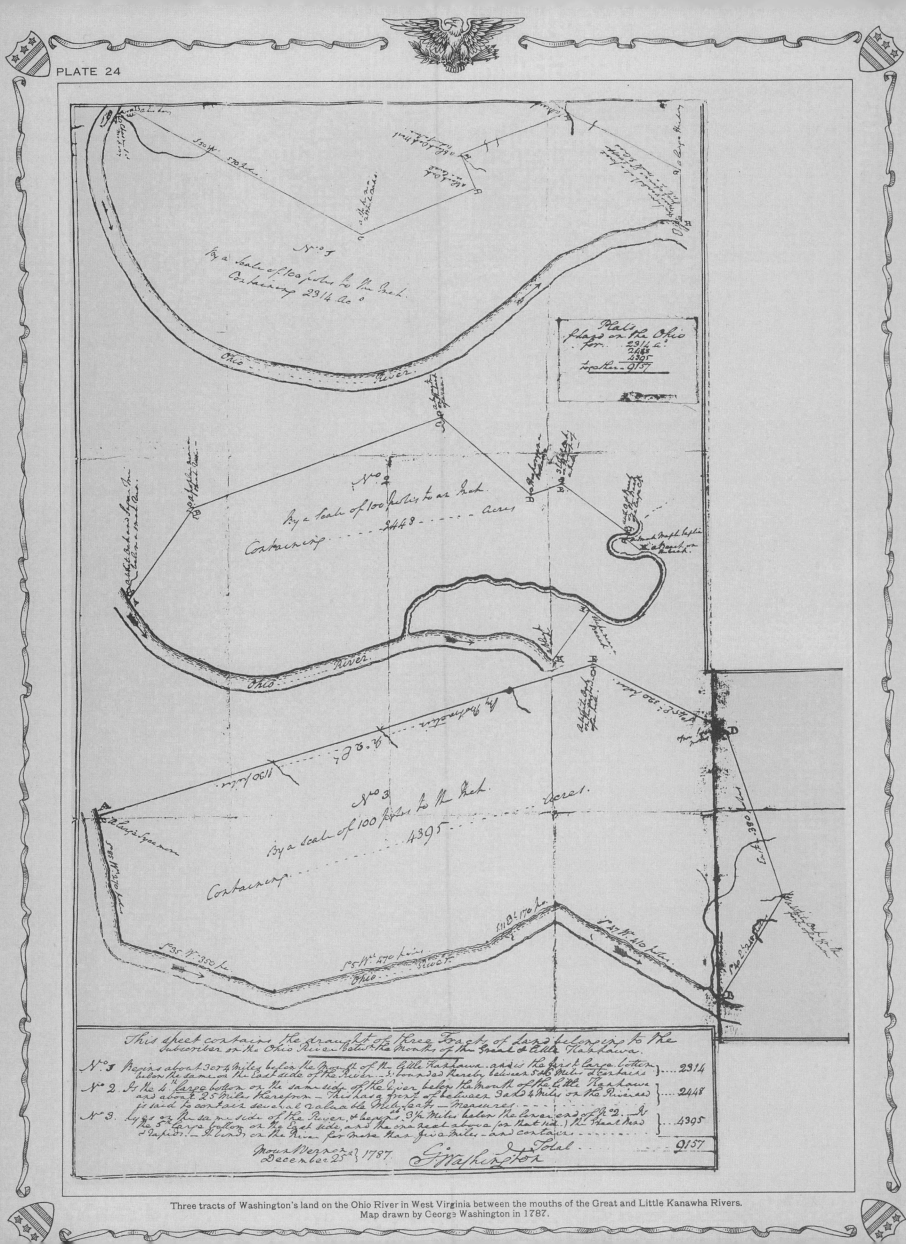

PLATE 24

Three tracts of Washington's land on the Ohio River in West Virginia between the mouths of the Great and Little Kanawha Rivers.
Map drawn by George Washington in 1787.

George Washington presiding over the Constitutional Convention.

John Jay had begun negotiating with Gardoqui in the summer of 1785, presumably with the objectives, specified by Congress, of opening the Mississippi for American trade and establishing the 31st parallel as the border between the United States and Spanish Florida. However, Jay shared Washington's conviction that free navigation of the Mississippi should be postponed until stronger ties between the eastern and western parts of the United States had been created by improving inland navigation. On August 3, 1786, Jay expressed these views before Congress, which provoked the fury of southerners and westerners against the eastern commercial elite and doomed ratification of any treaty he might negotiate with Spain.[60]

"The British still occupy our posts to the westward, and will, I am persuaded, continue to do so under one pretence or another, no matter how shallow, as long as they can," Washington told Lafayette in May 1786. This had been their intention all along, Washington suspected, since the negotiation of the Treaty of Paris in 1783, "to inflame the Indian mind, with a view to keep it at variance with these states for the purpose of retarding our settlements to the westward and depriving us of the fur and peltry trade of that country."[61]

But this strategy would backfire, Washington declared. "Great Britain, viewing with eyes of chagrin and jealousy the situation of this country, will not, for some time yet if ever, pursue a liberal policy towards it," Washington told William Carmichael, an American envoy to Spain. "But unfortunately for her the conduct of her ministers defeats their own ends: Their restriction of our trade with them will facilitate the enlargement of Congressional powers in commercial matters more than half a century would otherwise have effected. The mercantile interests of this country are uniting as one man to vest the federal government with ample powers to regulate trade and to counteract the selfish views of other nations."[62]

The impetus also came from internal threats to the young republic. Shays' Rebellion in 1786–87—an armed uprising of poor farmers in Massachusetts against a cycle of taxation, debt, property seizures by the state government, and debtors' prison—prompted calls from the elite for more federal power to carry out the laws and maintain order. John Jay told Washington in the spring of 1786 that "an opinion begins to prevail that a general convention for revising the Articles of Confederation would be expedient."[63] Washington agreed that "something must be done, or the fabric must fall. It certainly is tottering!"[64] While he did not publicly advocate more power for Congress, his private statements were influential. He argued for strong government through the impost, which would allow Congress to collect a 5 percent tax on imports; and he believed the sale of western lands ceded by the states to Congress would help it financially.[65] Washington continued to believe that "the burdens of war shall be in a manner done away by the sale of western lands" (for the nation as well as for himself personally).[66]

Washington was asked to preside over the Constitutional Convention in 1787, an indication of the high esteem in which he was held by virtually all Americans. And while he had little to do with drafting the Constitution, his presence lent credibility to the proceedings in the public eye. He was not associated with any faction or local interest, but instead regarded as a selfless public servant. He had held the army together, through nakedness and starvation, through crises that might have been averted if Congress had not been utterly dependent on the states to raise revenue.

Memories of those trying times came flooding back during a ten-day recess in July and August when Washington traveled outside Philadelphia with Gouverneur Morris to go trout fishing on a stream at Valley Forge. "Whilst Mr. Morris was fishing I [rode] over the old cantonment of the American army of the winter 1777 and 8," Washington noted in his diary. "Visited all the works, which were in ruins, and the encampments in the woods where the ground had not been cultivated." (See *A Map of Pennsylvania, Detail #6*, page 150.) Washington also recorded a trip to Trenton "on another fishing party. Lodged at Colonel Sam Ogden's at the Trenton Works," which had supplied the army with cannon and shot during the Revolution. (See *A Map of the Province of New York, Detail #6*, page 141.) After the Convention had resumed, Washington rode on a Sunday up to Whitemarsh, he wrote. "Traversed my old encampment, and contemplated on the dangers which threatened the American army at that place. Dined at Germantown."[67] (See *A Map of Pennsylvania, Detail #7*, page 152.)

During the summer of 1787, while the Constitution was being debated, Congress passed the Northwest Ordinance, establishing a government and providing for eventual statehood for the areas north and west of the Ohio River.[68*] Arthur St. Clair was named governor of the Northwest Territory. He had served in the Revolution—controversially—abandoning Ticonderoga in the face of Burgoyne's advance. It may have been prudent, but it put a cloud over his reputation that his performance in the next few years would darken rather than dispel.[69] St. Clair would arrive at Fort Harmar in July 1788.[70]

Once the Convention was over and the Constitution was sent to the state legislatures for ratification, Washington's name became the main argument put forward for approving the document.[71] Under the threat of southern withdrawal from the Convention, the Constitution included major concessions to slaveholders, and despite his growing disgust with the institution and his desire to extricate himself from it, Washington had made no public pronouncements and took no action privately that might have alienated his fellow planters and put the framework for the new national government in jeopardy. In determining a state's population, and thus the size of its delegation in the House of Representatives, the Constitution counted each slave as three fifths of a person. And slaveholders were guaranteed that there would be no federal interference with the slave trade until 1808. For a slave-breeding state like Virginia, the ban on importing and exporting slaves from the United States, to take effect that year, would actually be beneficial.[72]

Toward the end of the war, Lafayette had written to Washington proposing that they "unite in purchasing a small estate, where we may try the experiment to free the Negroes, and use them only as tenants. Such an example as yours might render it a general practice; and if we succeed in America, I will cheerfully devote a part of my time to render the method fashionable in the West Indies." Washington had replied that he would be "happy to join you in so laudable a work," but never followed through. Lafayette did, however, and Washington had congratulated him in May 1786 for purchasing "an estate in the colony of Cayenne with a view of emancipating the slaves on it." This, Washington wrote, "is a generous and noble proof of your humanity. Would to God a like spirit would diffuse itself generally into the minds of the people of this country, but I despair of seeing it. Some petitions were presented to the Assembly at its last session, for the abolition of slavery, but they could scarcely obtain a reading. To set [the slaves] afloat at once would, I really believe, be productive of much inconvenience and mischief, but by degrees it certainly might, and assuredly ought to be effected, and that too by legislative authority."[73]

The Confederation Congress announced ratification of the Constitution on July 2, 1788 (by all but Rhode Island and North Carolina), exactly twelve years after the Declaration of Independence was approved by the Continental Congress, and national elections for the Constitutional Congress and the Executive were scheduled for January 1789. During the six months between ratification and the election, Washington was deluged at Mount Vernon with letters urging him to accept the presidency, but he remained silent, creating an aura of reluctance that reinforced his image as a selfless public servant who did not grasp for power. And while this ritual may have gratified his own desire for fame, it also enhanced his authority—his ability to lead the whole nation.[74]

Arthur St. Clair.

* The Northwest of the eighteenth century is today's Midwest: Ohio, Indiana, Illinois, Michigan, and Wisconsin. The Southwest of the eighteenth century is today's Alabama, Mississippi, Tennessee, and parts of Louisiana and Florida. As the United States expanded past the Mississippi toward the Pacific, these regions were called the Old Northwest and Old Southwest. In between the two, Kentucky was formed (from the western parts of Virginia) and shared their turbulent history.

In January, Washington finally indicated that he would stand for election, and on February 4, in accordance with the Constitution, the members of the electoral college in each state (chosen as directed by the state's legislature) met and cast their ballots. Now Washington was forced to wait for two and a half months for confirmation of the vote, as the ballots were sent to the Senate in New York City but could not be opened for lack of a quorum. The "stupor or listlessness" of the legislators who trickled into the new capital did not bode well for the Constitution, Washington remarked to Knox. When the ballots were finally opened, Washington was elected unanimously: Each elector, required to vote for two people, had cast one vote for Washington. John Adams, having lost to Washington 69–34 but having garnered the second largest number of votes among all the candidates, was elected vice president.[75]

A messenger from the Senate arrived with the news at Mount Vernon on April 14, and Washington was ready to leave two days later. "About ten o'clock I bade adieu to Mount Vernon, to private life, and to domestic felicity," Washington wrote in his diary on the 16th, "and with a mind oppressed with more anxious and painful sensations than I have words to express, set out for New York."[76] The trip took an entire week, as people turned out to cheer Washington and the towns along the route offered celebratory feasts.[77]

Arriving at Elizabethtown, New Jersey, on April 23, Washington was greeted by a delegation of senators, congressmen, and state and local officials, the *New York Daily Advertiser* reported. (See *A Map of the Province of New York, Detail #2*, page 127, left center.) Together they boarded a barge and were rowed into the Upper Bay toward Manhattan "by thirteen pilots of this harbor, dressed in white uniform . . . His Excellency's barge was accompanied by the barge of the Honorable General Knox, and a great number of vessels and boats from Jersey and New-York, in his train." As they passed Bedloe's Island on their left and Governors Island on their right, a sloop under full sail approached the barge, and Washington was serenaded by a quartet of men and women singing to the tune of "God Save the King":

Joy to our native land,
Let every heart expand,
For Washington's at hand,
With glory crowned.

(See *A Plan of the City of New-York, Detail #2*, page 126. Bedloe's is labeled *Kennedys or Corporation I.*) As Washington took off his hat and bowed, a second boat pulled up next to the sloop and an expanded chorus sang another ode to Washington while porpoises leaped in front of his barge.

Striking a discordant note, another vessel appeared, displaying on it deck "Dr. King from South Africa with a collection of natural curiosities," one newspaper reported. Two orangutans stared back at Washington, while the anti-Federalist journalist Philip Freneau, standing near them, bowed to the president-elect. It was the day's only omen of the bitter partisan attacks that would wound Washington so deeply during and after his presidency.

As Washington approached the southern tip of Manhattan, the Spanish sloop of war *Galveston*, anchored north of Governors Island, fired a thirteen-gun salute, which was answered by another from the Battery. Governor George Clinton and other officials greeted Washington at the foot of Wall Street, at the stairs of Murray's Wharf, which were carpeted and the rails draped with crimson for his arrival. The dignitaries then paraded through Queen Street to the president's house on Cherry Street, the *Daily Advertiser* noted, "followed by an amazing concourse of citizens." (See *A Plan of the City of New-York, Detail #1*, page 125. Murray's Wharf stood at the opposite end of Wall Street from Trinity Church, marked *P*. The continuation of Dock Street, two streets in from the wharves, was Queen Street. Washington's residence, Franklin House at No. 3 Cherry Street, was near the East River shore just beyond the shipyards, *H*, near today's Brooklyn Bridge.)

After a short wine and punch reception at Washington's residence, he changed clothes and rode in Governor Clinton's coach to his mansion for a banquet. "In the evening, the houses of the citizens were brilliantly illuminated," the *Daily Advertiser* reported, and Washington went out to inspect them. Undoubtedly exhausted, and overwhelmed by the day's tributes, Washington's mind reeled as he faced the people's exalted expectations of his leadership. "The display of boats which attended and joined us on this occasion, some with vocal and some with instrumental music on board, the decorations of the ships, the roar of cannon, and the loud acclamations of the people which rent the skies, as I passed along the wharves, filled my mind with sensations as painful (considering the reverse of this scene, which may be the case after all my labors to do good) as they are pleasing."

George Washington arriving in New York City for his inauguration.

CHAPTER EIGHT

DANGER ON THE FRONTIERS,

UPHEAVAL IN EUROPE

"My movements to the chair of Government will be accompanied by feelings not unlike those of a culprit who is going to the place of his execution," Washington told Henry Knox on April 1, 1789, "so unwilling am I, in the evening of a life nearly consumed in public cares, to quit a peaceful abode for an ocean of difficulties." As he had when he assumed command of the Continental army, Washington deprecated his own competence but promised "integrity and firmness," which, "be the voyage long or short, never shall forsake me although I may be deserted by all men."[1] Thirteen guns saluted at dawn on Inauguration Day, April 30, and Washington was sworn in at Federal Hall on the corner of Broad and Wall streets. (See *A Plan of the City of New-York, Detail #1*, page 125, center left. Federal Hall is labeled *I, City Hall*, because the federal and city governments were both housed in this building.)

Washington's weariness aside, the mood of the country was buoyant. The thirteen guns at dawn suggested that the eleven states in the Union were justly confident of North Carolina's and Rhode Island's eventual ratification of the Constitution. And Washington assumed office during a period of relative calm on all fronts. "Our prospects have been gradually meliorating. Unanimity increases. Economy has succeeded to profusion. Industry prevails. Such is the general picture of the United States," Washington told Rochambeau. The recovery of the economy after the war and the venting achieved by Shays' Rebellion, as well as confidence in Washington and the new, stronger government, all helped. The Northwest Ordinance of 1787 also contributed to a sense of orderly expansion and progress for Americans. And with France headed toward revolution, the monarchies of Britain and Spain became alarmed, and focused on European affairs instead of fomenting intrigue and border warfare with the Native Americans on the U.S. frontiers in the Northwest and the Southwest.[2]

Nonetheless, Washington carefully monitored developments on the frontiers and in Europe. He could afford to postpone military measures and action, and he had to because Congress had not yet established the defense infrastructure. Knox, a holdover from the Confederation government, continued as head of the War Department and kept Washington informed, particularly about tensions with the Indians in the Northwest. In the opening days of his first term Washington also met with St. Clair, the ill-starred governor of the Northwest Territory.[3]

St. Clair had returned from the Northwest for the inauguration after concluding a new treaty with the Wyandots and their allies at Fort Harmar in January 1789. Congress viewed the agreement as a confirmation of the treaties of Fort Stanwix in 1784 and Fort McIntosh in 1785 in which the Indians made concessions north of the Ohio River and east of the Muskingum River. (See Hutchins, *A New Map*,

Detail #1, page 204. The Muskingum flows into the Ohio on the lower right.) An apparent gain for white settlers and speculators, this new concession ultimately triggered more Indian attacks.

However, both sides violated the treaty, the Native Americans refusing to be hemmed in, and whites encroaching on tribal land with an eye to further expansion. Land speculators, including many powerful officials in the federal government, had seen to it that St. Clair had no leeway in his instructions to cede territory. Indeed his mission was to look for ways to pit the tribes against each other. St. Clair relayed advice to Washington from the Wyandots—who were evidently eager to subdue rival tribes—that "a post should be taken by the United States at the Miami Village as the surest means to overawe the nations on the Wabash. It is certainly well situated for that purpose, and would command the greatest part of the Indian trade." (See Hutchins, *A New Map, Detail #3*, page 213, center and lower left.)[4]

The Shawnees, Miamis, and Kickapoos, confined west of the Muskingum River by the treaty, became increasingly hostile to American settlers.[5] In the spring and summer of 1789, numerous reports flooded in describing Indian attacks on Kentucky settlers south of the Ohio River.[6] In May, Washington received a report "of some murders committed by the Indians . . . at Dunkard Creek which runs into the Monongahala River." (See Hutchins, *A New Map, Detail #2*, page 207, center and lower left.)

"It is with great concern that I learn this circumstance," Washington told Virginia governor Beverly Randolph, "as a treaty has been lately concluded by the governor of the western territory with the Wyandot, Delaware, Ottawa, Chippewa, Pottawattamie, and Sac nations of Indians, northwest of the Ohio." The raiders must have been "a party from the remnants of the Shawnee tribe, who are joined by a few renegade Cherokees," Washington concluded, and asked that in the future "the nearest post of the troops stationed on the Ohio" be notified immediately "in order if possible that the banditti be intercepted."[7]

One active raiding party was set up on the north side of the Ohio just above the mouth of the Scioto. (See Hutchins, *A New Map, Detail #1*, page 204, bottom center.)[8] Egged on by land speculators, the whites were as vicious and destructive in their raids as the Indians and often attacked indiscriminately, punishing hostile, neutral, and friendly tribes alike.

As the cycle of violence continued, the settlers drove away potential allies, and the Native Americans formed a confederation of tribes, which was supplied and encouraged by the British in the forts on the Canadian border. The Indians escalated their attacks to include not only settlements, but boats on the Ohio, Tennessee, and Cumberland rivers, which were the commercial arteries of the region. (See McMurray, *A Map of the United States, Detail #4*, page 217, left center, where the Tennessee

General Josiah Harmar.

and Cumberland rivers flow into the Ohio. This area between the Northwest and the Southwest was not a barrier but rather a link, a zone of communication traversed by the Native Americans above and below.)[9]

With Josiah Harmar's regiment of federal troops steadily losing men in its futile attempts to keep the Native Americans and settlers apart, Secretary of War Knox gave Washington an overview of the deteriorating situation on the frontiers in June 1789. The United States did not have the manpower or resources to launch a major offensive in the Northwest, Knox asserted, and it would be hypocritical to punish the Indians, given the provocations and atrocities committed by white settlers. Such an action would "stain the character of the nation," he wrote. Instead, Washington approved Knox's plan to move Harmar's units, which were not at full strength, further west on the Ohio to protect the Native Americans north of the river from attacks by Kentucky settlers (which had been the most brutal and random) while continuing to pursue a treaty involving every tribe between the Ohio and the Great Lakes. (See Bradley, *A Map of the United States, Detail #1*, page 216.)[10]

Knox told Washington that the United States was even less prepared for a military confrontation with the powerful Creek Indians in the Southwest, where North Carolina's refusal to ratify the Constitution left South Carolina's and Georgia's lines of supply and communication to the rest of the nation in doubt. Washington was even more concerned about the prospect of war here than in the Northwest. The Creeks were backed by the Spanish in border disputes with the state of Georgia. And the Creek confederation could field several thousand warriors—far more than the Northwest Indians—against the widely dispersed settlers on the western frontiers of the southern states and any force of militia or regulars the United States could muster there. (See *A General Map of North America, Detail #4*, page 163.)

Washington's other worry in the Southwest was that the Spanish might bribe some adventurous, acquisitive, and disloyal Americans to split off from the United States and set up a rogue republic. British attempts to involve Americans in anti-Spanish schemes presented a danger here as well. Even before he had entered office, Washington had been briefed at Mount Vernon about the "Spanish Conspiracy," which he was monitoring through coded messages with his informers.[11] Harry Innes had reported that Colonel John Connolly, a British spy, was in Kentucky trying to recruit Americans for an expedition to capture New Orleans and open the navigation of the Mississippi River. He promised British money, ammunition, and ships to support the operation.[12]

"As a friend to United America, I embrace, with extreme satisfaction the proposals you are pleased to offer of transmitting farther intelligence," Washington had told Innes in March. He hoped Innes would reveal "the machinations of all those, who, by sowing the seeds of disaffection, may attempt to separate any portion of the United States from the Union. I will only add, for myself, I have little doubt but that a perseverance in temperate measures and good dispositions will produce such a system of national policy, as shall be mutually advantageous to all parts of the American Republic."[13]

Hoping to insert the United States government as the mediator in the dispute between Georgia and the Creeks—and pry the Creeks away from the Spanish—Washington got congressional approval for Knox to send a commission led by Benjamin Lincoln to negotiate a treaty with the Creeks. "On the 15th of September next there is to be a treaty held in the State of Georgia, between the Indians on the southern frontiers and commissioners on the part of Georgia," Washington wrote to Lincoln. "At this treaty there will be a numerous and respectable concourse of Indians, two, and some say to the number of three thousand. Their famous counselor, the noted McGillivray is to be present." Washington told Lincoln that "the Treaty is to be held in Georgia at the Rock-Landing on the [Oconee] River."[14] (For the Oconee, see McMurray, *A Map of the United States, Detail #5*, page 231, center. The Rock-Landing was several miles south of the confluence of the Oconee and Crooked Creek, a few miles south of today's Milledgeville.) Lincoln would be up against a sophisticated opponent at the bargaining table: McGillivray, the mixed-race leader of the Creeks,

General Benjamin Lincoln.

Fort Washington.

had a foot in both worlds and was not one to be duped by land speculators and government agents.[15]

"We are recovering slowly from the calamities and burdens with which we were almost overwhelmed by a long and expensive war," Washington told La Luzerne after a year in office. "Our crops the year past have been more abundant, and our markets much better than usual. These circumstances will assist in enabling our citizens to extricate themselves from their private and public debts."[16] He had told Rochambeau that "the opposition offered to the reform of our federal Constitution has in a great measure subsided, and there is every reason to predict political harmony and individual happiness to the states and citizens of confederated America."[17]

As head of the War Department, with Indian affairs as part of his portfolio, Knox reported directly to Washington. "Many of your old acquaintances and friends are concerned with me in the administration of this Government," Washington wrote to Lafayette. "By having Mr. Jefferson at the Head of the Department of State, Mr. Jay of the Judiciary, Hamilton of the Treasury and Knox of that of War, I feel myself supported by able coadjutors, who harmonize extremely well together. I believe that these and the other appointments generally have given perfect satisfaction to the public."[18]

As Washington reported to his French friends on America's prosperity and success, France in 1789 erupted in revolution. The Bastille, a massive medieval prison and symbol of monarchical tyranny, was stormed by mobs on July 14, and Lafayette sent Washington the key.[19] "The revolution which has been effected in France is of so wonderful a nature that the mind can hardly realize the fact," Washington wrote to Gouverneur Morris in October, "but I fear though it has gone triumphantly through the first paroxysm, it is not the last it has to encounter before matters are finally settled." Washington continued presciently:

In a word the revolution is of too great magnitude to be effected in so short a space, and with the loss of so little blood. The mortification of the king, the intrigues of the queen, and the discontent of the princes and the nobility will foment divisions, if possible, in the National Assembly, and avail themselves of every faux pas in the formation of the Constitution if they do not give a more open, active opposition. To these the licentiousness of the people on one hand and sanguinary punishments on the other will alarm the best disposed friends to the measure, and contribute not a little to the overthrow of their object. Great temperance, firmness, and foresight are necessary in the movements of that body. To forbear running from one extreme to another is no easy matter, and, should this be the case, rocks and shelves not visible at present may wreck the vessel.[20]

The deployment of Harmar's regiment further westward did not provide adequate security on the frontier in the summer and fall of 1789, and settlers continued to demand more protection from the federal government in New York. Even though Harmar established new forts, designed to intimidate the Indians, his troops were spread too thin to go on the offensive, which angered white frontier leaders. Harmar's new headquarters was to be at Fort Washington (the site of present-day Cincinnati), named for the president, on the Ohio River between the Great Miami and Little Miami rivers.

St. Clair renamed the settlement next to the fort Cincinnatus, also in honor of Washington because he was compared to that Roman hero, a general who returned to his farm after victory rather than become a dictator. Harmar also strengthened the garrisons at Fort Finney and Fort Knox. (See Bradley, *A Map of the United States, Detail #1*, page 216. Fort Washington is at the center. Fort Finney, southwest of the mouth of the Great Miami, is shown but not labeled, across the Ohio from Louisville at Clarksville. Fort Knox is shown up the Wabash at Vincennes, left center.)[21]

Underlying the conflict in the Northwest was the British presence on the Canadian border, where they continued to hold posts on U.S. soil and to use them as bases for supplying the Indians. When Congress adjourned on September 29, 1789, many other issues with the British were still unresolved: the need for a commercial treaty, America's trade with the West Indies, and compensation for slaves carried away during the Revolution. Symptomatic of the troubled relationship, the British had sent no ambassador to the United States.[22]

During the congressional recess, Washington took a tour of the northeastern states from mid-October to mid-November, traveling through Connecticut, Massachusetts, and New Hampshire, and as far north as Kittery Point, Maine. (See *A Map of the Most Inhabited Part of New England*, page 83, upper right. Kittery Point is just north of Portsmouth, New Hampshire, across the Piscataqua River.) In Connecticut he noted that "the destructive evidences of British cruelty are yet visible both in Norwalk and Fairfield, as there are the chimneys of many burnt houses standing in them yet." And at Lexington he "viewed the spot on which the first blood was spilt in the dispute with Great Britain on the 19th of April 1775." Mostly, however, he looked to the present and future, recording in his diary the condition of roads and the state of agriculture and industry in the various towns.[23] He avoided Rhode Island—"Rogues Island"— the only state that had not ratified the Constitution,

since North Carolina joined in November. (Rhode Island joined in May 1790.)[24]

The New Year in 1790 brought a crowded agenda for Washington and his cabinet. Hamilton presented a controversial program for the national economy that called for the federal government to assume the states' war debts as well as its own, to fund the debt at face value, and to charter a national bank. The question of where to locate the permanent national capital came to the fore, and the final choice would be part of a compromise to win approval for Hamilton's economic program. Knox meanwhile was reorganizing the militia as per Washington's "Sentiments on a Peace Establishment" of 1783, and still waiting for the commissioners he had sent to Georgia to reach an accord with the Creeks.[25]

Washington began to suspect that McGillivray was playing the Spanish and the Americans off each other to see who would make a better offer. To woo him away from the Spanish, Washington approved a plan to bring McGillivray to New York for face-to-face negotiations. Meanwhile he sent three companies of troops to Georgia. "The proposed disposition of the said companies after their arrival in Georgia, to wit—'one company at the St. Mary's; one ditto at Beard's Bluff on the Altamaha; and one ditto at the Rock-Landing on the Oconee;' appears from the maps and information to be the best," he told Knox.[26] (For these three rivers, see

Alexander McGillivray.

McMurray, *A Map of the United States, Detail #5*, bottom center to center.)

In the Northwest, tensions ran high and armed conflict seemed imminent. Knox believed a punitive raid against a few hundred maverick warriors would improve the situation.[27] By April 1790, Knox had won congressional approval for only a slight increase of four hundred men in the federal army, to some twelve hundred enlisted soldiers. By May, with settlers appealing for help, he had given up on negotiation with the maverick Shawnees and Miamis. With Washington's approval, in June he ordered St. Clair to plan a cavalry attack by a combined force of four hundred regulars and militia, and to strike before winter.[28]

England continued to hold forts and incite the Native Americans in the Northwest while refusing to normalize diplomatic and commercial relations with the United States. However, after the Nootka Sound incident raised the prospect of war with Spain, in July 1790, the British needed American cooperation and sent an unofficial representative, Major George Beckwith, an aide to the governor-general of Canada, to New York, where he met with Secretary of the Treasury Alexander Hamilton.* Beckwith intimated that the British might be ready to form an alliance with the Americans and that if war broke out between England and Spain, the Americans would do well to side with the British. The British would want to pass through American territory down from Canada to the Mississippi to attack the Spanish in Louisiana, and Washington would have to decide whether or not to allow them through.

If they won, the British would control Florida and Louisiana, surrounding the United States from the north, west, and south, and from the east on the Atlantic with their navy, as Spain and England already did together.[29] "It seems to be our policy to keep in the situation in which nature has placed us," Washington wrote to Lafayette, "to observe a strict neutrality, and to furnish others with those good things of subsistence, which they may want, and which our fertile land abundantly produces, if circumstances and events will permit us so to do."[30]

Knowing that both sides needed their help, the Americans tried to play Spain and England off each other by not committing to either. Hamilton protested to Beckwith that the British were inciting the Native Americans in the Northwest. Meanwhile, Washington used various channels, including Lafayette in Paris and Secretary of State Thomas Jefferson, to convey to the Spanish that the United States would remain neutral if war broke out between Spain and England, but the Americans needed concessions from Spain, namely the opening of the Mississippi. The Spanish faced the constant threat of American frontiersmen scheming to arm themselves and capture New Orleans; that they might be backed by the British government, and the American, if war broke out was alarming.

The Spanish had been steadily attempting to create and maintain buffer zones between the American Southwest and the Mississippi by supporting both the indigenous Indian tribes and groups of white settlers who might split off from the United States.[32] The Yazoo Company was poised to do just that. Georgia claimed much of the same territory as Spain east of the Mississippi and Yazoo rivers—which was also the domain of the Choctaw and Chickasaw tribes and some of the Cherokees as well. Georgia had recently sold nearly sixteen million of these acres to land speculation companies, and then abdicated all responsibility for governing the region. A soldier of fortune named James O'Fallon was chosen by the speculators as their "governor." (See McMurray, *A Map of the United States, Detail #4*, page 217, bottom left to bottom center.)

However, the scheme soon fell through when the three main players in the region withdrew support. Facing a possible war with England, the Spanish did not want to antagonize the United States; McGillivray and the Creeks decided an alliance with Spain was imprudent under the circumstances; and Washington was not interested in O'Fallon's offer of troops to drive out the Spanish.[33] Washington issued a proclamation warning that "James O'Fallon is levying an armed force in that part of the State of Virginia which is called Kentucky, disturbs the public peace and sets at defiance the treaties of the United States with the Indian tribes . . . and my proclamations of the 14th and 26th days of August . . . and it is my earnest desire that those who have incautiously associated themselves with the said James O'Fallon may be warned of their danger . . . all persons violating the treaties . . . shall be prosecuted with the utmost rigor of the law."[34]

Since Washington had no troops in the area to prevent the Yazoo and other schemes in the future, he used the Creeks as his proxy. When Lincoln's commission could not get a new treaty with the Creeks, Knox sent Marinus Willett to negotiate, and he finally got McGillivray to visit New York with twenty-nine Creek chiefs. To make sure they were treated well on their long journey, Washington had Knox write to the governors of Virginia, Maryland, and Pennsylvania, asking that they provide the Creek delegation "with whatever might be deemed a proper respect that they might be kept in good humor."[35]

The delegation arrived on July 20, 1790, and by the beginning of August, with great ceremony, Washington had signed the resulting Treaty of New York, which settled the contested borders. "While I flatter myself that this treaty will be productive of present peace and prosperity to our southern frontier, it is to be expected that it will also in its consequences be the means of firmly attaching the Creeks and the neighboring tribes to the interests of the United States," Washington told the Senate. "At the same time it is to be hoped that it will afford solid grounds of satisfaction to the state of Georgia, as it contains a regular, full and definitive relinquishment, on the part of the Creek

* The British dispute with Spain over trade and navigation rights in the Pacific Ocean escalated when the Spanish commandant at Nootka Sound, off the Pacific coast of Canada, seized several British merchant ships.

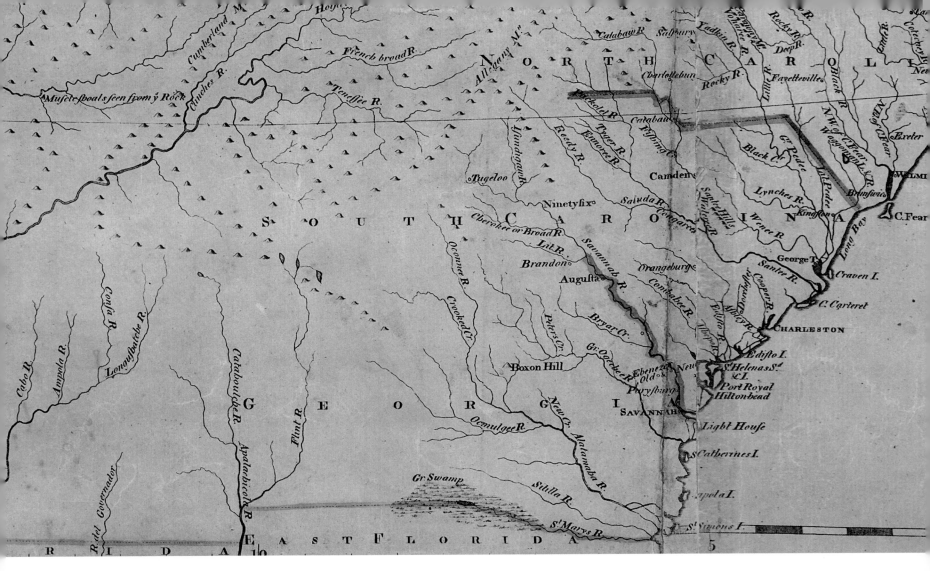

McMurray, *A Map of the United States, Detail #5:* Knox directed the talks that resulted in the Creeks ceding to Georgia disputed territory on the Oconee River while retaining hunting rights southwest of the junction of the Oconee and the Ocmulgee (center left).

Nation, of the Oconee Land, in the utmost extent in which it has been claimed by that state and thus extinguishes the principal cause of those hostilities from which it has more than once experienced such severe calamities."[36] (See McMurray, *A Map of the United States, Detail #5.*)

The treaty sowed the seeds of future conflict, however, Washington told the Senate. There was a

certain claim of Georgia arising out of the treaty, of land to the eastward of a new temporary line from the forks of the Oconee and Ocmulgee in a southwest direction to the St Marys River, which tract of land the Creeks in this city absolutely refuse to yield. This land is reported to be generally barren, sunken and unfit for cultivation, except in some instances on the margin of the rivers, on which by improvement rice might be cultivated, its chief value depending on the timber fit for the building of ships with which it is represented as abounding. While it is thus circumstanced on the one hand, it is stated by the Creeks on the other to be of the highest importance to them, as constituting some of their most valuable winter hunting ground.[37]

To enforce the treaty, McGillivray and his powerful army of Creek warriors were given the right to evict white settlers from Indian land. Secretly, the treaty also gave McGillivray a pension much larger than his retainer from the Spanish, and promised economic support to the Creeks if their fur trade was shut down by war between Spain and England. "In preparing the Articles of this treaty the present arrangements of the trade with the Creeks have caused much embarrassment," Washington told the Senate, since

said trade is almost exclusively in the hands of a company of British merchants, who by agreement make their importation of goods from England into the Spanish ports. As the trade of the Indians is a main mean of their political management, it is therefore obvious that the United States cannot possess any security for the performance of treaties with the Creeks, while their trade is liable to be interrupted or withheld at the caprice of two foreign powers. Hence it becomes an object of real importance to form new channels for the commerce of the Creeks through the United States. But this operation will require time, as the present arrangements can not be suddenly broken without the greatest violation of faith and morals. It therefore appears to be important to form a secret Article of a treaty similar to the one which accompanies this message.[38]

With the Treaty of New York in place, and the Yazoo land companies largely going out of business over the next few months, Washington felt he was making progress toward a more stable peace on the frontiers, north and south.[39] "I learn with pleasure, by your letter of [September 26] that the person supposed to have been the principal in the murder of the two Indians on Pine Creek has been

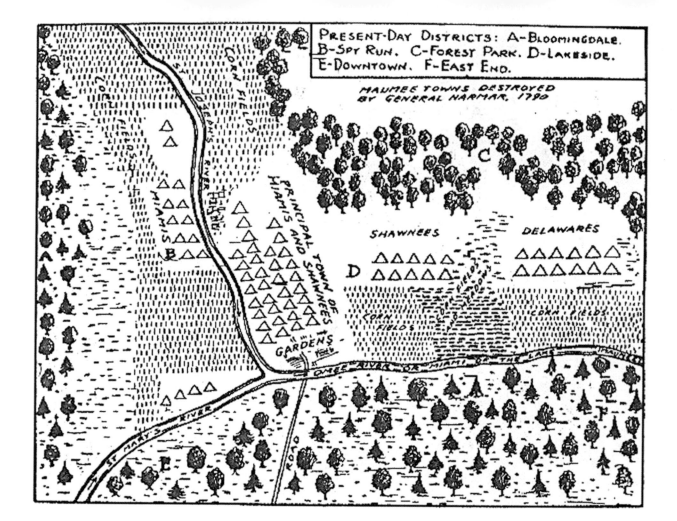

PRESENT-DAY DISTRICTS: A-BLOOMINGDALE. B-SPY RUN. C-FOREST PARK. D-LAKESIDE. E-DOWNTOWN. F-EAST END.

Miami Town, site of Fort Wayne, Indiana, today.

lodged in Lancaster [jail], and that it is very probable all the offenders will soon be apprehended," Washington wrote to Attorney General Edmund Randolph on October 3, 1790. "I cannot avoid expressing my wish that the proceedings, in bringing these persons to justice may be such as will vindicate the laws of our country, and establish a conviction, in the minds of the Indians, of our love of justice and good faith."[40]

To further secure the situation in the Southwest, Washington brought the foremost land speculators, schemers, and adventurers into top positions from the governor on down in the new territorial government formed that year by Congress when it established the Southwest Territory (just as it had formed the Northwest Territory three years earlier). Spain became less conciliatory when the threat of war with England passed, and conflict continued to simmer, but Washington's own scheming had brought a measure of peace. He had avoided war thus far, but as he made clear in a letter to Lafayette, he would wipe out any Indians who breached his arrangements.[41]

"McGillivray and about thirty of the Kings and Head Men are here: This event will leave us in peace from one end of our borders to the other; except where it may be interrupted by a small refugee banditti of Cherokees and Shawnees, who can be easily chastised or even extirpated if it shall become necessary," Washington told Lafayette. "But this will only be done in an inevitable extremity; since the basis of our proceedings with the Indian Nations has been, and shall be justice, during the period in which I may have anything to do in the administration of this government."[42]

At the end of August 1790, as the nation's capital moved to Philadelphia and Washington prepared to leave New York, St. Clair arrived to discuss the raid against the Northwest tribes ordered in June. He and Harmar had developed a more ambitious plan, by which Harmar was to command the federal troops, supported by militia, for a total of about fifteen hundred men. Instead of a raid, it was to be a major campaign to subdue these tribes, destroy their villages, and establish a fort at Miami Town to contest the area with the British at Detroit.[43] Despite his abiding interest in Miami Town's strategic location, Washington approved the mission but not the fort, which he thought would be too vulnerable and too expensive.[44] He then returned eagerly to Mount Vernon after seventeen months away.

By November, Washington's main concern was that he had received no news of Harmar's expedition against the western Indians. "I am a little surprised that we have

Little Turtle.

not heard (so long after the time appointed for the rendezvous) of the issue, the progress, or the commencement of the expedition against the Wabash Indians under the conduct of Brigadier General Harmar," Washington told Knox. "This, in my opinion, is an undertaking of a serious nature. I am not a little anxious to know the result of it, and therefore request, if any official or other accounts have been received by you relating thereto, that you would forward them to this place, provided they can reach it before Monday the 22d instant on which day I expect to leave home for Philadelphia."[45]

Two days later he added: "I am apprehensive that Governor St. Clair's communication of the object of the expedition to the officer commanding at Detroit has been unseasonable and may have unfavorable consequences." The purpose of notifying the British was to assure them that Detroit was not the target of the offensive. However, Washington observed, "It was certainly premature to announce the operation intended until the troops were ready to move; since the Indians, through that channel, might receive such information as would frustrate the expedition."[46] Washington would soon learn definitively that his administration's first major military campaign, in September and October 1790, was a disaster.

As Harmar's main force set off for Miami Town from Fort Washington in September, a detachment from Fort Knox was to move up the Wabash as a decoy. (See Bradley, *A Map of the United States, Detail #1*, page 216. In this 1796 map, Miami Town, top, center, is labeled *Fort Wayne*.) However, this second force departed behind schedule and later turned back to seek the safety of the fort. Little Turtle, forewarned of Harmar's column by the British, evacuated Miami Town. Learning of this, Harmar rushed a detachment forward to strike any Indians who remained. After destroying crops and villages, detachments of Harmar's men were ambushed and defeated by Little Turtle's warriors in and around Miami Town, suffering 180 casualties. Harmar and his army retreated in disorder, abandoning the wounded and leaving the dead unburied.

When preliminary reports of the defeat came in, Washington vented to Knox, declaring

without reserve that my forebodings with respect to the expedition against the Wabash Indians are of disappointment; and a disgraceful termination under the conduct of Brigadier General Harmar. I expected little from the moment I heard he was a drunkard. I expected less as soon as I heard that on this account no confidence was reposed in him by the people of the western country. And I gave up all hope of success, as soon as I heard that there were disputes with him about command. The latter information is from report only; but the report of bad news is rarely without foundation. If the issue

of this expedition is honorable to the concerters of it, and favorable to our arms, it will be double pleasing to me; but my mind, from the silence which reigns, and other circumstances, is prepared for the worst; that is, for expence without honor or profit.[47]

Harmar tried to put a positive spin on the result by focusing on the damage done to the Indians. "The substance of the work is this—our loss was heavy, but the headquarters of iniquity were broken up. At a moderate computation not less than 100, or 120 warriors were slain and 300 log-houses and wigwams burned. Our loss about 180. The remainder of the Indians will be ill off for sustenance [since] 20,000 bushels of corn in the ears were consumed, burned, and destroyed by the army with vegetables in abundance. The loss of Major Wyllys and Lieutenant Frothingham of the federal troops, and a number of valuable militia officers I sincerely lament."[48]

Ironically, rushing the detachment forward was the same mistake that Washington had urged on Braddock in 1755, and the result was the same. The western tribes soon declared all-out war, raiding throughout the Ohio Valley and into western Pennsylvania, making it the deadliest and most gruesome winter to date on the frontier. Blue Jacket, a Shawnee chief, with some two hundred warriors attacked the Cincinnati area in January 1791. Whites in turn shared stories of Indian atrocities, and pressure mounted in Congress and the administration to launch another offensive.[49]

Washington and Knox agreed on St. Clair to lead the next campaign, and he was confirmed by Congress as both governor and major general. Congress approved a vast expansion of funding and of federal power over the military between January and March 1791 in order to raise a force of three thousand men. It would take a few months to build this force, so to buy time and protect settlers Knox reversed his earlier policy and allowed eager Kentucky militia units to venture north of the Ohio to attack the Indians in the hope of reducing their raids on the frontier. Congress had just approved statehood for Vermont and Kentucky, which helped bind this territory to the Union, and also enabled Kentucky to assert its security needs loudly in Congress.

In addition to sanctioning these raids by irregular units, the administration focused on a diplomatic offensive to prevent a pan-Indian coalition from forming and possibly spreading to include the Six Nations, which would open another hostile front in western New York and Pennsylvania. Joseph Brant, the Mohawk whose influence had taken two thirds of the Iroquois to the British side during the Revolution, was of particular concern to Washington since he was angry about recent incursions by whites in his territory. By hosting chiefs in Philadelphia or sending agents to their villages, Washington and his administration pressed hard for peace, all the while

Joseph Brant.

preparing for a major offensive against Miami Town, still controlled by the Indians. This time the establishment of a fort there would be the top priority, despite the expense. And it would be supported by a chain of outposts stretching back to Fort Washington.[50]

In March 1791, Washington sternly instructed St. Clair to "beware of surprise" on his expedition, undoubtedly recalling his own encounters on the frontier some forty years earlier and the disaster of Braddock's campaign. "Trust not the Indian; leave not your arms for the moment; and when you halt for the night be sure to fortify your camp—again and again, General, beware of surprise." At the same time, Washington and Knox both underestimated the capabilities of Indian war leaders. On March 23, St. Clair left Philadelphia for the West.[51]

Assuming the campaign in the Northwest would begin that summer, Washington set off for the Potomac to supervise the survey of the land for the Federal District, as the future capital of the United States was called.[52] Then, in April, he set off on a three-month tour of the southern states.[53] Before he left, he continued to press the diplomatic offensive in the Northwest, but lacking regular relations with the British, he told Jefferson,

> You will readily agree with me that the best interests of the United States require such an intimation to be made to the governor of Canada, either directly or indirectly, as may produce instructions to prevent the Indians receiving military aid or supplies from the British posts or garrisons . . . [Major] Beckwith seems peculiarly designated to be the channel of an indirect intimation. Referring the mode and extent of communicating with him to your own discretion, I wish it may be suggested in such manner as to reach Lord Dorchester, or the Officer commanding in Canada, that certain information has been received of large supplies of ammunition being delivered to the hostile Indians, from British posts, about the commencement of the last campaign. And, as the United States have no other view in prosecuting the present war against the Indians, than, in the failure of negotiation, to procure, by arms, peace and safety to the inhabitants of their frontier, they are equally surprised and disappointed at such an interference.[54]

Washington admitted to Hamilton that Americans shared the blame for tensions on the frontier. And the federal government needed to speak as one voice for the nation:

> Every expedient, as I believe you know, is in operation to avert a war with the hostile Indian tribes, and to keep those who are in treaty with us in good temper; but I am nearly thoroughly convinced that neither will be effected, or, if effected, will be of short duration while land jobbing and the disorderly conduct of our borderers is suffered with impunity; and whilst the states individually are omitting no occasion to interfere in matters which belong to the general government. It is not more than four or five months since the Six Nations or part of them were assured (through the medium of Colonel [Timothy] Pickering) that thence forward they would be spoken to by the government of the United States only and the same thing was repeated in strong terms to the [Seneca chief] Cornplanter at Philadelphia afterwards. Now, as appears by the extract from Mr. King, the legislature of New York are going into some negotiations with these very people. What must this evince to them? Why, that we pursue no system, and that our declarations are not to be regarded. To sum the whole up in a few words: the interferences of states and the speculations of individuals will be the bane of all our public measures.[55]

At Richmond, news from his secretary, Tobias Lear, made Washington anxious that the slaves he had brought to Philadelphia would think themselves entitled to freedom because of a Pennsylvania law that emancipated adult slaves six months after their master moved to the state and became a citizen. This did not apply to Washington, but he worried, especially about the dower slaves, who were not his property, that they might learn about the law from abolitionists and think it applied to them. Washington instructed Lear to look into the situation further and if it seemed prudent to bring the slaves back to Mount Vernon. It should be done "under pretext that may deceive both them and the public."[56] As the enlistment of William Crawford to survey land in violation of the Proclamation of 1763 and the advice to Congress about acquiring Native American land had already shown, Washington was not averse to practicing deception when real estate or reputation was at stake.

True to his habit of mapping and measuring, Washington sketched his route as he moved south. He called the pinelands along the North Carolina coast "the most barren country I ever beheld." Wilmington, however, intrigued him for its potential to exploit the Cape Fear River as an artery to the interior as far as Fayetteville, which he was told was a bustling market for tobacco and flaxseed. (See *An Accurate Map of North and South Carolina, Detail #1*, page 165.) He traveled farther south across more "sand and pine barrens" to South Carolina and the prosperous rice plantation of William Alston above the Waccamaw River. He admired the trees and crops and noted the contrast with the areas he had passed through. General William Moultrie, Colonel William Washington, and John Rutledge escorted him to Georgetown and then

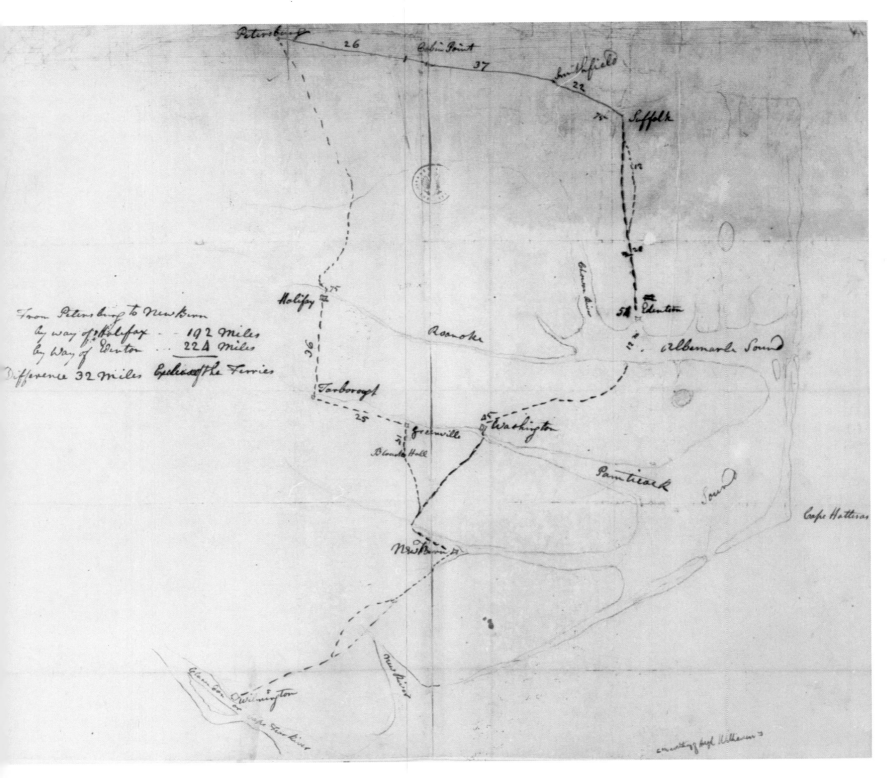

Washington's map of part of his southern tour: In April 1790, Washington sketched his route from Petersburg, Virginia, to Wilmington, North Carolina, noting the distances between towns. On the left, he compared the mileage for going and coming by different routes between Petersburg and Newbern.

to Charleston. The week of celebration there exceeded his welcome for the inauguration in New York. He visited the line of defense in the campaign of 1780 and the site of Fort Moultrie on Sullivan's Island. (See *An Accurate Map of North and South Carolina, Detail #2*, page 166.)[57]

He then headed for Savannah. He arrived at Purrysburg and was escorted down the Savannah River, stopping to visit Nathanael Greene's widow, who had fallen on hard times and lived on land given by the state of Georgia. He reached Savannah on May 12, where there were more festivities and he walked the ground of d'Estaing's and Lincoln's failed attempt to besiege and then storm the British-held city in October 1779. (See *A Map of South Carolina and a Part of Georgia, Detail #5*, page 215.)[58]

Moving north to Augusta, Columbia, and then to Camden, Washington intently studied the site of Greene's clash with Lord Rawdon on April 25, 1781, and concluded

that Greene, having picked a good spot to confront the enemy, had failed to dig in sufficiently. He was seemingly less critical of Gates's defeat at Camden by Cornwallis, excusing it because the two armies collided unexpectedly in the night. However, there was an implied criticism: Had Gates done better reconnaissance and planning, he might have advanced a half mile further and protected his force behind "an impenetrable swamp" until he had "formed his own plans." (See *An Accurate Map of North and South Carolina, Detail #4*, page 176.)[59]

On the way from Camden to Charlotte, North Carolina, Washington was visited by some Catawba chiefs who suspected that plans were being hatched to take away their land. (See *An Accurate Map of North and South Carolina, Detail #5*, page 178.) At Salem, he met with Governor Alexander Martin, who reassured the president that in the last state to ratify the Constitution, there was growing acceptance among the public. To Washington's further relief, Martin declared his opposition to the land companies that were bent on ignoring the borders set by the Indian treaties in order to lay claim to huge tracts in the West.[60]

The governor accompanied Washington on June 2 from Salem to Guilford, where Washington was able to visit the nearby battlefield. Here at Guilford Court House on March 15, 1781, Cornwallis had defeated Greene, but the victory had been costly, sending the British limping to the coast for supplies from the British navy. Now, ten years later, Washington replayed the battle in his mind with a different outcome. On seeing how strong a position the advance troops had taken, Washington implied that Greene should have placed regulars, not militia, in this first line: Had the militia stood their ground, instead of falling back, "the British must have been sorely galled in their advance, if not defeated." (See *An Accurate Map of North and South Carolina, Detail #8*, page 185.)[61]

Returning to Mount Vernon on June 12, his horses were "much reduced in flesh" after traveling 1,887 miles, but Washington had gained weight from all the festivities and dinners. And he was deeply contented for having made the trip. It had enabled him, he wrote, "to see with my own eyes the situation of the country through which we traveled, and to learn more accurately the disposition of the people than I could have done by any information." The American people were frugal and industrious, he concluded, and even outside Federalist New England they were becoming more inclined to support the new government as they began "to feel the good effects of equal laws and equal protection."[62]

Except for King's Mountain, Bennington, and the Canadian theater of operations, Washington had now visited all of the major American battlefields. The war in the South, which he had understood through maps and reports, was now tactile and three-dimensional for him. And so were the long barren stretches of land along the coast of the Carolinas, with their thin, sandy soil—which undoubtedly convinced him all the more that sooner or later, despite Indian treaties, the United States would expand to the fertile valleys of the West.[63]

Back in Philadelphia in late July 1791, Washington expected to hear that the Northwest campaign had begun, but was outraged to find disarray in the War Department instead and St. Clair's expedition mired in delays. The failure of the contractor and quartermaster to provide supplies and the dearth of troops (due to expired enlistments) meant the invasion could not begin until the fall. Washington insisted that the expedition proceed before the winter, even if it was not fully prepared.[64]

Washington also faced the prospect of war breaking out between England, Spain, and France, which would, at a minimum, endanger American commerce. France contended with social upheaval within its borders and a massive slave revolt in Santo Domingo (also called Hispaniola). The neighboring monarchies looked on anxiously, and were poised to intervene, to contain the spread of revolution. By the treaty of 1778, the United States would be obligated to ally with France against the British, or a British and Spanish coalition, thus cutting off markets and endangering the three land frontiers—North, West, and South.[65]

Washington's response was guided by a determination to preserve peace on the frontiers through treaties with the Indians and crushing those who refused. "It is my wish and desire that you would examine the laws of the general government which have relation to Indian affairs," he told Attorney General Randolph,

that is, for the purpose of securing their lands to them; restraining states or individuals from purchasing their lands; and forbidding unauthorized intercourse in their dealing with them. And moreover, that you would suggest such auxiliary laws as will supply the defects of those which are in being, thereby enabling the Executive to enforce obedience.

If Congress expect to live in peace with the neighboring Indians and to avoid the expenses and horrors of continual hostilities, such a measure will be found indispensably necessary; for unless adequate penalties are provided, that will check the spirit of speculation in lands and will enable the Executive to carry them into effect, this country will be constantly embroiled with, and appear faithless in the eyes not only of the Indians but of the neighboring powers also. For, notwithstanding the existing laws, solemn treaties, and proclamations which have been issued to enforce a compliance with both, and some attempts of the governments west of the Ohio to restrain their proceedings, the agents for the Tennessee Company are at this moment by *public advertisements* under the signature of a Zachariah Cox encouraging by offers of land and other inducements, a settlement at the Muscle-Shoals, and is likely to obtain emigrants for that purpose although there is good evidence that the measure is disapproved by the Creeks and Cherokees; and it is presumed is so likewise by the Chickasaws and Choctaws, unless they have been imposed upon by assurances that trade is the only object in view by the establishment.[66]

(See McMurray, *A Map of the United States, Detail #4*, page 217, left center.)

Aided by geographic distance and isolation, Washington also wanted to keep the United States out of European conflicts if possible. "The change of systems, which have so long prevailed in Europe, will, undoubtedly, affect us in a degree proportioned to our political or commercial connections with the several nations of it," he told Gouverneur Morris. "But I trust we shall never so far lose sight of our own interest and happiness as to become, unnecessarily, a party in their political disputes. Our local situation enables us to keep that state with them, which otherwise could not, perhaps, be preserved by human wisdom."[67]

Though distressed by the news that King Louis XVI had attempted to flee the country, only to be captured and returned to Paris, Washington exhibited great patience in dealing with the French revolutionary government, and warmly received the new minister to the United States, Jean-Baptiste de Ternant (who, as an inspector for the Continental army, had reported to Washington from the South during the war.)[68] In September 1791, Washington cheerfully informed Ternant that the United States would supply "our good friends and allies the French" with the arms and ammunition he requested to suppress "the alarming insurrection of the Negros in Hispaniola."[69] (See *A General Map of North America, Detail #2*, page 31, left center. The western half of the island, today's Haiti, is shown in green, indicating a French colony. The eastern half, today's Dominican Republic, is shown in yellow, as a Spanish colony.)

By the end of September 1791, with the first frost, St. Clair's forces had completed a new stockade fort on the Great Miami, named Fort Hamilton (site of today's Hamilton, Ohio), as the launch point, supply depot, and refuge in case of retreat. Knox informed Washington that in the meantime a decoy expedition of volunteers under General James Wilkinson had moved up the Wabash and destroyed L'Anguille, an Indian town near the junction of the Wabash and Anguille (Eel) rivers. (See Hutchins, *A New Map, Detail #3*, page 213, bottom left.)[70]

St. Clair's invasion force of 2,300 men, hampered from the start by supply shortages, set off from Fort Hamilton on October 4. On the 12th they built Fort Jefferson and waited for supplies. Desertion was rampant, as enlistments were to expire on November 3. They pushed on toward Miami Town on the 24th, then stopped, and started again on November 2 with only 1,500 men. On November 3 they camped on a mound overlooking the headwaters of the Wabash River's East Branch. (See Bradley, *A Map of the United States, Detail #2*, page 239.)

Here, on November 4, 1791, St. Clair's force was utterly defeated and massacred by a thousand Native American warriors well supplied by British agents and under the

Fort Hamilton.

ABOVE: Fort Jefferson.

OPPOSITE: Bradley, *A Map of the United States, Detail #2:* St. Clair's force started out from Fort Hamilton, lower left. Moving north, the army built Fort Jefferson before proceeding north again to the mound where they camped on November 3, 1791, left center (here labeled *Fort Recovery*, which was built two years later).

brilliant leadership of Little Turtle. The Miami chief had seized the initiative by attacking St. Clair en route instead of waiting for him to attack Miami Town. Striking at dawn, Little Turtle's thousand warriors killed many of the Kentucky militiamen who were camped as an advance guard across the stream from the main army, while the rest fled, running straight through the encampment on the mound. As the Indians enveloped the mound from the front and sides, pouring in volleys of musket fire and then scalping and dismembering their victims, St. Clair's camp became a horrific scene of panic and slaughter.

Nearly forty officers were killed among the nine hundred casualties. In addition to the dead and wounded, the road was strewn for miles with the guns and equipment shed by the fleeing men—even after the Indians had stopped pursuing them. It was the worst blow in losses and to morale suffered by whites at the hands of Native Americans since Braddock's disaster on the Monongahela on July 9, 1755. Worse than Braddock's defeat, it was the most lopsided Native American victory ever.[71]

Washington learned of the disaster in December while having dinner with guests at home in Philadelphia. Summoned from the table by an aide, he left the room to read the message. He then returned to the table and retained his composure for the rest of the evening. Only after he and his secretary, Tobias Lear, were alone in the president's study did he unleash a torrent of anger, his body shaking with rage as he paced the room. St. Clair had done exactly what Washington had warned him not to do—fallen prey to a surprise attack—resulting in the worst defeat American forces had ever suffered, with two thirds of the army killed or wounded. Little Turtle's victory was proportionally greater than any won by the British during the entire Revolutionary War.[72]

When St. Clair arrived in Philadelphia in mid-January 1792, the administration began combating the avalanche of criticism triggered by the failed campaign. Knox fended off accusations and proposed legislation to strengthen the army by recruiting high-quality long-term soldiers, with enlistment bonuses and higher pay, and increasing its size to five regiments. These would be organized on the legion system proposed by Baron von Steuben right after the Revolution in 1784. To provide greater flexibility of maneuver in the wilderness, the five-thousand-man army would contain four sub-legions—each with a combination of infantry, artillery, and cavalry, and led by a brigadier general—which could operate independently if necessary. Army procurement was taken away from Knox and his crony contractors, and assigned to Hamilton at Treasury, while political generals like St. Clair were to be replaced by competent military men. The militia was also to be reformed to create uniform national standards for training and equipment to be met by all the states.

In March, Congress reluctantly and narrowly voted to give the country the army Washington had been saying it needed since the end of the Revolution. And in May, Congress passed two bills reforming the militia system. One took strides toward uniform standards, which would be a long process. The other—which would soon play a big role—empowered the president to call out these state troops to uphold the law, to put down rebellions, and to repel invasions.[73]

Critics of the plan to expand the army had been mollified by a promise to pursue negotiations with the Indians, a clause that provided for disbanding the three new regiments when peace was achieved, and St. Clair's dismissal (though he was allowed to keep the governorship of the Northwest Territory).[74] Searching for a commander with experience, Washington turned to the veteran officers of the Revolution and at length settled on Anthony Wayne as major general of the army. "Mad Anthony," despite his reputation for impulsiveness, would ultimately prove to have just the right combination of aggressiveness and caution needed in a commander on the frontier.[75]

In June 1792 Wayne arrived in Pittsburgh, where he found only forty recruits and a few cavalrymen. While he began the colossal task of mustering and training the new Legion of the United States there, James Wilkinson, one of the four new brigadier generals and Wayne's deputy, was attempting to hold the line in the Northwest, where

St. Clair's defeat.

he had a mere seven hundred men for all of the posts on the Ohio and the forts north of Fort Washington. By August Wayne had more than a thousand men and was drilling them according to Baron von Steuben's manual. Like Washington creating the First Virginia Regiment at Fort Cumberland in the 1750s, Wayne got results with harsh discipline, including floggings and executions. Knox and Washington both condoned his efforts.

"So long as the vice of drunkenness exists in the army, so long I hope ejections of those officers who are found guilty of it will continue; for that and gaming will debilitate and render unfit for active service any army whatsoever," Washington told Knox. "Re-iterate, in your letters to Genl. Wayne, the necessity of employing the present calm in disciplining and training the troops under his command . . . He is not to be sparing of powder and lead (in proper and reasonable quantities) to make the soldiers marksmen." A few days later, Washington added: "I hope the recruiting officers will double their diligence to obtain the men and their vigilance to prevent desertion. The latter is shameful, and calls for vigorous pursuits and exemplary punishments."[76] However, Washington told Knox, "Concerning [Wayne's] idea of having a brand [for the foreheads of deserters] I have

great doubts, both as to the legality and policy of the measure; the bad impression it may make in the country, may considerably outweigh the good effects it may produce in the army."[77]

When Congress had voted for the new, million-dollar defense budget (a threefold increase) its members also began looking for more revenue, and early in 1792 had enacted an excise tax on domestically produced whiskey. Along with other factors, the tax—the first federal tax on a U.S. product—would be a source of turbulence, and geography was a major reason. Because the tax was on the product of distilled grain, it sparked conflict between merchants and farmers, urban and rural areas, North and South, East and West. Americans who lived beyond the Alleghenies and depended on whiskey for their livelihood were all the more incensed at being singled out for federal taxation. By the middle of 1792, violent resistance on a large scale had broken out in western Pennsylvania. Washington was determined to enforce the law, with troops if necessary, and he issued a proclamation in September warning the insurgents to disband.[78]

The whiskey tax also helped galvanize the Anti-Federalists, or Republicans, early in 1792, a nascent political party coalescing around Secretary of State

Thomas Jefferson, which objected to augmenting centralized power. Opposed to them were the Federalists, adherents of Secretary of the Treasury Alexander Hamilton, who had introduced the excise tax. Washington was a Federalist in his convictions, but tried to stay above the factionalism he feared would divide the country.[79]

The two parties were further polarized by their opposite reactions to developments in France, a country still closely bound to the United States commercially and politically by the treaty of 1778, which had helped the Americans win their independence. Republicans believed the French Revolution was realizing the same ideals of liberty as the American Revolution. The Federalists, who saw France descending into mob rule, favored closer ties to England.[80] "How unfortunate, and how much is it to be regretted then, that whilst we are encompassed on all sides with avowed enemies and insidious friends, that internal dissensions should be harrowing and tearing our vitals," Washington wrote to Jefferson. "The last, to me, is the most serious, the most alarming, and the most afflicting of the two."[81]

The British finally sent their first official ambassador to the United States, George Hammond, who had arrived in Philadelphia in October 1791. However, they were trying at the same time to create a single Indian nation in the Northwest, as a buffer state between Canada and the United States.[82] With the monarchies of Britain and Spain uniting in common cause over their shared hostility to the revolutionaries in France, Spain's officials in Florida and Louisiana felt they had a free hand to be more aggressive on the southwest border of the United States in the summer and fall of 1792. They had no scruples, Washington lamented to Knox, about provoking "a war which must expose helpless women and children to the relentless fury of savages, and to the cruelties of the tomahawk and scalping-knife."

Their agents tried to get the Creeks to abandon the Treaty of New York signed by McGillivray. "To accomplish which, these Indians, together with the Cherokees, Chickasaws and Choctaws, are invited to a grand council at Pensacola; where, if they will attend, it is intimated to them, they shall be furnished with arms, ammunition, and goods of all sorts," Washington wrote to Knox in August. "An agent of Spain, (a Captain Oliver) . . . supposed to be acting in concert with McGillivray, has *forbid* their running the line that was established by treaty with these people; promising them the support of Spain against any measures which may be pursued by the United States, in case of their refusal."[83]

Making matters worse for the United States government, southern chiefs who had fought alongside Little Turtle to defeat St. Clair returned and roused the warriors in the Tennessee region. Settlers in western Georgia were also violating the treaty and encroaching on Indian land. Washington protested to the Spanish envoy in Philadelphia on one hand and on the other urged Governor Edward Telfair of Georgia and the governor of the Southwest Territory, William Blount, to take action.

"I wish Governor Blount may have been able to terminate the conferences, which he was to have had at Nashville about the 25th of last month with the Cherokees, Chickasaws and Choctaws to the mutual advantage and satisfaction of all the parties concerned," Washington told Knox, "but the difficulty of deciding between lawless settlers and greedy (land) speculators on one side, and the jealousies of the Indian nations and their banditti on the other, becomes more and more obvious every day; and these, from the interference of the Spaniards . . . add not a little to our embarrassments."[84] With only a few federal troops available to deploy in the region, Washington could do little to prevent a likely outbreak of war.[85] Washington was becoming convinced that, "diabolical as it may seem," Madrid and London were coordinating their efforts "to check the growth of this rising country."[86]

In the Northwest, the strenuous diplomatic efforts the administration had promised to pursue were having little effect. Knox and Washington hosted delegations of chiefs in Philadelphia and sent agents with gifts to Indian villages. They distributed to the chiefs a silver medallion showing Washington smoking a peace pipe with an Indian who had laid down his tomahawk. Ultimately there was literally too much bad blood between the two sides to achieve peace until one side was further weakened. And the British thwarted several ambassadors by refusing to let them reach the villages, while others were killed

General Anthony Wayne.

Brigadier General James Wilkinson.

by Indians, even those under flags of truce. "The unhappy fate of our messengers is a lamentable proof of Indian barbarity, and a strong evidence of the bad dispositions of at least some of their tribes," Washington told Knox. "This ought to stimulate every nerve to prepare for the worst."[87]

In October 1792, when the tribes gathered for a grand council—at a site where the Auglaize River flowed into the Miami—they followed the lead of the Shawnees (spurred by the British) in demanding that all of the territory north and west of the Ohio River be restored to the Indians. (See Bradley, *A Map of the United States, Detail #2*, page 239, top center, where the Auglaize River is labeled *Gr. au Glaize R.*) The resounding victories of the Miamis under Little Turtle had emboldened the Indians to forge an alliance aimed at confining Americans south of the Ohio River.[88] At the end of the year, sporadic warfare continued, with Little Turtle leading successful raids.[89]

Wayne meanwhile had moved his troops out of Pittsburgh some twenty miles down the Ohio to a site he named Legionville. (See Bradley, *A Map of the United States, Detail #3*.) There, free from the distractions of Pittsburgh, he redoubled his training efforts and created a formidable army. Like the Continental army that was reborn under von Steuben's stern gaze at Valley Forge, the Legion was transformed into a professional force.[90] "Whatever Genl. Wayne may require towards the equipment of his troops . . . I think had better be granted," Washington told Knox.[91]

In December 1792 news arrived in Philadelphia that the radical French revolutionaries had taken over the Legislative Assembly. The defeat of French forces by Prussian and Austrian armies had led to widespread revolt in Paris, paving the way for the radical takeover. King Louis XVI was imprisoned. The Constitution was suspended. Lafayette fled, only to be captured by the Austrians. In America, Anti-Federalists rejoiced in the streets, while Washington worried about his adoptive son. Washington also felt constrained as president not to alienate the new French regime, since France had long been a staunch ally and served as a counterweight to the British. He gave instructions for Gouverneur Morris, the American envoy in Paris, to express "informally the sentiments and wishes of this country respecting the M. de la Fayette." And he asked Jefferson to reply for him to a letter from Lafayette's wife—to convey to her "all the consolation I can with propriety give her consistent with my public character and the national policy."[92]

Soon came the Reign of Terror in France, the mass executions by guillotine. The Republicans took the bloodletting in stride, while the Federalists were horrified.[93] Marking the letter private and leaving blanks to avoid committing his views officially to paper, Washington wrote to Henry Lee that "the affairs of [France]" were "in the highest paroxysm of disorder, not so much from the pressure of foreign enemies (for in the cause of liberty this ought to be fuel to the fire of a patriot soldier, and to increase his ardor) but because those in whose hands the g[overnmen]t is entrusted are ready to tear each other to pieces, and will, more than probably prove the worst foes the country has."[94]

As Washington's first term came to a close at the end of 1792, he was walking a diplomatic tightrope to keep the United States out of the conflict engulfing Europe and to cope with the challenges that faced the country on all fronts. Apologizing to Gouverneur Morris for not replying fully to his letters of December and January, Washington wrote that "you will readily believe, my dear sir, that, what with the current affairs of the government, the unpleasant aspect of matters on our Indian frontiers, and the momentous occurrences in Europe, I am not only pressed with the quantity of business, but that the nature of a great part of it is peculiarly delicate and embarrassing."[95]

Silver medallion showing President George Washington smoking a peace pipe with an Indian, symbolizing the hoped-for better relations with native tribes.

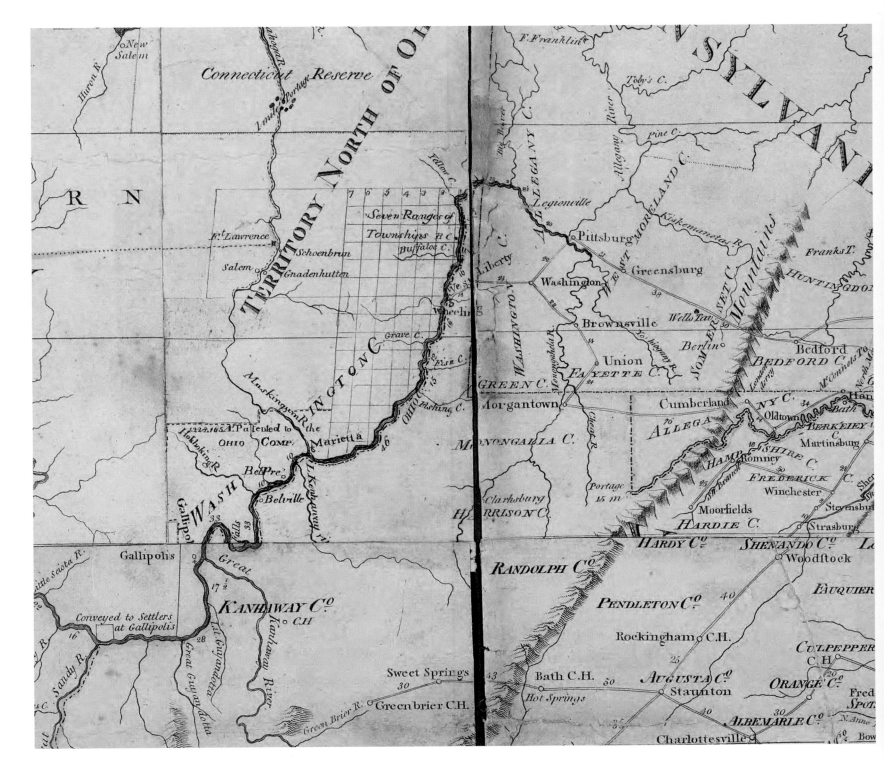

Bradley, *A Map of the United States, Detail #3:* Seeking a more isolated
post in which to train and discipline his troops, Wayne moved the army
from Pittsburgh to Legionville, upper right.

CHAPTER NINE

GAINS IN THE NORTHWEST AND SOUTHWEST, TROUBLE WITH FRANCE

"A mind must be insensible indeed, not to be gratefully impressed by so distinguished, and honorable a testimony of public approbation and confidence," Washington wrote to Henry Lee in January 1793, after the presidential election. Despite his longing to retire to Mount Vernon, Washington had consented to a second term and was elected unanimously. "And, as I suffered my name to be contemplated on this occasion, it is more than probable that I should, for a moment, have experienced chagrin if my re-election had not been by a pretty respectable vote," he admitted to Lee. "But to say I feel pleasure from the prospect of commencing another tour of duty would be a departure from truth."[1] Too much had been left unsettled for him to depart: the frontier, building the army, the growing unrest over the whiskey tax, political parties, and foreign relations.[2]

Edmond Charles Genet.

On March 16 came the grim news that King Louis XVI had been guillotined. Then, as Washington was leaving for Mount Vernon, word arrived that France had declared war on England, Russia, and the Netherlands, signaling that the conflict would become a naval contest as well and would impact the United States. French agents were having no trouble arranging for armed vessels to sail from American ports as privateers against British shipping. Americans were siding with the French, seeing that revolution as an outgrowth of their own. Washington had to act quickly to prevent the United States from being dragged into war against England and Spain, the hostile behemoths that loomed at the nation's borders. (See McMurray, *A Map of the United States, Detail #1*, page 201, which delineates the United States as a single entity, highlighting its borders.)

He rushed back to Philadelphia and gathered his cabinet. Congress was in recess and the president had no war powers, but the cabinet decided he would not be exceeding his constitutional authority by simply continuing the existing state of peace. On April 22, 1793, he signed what has come to be known as the Proclamation of Neutrality, though it avoided that word. The United States, Washington declared, would "pursue a conduct friendly and impartial towards the belligerent powers," and Americans who violated this policy would be prosecuted.[3]

The proclamation would soon be put to the test by the new French ambassador to the United States, Citizen Edmond Charles Genet, who had arrived not at Philadelphia but at Charleston in April—deliberately sidestepping the federal government and taking his business directly to the people, who flocked to him euphorically, as he bestowed French commissions on Americans to prey on British vessels and help France seize territory from the Spanish in Florida and Louisiana. Instead of sailing north, he proceeded slowly by land, basking in the adulation of the cheering crowds along the way. At Richmond he learned about Washington's proclamation of neutrality, and he finally moved on to present himself officially in mid-May at Philadelphia, where he was greeted by the people ecstatically.

He had put the administration in a quandary: The British ambassador was furious about French ships capturing British vessels in American waters. Searching for a resolution, Washington declared that the proclamation of neutrality forbade any more privateering, but prizes taken before it was issued would not have to be returned. Patronizing to the president when they met, Genet proceeded to ignore the government and set up French courts to divide the profits from the British ships his privateers captured. He also plotted to spark a revolt against the Spanish by French settlers on the Mississippi. Jefferson did not intervene or tell Washington, since he and his Republicans were supportive of the French, just as Hamilton and the Federalists favored the British. The split had polarized the country, and mobs of both persuasions roamed Philadelphia that summer, causing concern for the safety of Washington and other officials, and some began to arm themselves.[4]

Genet continued his attempts to drag the United States into the war, and Washington finally took the drastic step of asking France to recall its ambassador. Genet's popularity collapsed quickly, and revelations of his disrespectful behavior to the president demolished what was left of it. (Washington magnanimously granted him political asylum, since he would have been guillotined had he returned to France.) Late in the summer an epidemic of yellow fever in the capital left thousands dead and emptied the city as people fled. The crowds were dispersed, and the allure of the French Revolution and its guillotine were diminished by the horrific death toll in Philadelphia. Washington did not reconvene his cabinet until November 1, 1793, at Germantown.[5]

With the collapse in August of eighteen months of further diplomatic efforts with the Indians at a conference at Sandusky—backed by the British, they insisted once again on the Ohio River as their southern and eastern border—Washington would have to rely on Wayne's ability to wage war. In May Wayne had brought his troops down the Ohio from Legionville to Fort Washington and during the summer and fall had improved St. Clair's road. His two thousand Legionnaires were later joined by a thousand mounted Kentucky militiamen, as they gradually penetrated northward.

However, Wayne no longer intended to launch a campaign in 1793. The administration's insistence on giving negotiations a chance had hampered his logistical preparations, and it was now too late in the season. He could not afford to attack unprepared and risk a third defeat, which Washington admonished him would be "inexpressibly ruinous to the reputation of the government." Instead, he pressed on a few miles beyond the last fort, Fort Jefferson, and established a strong base, which he named Fort Greeneville (today's Greenville, Ohio) in honor of the late Nathanael Greene, with whom he had served in the Revolution. Here, deep in Indian territory, Wayne would wait until spring, build up his supplies, and launch his offensive. (See Bradley, *A Map of the United States, Detail #2*, page 239.)[6]

To the south as well, war seemed imminent. The Indian tribes had all become more combative, caught between hostile American settlers to the north and east and the Spanish to the south and west, who were encouraging them, especially the Creeks. Genet's agitation had inspired the formation of Democratic Societies throughout the United States, organizations espousing republican ideals and support for the French Revolution. In December 1793, the Kentucky Democratic Society, led by militant anti-Spanish and pro-French agitators, issued a resolution to Americans on the frontier, calling them to arms against the Spanish on the Mississippi. The appeal also condemned the federal government and called for resistance to the whiskey tax—and possibly even secession. George Rogers Clark, a hero of the Revolution, had accepted a commission from Genet as a general in the French army and, with volunteers from Kentucky, Georgia, and South Carolina, was planning an incursion into Spanish territory.[7]

As the year ended, Washington was also faced with Americans being taken prisoner by Algerian raiders in the Mediterranean Sea, and by the British, who, in addition to their machinations in the Northwest, were seizing American ships in the French West Indies and keeping their crews in suffocating, disease-ridden prison ships in the Caribbean, much as they had in New York during the Revolution.[8]

Washington continued to seek buyers for his own western lands, and on December 12, 1793, he also wrote to Arthur Young, an English agricultural reformer, that if expert English farmers could be found as tenants, he would rent out all of the farms at Mount Vernon while keeping the Mansion House Farm "for my own residence, occupation, and amusement in agriculture." Washington explained this momentous decision to relinquish direct control of his beloved estate as stemming from his advancing age and desire to simplify his affairs "and from other causes which it is not necessary to detail."[9]

Hoping that his former secretary Tobias Lear might also find such suitable tenants in his travels "through England, Scotland, and elsewhere," Washington later sent him a copy of the letter to Young—with a more revealing cover letter. Since the public assumed Washington possessed "a good and clear estate," and regularly asked him for charitable contributions, he wanted rental income to avoid the embarrassment of having to decline, he told Lear. However, the impetus "more powerful than all the rest," he wrote, in a paragraph marked "private," was "to liberate a certain species of property which I possess very repugnantly to my own feelings." Washington wanted to free his slaves—between two hundred and three hundred of them—but needed to compensate for the huge financial sacrifice it would entail. The president's desire to free his slaves was a revolutionary challenge to the established order that would have sent shock waves through the slaveholding states were it known, and he was careful to keep it a secret. In making a copy of the letter for his files, Washington left out the private paragraph.[10]

However, when Young wrote back to ask if the Mount Vernon slaves would be included in the rental of the farms, Washington replied candidly: "I have something better in view for them." The renters could "hire them as they would any other laborers." At the Mansion House Farm too, all of the slaves would become hired help. Washington's plan gave him the income he needed and ensured that the slaves would not simply be cast out into white society to fend for themselves.[11]

His prior decision to not sell his slaves already meant that he supported them, albeit in abject squalor, while forgoing their commercial value: Selling one able-bodied male could have paid for a small city lot, a ton and a half of beef, three hundred gallons of whiskey, or Washington's tax liability for two years. And freeing his slaves would cost him far more. He would not only lose their cash value and the income from their labor, but would continue to be responsible for the support of the minors until they came of age and for the elderly for as long as they lived. Together, these two age groups made up more than half of Mount Vernon's slaves.

Securing rental income from the farms was therefore crucial. Since ideally all of the slaves would be freed at once, Washington's plan depended on finding four renters and having them arrive simultaneously. Each of the farms was substantial and would need a renter who was both skilled and well financed, enabling him to make the land productive without delay. And such renters would probably have to be found abroad, since few American farmers

Yellow fever in Philadelphia, summer 1793.

in the South would be eager to hire emancipated slaves. The thorniest problem of all was that Washington owned only about half the slaves at Mount Vernon, who had intermarried with the rest, belonging to Martha as part of her dowry. He could hardly free his own slaves while the dower slaves remained in bondage.

Washington did not expect all of these elements to come together right away, and in any case, he did not plan to free his slaves while still in office. That might have been his boldest stroke, setting a moral example for the nation, but Washington was loath to give ammunition to the administration's political opponents, the Virginia Republicans, Jefferson in particular, who celebrated the liberty, brotherhood, and equality of the French Revolution, but were not about to free their own slaves.[12]

While Wayne had postponed his offensive, he still hoped to send a signal of strength to the Indians and throw them off balance. On Christmas Day 1793, he arrived with a contingent of troops at the site of St. Clair's defeat at the headwaters of the Wabash River's East Branch. While burying the remains of the dead after two years, he built a fortified post on the knoll where the massacre took place and named it Fort Recovery. The fort was a two-day march from Fort Greeneville in the direction of Miami Town and signaled that the United States was determined to persevere in the fight for the Northwest. (See Bradley, *A Map of the United States, Detail #2*, page 239.) Wayne forced the Indians to prepare for a possible winter campaign, causing further hardship and starvation, as warriors and provisions were pulled together from the various villages.[13] However, in January 1794, Knox presented Washington with discouraging reports from General Wayne at Fort Greeneville, where his Legion was suffering through the winter with meager pay, rations, and supplies.

The force stood on the brink of disintegration as enlistments expired, criticism swirled around Wayne, and even his officers became insubordinate. Wayne did not know that his ambitious, disloyal second in command, James Wilkinson, was pursuing a smear campaign to unseat him and take his place.[14]

Despite Genet's fall from power in late February, the plans he had set in motion with George Rogers Clark seemed to have lost no momentum, and threatened to provoke war with Spain.[15] The scheme was apparently a two-pronged offensive: The South Carolinians and Georgians under Samuel Hammond were to invade East Florida and capture St. Augustine (see *A General Map of North America, Detail #4*, page 163, lower right), while Clark and the westerners were to take St. Louis before descending the Mississippi to attack Natchez and New Orleans (see McMurray, *A Map of the United States, Detail #4*, page 217, upper left to lower left). Clark, commissioned as a major general in the service of France, published a call for recruits, promising a dollar a day or

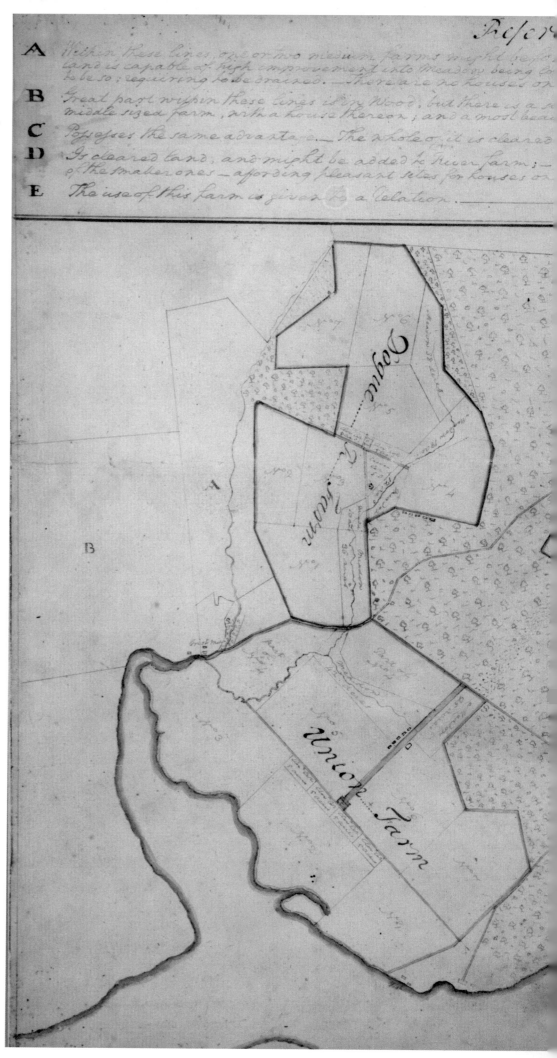

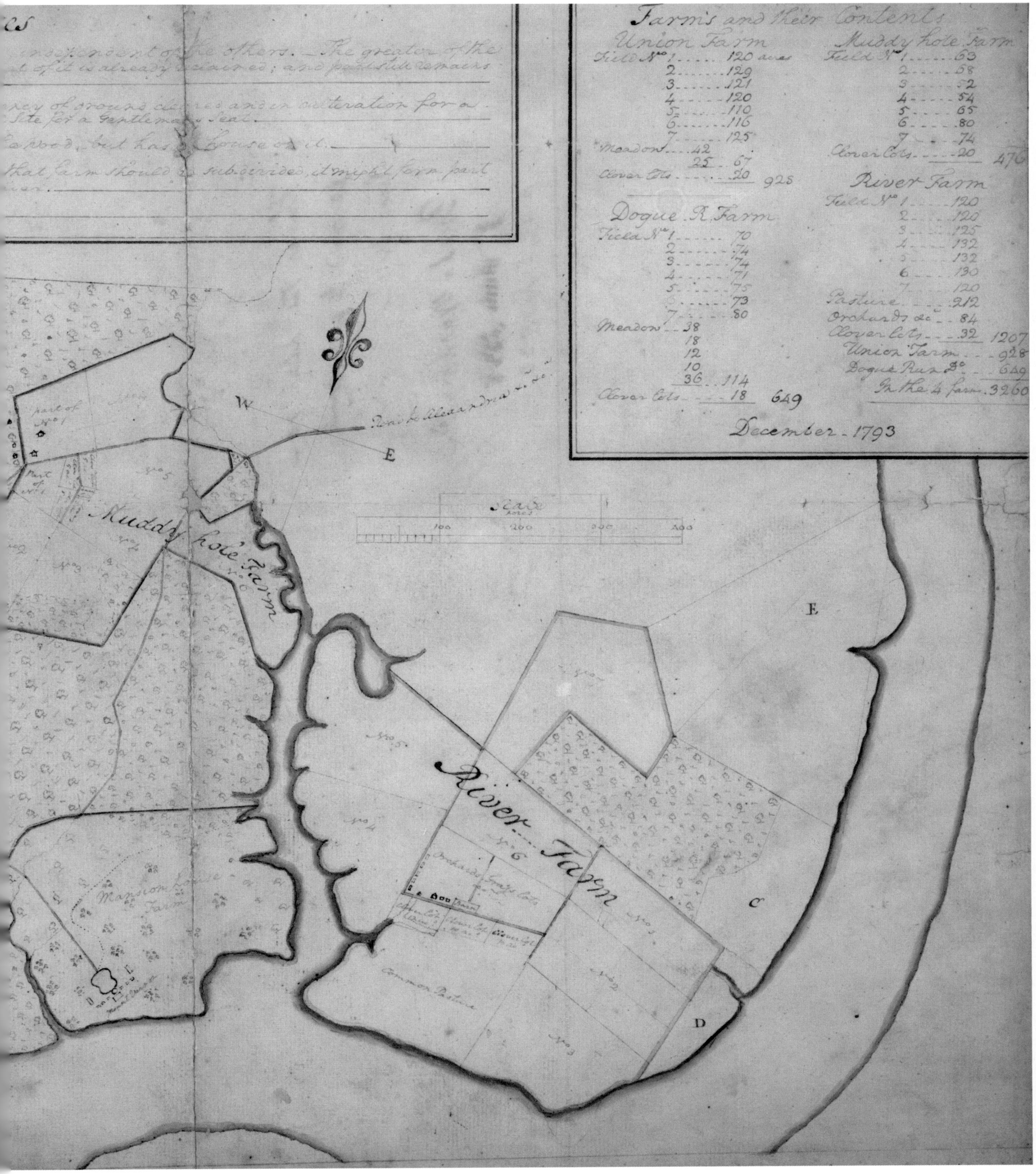
Farms and their Contents
Union Farm
Field No 1 ...... 120 acres
2 129
3 121
4 120
5 110
6 116
7 125
Meadow ... 42
25 ... 67
Clover Lots ... 20 928
Dogue R. Farm
Field No 1 70
2 74
3 74
4 71
5 75
6 73
7 80
Meadow ... 38
18
12
10
36 ... 114
Clover Lots ... 18 649
Muddy hole Farm
Field No 1 63
2 58
3 52
4 54
5 65
6 80
7 74
Clover Lots ... 20 476
River Farm
Field No 1 120
2 120
3 125
4 132
5 132
6 130
7 120
Pasture ... 212
Orchards &c ... 84
Clover Lots ... 32 1207
Union Farm ... 928
Dogue Run Do ... 649
In the 4 farms 3260
December 1793
Scale
100 200 300 400
Muddy hole Farm
River Farm
Mansion House Farm
Common Pasture
W
E
C
D

Washington's own survey of Mount Vernon, 1793: Washington proposed to keep the Mansion House Farm (bottom center) while renting out the other four: Union Farm (lower left), Dogue Run Farm (left center), Muddy Hole Farm (center), and River Farm (lower right). References *A–D* (upper left) describe the advantages of these additional tracts (left center and lower right) as separate farms or additions to the others. The use of farm *E* "is given to a relation," Washington noted, referring to his nephew Major George Augustine Washington.

a thousand acres of any territory captured from Spain. Kentucky governor Isaac Shelby insisted he had no authority to disrupt Clark's enterprise: No law prevented men from arming themselves and leaving the state. At the end of February the crisis was heightened by reports that Clark was actually mobilizing his troops for the expedition.

The new French minister, Joseph Fauchet, obliged the administration by issuing a proclamation on March 6 withdrawing all of the commissions that Genet had conferred on Clark and his officers. The Federalists managed to push a bill through the Senate that criminalized filibustering expeditions like Clark's, but the Republican-controlled House refused to act on it. Washington now decided to act on his own, risking a political backlash from Republicans in the West and South. On March 24, he issued a proclamation warning American citizens to "refrain from enlisting, enrolling, or assembling themselves for such unlawful purposes" or suffer prosecution to the full extent of the law for "such dangerous and daring violations."

He also ordered Wayne to deploy troops at Fort Massac, on the Ohio River, to cut Clark off if he came by that route. (See Hutchins, *A New Map, Detail #4*.) Within a week, however, it was clear that Clark and his freebooters had canceled their plans. Among other factors, Fauchet's withdrawal of the commissions and the lack of French funds had been decisive. Washington's belated proclamation had a negligible effect, but he was happy to have pulled the country back from the precipice of war.[16]

No sooner had the potential clash with Spain been forestalled than the threat of war flared in the Northwest. The English governor-general of Canada, Sir Guy Carleton, elevated to the peerage as Lord Dorchester, had recently received a delegation of western Indians at Quebec and informed them that since Britain and the United States would soon be at war, this would be a golden opportunity for the Indians to put warriors in the field and recapture the lands they had lost in the Ohio country. Washington's main concern was that the British might convince friendly Indian nations to join the coalition of hostile ones—the Delaware, Shawnees, and Miamis—arrayed against Wayne's Legion. Washington repeatedly told Knox and reiterated in April 1794 that the federal agent to the Iroquois, General Israel Chapin, "should be instructed to leave no means unassayed to keep the Six Nations well disposed . . . and to buy Captain Brant off at almost any price." At the same time, Congress resolved to mobilize eighty thousand militiamen and establish an auxiliary army of twenty-five thousand troops to meet the British threat in the Northwest.[17]

War with England could only bring harm to the young nation, Washington told the Senate in mid-April, and since "peace ought to be pursued with unremitted zeal . . . I have nominated John Jay as envoy extraordinary of the United States to his Britannic Majesty." Washington still had full confidence in the ambassador to England, Thomas Pinckney, he explained, but Jay's appointment would "announce to the world a solicitude for a friendly adjustment of our complaints and a reluctance to hostility. Going immediately from the United States, such an envoy will carry with him a full knowledge of the existing temper and sensibility of our country, and will thus be taught to vindicate our rights with firmness and to cultivate peace with sincerity." It was precisely Jay's degree of firmness in negotiating with the British that would ultimately become the target of Republican attacks at home, fueling a political firestorm.[18]

On May 20 news arrived in Philadelphia that Lord Dorchester's threat seemed on the verge of becoming reality. Lieutenant Governor John Graves Simcoe had dispatched three companies of British troops sixty miles south from Detroit (see Hutchins, *A New Map, Detail #1*, page 204, top center) to reoccupy Fort Miami below the rapids of the Miami River near the southern shore of Lake Erie (see Bradley, *A Map of the United States, Detail #2*, page 239, upper right corner. Fort Miami is labeled *British Garrison*). Presumably the incursion deeper into U.S. territory was to fend off a possible attack on Detroit by Wayne's Legion.

The British ambassador in Philadelphia, George Hammond, protested that Lord Dorchester's speech had been misconstrued, and Simcoe's supposed invasion had yet to be confirmed. Washington helped defuse the crisis by asking Governor Thomas Mifflin

George Rogers Clark.

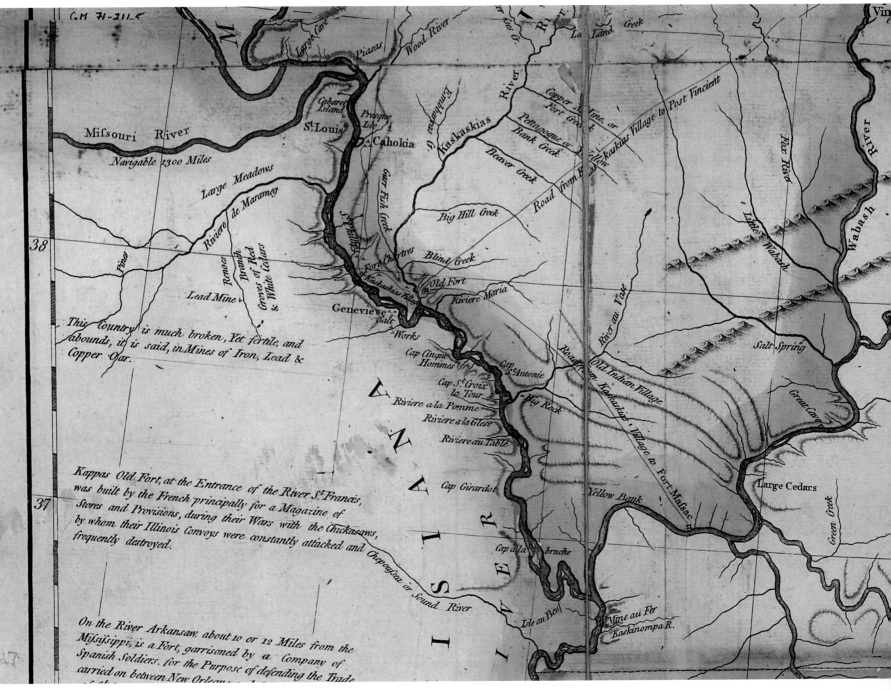

The map contains the following labels and notations:

GM 71-211.5

Missouri River
Navigable 1300 Miles

St. Louis
Cahokia

Large Meadows

Rivière de Marameg

Renaux Branch
Groves of Red & White Cedars

Lead Mine

This Country is much broken, Yet fertile, and abounds, it is said, in Mines of Iron, Lead & Copper Oar.

Genevieve Salt
Works

Fort Chartres
Kaskaskias River
Old Fort

Riviere Maria

Cap Cinque Hommes
Cap St Antonie
Cap St Croix le Tour
Riviere a la Pomme
Riviere a la Glaise
Riviere au Table

Cap Girardot

Kappas Old Fort, at the Entrance of the River St. Francis, was built by the French principally for a Magazine of Stores and Provisions, during their Wars with the Chickasaws, by whom their Illinois Convoys were constantly attacked and frequently destroyed.

Chepoysea or Sound River

Cap à la bruche

On the River Arkansaw, about 10 or 12 Miles from the Missisippi, is a Fort, garrisoned by a Company of Spanish Soldiers, for the Purpose of defending the Trade carried on between New Orlean

Isle au Beuf
Mine au Fer
Kaskinompa R.
Yellow Bank
Big Rock

Road from Kaskaskias Village to Fort Massac
Road from Kaskaskias Village to Fort Massac
Old Indian Village

River au Vase

Salt Spring

Large Cedars
Green Creek
Great Cave

Little Wabash
Wabash River

Large Cave
Piasas
Wood River
Presque Isle
Cabaret Island

Kaskaskias River
Copper Mine or Fort Gage
Pettecoque or
Bank Creek
Beaver Creek
Road from Kaskaskias Village to Post Vincent
La Land Creek
Fox River
Vin

Big Hill Creek
Blind Creek

Goar Fish Creek

Pines

38
37

MISSIRI

Hutchins, *A New Map, Detail #4:* Washington hoped to block the western prong of Clark's invasion force by strengthening the garrison at Fort Massac on the Ohio River (lower right). St. Louis is shown in the upper left.

of Pennsylvania to refrain from sending a thousand militiamen to Presque Isle as he had planned—a move certain to inflame British hostility on the Canadian frontier. Presque Isle, on the southern shore of Lake Erie, had been a French outpost, just north of Fort Le Boeuf, when Washington had traveled there on his first mission in 1753. (See *A General Map of the Middle British Colonies, Detail #5,* page 43.) Now it was a town in U.S. territory, and Mifflin was eagerly promoting settlement there. These settlers would certainly denounce Washington for denying them militia protection, but that was a price he was willing to pay for peace with the British.[19]

Privately, however, Washington was losing patience with the British. He wrote to John Jay in August, expressing relief at his safe arrival in London and informing him of the latest British provocation in the Northwest: Simcoe's official protest against Americans occupying land that was plainly within the borders of the United States. Washington complained that "all the difficulties we encounter with the Indians, their hostilities, the murders of helpless women and innocent children along our frontiers, results from the conduct of the agents of Great Britain in this country," who were arming and supplying the hostile tribes and instigating their attacks. "Can it be expected I ask, so long as these things are known in the United States . . . and suffered with impunity by Great Britain, that there ever will, or can be any cordiality between the two countries? I answer no!" Washington predicted that war would be inevitable if the northwestern posts were not surrendered soon.[20]

The latest reports from the Georgia frontier warned that the militia could not be held back much longer from attacking the Creeks. For Washington, the behavior of the pioneers was as troublesome as that of the Indians. Just as the Creeks were making incursions into Georgia, whites were violating treaties by settling on Indian land. In mid-July the cabinet agreed that Governor George Mathews (elected in 1793) should be reprimanded and ordered to prevent new settlements on Indian land, and promised federal aid if necessary. And in Kentucky, the Republicans had issued a "Remonstrance to the President . . . and Congress" in which they declared they could wait no longer for the opening of the Mississippi through diplomacy.

If Washington could not soothe the westerners on one hand and the Spanish on the other, he knew he might be faced with the dreadful choice of supporting military action against the Spanish colonies—which would lead to war with both Spain and England—or watching Kentucky break away from the Union. For the moment, Washington followed his cabinet's advice and made no official response to the Kentuckians' protest.[21]

Soon the Kentuckians' Remonstrance looked mild in comparison to the discontent that boiled over into a revolt in the western counties of Pennsylvania, where armed mobs resisted the excise tax on whiskey. The Whiskey Rebellion and Washington's measures to suppress it would unfold on the terrain of his early military career and land acquisitions.

For the mainly Scottish and Irish immigrants in this still remote area, distilling grain into whiskey was their economic mainstay. A wagonload of wheat cost as much to transport across the mountains as it would sell for at market. And while a horse could carry only four bushels of grain at a time, it could carry enough whiskey to equal twenty-four bushels, and so bring a profit. Whiskey was also currency in this largely barter economy, and a tax in cash struck the distillers as an unbearable burden.

Opposition to the excise laws introduced by Hamilton had been simmering in the Allegheny region since the end of Washington's first administration, and he had predicted that all it would take was a forceful demagogue to ignite an insurrection. Now, as violent resistance arose, he blamed Genet and the Democratic Societies he had inspired for breeding "distrust of government among the people" and providing an organizational structure for the rebellion.[22] Here too was the sectional dissolution Washington warned against when he promoted improved inland navigation, especially of the Potomac River: Westerners deterred by bad roads from marketing their goods in the East would turn elsewhere. Some of the protesters had reportedly sold everything and moved to Detroit.[23]

On July 17, 1794, the insurgents burned the mansion of a federal officer on Chartiers Creek and two weeks later assembled a small army at Braddock's Field. Washington sent four commissioners to Pittsburgh, where they negotiated with a delegation sent by the protesters on August 21. These delegates, representing Westmoreland, Washington, Fayette, and Allegheny counties, reported back to a larger committee a week later at Brownsville (on the Monongahela at the mouth of Red Stone Creek) that the government offered amnesty in exchange for full compliance with the excise law. After a second meeting of the commissioners and delegates at Pittsburgh the prospect of a peaceful settlement grew dim, and

on September 9 Washington approved Hamilton's plan to mobilize the militia of New Jersey, Maryland, and Virginia in addition to Pennsylvania's. On September 30 Washington, accompanied by Hamilton, set out from Philadelphia for Carlisle to inspect the Pennsylvania and New Jersey militia who were to rendezvous there. He would then proceed to Fort Cumberland, in Maryland, to see the Virginia and Maryland militia, before heading north to Bedford, Pennsylvania, where the entire force would assemble. (See *A Map of Pennsylvania, Detail #1*, page 38, and *Detail #3*, page 55.)[24]

That evening, Washington received word of Anthony Wayne's momentous victory on August 20 over Little Turtle and some two thousand Indians at Fallen Timbers, near the rapids of the Miami River, west of Lake Erie. Washington noted in his diary that his party was "overtaken by Major Stagg, principal clerk in the Department of War with letters from General Wayne and the Western Army containing official and pleasing accounts of his engagement with the Indians near the British post at the Rapids of the Miami of the Lake and of his having destroyed all the Indian settlements on that river in the vicinity of the said post quite up to the Grand Glaize—the quantity not less than 5,000 acres—and the stores, etc. of Colonel McGee, the British agent of Indian affairs, a mile or two from the garrison."[25]

(See Bradley, *A Map of the United States, Detail #2*, page 239. Wayne's force built Fort Adams, Fort Wayne, and Fort Defiance as it proceeded to the Rapids of the Miami River. In the upper right, the map claims the decisive clash of Wayne's army with the Indians took place on August 10, 1794, rather than August 20, at Fallen Timbers, an area, not labeled, where trees had been felled by a tornado and the Indians lay in ambush. Before the defeated Indians could enter the British garrison, the commander closed the gates. Pursuing the Indians as they fled on foot across an open field, American cavalrymen slaughtered them with their sabers.)[26]

While en route to inspect the militia, Washington stopped to observe construction work on a canal to link the Schuylkill and the Susquehanna rivers. On October 4, he arrived at Carlisle, where he met with representatives of the insurgents on the 9th and 10th. Despite their pleas, he insisted that the army would proceed over the mountains. On the 12th he set out for Cumberland, arriving four days later, after stopping at familiar ground: Bath and then Old Town (Cresap's, where Washington had first encountered the frontier forty-six years earlier; Cresap had died in 1790). At Cumberland he turned over the army to Governor Henry Lee of Virginia, who became commander in chief, and to Hamilton.

With Lee and Hamilton, Washington set off for Bedford along Wills Creek on October 19. "The road from Cumberland to this place is, in places, stony but in other respects not bad. It passes through a valley the whole way, and was opened by troops under my command in the autumn of 1758." This was the road from Cumberland to Raystown that Washington cut when taking his troops to join the Forbes expedition. (See *A Map of Pennsylvania, Detail #1*, page 38.)[27]

From Bedford, Washington returned to Philadelphia while Lee and Hamilton led the militia westward toward Pittsburgh, where they encountered no resistance. Despite Washington's parting admonitions to uphold the law, the army was undisciplined and treated the local population roughly, arresting about 150 people, dragging many from their homes in the middle of the night. After harsh confinement and interrogation, all but twenty were released for lack of evidence. Leaving a detachment camped on the Monongahela for the winter, the army marched home, taking the twenty alleged insurgents to Philadelphia, where they were paraded through the streets in December.

Their trials lasted through most of the next year, but only two men were convicted. Washington ultimately pardoned them, and vented his wrath in his State of the Union address, lashing out against "certain self-created societies" that had "assumed the tone of condemnation" against the government. His dubious claim that the Republicans' Democratic Societies were responsible for the Whiskey Rebellion deepened the partisan divide. Jefferson declared that Washington, once "the head of a nation," was now merely the leader of the Federalist Party.[28]

In the Northwest, Wayne, despite his victory in August, reported problems with recruitment and appealed to the government for a large permanent army to secure the frontier. And Timothy Pickering, a seasoned negotiator who had gone to Canandaigua in Iroquois country to see Joseph Brant, had not reported any progress in his struggle to counter British influence over the Six Nations.[29]

However, in his latest letter to Washington, written in August 1794, John Jay indicated that the British seemed more amenable to meaningful negotiation than at any point since his arrival. Washington wrote back in early November, saying that "no man more ardently wishes you complete success than I do." However, many factors in the negotiation remained beyond Jay's control, Washington wrote. He should simply do his best and reasonable people would support him. "Against the malignancy of the discontented, the turbulent, and the vicious, no abilities, no exertions, nor the most unshaken integrity are a safeguard."[30]

As he had done in sending Jay to London, Washington now prepared to send Thomas Pinckney to Spain as a special envoy to accelerate the talks on navigation of the Mississippi. Washington also sent Colonel James Innes to Lexington, Kentucky, to convince the restive westerners that the federal government was doing all it could on their behalf.[31]

The Whiskey Rebellion, July 1794. A tax collector is tarred and feathered and ridden on a rail.

John Jay.

Thomas Pinckney.

Timothy Pickering.

The dawn of the New Year in 1795 brought Washington news of progress on several fronts. On January 2, he was able to lay before the Senate the fruits of Timothy Pickering's trip to Iroquois country: two treaties signed at Canandaigua in November that secured the friendship of the Six Nations, diminished British influence, and allowed the United States to fortify Presque Isle, on the southern shore of Lake Erie. On that same day, Washington nominated Pickering as secretary of war and the Senate confirmed him to replace Knox, who had just resigned.[32]

On March 7, 1795, the text of a treaty negotiated in London by John Jay with Lord Grenville arrived in Philadelphia. Jay wrote to Washington that these twenty-eight articles were the best terms he could get. Overall, the treaty seemed more favorable to the British, except for Article Two, which required them to finally evacuate the posts they still held in the Northwest. However, they could drag out the withdrawal until the middle of 1796. The next article allowed Canadian trappers, traders, and Indians full use of the Northwest Territory including the Mississippi River, a right far more valuable than the reciprocal privilege in Canada granted to Americans. And among other omissions, the treaty failed to address the complaint that Britain's refusal to leave the western posts for more than ten years had inflicted losses on Americans for which they should be compensated. The bulk of the treaty dealt with regulation of maritime commerce between Britain and the United States, and many of the provisions were blatantly against American interests.

Nonetheless, the document patched up relations with England enough to prevent the outbreak of war, and for this alone Jay's treaty was regarded as a success by Washington and the Federalists. If war with England could not be avoided in the long run, the treaty would buy time for the fledgling United States to gain strength. Nonetheless, Washington realized that his Republican opponents—Anglophobes and Francophiles—would tear the treaty apart in the press, so he and Secretary of State Randolph resolved to keep its contents secret until the Senate could approve it and the president could ratify it with his signature.[33]

As he prepared to leave for Mount Vernon during the congressional recess, Washington wanted to have a plan in place for dealing with the ongoing problem of Indian relations on the frontiers. He pressed his new secretary of war to draft a comprehensive strategy. By late March 1795, Pickering had drawn up specific instructions for Governor Blount of the Southwest Territory and for James Seagrove, Indian agent in Georgia. Washington also wanted to manage developments in the Northwest, and had Pickering spell out how the fort at Presque Isle would be built and garrisoned, in addition to writing instructions for General Wayne's peace negotiations with the defeated Indians.[34]

Those talks with the Ohio Indians bore fruit on August 9, 1795, in the Treaty of Greeneville, which Washington was pleased to learn about from Pickering in September. While waiting for details of the treaty in the Northwest, Washington had Pickering dispatch Agent Seagrove to the Southwest border to mediate a cease-fire between the Creeks and the Chickasaws. The president hoped to report to Congress in November that the administration had brought about peace on the frontiers.[35]

In his Seventh Annual Address to Congress, Washington celebrated the end of the long war with the Northwest Indians and pointed to hopeful signs that the Creeks and Cherokees in the Southwest were ready for peace. However, he condemned "the violences of the lawless part of our frontier," the taking of Indian land by white pioneers, which perpetuated the cycle of raids and retribution and cost the government dearly to mobilize troops and secure the border.[36] Soon Pickering was advising the president that the federal government would have to take action, and on February 2, 1796, Washington addressed Congress to denounce the "daring designs of certain persons to take possession of lands belonging to the Cherokees, and which the United States have by Treaty solemnly guaranteed to that Nation. The injustice of such intrusions, and the mischievous consequences, which must necessarily result therefrom demand that effectual provision be made to prevent them."[37]

By this time, word had reached Philadelphia that Thomas Pinckney's mission as special envoy to Madrid had produced a treaty, but the text had not yet crossed the Atlantic. Washington wrote Pinckney that "we are in daily and anxious anticipation of its arrival," since it would be "soothing to the inhabitants of the Western Waters, who were beginning to grow restive and clamorous." The arrival of the Treaty of San Lorenzo in Philadelphia on February 22, 1796, also made a fine sixty-fourth-birthday gift for the president, since it contained every concession by the Spanish that Americans had hoped for: free navigation of the Mississippi; the right to deposit goods for export at New Orleans, tax free; the southwest boundary of the United States at the 31st parallel; and a promise to curb Indian incursions into the United States along the frontier.[38] On June 1, 1796, Washington signed the bill admitting the Southwest Territory to the Union as the sixteenth state, Tennessee. In the Northwest, the last posts were transferred from British to American control by the middle of the summer.[39]

On September 19, 1796, as Washington rode home to Mount Vernon in his carriage for a six-week vacation, his open letter "To the PEOPLE of the United States, Friends and fellow citizens," which came to be known as his Farewell Address, appeared in a Philadelphia newspaper. The address definitively announced his retirement, for anyone who thought he might serve a third term. In reiterating the policy of neutrality he had spelled out three years earlier, the address served as a kind of second declaration of independence, calling impartially for the United States and its political factions to avoid being drawn into any sphere of foreign influence, French, English, or Spanish.[40]

Washington urged the American people to maintain a strong central government and the integrity of the Union in order to preserve their liberty. Beware of "characterizing parties by *geographical* discriminations—*Northern* and *Southern*, *Atlantic*, and *Western*," he warned, "whence designing men may endeavor to excite a belief that there is a real difference of local interests and views." Washington cited the Pinckney Treaty with Spain as "decisive proof" for westerners that the federal government and the eastern states did not support policies "unfriendly to their interests in regard to the Mississippi." The two treaties, with Britain and Spain, secured for the western states "everything they could desire in respect to our foreign relations toward confirming their prosperity."[41]

Back in Philadelphia on October 31, Washington was confronted with an international crisis of major proportions. The French government, furious over America's rapprochement with the British in the recently ratified Jay Treaty, accused the administration of abandoning the 1778 treaty with France and denounced Washington's Farewell Address. Ignoring American claims of neutrality, the French would retaliate by seizing British goods carried on American ships. From the numerous French ports in the West Indies, American vessels would come under attack, with grave effects on American commerce.[42] (See *A General Map of North America, Detail #2*, page 31. The French islands are shown in green.)

With three months left in his term, Washington delivered his Eighth Annual Address to Congress on December 7, 1796—his last official appearance. While noting that outstanding differences with the British were gradually being resolved by implementation of the Jay Treaty, Washington presented a bleak picture of relations with France. "Our trade has suffered and is suffering extensive injuries in the West Indies from the cruisers and agents of the French republic," he reported. Observing that "the most sincere neutrality is not sufficient to guard against the deprivations of nations at war," Washington urged Congress to establish a navy to "secure respect to a neutral flag" and "prevent the necessity of going to war by discouraging belligerent powers."

Washington ended the speech on a celebratory note, however, recalling "the period when the administration of the present form of government was commenced" in 1789, and congratulating the representatives "and my country on the success of the experiment."[43] Washington conscientiously withheld his detailed report on French aggression until January 19, 1797, so it would not be perceived or used as Federalist propaganda during the presidential election—to tarnish the Republicans and their embrace of the French. Despite an unrestrained campaign of French and Republican propaganda aimed at electing Jefferson, he took second place, becoming vice president, with John Adams, a Federalist, as president.[44]

The new ambassador to France from the United States, Charles Cotesworth Pinckney, was to carry the document detailing French violations of American neutrality to Paris, but in February, Washington learned unofficially that the French had refused to recognize his credentials. Even before this latest insult, Washington had told Hamilton that he considered the behavior of the French "outrageous beyond conception." By the time the rumors from Paris could be confirmed, however, the problem would be on the shoulders of the new president. Washington's final birthday in office, February 22, 1797, began with the ringing of bells and the firing of cannon, and was celebrated with great emotion by his supporters, some twelve thousand of them crowding into Rickett's Amphitheater in Philadelphia that evening for a ball in his and Martha's honor. Washington was reportedly very moved by the thunderous applause when the couple arrived, and rendered speechless at various times throughout the evening by the overwhelming display of affection.

Privately, as he revealed in a letter to Knox, Washington was also deeply wounded by the personal attacks in the press by French and Republican partisans who were determined to "misrepresent my motives, to reprobate my politics, and to weaken the confidence which has been reposed in my administration." He told Knox that "the prospect of retirement is most grateful to my soul, and I have not a wish to mix again in the great world or to partake in its politics."

The man who had inaugurated Washington's rise to fame twenty-two years earlier by proposing his appointment as commander in chief of the Continental army, President-elect John Adams, took the oath of office in March with Washington sitting on one side of the dais and Jefferson on the other. After the ceremony, Adams walked out, and Washington insisted that Jefferson exit ahead of him. As he did when he resigned his commission at Annapolis after the Revolution, Washington again personified the peaceful transfer of power that so distinguished the great experiment in republican government.[45]

he farms, independent of the others. — The greater of the
ng low; part of it is already cleared; and part still remains
s on it.

s a sufficiency of grounds cleared and in cultivation for a
beautiful site for a Gentleman's Seat.

rea of the wood, but has a house on it.

m; — or if that farm should be sub-divided, it might form part
s on the River.

Union
Field Nᵒ 1.
2.
3.
4.
5.
6.
7.
Meadow
Clover Lots

Dogue
Field Nᵒ 1.
2.
3.
4.
5.
6.
7.
Meadow
Clover Lots

W ——— E
Road to Alexandria &c. &c.

Scale
Poles
100   200   300   400

part of Nᵒ 1
Part of Nᵒ 1
Nᵒ 2
Nᵒ 3
Nᵒ 5
Muddy hole Farm Nᵒ 6

Mansion House Farm

River Farm Nᵒ 6
Nᵒ 5
Nᵒ 4
Orchard Grass Lots
Common Pasture

CHAPTER TEN

BACK TO THE LAND, DIVIDING

MOUNT VERNON

The six-day journey home to Mount Vernon, in the company of Martha, his step-granddaughter Nelly Custis, and the marquis de Lafayette's son, George Washington Motier Lafayette, was punctuated by "parades and escorts," which Washington found "very flattering" but avoided as much as possible when he had advance notice, he later told Secretary of War James McHenry. He was anxious to return to his "long forsaken residence" which would "require considerable repairs," and the general would soon be attempting to command an army of "joiners, masons, painters, etc." Washington was also eager to be free "from the toil, the cares and responsibility of public occupations and engaged in rural and agricultural pursuits." As Nelly wrote to a friend after they arrived at Mount Vernon on March 15, "Grandpapa is very well, and much pleased with being once more *Farmer Washington*."[1]

On a typical day at Mount Vernon, Washington told McHenry, he rose at dawn, and "if my hirelings are not in their places at that time I send them messages expressive of my sorrow for their indisposition. Then, having put these wheels in motion, I examine the state of things further, and the more they are probed, the deeper I find the wounds are which my buildings have sustained by an absence and neglect of eight years." Breakfast was at seven, and then "I mount my horse and ride round my farms, which employs me until it is time to dress for dinner, at which I rarely miss seeing strange faces, come, as they say, out of respect to me . . . And how different this, from having a few social friends at a cheerful board? The usual time of sitting at table; a walk, and tea, brings me within the dawn of candlelight," when he would usually "retire to my writing table and acknowledge the letters I have received."[2] (See *Washington's own survey of Mount Vernon, 1793*, page 249. Mount Vernon was an eight-thousand-acre plantation, so even inspecting a portion of the five farms—each with its own overseers, slaves, livestock, equipment, and buildings—occupied the bulk of his day, between breakfast at seven A.M. and his return for dinner at two P.M.)[3]

While he tolerated the stream of visitors who came to dine or to stay at Mount Vernon, Washington craved the company of old friends, virtually all of whom had moved away, or were now dead. George and Sally Fairfax had long since moved to England, and

Mount Vernon.

the mansion at Belvoir, just south of Mount Vernon across Dogue Creek, lay in ruins, having burned down in 1783, probably struck by lightning. Washington toured the site on horseback and wrote to the Fairfaxes that he "could not trace a room in the house [in the ruins] that did not bring to my mind recollections of pleasing scenes."[4]

When George Fairfax died and his brother Bryan sailed for England, Washington asked him to take a letter to Sally from Martha since they were old friends and neighbors. Washington quietly slipped a letter of his own to Sally into the envelope, revealing that his passion for her was unabated, despite his strong and stable marriage to Martha. Looking back over the past twenty-five years, he wrote to Sally, "many important events have occurred and such changes in men and things have taken place as the compass of a letter would give you but an inadequate idea of. None of which events, however, nor all of them together, have been able to eradicate from my mind the recollection of those happy

moments, the happiest in my life, which I have enjoyed in your company."

Washington continued, "It is a matter of sore regret, when I cast my eyes towards Belvoir, which I often do, to reflect that the former inhabitants of it, with whom we had lived in such harmony and friendship, no longer reside there, and that the ruins can only be viewed as the memento of former pleasures." Since Sally still had relatives in America, "I have wondered often," Washington wrote, "that you should not prefer spending the evening of your life among them rather than . . . in a foreign country, numerous as your acquaintances may be, and sincere, as the friendships you may have formed."[5]

Preventing Mount Vernon from falling into ruins like Belvoir was Washington's new focus, and it was both time-consuming and expensive. His salary as president, the profits from agriculture at Mount Vernon, and rental income from his lands in the West had not covered his expenses during the previous eight years. In retirement he had fewer expenses, since he did not have to maintain a residence in Philadelphia in addition to Mount Vernon,

but he also had no salary or pension. The budget shortfall in these final years of his life was covered by the "occasional supplies of money in payment for lands sold," he noted, "to the amount of upwards of $50,000." The tracts of land he had acquired as a young man, as bounties for military service or through purchase, provided the cash flow in retirement that kept him out of "debt and difficulties."[6]

Every sale was fraught with difficulty, however, and much of his forty-five thousand acres, including the parcels along the Kanawha River, remained unsold. The war in Europe had initially produced a flood of immigration to America and a sellers' market for land, but hostilities on the high seas had reduced the number of new settlers. As American trade was strangled by French retaliatory measures, the supply of cash dried up, and American land speculators asked for long-term credit with little down payment for large parcels. Washington complained of the "vague, speculative, and unmeaning offers of men who have no wherewithal to fulfill an engagement and do not mean (more than probably) to do it."[7] Of one buyer, Washington wrote: "He has sold part of the land for nearly double what he was to give me, and yet, instead of paying

The Great Falls of the Potomac, a painting by George Beck that was owned by George Washington and still hangs at Mount Vernon.

George Washington's sketch of the rapids at Harpers Ferry in 1754, beginning his lifelong interest in making the Potomac River navigable.

me according to the installments, he sends the money (always short) by such driblets, and is such manner as to be of no real use to me."[8]

Crucial to the future value of Washington's land was the success of the Potomac improvement project, which he believed would put his acreage on the principal commercial route connecting the eastern seaboard with the fertile Ohio country and the Great Lakes. And while the Potomac Company limped along, Washington continued to promote it vigorously, pointing out the progress achieved and omitting the obstacles that remained. The river had been cleared as far westward as Fort Cumberland—more than two hundred miles—he wrote to Sally Fairfax, without mentioning that the route still had to cross the Allegheny Mountains, or that all goods transported eastward to the Atlantic Ocean would have to be hauled by land around Great Falls. (See *A Map of . . . Virginia, Detail #3*, page 27, right center, for Great Falls. See *Detail #4*, page 29, upper left, for the site of Fort Cumberland, at Wills Creek.)[9]

Displaying his enthusiasm for inland navigation (and jogging what he described as his failing memory), Washington impressed one visitor at Mount Vernon by naming all of the rivers, creeks, and lakes from Maine southward that could connect the West with the Atlantic Ocean. He remained convinced that the Potomac trumped all other routes, but canal projects springing up across the country would cast this vision into doubt. As the Potomac

Company faltered, Washington loaned it almost $3,500, from the sale of all his "six percent stock of the United States." All of his prestige, however, was not enough to induce the State of Virginia to lend the company money.

Washington scraped together enough to pay the assessment of one hundred dollars per share agreed on by the shareholders, but many of them backed out. Washington never wavered, however, in his conviction that the stock would ultimately rise in value, and bequeathed his shares as the endowment for a national university, another of his most cherished projects. It would take another quarter of a century, but "the Yorkers," as Washington had called them, would triumph in the canal race, completing the Erie Canal across the relatively flat Mohawk River Valley. The Potomac Canal served a local function for a number of years without turning a profit, and the company folded without managing to get across the mountain barrier to the West.[10]

Progress was equally sporadic on another Potomac River project in which the retired president took a keen interest: building the city of Washington, which, out of modesty, he still referred to as the Federal City. The federal government was scheduled to move there in 1800, but small investors had purchased few of the city's lots; Washington had felt relieved when three wealthy speculators—James Greenleaf, Robert Morris, and John Nicholson—agreed to buy thousands of lots and build houses on them in addition to lending money for the construction of the public buildings. The speculators had agreed to pay for these commitments in installments, the first of which they made on time in 1794.

However, their operations were highly leveraged, with loans from the Dutch, and when France invaded Holland and a credit contraction ensued, the speculators could not make their second payment, in 1795. Washington was furious at his old friend Morris, who had steered the nation's finances during the Revolution, and the worst was yet to come. The following year construction restarted briefly, and then stopped again as the credit markets froze up and the speculators' house of cards collapsed. Greenleaf was thrown into debtor's prison in October 1797. Morris and Nicholson holed up in their houses, resisting arrest for only a few months longer. Washington later commented in disgust that "it has always been my opinion, and so I have expressed it, that the proprietors of the city of Washington (with some exceptions) are, by their jealousies, and the modes they pursue to promote their local interests, among its worst enemies."[11]

Before he left office, Washington had extracted a loan guarantee from Congress and a $100,000 loan from Maryland, which allowed work to proceed slowly amid the swamp, mud, and forest of the future capital. In retirement, Washington purchased lots near the Capitol to build a boardinghouse for members of Congress, a business venture that also set a patriotic example and inspired other investors to buy lots as well.[12]

"Various conjectures have been formed relative to the causes which have induced the president to convene the Congress at this season of the year," Washington wrote to Secretary of the Treasury Oliver Wolcott on May 15, 1797, the day before a special session called by John Adams. Even as Washington pressed Wolcott for the inside story, he claimed to be contented with his new role outside the halls of power: "For myself, having turned aside from the broad walks of political, into the narrow paths of private life, I shall leave it to those whose duty it is to consider subjects of this sort, and (as every good citizen ought to do) conform to whatsoever the ruling powers shall decide."

In his final years, Washington did not expect to travel more than twenty miles from Mount Vernon, he told Wolcott. "To make and sell a little flour annually; to repair houses (going fast to ruin); to build one for the security of my papers of a public nature; and to amuse myself in agricultural and rural pursuits will constitute employment for the few years I have to remain on this terrestrial globe."[13]

While President Adams now bore the burden of dealing with the French government—its policy of retaliation against American ships and sailors, and its obstinate refusal to recognize Charles Cotesworth Pinckney as ambassador—the continuing crisis would soon draw Washington back into a public role, as the United States came to the brink of war with France. In his address to Congress on May 16, Adams took a firm, combative stance, designed to "convince France and the world that we are not a degraded people, humiliated under a colonial spirit of fear and a sense of inferiority, fitted to be the miserable instruments of foreign influence."[14]

Washington lauded the speech, in which Adams, while calling for peace, had advised merchants to arm their vessels for self-defense. Adams also recommended that Congress expand the navy and overhaul the militia system to create a stronger fighting force. Washington hoped the speech would inspire an outpouring of public support and show the French government that, contrary to Republican propaganda, most Americans did not want the United States submitting to French influence. "A little

Robert Morris.

time will show who are [America's] true friends, or what is synonymous, who are true Americans," Washington wrote to Thomas Pinckney, "those who are stimulating a foreign nation to unfriendly acts, repugnant to our rights and dignity, and advocating all its measures, or those whose only aim has been to maintain a strict neutrality, to keep the United States out of the vortex of European politics, and to preserve them in peace."[15]

Adams expanded the delegation to France, naming Elbridge Gerry, a Republican, and John Marshall, a Federalist, to serve with Charles Cotesworth Pinckney. Washington naturally approved, since this was a step he had contemplated before leaving office, and Marshall was one of his protégés. Not until December did Washington receive a letter from Pinckney, dated September 19th, saying that the delegation had arrived safely in Rotterdam on

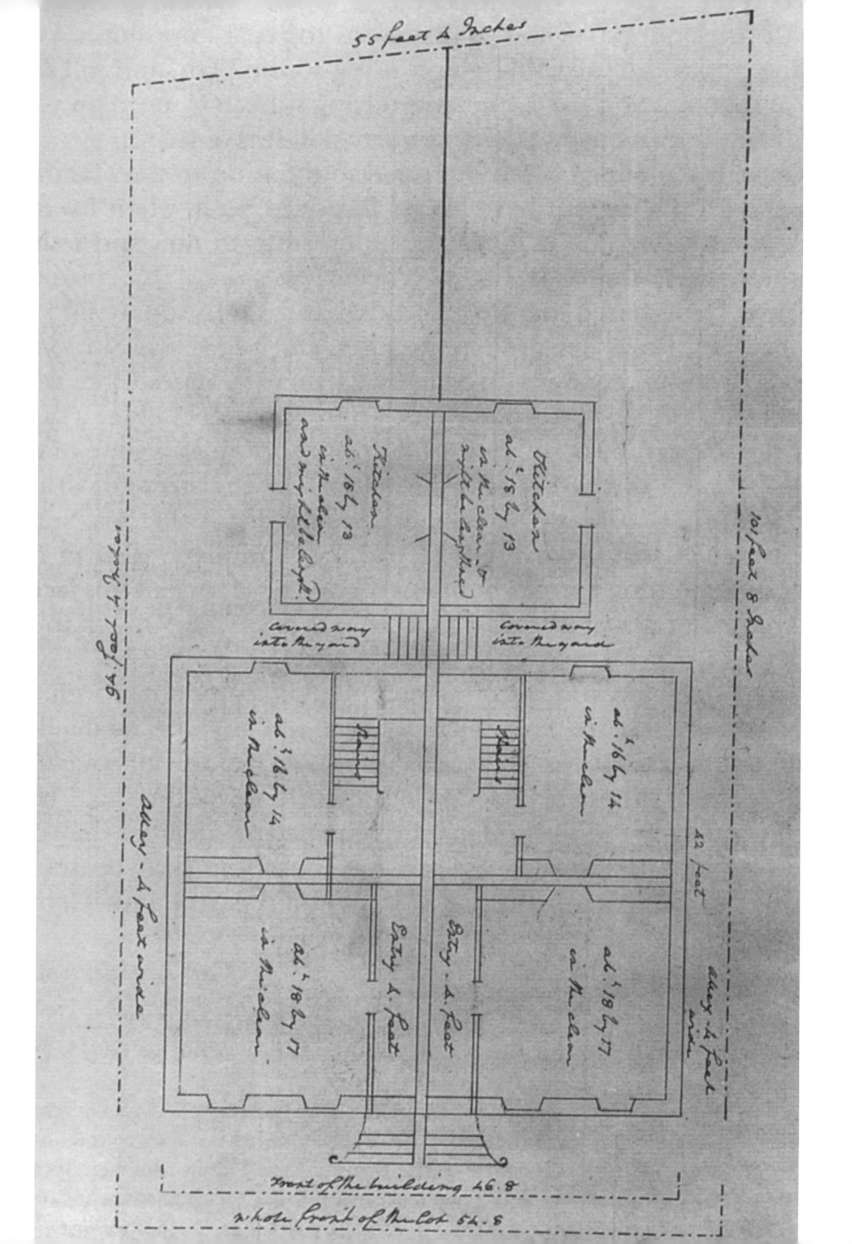

ABOVE, LEFT: President John Adams.

ABOVE: Charles Cotesworth Pinckney.

OPPOSITE: George Washington's plan for his Capitol Hill houses.

their way to Paris and that he and Marshall had developed an excellent rapport. "That the government of France views us as a divided people, I have little doubt," Washington replied to Pinckney, "and that they have been led to entertain that opinion from representations and the conduct of many of our own citizens is still less doubtful. But I shall be very much mistaken indeed in the mass of the people of the United States, if an occasion should call for an unequivocal expression of the public voice, if the [French government] would not find themselves very much deceived."[16]

For that occasion Washington would have to wait through the long, severe winter on the Potomac. "Since the first of November we have hardly experienced a moderate day," he wrote to Marshall in December. "Heavy rains following severe frosts have done more damage to the winter grain, now growing, than I can recollect ever to have seen. At this moment and for several days past, all the creeks and small waters are hard bound with ice, and the navigation of the river, if not entirely stopped is yet very much impeded by it."[17] Washington did have the satisfaction of learning in December that the Austrians had released Lafayette from his harrowing confinement in the dungeon at Olmutz and he was bound either for Holland or America.[18]

Washington also had to endure the attacks in the press by Republicans and their French allies—including Thomas Jefferson, former French ambassador Fauchet, and James Monroe, the ambassador to France recalled to America by Adams—who denounced Washington and his administration as well as the current one for betraying the French and favoring the British. "I think it is in vain to expect any change in the sentiments or political conduct of those who are, in every form it can be tried, opposing the measures of government and endeavoring to sap the foundation of the Constitution," Washington wrote to James Ross in February 1798. "A little time now must decide what their ulterior movements will be, as they have brought matters to a crisis."[19]

Snowbound in the mansion at Mount Vernon in early March 1798, Washington began to wonder if the delegation had been guillotined, since there appeared to be no news from France across the stormy Atlantic. In Philadelphia, Adams had just received word of further French intransigence. Aggravated by Adams's inaugural speech, the French government had declared it would receive the delegation only if the United States publicly espoused a new policy. Pinckney and his fellow delegates reported that three French agents, designated X, Y, and Z in the dispatch, had paid them a visit to make further demands: The delegation had to renounce the belligerent policy of the Adams administration, present foreign minister Charles-Maurice de Talleyrand with a large bribe, and arrange a massive loan from the United States.[20]

Adams curbed his initial impulse to declare war, and withheld many of the details of the situation from Congress in order to prevent a public uproar against the French—and keep his diplomatic options open. However, Republicans suspected the president was concealing information that gave a benign explanation for the behavior of the French, and the House majority pressured him to release the complete dispatches. "What a scene of corruption and profligacy has these communications disclosed in the directors of a people with whom the United States has endeavored to treat upon fair, just and honorable ground!" Washington wrote to Maryland senator James Lloyd, who had sent him copies of the dispatches. He hoped with Lloyd that the news would have the effect of "speedily uniting our fellow-citizens in a firm determination to support our government and preserve our independence."[21]

James McHenry, Secretary of War.

Indeed, when Adams had the full record published in early April, a firestorm of protest spread through the country. The French were loudly denounced at massive rallies and in written addresses that deluged the White House. Just as the Republicans had inflamed public opinion against the British when the Jay Treaty was unveiled, the Federalists now added to the hysteria for war against France with warnings of a French invasion. In the coming months, the Federalists pushed the infamous Alien and Sedition Acts through Congress, defining criticism of the administration as libel and providing for stiff jail terms. In the name of national security, the Federalists were able to gag Republican rivals in the press and in the government.

In addition to strengthening coastal fortifications and the navy, measures approved in a previous session, Congress now agreed to expand the three-thousand-man army with an "additional army" of ten thousand troops, and to create a "provisional army" of fifty thousand men to be mustered in the event of a French invasion. Adams favored a strong navy but opposed the creation of a large standing army as a danger to the republic. He was overridden by the dominant wing of the Federalist Party, controlled by Alexander Hamilton.[22]

Washington wrote to Secretary of War James McHenry in May to ask why the mouth of the Shenandoah River (at present-day Harpers Ferry in West Virginia) was not being considered along with other sites for arsenals and cannon foundries. "I will pledge myself that there is not a spot in the United States which combines more, or greater prerequisites . . . considered either as a place of immense strength against, and inaccessible by an enemy, although open to inland navigation in all directions, as well as crosswise as to the shipping port at the Federal City, and water transportation to the western country; for its centrality among furnaces and forges; for its inexhaustible supply of water, having the whole Shenandoah River as a resource; and for the populous and plentiful country in which it lies."[23] (See *A Map of . . . Virginia, Detail #3*, page 27, top center, where the Shenandoah flows into the Potomac.) As the administration braced for war, Washington was eager to connect his vision for improving the Potomac with the country's nascent military-industrial complex.

Regarding the immense challenges facing his administration, Adams wrote to Washington in June: "I have no qualifications for the martial part of it, which is like to be the most essential . . . I must tap you sometimes for advice. We must have your name if you will, in any case, permit us to use it. There will be more efficacy in it than in many an army." Secretary of War McHenry wrote that the United States would soon retaliate by authorizing American privateers to attack French ships. "You see how the storm thickens and that our vessel will soon require its ancient pilot," he told Washington. "Will you, may we flatter ourselves that in a crisis so awful and important you will accept the command of all our armies? I hope you will, because you alone can unite all hearts and hands, if it is possible that they can be united."[24]

Washington replied to Adams that he had never imagined anything would arise during his retirement that "could turn my eyes from the shades of Mount Vernon." For inscrutable reasons, however, Providence had "reserved for lawless France . . . to slaughter its own citizens and to disturb the repose of all the world besides." If the French actually invaded, "I certainly should not entrench myself under the cover of age and retirement," he wrote. Washington thought such an event unlikely, however, and hoped that the outrage displayed by the American people about the XYZ affair would puncture any illusions the French might have that a majority of the country stood ready to welcome their troops and help overthrow the government.[25]

Adams, however, had not waited for Washington's reply. Pressured by Hamilton's allies to put him in charge of the military, and convinced that he had dictatorial ambitions, Adams boxed him out on July 2, 1798, by abruptly nominating Washington as lieutenant general and commander of all United States forces. The Senate unanimously confirmed him the following day, and his commission was dated July 4th. When Washington picked up a newspaper and learned of his appointment, he was stunned. McHenry urged him to make this "crowning sacrifice . . . for the sake of your country, and to give the last finish to a fame that nothing short of such a call, and the present occasion, could have been capable of increasing." In a letter to Adams, Washington accepted the appointment on the condition that he would "not be called into the field until the army is in a situation to require my presence, or it becomes indispensable by the urgency of circumstances."[26]

Washington's main concern was that Adams might name the three major generals to serve under him, again without any consultation. While Hamilton, Charles Cotesworth Pinckney, and Knox were the only serious contenders, the order of their rank became a matter of bitter dispute, since the aging Washington might primarily be a figurehead, with his second in command effectively controlling the military.

Washington's preference was largely shaped by geographical considerations. Any French invasion was sure to be directed at the South, he told Secretary of State Timothy Pickering, because it was closest to their West Indian possessions and to Louisiana, which they hoped to recapture. (See *A General Map of North America, Detail #1*, page 18, and *Detail #2*, page 31.) Even though Hamilton would be slighted, Washington thought Pinckney, now on his way back from France, should be second in command because he was from South Carolina and his powerful influence would be needed to fully mobilize the defense of the South. And Pinckney was unlikely to serve under Hamilton since he had outranked him during

the Revolution. Knox had the most seniority of the three candidates, but Washington slotted him below the others, since he had always been obese and had lately become very sedentary. Conferring with McHenry, Washington agreed that Congress should be presented with the names Hamilton, Pinckney, and Knox—in that order—but with the understanding that the slate should be approved, leaving the order of their rank to President Adams.[27]

Informed by McHenry of Washington's preference, Adams might have found common ground with him in putting Hamilton below Pinckney. Instead, upon seeing the list, with Knox at the bottom, Adams felt New England

Alexander Hamilton.

was being insulted. Harking back to the appointment of Washington to lead the Continental army in 1775, Adams insisted on the principle of geographical balance between New England and the South, and moved Knox to the top of the list, with Hamilton at the bottom. Adams was also receptive to Knox's argument that his seniority gave him a legal right to be second in command.[28]

Adams still had most of the cabinet members from Washington's administration in place, and by now had grown disgusted with the back-channel communication they kept up with the former president. (Hamilton, back in New York practicing law, continued to exert an even greater influence over Pickering and McHenry.) Washington, who began with strict propriety in telling McHenry, Pickering, Wolcott, and Hamilton to show him only documents that were appropriate to share, without breaking official rules, had abandoned these scruples and was using the cabinet to advise him as if he were still in office. In a letter marked "private, and quite confidential," Washington wrote to McHenry in October:

If Colonel Pickering, and the gentlemen who act with you, are minutely acquainted with all the circumstances of the case, it would be satisfactory to me to know their opinions also, with respect to my eventual resignation, but not as a matter required by me, but as questions propounded by yourself, entirely and absolutely . . . I should like to have seen a copy of Mr. Wolcott's letter to the president, but as it was not sent, I presume there was some reason for withholding it, and do not repeat the request. I wish to hear from you on the subject of this letter as soon as possible. Burn it, as soon as it is perused, as I will do your answer.

He was also reading Adams's mail. In September, McHenry showed Washington a letter he had received from Adams insisting that he had the final word on these military appointments. Adams had closed the letter angrily, saying there had been "too much intrigue in this business with General Washington and me," and he did not plan "to be the dupe in it."[29]

Furious, Washington wrote to Adams directly on September 25th that Hamilton should be first, Pinckney second, and Knox third, or else, he made clear, he would resign his commission. Washington, whose memory was indeed failing, had forgotten his agreement with McHenry to let Adams decide on the order of the major generals. Hamilton had flatly refused to serve unless he was second in command, and Washington had succumbed to the influence of his allies.

The hero of the Revolution who had gracefully resigned his commission at Annapolis in 1783 in deference to the civilian authority of the new republic was now strong-arming the president—over a relatively minor dispute about rank. Had Adams decided to have a showdown with Washington and force his resignation, the country might have faced a severe crisis. The authority of the government could have been undermined and its ability to wage war seriously impaired. Fortunately, for Washington's reputation and for the United States, Adams was magnanimous enough to back down. While asserting his authority as president over military appointments, Adams agreed to delegate the choice of major generals to Washington.[30]

Breaking his resolution that he would never again travel more than twenty miles from Mount Vernon, on November 5, 1798, Washington departed for Philadelphia to organize the new army, and the work kept him there for five weeks. "Making selection of the officers for the twelve new regiments and arranging them to the different states," he wrote, "is a work of infinitely more difficulty than I had any conception of." With Hamilton, Pinckney, and McHenry, Washington also discussed the latest tactics and weaponry, as they forged a new military establishment informed by their experience during the Revolution but not limited by it. Washington brought up the possibility that the French, even if they did not attempt to invade the United States, might get a foothold in North America by taking the Floridas and Louisiana. Did he have the authority to invade immediately and expel them, Washington asked, or did he have to wait for approval from Congress or the president?[31]

Washington warned Adams that the United States had to adopt a different strategy than the kind that succeeded against the British during the Revolution. Then, "time, caution, and worrying the enemy until we could be better provided with arms and other means, and had better disciplined troops to carry on, was the plan for us." The French, however, "ought to be attacked at every step, and, if possible, not suffered to make an establishment in this country, acquiring thereby strength from the disaffected and the slaves."[32]

Impatient to get back to Mount Vernon, Washington left Philadelphia on December 14, and not until adverse winds kept him waiting to cross the Susquehanna did he write to McHenry, explaining how he planned to run the military. While he would take no "direct agency" in raising the army, he did not abdicate all responsibility to his second in command, Hamilton. Pinckney's sphere was to be Georgia, the Carolinas, and Virginia too if he was willing. And while Hamilton was in charge of the northeastern states, because he was near the seat of government, he was to take orders directly from the president. Washington further checked Hamilton's power by directing that General Wilkinson, who had replaced Anthony Wayne as commander of the western army, send all of his dispatches through McHenry, ostensibly so the secretary of war could "give immediate orders in cases which may be too urgent to wait for the agency of General Hamilton." Given Washington's suspicion that the French would try to seize New Orleans and control the mouth of the Mississippi, he may also have been disconcerted by rumors Hamilton's political enemies had circulated, claiming that he planned to take control of the army and establish himself as emperor of the Southwest.[33]

Any such ambitions Hamilton may have harbored were thwarted by early 1799 as the threat of war with France subsided, and President Adams took back control of military affairs by simply declining to mobilize the army. Hamilton was left idle, as were the many other appointed officers who wrote to Washington that they had put aside their jobs for commissions that never materialized. With plenty of militia on the southern frontier, where the greatest danger loomed from a French invasion, Washington was not alarmed but merely embarrassed and annoyed that organizing the regular army had been a fruitless exercise. The call of duty had drawn him away from Mount Vernon to lead the army, he complained to McHenry, and had cost him precious time that he needed to get his estate and those of which he was a trustee "in such a clear and distinct form as that no reproach may attach itself to me when I have taken my departure for the land of spirits."[34]

In February Adams wrote to Washington, relaying the momentous news that he had just appointed the American minister to Holland, William Vans Murray, as "minister plenipotentiary to the French republic." Acting on unofficial assurances from Talleyrand to a third party that an American ambassador would be received in Paris, Adams had taken a big risk to achieve a diplomatic breakthrough, braving what was sure to be a storm of Federalist denunciations at home—especially since the president had not consulted his cabinet or any Federalist leaders before submitting Murray's name to the Senate for confirmation. To avoid being duped and to ensure that Murray was honorably received, Adams instructed him to remain in Holland until the French had officially confirmed their intentions. With a sexist line his wife, Abigail, undoubtedly would have frowned on, Adams assured Washington he had done nothing that could be construed as "babyish and womanly blubbering for peace."[35]

The Senate confirmed Murray on the condition that Adams appoint two other envoys as part of a delegation, and that they remain in America until definitive word arrived from France. As the French failed to come forward with unequivocal assurances, however, Federalist criticism of Adams mounted, and Washington hoped the president could somehow reverse course without giving the Republicans ammunition to attack him. By July, the Federalists were asking Washington to run for a third term as president, since Adams could no longer unite the party.[36]

To Governor Trumbull of Connecticut, Washington replied that it no longer made any difference who was nominated, as long as every Federalist voted for him. He was no longer indispensable. Sadly, since factions dominated American politics, the Republicans could "set up a broomstick and call it a true son of liberty, a democrat, or give it any epithet that will suit their purpose and it will command their votes in toto," he wrote. It was now both sufficient and necessary that the Federalists do the same: vote unanimously for any candidate, whose qualifications were irrelevant. Washington had concluded not only that his time had passed—a time when a president, rising above faction, represented and united the American people—but also that his faculties were in decline. If he agreed to run, he "should be charged not only with irresolution, but with concealed ambition which waits only for an occasion to blaze out; and, in short, with dotage and imbecility."[37]

British admiral Horatio Nelson's decisive victory in the Battle of the Nile (August 1–2, 1798) had stirred the European enemies of France to launch the War of the Second Coalition (1799–1802) and roll back the conquests made by the French revolutionary government, which now seemed on the verge of collapse. In America, the Federalists looked forward to a restoration of the French monarchy and were stunned when Adams decided the time was ripe to finally send Murray's delegation to Paris. Washington was baffled, having thought this was the perfect opportunity for Adams to do the opposite—to back away from the premature overtures he had initiated in the face of outrageous French insults to the United States on the high seas and in the XYZ affair.

The Federalists were so upset that they beseeched Washington to step in and exert all of his influence to stop Adams, to save the United States from a military alliance with the beleaguered revolutionaries in France and a resurgence of the Republicans at home. Adams's maneuver would prove to be a brilliant piece of diplomacy—checking the extremists in his own party and averting war—and to his credit, Washington did not oppose the president. Washington had petulantly given Adams an ultimatum over the military appointments, but he now told McHenry: "I have been stricken dumb, and I believe it is better that I should remain mute." He conceded that while the American ship of state seemed to be "moving by hasty strides to some awful crisis," the "vessel remained afloat or very nearly so, and considering myself a passenger only, I shall trust to the mariners whose duty it is to watch, to steer it into a safe port."[38]

Washington had tried at various times since 1793, in the wake of his proposal to Arthur Young, to rent out Mount Vernon's farms and have his freed slaves labor on them as hired hands. And while he had not intended to emancipate his slaves while still in office, in 1796 the sale by one of the Custis heirs of some dower slaves had spurred him to hatch a secret rescue plan that would free all of them as well as his own slaves—a plan that involved Washington's land in the West as well as Mount Vernon.

Washington's stepson, Jacky Custis, had died shortly after the Battle of Yorktown, leaving behind a widow and four children: Martha, Eliza, Eleanor (Nelly), and George Washington (Wash) Parke Custis. Martha Custis had married Thomas Peter in 1795, and as her property came under his control he began, in the most brutal and exploitive fashion, selling off her share of the dower slaves from Mount Vernon—not only breaking up families but separating out the young girls, some between the ages of four and thirteen, for individual sale. These kinds of sales were standard practice, and Washington had either anticipated Peter's transactions, which began in February 1796, or had advance information about them.

A few months earlier, Washington had approached Dr. David Stuart, the second husband of Jacky Custis's widow, and begun negotiating a manumission agreement that was intended eventually to include all of the Custis heirs. At the same time, Washington was gathering information through his manager at Mount Vernon about a neighboring plantation that reportedly had been subdivided into small tenements for rent; he also asked

George Washington ("Wash") Parke Custis.

his manager to make a list of all the dower slaves' marriages—among themselves, to his own slaves, and to "neighboring Negros." With a newspaper advertisement, Washington also renewed his effort to rent or sell his properties in the West.

The plan was for Stuart to hire the Custis slaves from Mount Vernon to work on the old Custis plantation on Virginia's Eastern Shore as a first step to setting them free. (For the Eastern Shore of Chesapeake Bay, see *A Map of . . . Virginia, Detail #8*, page 190, center right.) Washington also hoped to find settlers, preferably English farmers, for his tracts in the West and have them hire some of the emancipated Mount Vernon slaves. While the immediate removal of the Custis slaves to the Eastern Shore would break up families, it would only be a temporary separation, to prevent the sale of the individuals. Once Washington had left office a year later, he would liberate his own slaves and, with the aid of his manager's list, reunite the families.

Washington insisted on waiting because his administration was, in 1796, in the midst of a major crisis that he feared would worsen if he freed his own slaves immediately. The Republicans in Congress had threatened to block funding for the Jay Treaty because it required Americans to pay their prewar debts to British creditors but did not honor the British promise to pay for slaves they freed and evacuated abroad at the end of the Revolution. Led in the House by Virginia's James Madison, most of the aggrieved American debtors and slaveholders were southerners like Washington, and he feared that freeing his slaves would be perceived as a betrayal, particularly of his own social class, sparking outrage and further opposition to the treaty.

Nonetheless, with Peter selling slaves, the marriages of Eliza and Nelly looming, and Wash in line to inherit the remaining slaves upon his grandmother Martha Washington's death, Washington was anxious to move forward right away with the first phase of the plan, the hiring and freeing of the Custis slaves. Despite Washington's careful consideration of every detail, however, the plan fell through. He was unable to find the tenants or buyers he needed for his western properties, and unwilling to free his own slaves immediately. More important, it appears that he could not convince the interested parties—the Custis heirs—to cooperate.

Given that Washington's scheme was motivated by his distrust of the Custis heirs, and his revulsion at their willingness to sell off human beings, he could hardly have been surprised that they refused to make a financial sacrifice for the benefit of their slaves. He may have persisted in the scheme as long as he did because the Custis heirs' cooperation would have given him allies from his own social milieu—not Quakers or other northern abolitionists regarded in the South as outsiders and extremists. With these familial allies at his side, he might have welcomed the political fallout from emancipating the Mount Vernon slaves, and used it as a catalyst for social change.[39]

Three years later, in July 1799, as Washington sat down to write his will, Mount Vernon still had more than three hundred slaves, only half of them his own. And he still possessed most of his speculative land purchases totaling some forty-five thousand acres: twelve parcels in Virginia, four on the Ohio, five on the Kanawha, two in Maryland, one in Pennsylvania (the site of Fort Necessity), one on the Mohawk, three in the Northwest Territory, and two in Kentucky. (He had been able to sell only two tracts in Pennsylvania and part of his Mohawk Valley land.)

Having failed in his attempts to bring the land and the slaves together in an arrangement that would turn them into free laborers or sharecroppers, Washington emancipated them in his will. The young, the old, and the infirm were to be supported by Washington's heirs. Any orphans were to be indentured until the age of twenty-five, taught to read and write, and given vocational training. Revealing his fear that these radical directives would not be obeyed, Washington reinforced them with exceptionally emphatic language. "And I do moreover most pointedly and most solemnly enjoin it upon my executors hereafter named, or the survivors of them, to see that this clause respecting slaves and every part thereof be religiously fulfilled at the epoch at which it is directed to take place, without evasion, neglect, or delay."[40]

However, to avoid a painful and untenable situation in which the dower slaves lived and worked at Mount Vernon among free blacks, with whom they were intermarried, the provision freeing Washington's slaves was only to take effect upon Martha Washington's death and the division of the plantation into three parts. Martha was to have the "use, profit, and benefit of my whole estate, real and personal, for the term of her natural life," Washington wrote, and he gave "to her and her heirs forever" a town lot in Alexandria, along with the household and kitchen furniture at Mount Vernon.[41]

Washington had survived all of his siblings, so upon Martha's death, his nephew Bushrod, the son of John Augustine Washington, was to receive the core of the plantation, as described by Washington in his will. "Beginning at the ford of Dogue Run, near my mill, and extending along the road, and bounded thereby as it now goes, and ever has gone since my recollection of it, to the ford of Little Hunting Creek at the gum spring until it comes to a knoll, opposite to an old road which formerly passed through the lower field of Muddy Hole Farm, at which on the north side of said road are three red or Spanish oaks marked as a corner and a stone placed hence by a line of trees to be marked, rectangular to the back line."[42] Washington's life had come full circle: In his final months, he was using the skills he had learned as a young surveyor to select markers and plot out boundaries. (See *Washington's own survey of Mount Vernon, Detail #1*.)

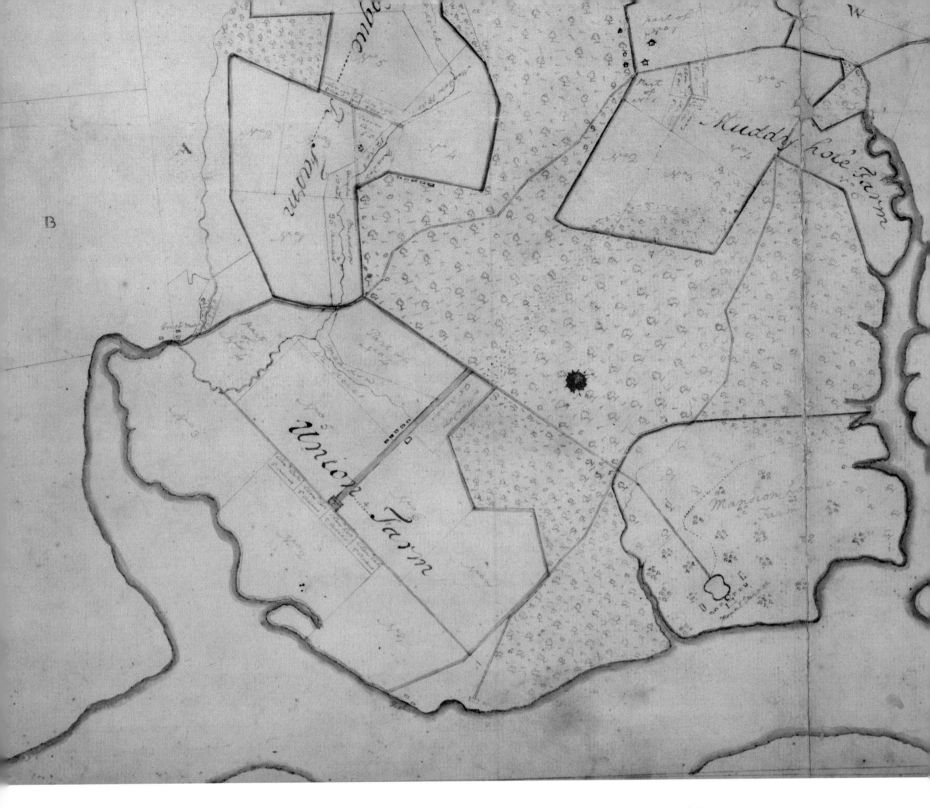

The second portion of the plantation, "my estate east of Little Hunting Creek, lying on the Potomac River, including the farm of 360 acres leased to Tobias Lear," comprised some two thousand acres and was left to his and Martha's double nephews, George Fayette and Charles Augustine, the two sons of George Augustine Washington and Frances "Fanny" Bassett.[43] (See *Washington's own survey of Mount Vernon, Detail #2*, page 270.)

Washington left the rest of Mount Vernon to Martha's granddaughter Eleanor "Nelly" Parke Custis and her husband, Washington's nephew Lawrence Lewis. Washington noted that "it has always been my intention, since my expectation of having issue has ceased, to consider the grandchildren of my wife in the same light as I do my own relations," and through the marriage of Nelly and Lawrence "the inducement to provide for them both has been increased." They were to inherit "all the land north of the road leading from the ford of Dogue Run to the Gum

Spring as described in the devise of the other part of the tract, to Bushrod Washington . . . making together about two thousand acres."[44] (See *Washington's own survey of Mount Vernon, Detail #3*, page 271.)

Aside from other specific, more minor bequests the rest of Washington's estate "real and personal" which included his thousands of acres in the West, was to be sold by his executors and the proceeds divided equally among twenty-three heirs, mainly the children of his four siblings: John Augustine, Betty, Samuel, and Charles, and of his half brother Augustine.[45]

In December 1799, five months after he completed his will, Washington died as he had lived, pursuing the intimate connection to the land that had made maps so central to his life.[46] "On Thursday, December 12th, the General rode out to his farms about ten o'clock," Tobias Lear recalled. Washington noted in his diary that the

Washington's own survey of Mount Vernon, Detail #1: Bushrod inherited the portion of Mount Vernon below the main road (top) between Dogue Creek (left) and Little Hunting Creek (right) all the way to the Potomac River (bottom). This included Union Farm, Muddy Hole Farm, and the Mansion House Farm—some four thousand acres "with the Mansion House and all other buildings and improvements thereon." This bequest included one of the more lucrative elements of the plantation, the fishery (bottom center), where the herring catch was packed into barrels with salt and sent to market.

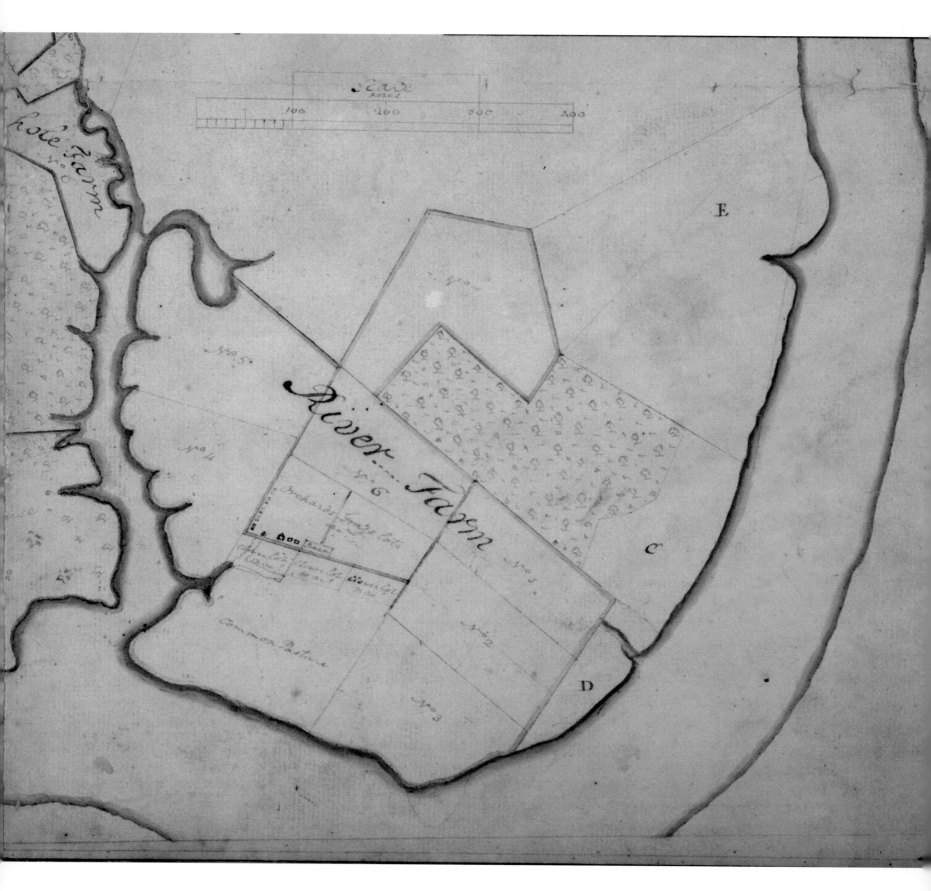

Washington's own survey of Mount Vernon, Detail #2: In 1786 Washington had promised to bequeath this land to his nephew George Augustine Washington, who had just married Martha's niece, Frances Bassett. Washington immediately urged George Augustine to take over the 360-acre section at the northeast corner of River Farm (labeled *E*, upper right), which he did. George Augustine died in 1793, leaving Fanny in control of the farm. Fanny married Tobias Lear two years later, and he took charge of the farm when she died in the spring of 1796. Lear settled there with his own son and the children of George Augustine and Fanny: Anna Maria and the heirs to River Farm, her brothers George Fayette and Charles Augustine.

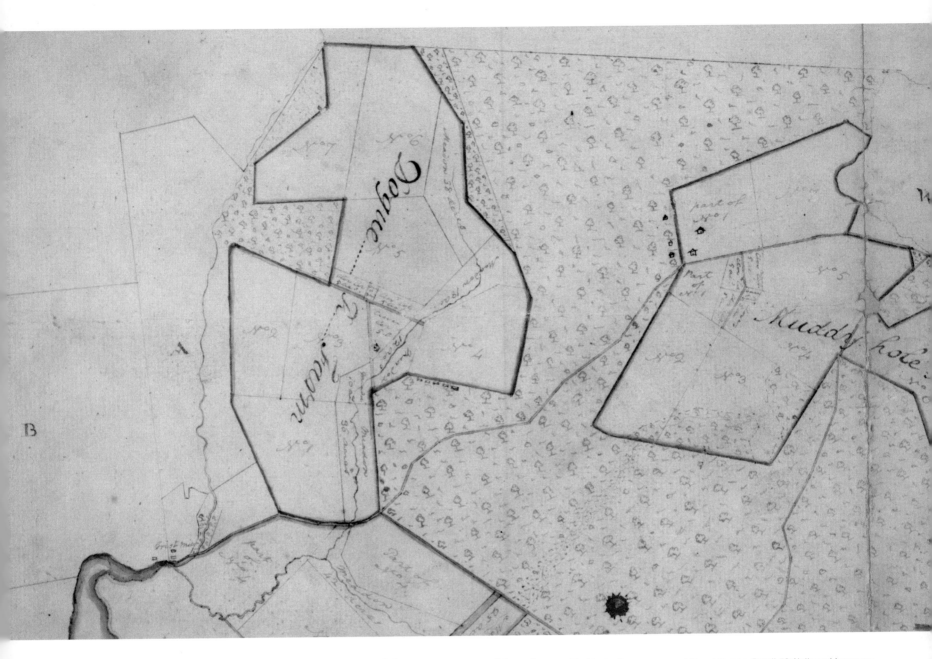

morning was cloudy, with the wind at the northeast, and the temperature at thirty-three degrees. "About one o'clock it began to snow—soon after to hail and then turned to a settled cold rain," he wrote, but he did not stop riding his horse around his beloved acres at Mount Vernon and supervising the winter activities on the various farms. He did not return to the mansion until after three P.M., Lear noted. "I observed to him that I was afraid he got wet, he said no, his great coat had kept him dry; but his neck appeared to be wet, and the snow was hanging from his hair. He came to dinner without changing his dress. In the evening he appeared as well as usual."

Only a heavy snowfall the following day prevented Washington "from riding out as usual," Lear wrote. "He had taken cold (undoubtedly from being so much exposed the day before) and complained of having a sore throat. He had a hoarseness, which increased in the evening, but he made light of it, as he would never take anything to carry off a cold, always observing, 'let it go as it came.'" Washington noted in his diary that the snow

Washington's own survey of Mount Vernon, Detail #3: Nelly and Lawrence Lewis inherited all of the plantation north and west of the road to Alexandria (lower left to right center). While much of the land was wooded, and the land around Dogue Run would need to be drained, this bequest included the mill and distillery, which, along with the fishery, were the features of the plantation that generated the most cash income. (Dogue Run flows through section *A*, down to the Grist Mill and Dogue Creek. The distillery is not labeled.) Section *B*, Washington noted in the References, would make "a beautiful site for a gentleman's [country] seat."

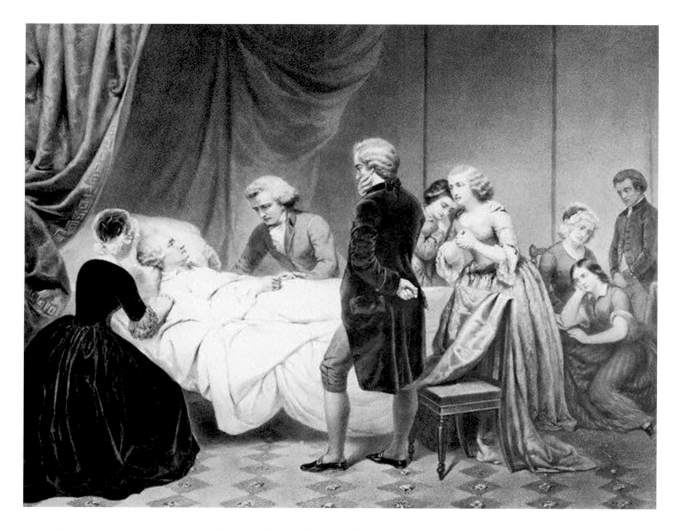

stopped at one P.M., with an accumulation of about three inches, and by four P.M. the weather was "perfectly clear." Despite his symptoms, Washington went out that afternoon "into the ground between the house and the river" to mark some trees for cutting. (See **Washington's own survey of Mount Vernon, Detail #1**, page 269. The mansion is on the lower right. The pear-shaped form in front of the main entrance indicates the driveway. Washington's last walk was on the other side—the front lawn leading down to the river.)

"On his retiring to bed, he appeared to be in perfect health, excepting the cold before mentioned, which he considered as trifling, and had been remarkably cheerful all evening," Lear wrote. However, "about two or three o'clock Saturday morning he awoke Mrs. Washington and told her he was very unwell . . . She observed that he could scarcely speak, and breathed with difficulty." Three doctors came to Mount Vernon that day, including his lifelong friend, James Craik. When the standard treatments, including bleeding the patient, did not help, one of the other doctors recommended performing a tracheotomy—cutting an opening at the base of Washington's neck that would allow him to breathe.

The procedure was rejected as too radical, and it probably would not have saved his life, since he evidently had

an acute infection, for which there was no effective treatment. The tracheotomy might have made Washington's death less torturous, however. Instead, he suffocated slowly as his throat swelled shut, enduring the agony with the same heroic composure he had displayed in the heat of battle and during the many other trials of his eventful life.

"About ten minutes before he expired," which was between ten and eleven P.M. on December 14th, "his breathing became easier," Lear reported. "He lay quietly; he withdrew his hand from mine, and felt his own pulse. I saw his countenance change. I spoke to Dr. Craik, who sat by the fire; he came to the bedside. The General's hand fell from his wrist—I took it in mine and put it into my bosom. Dr. Craik put his hands over [Washington's] eyes and he expired without a struggle or a sigh."

According to Lear, Martha Washington was sitting at the foot of the bed and asked "with a firm and collected voice, 'Is he gone?' I could not speak, but held up my hand as a signal that he was no more. 'Tis well,' she said in the same voice, 'All is now over; I shall soon follow him.'" Their stable marriage and mutual affection had been a great source of strength for Washington over the course of forty-five years. She could have been speaking for them both when she added, "I have no more trials to pass through."

ABOVE: Tobias Lear, Dr. James Craik, and others at George Washington's bedside, December 14, 1799.

OPPOSITE: The last life portrait of George Washington, by Charles de Saint-Mémim, in November 1798. The occasion was Washington's visit to the capital to confer with President Adams about military preparations for the looming war with France.

APPENDIX

CONTENTS OF THE YALE *GEORGE WASHINGTON ATLAS*

Paper conservator Sarah Dove recently disassembled Yale's *George Washington Atlas* and restored the maps. The appendix is drawn from her examination report, compiled before she began cleaning and repairing the maps. The maps from the Yale atlas reproduced in this book were photographed after she completed her work.

Map 1: *A General Map of North America* (north part)
Artist: John Rocque; published by M. A. Rocque in the Strand
Date: c. 1754–61
Plate size: H: 17¾" W: 35" (approx.)
Paper size: Two sheets joined through center; overall size: H: 21½" W: 37" W: 17½" W: 19"
Media: Hand coloring with pink, yellow, and light green watercolors
Description: Folded in 3 sections with edges folding into the center

Map 2: *A General Map of North America* (south part)
Media: Hand coloring with pink, dark pink, yellow, and light green watercolors

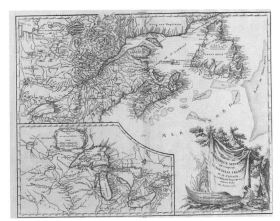

Map 3: *Partie de L'Amerique Septent? qui comprend La Nouvelle France ou Le Canada*
Artist: Sr. Robert de Vaugondy
Date: 1755
Plate size: H: 19¾" W: 23" (approx.)
Paper size: H: 21" W: 28"
Media: Some hand coloring with light green watercolor, some borders delineated in turquoise
Description: Horizontal map folded at center

Map 4: *A Correct Plan of the Environs of Quebec*
Artist: Drawn from the original surveys taken by the engineers of the army; engraved by Thomas Jefferys; published, the corner of St. Martins Lane, Charing Cross
Date: 1759
Plate size: H: 17¾" W: 35" (approx.)
Paper size: Two sheets joined to right of center crease, overall size: H: 18⅝" W: 38"
Media: Hand coloring with light green, brown, and blue watercolor, with Quebec City borders delineated in rust-red gouache
Description: Horizontal map folded twice into 3 sections

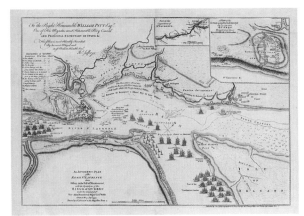

Map 5: *An Authentic Plan of the River St. Laurence*
Artist: Richard Gridley; published by Thomas Jefferys
Date: September 5, 1755
Plate size: H: 15¾" W: 21" (approx.)
Media: Hand coloring with light green, light blue, and Quebec City borders delineated in rust-red gouache
Description: Horizontal map on a single sheet

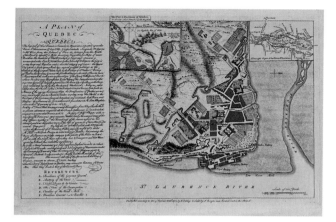

Map 6: *A Plan of Quebec*
Artist: Published by Edward Oakley
Date: October 1759
Plate size: H: 12⅝" W: 20¼"
Size: H: 15½" W: 21¼"
Media: Hand coloring with light green, light blue, and yellow, with
Quebec City in rust-red gouache
Description: Horizontal map on a single sheet

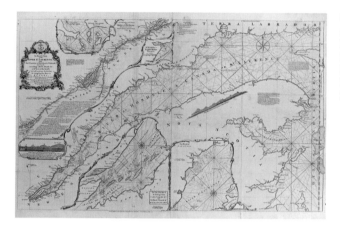

Map 7: *An Exact Chart of the River St. Laurence*
Artist: Thomas Jefferys; published by Robert Sayer
Date: after 1755
Plate size: H: 28½" W: 21¼"
Paper size: Two sheets joined at center, overall size: H: 28½" W: 37" (approx.)
Media: Hand coloring with light green, light pink, turquoise, and yellow
Description: Horizontal map, folded 3 times resulting in 6 sections

Map 8: *A Chart of the Gulf of St. Laurence*
Artist: Thomas Jefferys; published by Robert Sayer
Date: 1755
Plate size: H: 23½" W: 20"
Paper size: H: 28" W: 21¼"
Media: Hand coloring with light green, light blue, yellow, and light brown
Description: Vertical map folded in half

Map 9: *A General Chart of the Island of Newfoundland*
Artist: Thomas Jefferys; published by Robert Sayer; surveyed by James Cook and Michael Lane
Date: 1755
Plate size: H: trimmed W: 21½"
Paper size: H: 21⅜" W: 28½"
Media: Hand coloring with light green, turquoise, yellow, and light brown
Description: Horizontal map folded in half

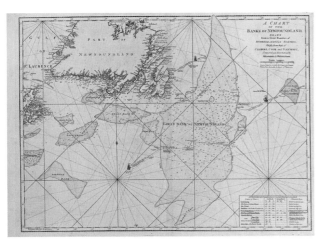

Map 10: *A General Chart of the Banks of Newfoundland*
Artist: Thomas Jefferys; published by Robert Sayer
Date: 1755
Plate size: H: 20" W: 26"
Paper size: H: 21¼" W: 28¾" (approx.)
Media: Hand coloring with light green, turquoise, yellow, and light brown
Description: Horizontal map folded in half

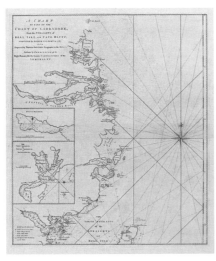

Map 11: *A Chart of the Coast of Labradore*
Artist: Thomas Jefferys
Date: 1755
Plate size: H: 20" W: 26'
Paper size: H: 21¼" W: 28¾" (approx.)
Media: Hand coloring with light green, turquoise, yellow, and light brown
Description: Vertical map folded in half

Map 12: *Map of Nova Scotia or Acadia* (top half)
Artist: London, printed and sold by A. Dury in Dukes Court, St. Martins Lane
Date: 1768
Plate size: H: 28½" W: 21¼"
Paper size: Two sheets joined at center, overall size: H: 21¹³⁄₁₆' W: 53" (approx.)
Media: Hand coloring with light green, light pink, yellow, and 3 areas of red gouache
Description: Folded in 4's

Map 13: *Map of Nova Scotia or Acadia* (lower half)
Plate size: H: 20¼" W: 21¼"
Paper size: Two sheets joined at center, overall size: H: 21¹³⁄₁₆" W: 54" (approx.)
Media: Hand coloring with light green, light pink, yellow, and 2 areas of red gouache
Description: Folded in 4's

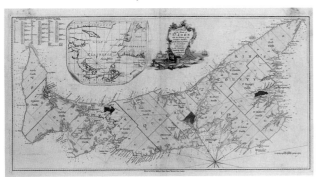

Map 14: *A Plan of the Island of St. John*
Artist: Printed and sold by A. Dury in Dukes Court, St. Martins Lane, London; surveyed by Captain Holland, 1775
Date: 1775
Plate size: H: 14¾" W: 28"
Paper size: H: 21¼" W: 29"
Media: Hand coloring with light green, yellow, and pink with rust-colored gouache in three areas
Description: Horizontal map folded in half

Map 15: *A Large and Particular Plan of Shegnekto Bay*
Artist: Thomas Jefferys; printed for R. Sayer in Fleet Street and T. Jefferys in the Strand
Date: 1775
Plate size: H: 14⅝" W: 21½"
Paper size: H: 21¼" W: 28½"
Media: Hand coloring with light green, yellow, and pink, with rust-colored gouache in two areas
Description: Horizontal map folded in half

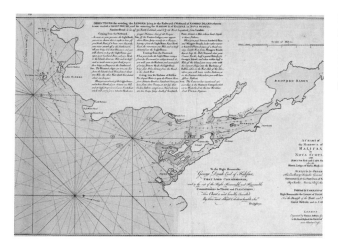

Map 16: *A Chart of the Harbour of Halifax, in Nova Scotia*
Artist: Thomas Jefferys
Date: 1775
Paper size: H: 16½" W: 24"
Media: Hand coloring with brown, light brown or faded pink, and yellow
Description: Horizontal map folded in half

Map 17: *Chart of the Coast of New York to Cape Breton Island* (first part)
Title: *An Actual Survey of the Sea Coast from New York to the I. Cape Breton* (upper part)
Artist: Sold by I. Mount, T. Page, and W. Mount, Tower Hill, London
Date: 1768
Plate size: H: 28½" W: 21¼"
Paper size: Two sheets joined at center, overall size: H: 21¹³/₁₆" W: 53" (approx.)
Media: Hand coloring with yellow and turquoise
Description: Folded in 4's

Map 18: *Chart of the Coast of New York to Cape Breton Island* (second part)
Title: *An Actual Survey of the Sea Coast from New York to the I. Cape Breton* (lower part)

Map 19: *Chart of the Coast of New York to Cape Breton Island* (third part)
Title: *A Map of the British Empire in America with the French and Spanish Settlements adjacent thereto* (upper half)
Artist: Henry Popple
Plate size: H: 21" trimmed W: 21¼"
Paper size: Two sheets joined at center, overall size: H: 21⅝" W: 53" (approx.)
Media: Hand coloring with yellow and turquoise
Description: Folded in 4's

Map 20: *Chart of the Coast of New York to Cape Breton Island* (fourth part)
Title: *A Map of the British Empire in America with the French and Spanish Settlements adjacent thereto*
(lower half)
Plate size: H: 21" trimmed W: 52"
Media: No hand coloring

Number 21: The Index (table of contents) in the atlas skips 21. The last map sheet is numbered 44, but there are only 43 map sheets in the atlas.

Map 22: *The Seat of War in New England, by an American Volunteer*
Artist: Printed for R. Sayer and J. Bennet, London
Plate size: H: 21" W: 20"
Paper size: H: 21" W: 30" (approx.)
Media: Pink, green, light brown, and yellow watercolor
Description: Horizontal map folded in half

Map 23: *A Map of the Most Inhabited Part of New England* (lower half)
Artist: Braddock Mead alias John Green / Thomas Jefferys
Plate size: H: 20" W: 34"
Paper size: H: 21¼" W: 36" (approx.)
Media: Pink, green, and yellow watercolor
Description: Horizontal map folded in 3's

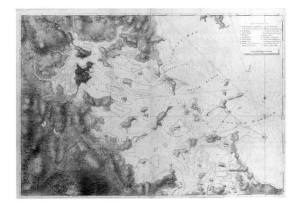

Map 24: *A Map of the Most Inhabited Part of New England* (top half)
Plate size: H: 20" W: 34" (lower edge trimmed)
Paper size: H: 21¼" W: 34" (approx.)
Media: Pink, green, yellow, and turquoise watercolor
Description: Horizontal map folded in 3's

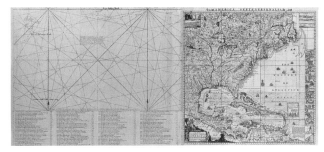

Map 25: *Boston Harbor*
Artist: J. F. W. Des Barres
Date: August 5, 1775
Technique: Mezzotint rocker with burnishing and engraving, hand colored
Plate size: H: 28¼" W: 41" (lower edge trimmed)
Paper size: H: 30" W: 42" (approx.)
Media: Brown, green, yellow, and turquoise watercolor with rust-colored gouache
Description: Horizontal map folded in 3's

Map 26: *A General Map of the Middle British Colonies in America*
Artist: Published by Lewis Evans, Philadelphia
Date: June 15, 1775
Plate size: H: 19" W: 26"
Paper size: H: 21¼" W: 29" (approx.)
Media: Pink, green, blue, and yellow watercolor
Description: Horizontal map folded in half

Map 27: *A Map of the Province of New York with Part of Pennsylvania and New England* (north part)
Artist: P. Andrews; published by A. Dury Dukes; surveyed by John Montresor
Date: June 10, 1775
Plate size: H: 28¾" W: 36"
Paper size: H: 29¾" W: 36" (approx.)
Media: Pink, green, and yellow watercolor
Description: Horizontal map folded in 3's

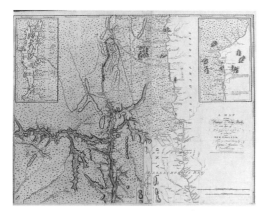

Map 28: *A Map of the Province of New York with Part of Pennsylvania and New England* (south part)
Plate size: H: 28⅜" W: 36¼"
Paper size: H: 29⅞" W: 37" (approx.)

Map 29: *A Plan of the City of New-York and Its Environs*
Artist: P. Andrews; sold by A. Dury; surveyed by John Montresor
Date: 1775
Plate size: H: 24½" W: 20¾"
Paper size: H: 29¼" W: 21¼"
Media: Hand coloring with light green, yellow, and pink
Description: Vertical map folded in half

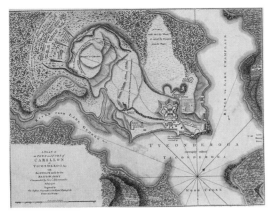

Map 30: *A Plan of the Town and Fort of Carillon at Ticonderoga: With the Attack Made by the British Army Commanded by General Abercrombie*
Artist: Thomas Jefferys
Date: July 8, 1758
Plate size: H: 24½" W: 20¾"
Paper size: H: 29¼" W: 21¼"
Media: Hand coloring with brown, turquoise, and yellow with rust-colored gouache in small areas
Description: Unfolded map (horizontal)

Map 31: *A Map of Pennsylvania*
Artist: Printed for R. Sayer and J. Bennet, London
Date: June 1775
Plate size: H: 27½" W: 52"
Paper size: H: 28⅝" W: 53" (approx.) 3 sheets joined
Media: Yellow, green, pink, turquoise, and green
Description: Folded in 4's

Map 32: *A Map of the Most Inhabited Part of Virginia* (lower half)
Artist: Joshua Fry and Peter Jefferson / Thomas Jefferys
Date: 1775
Plate size: H: 27½" W: 52"
Paper size: H: 21¼" W: 51"
Media: Yellow, green, and brown watercolor
Description: Folded in 2's (4 sections)

Map 33: *A Map of the Most Inhabited Part of Virginia* (upper half)
Plate size: H: 15½" W: 48"
Paper size: H: 21¼" W: 51"
Media: Yellow, green, and pink watercolor

Map 34: *An Accurate Map of North and South Carolina witn their Indian Frontiers* (upper half)
Artist: Henri Mouzon / Thomas Jefferys
Date: May 30, 1775
Plate size: H: 15½" W: 48"
Paper size: H: 21¼" W: 51"
Media: Yellow, green, and pink watercolor
Description: Folded in 2's (4 sections, each H: 21¼" x W: 13⅞")

Map 35: *An Accurate Map of North and South Carolina with Their Indian Frontiers* (lower half, with insets of Hilton Head and the harbor of Charleston)

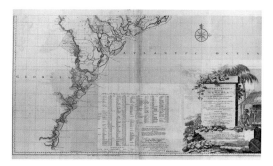

Map 36: *A Map of South Carolina and a Part of Georgia* (south part)
Artist: William De Brahm / Thomas Jefferys
Date: October 20, 1757
Plate size: H: 15½" W: 48"
Paper size: H: 21¼" W: 51"
Media: Yellow, green, and pink watercolor
Description: Folded 3 times and at the center, resulting in 8 sections

Map 37: *A Map of South Carolina and a Part of Georgia* (north part)
Plate size: H: 26⅝" W: 49"
Paper size: H: 28¼" W: 49"

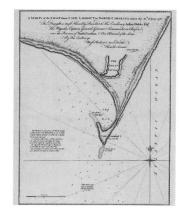

Map 38: *A Survey of the Coast About Cape Lookout in North Carolina*
Artist: Thomas Jefferys
Date: June 29, 1756
Plate size: H: 14¼" W: 11"
Paper size: H: 21¼" W: 16"
Media: Hand colored with yellow watercolor
Description: Unfolded map (vertical)

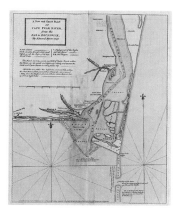

Map 39: *A New and Exact Plan of Cape Fear River*
Artist: Edward Hyrne / Thomas Jefferys
Date: 1749; published March 20, 1753
Plate size: H: 15½" W: 12½"
Paper size: H: 19⅛" W: 24"
Media: Hand colored with yellow watercolor
Description: Horizontal map folded at center

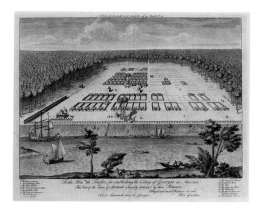

Map 40: *A View of Savannah as It Stood the 29th of March 1734*
Artist: Peter Gordon, engraved by P. Foudrinier
Date: c. 1750
Plate size: H: 18" W: 22¾"
Paper size: H: 21¼" W: 29"
Media: Black printer's ink, no hand coloring
Description: Horizontal map folded at center

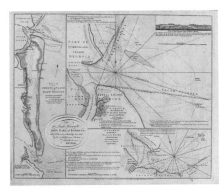

Map 41: *A Chart of the Entrance into St. Mary's River*
Artist: William Fuller for Thomas Jefferys
Date: c. 1750
Plate size: H: 20½" W: 24"
Paper size: H: 21¼" W 28"
Media: Yellow, green, light brown, and pink watercolor over black printer's ink
Description: Horizontal map folded in half

Map 42: *The Coast of West Florida and Louisiana / The Peninsula and Gulf of Florida or Channel of Bahama with the Bahama Islands*
Artist: Thomas Jefferys
Date: February 20, 1775
Plate size: H: 21⅝" W: 48"
Paper size: Two sheets joined at center, overall size: H: 21¼" W: 51"
Media: Yellow, green, and pink watercolor
Description: Folded in 2's (4 sections)

Map 43: *Course of the River Mississippi*
Artist: Printed for Robert Sayer in London
Date: 1765
Plate size: H: 43½' W: 14¼"
Paper size: H: 44" W: 21¼"
Media: Yellow and pink watercolor
Description: Vertical map comprised of two joined sheets; folded in 2's (4 sections)

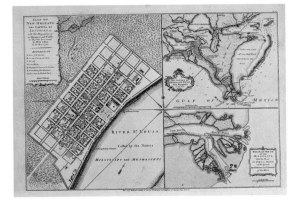

Map 44: *Plan of New Orleans the Capital of Louisiana*
Artist: Thomas Jefferys
Date: November 1759
Plate size: H: 13¼" W: 19¾"
Paper size: H: 15" W: 21⅜"
Media: Hand coloring with yellow and green watercolor and rust-colored gouache
Description: Unfolded map (horizontal)

ACKNOWLEDGMENTS

I first learned of Yale's *George Washington Atlas* in an article about Sterling Library's Map Collection by Kathrin Day Lassila in the July/August 2007 issue of the *Yale Alumni Magazine*. Ramsey Walker, former president of Walker & Company, also saw the article and suggested to George Gibson, publishing director of Bloomsbury USA, that I go up to Yale and see if the atlas could be the basis for a book. With his keen editorial eye and passion for history, George encouraged me as the book grew into a full biography, and he committed the resources, time, and effort to make the book, visually, all that it could be. At Walker/Bloomsbury, Patti Ratchford, Michael O'Connor, Beth Jordan, and Margaret Maloney also deserve my thanks. Michele Lee Amundsen skillfully researched the illustrations. I am also grateful to Sabine Hrechdakian and Susan Golomb at the Susan Golomb Literary Agency.

My thanks also go to Abraham Kaleo Parrish, head of the Map Department at Sterling Library, for making the book possible and coordinating the restoration and reproduction of the *George Washington Atlas*; Sarah Dove, the paper conservator who painstakingly repaired and restored the maps; and the Map Collection staff: Stacey Maples, Margit Kaye, and Oliver Schowalter-Hay. At Yale's Beinecke Rare Book and Manuscript Library, I would like to thank George Miles, curator of the Yale Collection of Western Americana, and Chris Edwards, the digital studio production manager, as well as photographers Robert Halloran, Meredith Miller, and David Driscoll for their help in reproducing the maps.

Edward James Redmond, in the Geography and Map Division at the Library of Congress, generously provided assistance, as did Joan Stahl, the head librarian at Mount Vernon, and William Reese, of William Reese Company in New Haven.

As an independent scholar, I am especially grateful to Kenneth Jackson, Lisa Keller, and Abigail Joseph of Columbia University's Seminar on the City, which fosters an exchange of ideas among urban historians. My research was made easier by the circulation staff of Columbia's Butler Library: Jose Hernandez, Andrea Barnes, Cathy Parker, Dorian Hernandez, Ben Gonzales, Erin Petrella, David Xia, Tyrrome Nelson, and Renata Johnson.

At the New York Society Library, I would like to thank the head librarian, Mark Bartlett, the assistant head librarian, Jane Goldstein, and the staff: Susan Chan, Andrew Corbin, Diane Srebnick, Patrick Rayner, Linnea Savapoulas, Janet Howard, Latria Graham, Carolyn Waters, and Marie Honan. At the New York Public Library, the staff in the Milstein Division at the Humanities Library was especially helpful: Ruth Carr, James Falconi, Maira Liriano, Asa Rubenstein, Charles Scala, and Robb Scott.

I am also grateful for the advice and input of fellow writers and historians, especially Andrew Page, Peter Duffy, Edward O'Donnell, Michael Miscione, Richard Mooney, and Francis Morrone. Michael Shafer's advice and assistance during the writing of my first book carried me through the second and third as well. The same is true of Sloan Walker, Polly Passonneau, William Petrick, Peter Brightbill, Peter Coston, Martha Cooley, Peter Marcotullio, and Danielle Smoller.

My parents, Jerrold and Leona Schecter, have always provided extraordinary support and encouragement, and their passion for history has been my greatest influence. My in-laws, Yolanda Torrisi Adler and Fred and Judy Adler, have also been tremendously generous and supportive. The same is true of my cousin Marsha Gray. Last but not least, I thank my wife, Vanessa Adler Schecter, for her advice and support. The love and laughter we share with our daughter, Naomi Piera Schecter, are my greatest joy.

ABBREVIATIONS

DGW: *Diaries of George Washington*. Boston: Houghton Mifflin, 1925.

DGW, UPV: *Diaries of George Washington*. Charlottesville: University Press of Virginia, 1983.

EAR: *Encyclopedia of the American Revolution*. New York: Scribner's/Thomson Gale, 2006.

GW: George Washington.

PGW: *Papers of George Washington*. Charlottesville: University Press of Virginia, 1997.

WPLC: George Washington Papers at the Library of Congress, 1741–99. http://memory.loc.gov/ammem/gwhtml/gwhome.html.

WGW: *Writings of George Washington from the Original Manuscript Sources, 1745–1799*. Washington, DC: Government Printing Office, 1931–44.

INTRODUCTION: AN ATLAS TELLS A LIFE STORY

[1] *DGW*, 1:439.

[2] Boston Athenaeum, *A catalogue of the Washington collection in the Boston Athenæum; compiled and annotated by Appleton P. C. Griffin . . . With an appendix, The inventory of Washington's books drawn up by the appraisers of his estate; with notes in regard to the full titles of the several books and the later history and present ownership of those not in the Athenæum collection, by William Coolidge Lane* (Cambridge, Mass.: University Press, J. Wilson and Son, Boston Athenaeum, 1897), 562–64.

[3] Flexner, *George Washington*, 4:113–14.

[4] Wiencek, *An Imperfect God*, 236; *PGW*, Rev. War Series, 3: 386.

[5] Pedley, "Maps, War, and Commerce," 161–73.

[6] Harley, *Mapping the American Revolutionary War*, 99–100.

1. VIRGINIA, BARBADOS, AND THE OHIO COUNTRY

[1] *PGW*, Colonial Series, 1:56–61.

[2] Anderson, *The War That Made America*, xxii–xxiii.

[3] Anderson, 29–31 and 39.

[4] Anderson, 28; *PGW*, Colonial Series, 1:7.

[5] *PGW*, Colonial Series, 1:7.

[6] *DGW*, 1:2–4.

[7] *PGW*, Colonial Series, 1:12–14.

[8] *DGW*, 1:5–7.

[9] *DGW*, 1:7–9.

[10] *DGW*, 1:11–12.

[11] *PGW*, Colonial Series, 1:8–10.

[12] *PGW*, Colonial Series, 1:6–7; *DGW*, 1:16; Freeman, *George Washington*, 1:241–48.

[13] *DGW*, 1:16–29.

[14] *DGW*, 1:29–36.

[15] *PGW*, Colonial Series, 1:51–53.

[16] Quoted in Flexner, *George Washington*, 4:113–14.

[17] *PGW*, Colonial Series, 1:16–18, 50–51, 53, and 55.

[18] *PGW*, Colonial Series, 1:56–57; Anderson, 29–35.

[19] Anderson, 7–10; *DGW*, UPV, 4:70 n. 17.

[20] Anderson, 7–10.

[21] Anderson, 13–20.

[22] Anderson, 19–23.

[23] *PGW*, Colonial Series, 1:58–59; *WGW*, 1:19–20; Anderson, 27–35.

[24] *DGW*, 1:43–46.

[25] *DGW*, 1:45–46.

[26] *DGW*, 1:46–47.

[27] *DGW*, 1:47–49.

[28] *DGW*, 1:50–54.

[29] Anderson, 43.

[30] *DGW*, 1:54–56.

[31] *DGW*, 1:56–59.

[32] *DGW*, 1:61–64.

[33] *DGW*, 1:64–67.

[34] *PGW*, Colonial Series, 1:58 and 63; Axelrod, *Blooding at Great Meadows*, 137–38.

2. FROM THE MONONGAHELA TO MASSACHUSETTS

[1] *PGW*, Colonial Series, 1:64.

[2] *PGW*, Colonial Series, 1:67–68.

[3] *PGW*, Colonial Series, 1:63–65 and 67 n. 12.

[4] *PGW*, Colonial Series, 1:70–71, 74–75 n. 3, and 75–76.

[5] *DGW*, 1:73–74 and 73 n. 3 and n. 5.

[6] *DGW*, 1:75–76; *PGW*, Colonial Series, 1:87.

[7] *DGW*, 1:76–77.

[8] *PGW*, Colonial Series, 1:93–95.

[9] *DGW*, 1:80–81; *PGW*, Colonial Series, 1:96–97.

[10] *PGW*, Colonial Series, 1:97 and 100.

[11] *DGW*, 1:84–87.

[12] *DGW*, 1:84–87.

[13] Anderson, *The War That Made America*, 47–48; Lengel, *General George Washington*, 36–38.

[14] *PGW*, Colonial Series, 1: 110–11 and 119.

[15] *PGW*, Colonial Series, 1: 118 and 124.

[16] *PGW*, Colonial Series, 1:126–27, 127 n. 1, and 136–38.

[17] *DGW*, 1:93, 99, 101, and 101 n. 1; *PGW*, Colonial Series, 1:137–38 and 143.

[18] *PGW*, Colonial Series, 1:155–56 n. 1.

[19] *PGW*, Colonial Series, 1:157–58.

[20] *PGW*, Colonial Series, 1:158–60.

[21] Anderson, 52.

[22] Anderson, 55–57, 64, and 67; *PGW*, Colonial Series, 1:247 and 248 n. 6; Freeman, *George Washington*, 1:422–24.

[23] Anderson, 64 and 67; *PGW*, Colonial Series, 1:277–78.

[24] Anderson, 67–68.

[25] *PGW*, Colonial Series, 1:293–97.

[26] *PGW*, Colonial Series, 1:300–301.

[27] *PGW*, Colonial Series, 1:316 and 327–30.

[28] *PGW*, Colonial Series, 1:330 and 332; Anderson, 69–70.

[29] Anderson, 70; *PGW*, Colonial Series, 1:338 and 341.

[30] *PGW*, Colonial Series, 1:326, 331, 332, 336, and 339; Anderson, 70–71.

[31] *PGW*, Colonial Series, 1:332–33 and 342; Anderson, 71; Lengel, 60.

[32] Anderson, 71–72; *PGW*, Colonial Series, 1:342.

[33] *WPLC*, William Fairfax to GW, July 26, 1755, with postscript from Fairfax Ladies; Flexner, *George Washington*, 4:354–55.

[34] *PGW*, Colonial Series, 1:340; Anderson, 70–72 and 152–57; Lengel, 62–64.

[35] Lengel, 63–69; Anderson, 74–87.

[36] Anderson, 119–25 and 155–56; Lengel, 69–70.

[37] Anderson, 126–28; Lengel, 69.

[38] Anderson, 133–63; *WPLC*, Joseph Chew to GW, September 11, 1758.

[39] Lengel, 69–70; Anderson, 163–66.

[40] Anderson, 163–66; *PGW*, Colonial Series, 1:300 n. 4; Lengel, 71–73.

[41] Lengel, 73–74.

[42] Anderson, 163–70.

[43] Anderson, 170 and 174–75; Lengel, 75.

[44] Lengel, 75–77 and 81; *WPLC*, GW to Francis Fauquier, November 28, 1758; Anderson, 171–75; Hirschfeld, *George Washington and Slavery*, 11–12.

[45] *WPLC*, GW to Richard Washington, August 10, 1760, Account Book 1.

[46] Anderson, 179–83.

[47] Anderson, 210–11.

[48] Anderson, 228–29; *WPLC*, GW to Richard Washington, August 10, 1760, Account Book 1.

[49] *WPLC*, GW to Robert Stewart, August 13, 1763; Anderson, 231–33.

[50] *WPLC*, GW to Robert Stewart, August 13, 1763; Anderson, 236–40; *DGW*, UPV, 1:162 n. 2.

[51] Anderson, 251–52; Abbot, "George Washington, the West, and the Union," 201.

[52] *WPLC*, GW to Francis Dandridge, September 20, 1765, Account Book 1.

[53] *WPLC*, GW to Capel & Osgood Hanbury, July 25, 1767, Account Book 2.

[54] *WPLC*, William Crawford to GW, September 29, 1767.

[55] Redmond, *WPLC* ; Abbot, 202; Ambler, *George Washington and the West*, 137.

[56] *WPLC*, GW to George Mason, April 5, 1769, Account Book 2.

[57] Ambler, 139–40; Abbot, 202–3; Anderson, 252.

[58] Abbot, 203 and 206–7; Anderson, 252–53; Chase, "A Stake in the West," 185–86.

[59] Anderson, 254.

[60] Anderson, 254–55.

[61] Anderson, 255–56.

[62] Flexner, 4:114; Hirschfeld, 12.

[63] Anderson, 256–57.

[64] Anderson, 257–58.

[65] Anderson, 258–59; *WPLC*, GW to John Murray, Lord Dunmore, April 3, 1775, Account Book 2.

[66] Lengel, 84–88.

[67] *PGW*, Revolutionary War Series, 1:12–13.

3. THE SIEGE OF BOSTON

[1] Flexner, *George Washington*, 2:23–25.

[2] *PGW*, Revolutionary War Series, 1:85 and 92.

[3] *PGW*, Revolutionary War Series, 1:51, 85–86, and 99.

[4] Flexner, 4:115–18.

[5] *PGW*, Revolutionary War Series, 1:50–51 and 86; Pedley, "Maps, War, and Commerce," 167.

[6] *PGW*, Revolutionary War Series, 1:103–4, 183–84, and 186–87.

[7] *PGW*, Revolutionary War Series, 1:116–18, 142.

[8] *PGW*, Revolutionary War Series, 1:116–18.

[9] *PGW*, Revolutionary War Series, 1:151–52.

[10] *PGW*, Revolutionary War Series, 1:205–8 and 226–27.

[11] *PGW*, Revolutionary War Series, 1:201, 226, and 231.

[12] *PGW*, Revolutionary War Series, 1:226.

[13] *PGW*, Revolutionary War Series, 1:209–11, 2:271–76 and 437–42.

[14] *PGW*, Revolutionary War Series, 1:349–51.

[15] *PGW*, Revolutionary War Series, 1:221–22.

[16] *PGW*, Revolutionary War Series, 1:178, 228, and 233–37.

[17] *PGW*, Revolutionary War Series, 1:238, 318, and 330–31.

[18] *PGW*, Revolutionary War Series, 1:274–75, 280–81, 297–98, and 353–54.

[19] *PGW*, Revolutionary War Series, 1:308.

[20] *PGW*, Revolutionary War Series, 1:336.

[21] *PGW*, Revolutionary War Series, 1:332–33 and 345 n. 6.

[22] *PGW*, Revolutionary War Series, 1:362–63.

[23] *PGW*, Revolutionary War Series, 1:372.

[24] *PGW*, Revolutionary War Series, 1:432–34 and 450–51.

[25] *PGW*, Revolutionary War Series, 2:3.

[26] *PGW*, Revolutionary War Series, 2:26–29.

[27] *PGW*, Revolutionary War Series, 1:432–34; 2:34 and 72–73.

[28] *PGW*, Revolutionary War Series, 3:16.

[29] *PGW*, Revolutionary War Series, 2:90–92.

[30] *PGW*, Revolutionary War Series, 2:94–95 and 100–101.

[31] *PGW*, Revolutionary War Series, 2:108–9.

[32] *PGW*, Revolutionary War Series, 2:119.

[33] *PGW*, Revolutionary War Series, 2:161.

[34] *PGW*, Revolutionary War Series, 2:184–87.

[35] *PGW*, Revolutionary War Series, 2:206 and 212–35.

[36] *PGW*, Revolutionary War Series, 2:282.

[37] *PGW*, Revolutionary War Series, 2:344, 350–51, 358–59, and 463–64.

[38] *PGW*, Revolutionary War Series, 2:384–85.

[39] *PGW*, Revolutionary War Series, 2:391–92.

[40] *PGW*, Revolutionary War Series, 2:495–96 and 519.

[41] *PGW*, Revolutionary War Series, 2:553, 557, and 561.

[42] *PGW*, Revolutionary War Series, 2:563–66.

[43] *PGW*, Revolutionary War Series, 2:589–90.

[44] *PGW*, Revolutionary War Series, 2:614.

[45] *PGW*, Revolutionary War Series, 3:3 n. 1.

[46] *PGW*, Revolutionary War Series, 3:19.

[47] *PGW*, Revolutionary War Series, 3:29 and 34.

[48] *PGW*, Revolutionary War Series, 3:88–89.

[49] *PGW*, Revolutionary War Series, 3:29–30 n. 1, 103, and 174.

[50] *PGW*, Revolutionary War Series, 3:290, 295, and 298 n.

[51] *PGW*, Revolutionary War Series, 3:364–65.

[52] *PGW*, Revolutionary War Series, 3:370–71 and 376 n. 5; *EAR*, 1:180 and 353.

[53] *PGW*, Revolutionary War Series, 3:372–73 and 377 n. 9.

[54] *PGW*, Revolutionary War Series, 3:373 and 377–78 n. 10 and n. 11.

[55] *PGW*, Revolutionary War Series, 3:422.

[56] *PGW*, Revolutionary War Series, 3:421.

[57] *PGW*, Revolutionary War Series, 3:425 and 434.

[58] *PGW*, Revolutionary War Series, 3:425 and 440–41.

[59] *PGW*, Revolutionary War Series, 3:463 and 539.

[60] *PGW*, Revolutionary War Series, 3:427–28 n. 19.

[61] *PGW*, Revolutionary War Series, 3:459 and 467.

[62] *PGW*, Revolutionary War Series, 3:461 n. 2 and n. 5, 463, 490, and 493.

[63] *PGW*, Revolutionary War Series, 3:489–90.

[64] *PGW*, Revolutionary War Series, 3:545–47.

[65] *PGW*, Revolutionary War Series, 3:483 and 496.

[66] *PGW*, Revolutionary War Series, 3:505–7 and 522–23.

[67] *PGW*, Revolutionary War Series, 3:508–9 and 530–31.

[68] *PGW*, Revolutionary War Series, 3:518.

[69] *PGW*, Revolutionary War Series, 3:543–44 and 555–57.

4. THE AMERICAN INVASION OF CANADA

[1] *PGW*, Revolutionary War Series, 1:455–59.

[2] Roberts, *March to Quebec*, v. The natives called the rattlesnake Manitou-Kinnibec, probably the source of the name for the Kennebec River.

[3] *PGW*, Revolutionary War Series, 2:73, GW to his brother Samuel Washington, September 30, 1775.

[4] Desjardin, *Through a Howling Wilderness*, 2–3 and 21.

[5] *EAR*, 2:957–58; Faragher, *Encyclopedia of Colonial and Revolutionary America*, 348–49; Desjardin, 3–5.

[6] *PGW*, Revolutionary War Series, 2:73; Desjardin, 5.

[7] *PGW*, Revolutionary War Series, 2:218.

[8] Hamilton, *Fort Ticonderoga*, 5.

[9] *PGW*, Revolutionary War Series, 1:42–43.

[10] Desjardin, 8–12.

[11] Desjardin, 13–14.

[12] *PGW*, Revolutionary War Series, 1:182–83; Desjardin, 53.

[13] Desjardin, 12–13; *PGW*, Revolutionary War Series, 1:334, n. 6. Montresor's journal is reproduced in Roberts, *March to Quebec*, 5–24.

[14] Roberts, *March to Quebec*, map caption facing 5.

[15] *PGW*, Revolutionary War Series, 1:182–83, letter written by Stephen Moylan for Washington.

[16] Roberts, *March to Quebec*, 3.

[17] Desjardin, 14.

[18] *PGW*, Revolutionary War Series, 1:332–33.

[19] *PGW*, Revolutionary War Series, 1:393–94; *EAR*, 1:162; Warc, *The War of the Revolution*, 1:149–50.

[20] *EAR*, 2:1017–18.

[21] *PGW*, 2:153.

[22] *PGW*, Revolutionary War Series, 1:455–59.

[23] *PGW*, Revolutionary War Series, 1:461–62.

[24] *PGW*, Revolutionary War Series, 1:460 n. 2 and 2:43 n. 2; Desjardin, 22–25; Ward, 1:168–69.

[25] *PGW*, Revolutionary War Series, 2:27–28, 30 n. 10; *Papers of the Continental Congress*, Item 152 (Columbia University Library microfilm).

[26] Desjardin, 53.

[27] Desjardin, 26–27.

28 Desjardin, 53–54.

29 *PGW*, Revolutionary War Series, 2:41; Desjardin, 54.

30 *EAR*, 1:162 and 2:1018.

31 Desjardin, 27.

32 *PGW*, Revolutionary War Series, 2:120.

33 *PGW*, Revolutionary War Series, 2:147–48 and 149 n. 10. "Mr. Brice" was probably James Price, a merchant in Montreal who was helping the American invasion.

34 *EAR*, 1:162 and 2:1018; Desjardin, 27.

35 Desjardin, 54–60; *PGW*, Revolutionary War Series, 2:155.

36 Desjardin, 60–64; *EAR*, 1:30–32; *PGW*, Revolutionary War Series, 2:155; Roberts, *March to Quebec*, 22–23.

37 Roberts, *March to Quebec*, 23 n. 35.

38 Clark, 70 (caption for "Map of Lake Megantic and Height of Land Border Country").

39 Desjardin, 82; *EAR*, 1:30–32.

40 *PGW*, Revolutionary War Series, 2:244–45.

41 Desjardin, 65; *PGW*, Revolutionary War Series, 2:59–60 and 95–96.

42 Allen, *Naval History of the American Revolution*, 59–62.

43 *PGW*, Revolutionary War Series, 2:106–7 and 179–80.

44 *PGW*, Revolutionary War Series, 2:240–42.

45 *PGW*, Revolutionary War Series, 2:324; *EAR*, 1:162 and 2:1018.

46 *PGW*, Revolutionary War Series, 2:324, 332, and 344.

47 *PGW*, Revolutionary War Series, 2:386.

48 *PGW*, Revolutionary War Series, 2:399.

49 *PGW*, Revolutionary War Series, 2:284–85.

50 *PGW*, Revolutionary War Series, 2:170, 250, 284–85, and 311–12.

51 *EAR*, 1:31.

52 *PGW*, Revolutionary War Series, 2:358; *EAR*, 1:31; Desjardin, 135–37.

53 Desjardin, 137–38; *EAR*, 1:162.

54 *PGW*, Revolutionary War Series, 2:403–4 and 453; *EAR*, 1:162–63; Desjardin, 141 and 145–46.

55 *PGW*, Revolutionary War Series, 2:424–25.

56 Allen, 65–66; *PGW*, Revolutionary War Series, 2:504–7.

57 *PGW*, Revolutionary War Series, 2:485.

58 *PGW*, Revolutionary War Series, 2:508–9.

59 *PGW*, Revolutionary War Series, 2:452–53 and 494.

60 *PGW*, Revolutionary War Series, 2:447 and 452.

61 *PGW*, Revolutionary War Series, 2:495.

62 *PGW*, Revolutionary War Series, 3:35.

63 *PGW*, Revolutionary War Series, 2:493 and 498 and 3:84.

64 *PGW*, Revolutionary War Series, 2:623; *EAR*, 1:164.

65 *PGW*, Revolutionary War Series, 3:112.

66 *PGW*, Revolutionary War Series, 3:78–79.

67 *PGW*, Revolutionary War Series, 3:141.

68 *EAR*, 1:164; *PGW*, Revolutionary War Series, 3:78–79 and 197–98.

69 *PGW*, Revolutionary War Series, 3:228.

70 *PGW*, Revolutionary War Series, 3:197–98.

71 *PGW*, Revolutionary War Series, 3:16.

72 *PGW*, Revolutionary War Series, 3:17.

73 *PGW*, Revolutionary War Series, 3:191–92, 206–7, and 212.

74 *PGW*, Revolutionary War Series, 3:277–88.

75 *PGW*, Revolutionary War Series, 3:306–9.

76 *PGW*, Revolutionary War Series, 3:382; *EAR*, 1:164.

77 *PGW*, Revolutionary War Series, 4:22.

78 *EAR*, 1:164.

79 *EAR*, 1:164; *PGW*, Revolutionary War Series, 4:22.

80 *PGW*, Revolutionary War Series, 4:172.

81 *EAR*, 1:164.

82 *EAR*, 1:164.

83 *EAR*, 1:164; *PGW*, Revolutionary War Series, 4:373.

84 *PGW*, Revolutionary War Series, 4:382–83.

85 *EAR*, 1:164.

86 *PGW*, Revolutionary War Series, 4:433 and 442.

87 *PGW*, Revolutionary War Series, 4:510 n.

88 *EAR*, 1:164–65.

89 *EAR*, 1:165.

90 *EAR*, 1:165.

91 *PGW*, Revolutionary War Series, 7:14–15.

92 *PGW*, Revolutionary War Series, 7:82–83.

93 *PGW*, Revolutionary War Series, 7:86, 93, and 143.

94 *PGW*, Revolutionary War Series, 2:493 and 3:112.

5. FROM THE HUDSON TO PHILADELPHIA AND BACK

1 *PGW*, Revolutionary War Series, 3:30–31.

2 *PGW*, Revolutionary War Series, 3:36–37; Augustyn and Cohen, *Manhattan in Maps*, 70–72.

3 *PGW*, Revolutionary War Series, 3:53, 310, and 470.

4 *PGW*, Revolutionary War Series, 3:310.

5 *PGW*, Revolutionary War Series, 3:339.

6 *PGW*, Revolutionary War Series, 3:339–40.

7 *PGW*, Revolutionary War Series, 3:340.

8 *PGW*, Revolutionary War Series, 3:340.

9 *PGW*, Revolutionary War Series, 3:312 n. 4.

10 *PGW*, Revolutionary War Series, 3:470–71 and 498.

11 *PGW*, Revolutionary War Series, 4:40–42 and 59–60.

12 *PGW*, Revolutionary War Series, 4:368–69.

13 *PGW*, Revolutionary War Series, 4:286.

14 *PGW*, Revolutionary War Series, 4:356.

15 *PGW*, Revolutionary War Series, 4:323–25.

16 *PGW*, Revolutionary War Series, 5:57–58.

17 *PGW*, Revolutionary War Series, 5:183–84 and 482.

18 *PGW*, Revolutionary War Series, 5:370.

19 *PGW*, Revolutionary War Series, 5:533–34.

20 *PGW*, Revolutionary War Series, 5:136–37, 143, 156, 160, and 169–72.

21 *PGW*, Revolutionary War Series, 5:189–90 n. 1.

22 *PGW*, Revolutionary War Series, 5:180.

23 *PGW*, Revolutionary War Series, 5:200.

24 *PGW*, Revolutionary War Series, 5:196–97 and n. 2.

25 *PGW*, Revolutionary War Series, 5:197 n. 2 and 244–45.

25 *PGW*, Revolutionary War Series, 5:280–83.

27 *PGW*, Revolutionary War Series, 5:394.

28 *PGW*, Revolutionary War Series, 5:291 and 306–7.

29 *PGW*, Revolutionary War Series, 5:408–9.

30 *PGW*, Revolutionary War Series, 5:429–30.

31 *PGW*, Revolutionary War Series, 5:482, 549–50, and 553–54 and n. 1.

32 *PGW*, Revolutionary War Series, 5:553–54 and n. 1 and 568–69 and n. 6.

33 *PGW*, Revolutionary War Series, 5:631.

34 *PGW*, Revolutionary War Series, 5:682.

35 *PGW*, Revolutionary War Series, 5:21.

36 Quoted in Wheeler, *Voices of 1776*, 138.

37 *WPLC*, GW to William Livingston, November 7, 1776; GW to Nathanael Greene, November 7, 1776.

38 Boudreau and Bleimann, *George Washington in New York*, 10–11; *PGW*, Revolutionary War Series, 7:176–78 n. 1.

39 *PGW*, Revolutionary War Series, 7:182–83 and 193.

40 *PGW*, Revolutionary War Series, 7:233.

41 Ward, *The War of the Revolution*, 1:281.

42 Quoted in Commager and Morris, *The Spirit of 'Seventy-six*, 499.

43 *WGW*, 8:234 and 324–26.

44 *WGW*, 8:407; Symonds and Clipson, *A Battlefield Atlas*, 41.

45 *WGW*, 8:449, 460, and 477–78.

46 Symonds and Clipson, 41; *WGW*, 8:458.

47 *WGW*, 8:448 and 456–59.

48 *WGW*, 8:449 and 506.

49 *PGW*, Revolutionary War Series, 4:517.

50 *WGW*, 9:106 and 154.

51 Symonds and Clipson, 45; *WGW*, 9:76–77.

52 *WGW*, 9:76 and 123.

53 *WGW*, 9:276–77 and 285.

54 *WGW*, 9:339–40.

55 *WGW*, 9:377–78.

56 *WGW*, 9:372 and 391.

57 *WGW*, 10:467–68.

58 Quoted in *EAR*, 2:703.

59 *WPLC*, GW to Congress, September 3, 1777.

60 *EAR*, 1:269.

61 *WPLC*, GW to Congress, September 9, 1777; *PGW*, Revolutionary War Series, 11:175.

62 *WPLC*, GW to Congress, September 11, 1777; Symonds and Clipson, 53; *EAR*, 1:105; Lengel, *General George Washington*, 228.

63 *WPLC*, General Orders, September 12, 1777; Symonds and Clipson, 53.

64 Symonds and Clipson, 53.

65 *WPLC*, GW to Thomas Nelson Jr., September 27, 1777.

66 Quoted in *EAR*, 2:1185.

67 Washington's route to Monmouth: *PGW*, Revolutionary War Series, 16:2–3; Symonds and Clipson, 64–65.

68 *PGW*, Revolutionary War Series, 15:590; Symonds and Clipson, 61–62.

69 *PGW*, Revolutionary War Series, 16:68, 133, and 249; Boudreau and Bleimann, 13; Symonds and Clipson, 67.

70 *PGW*, Revolutionary War Series, 16:177–79 and 243–45.

71 *PGW*, Revolutionary War Series, 16:289, 350–51, and 396–99; *EAR*, 2:815–19.

72 Williams, *Year of the Hangman*, passim.

73 Flexner, *George Washington*, 2:328–29; *EAR*, 1:202–3 and 2:1286–87; Williams, 114–87.

74 Williams, passim; Flexner, 2:329–31.

75 Flexner, 2:324, 332–33, 335, and 343.

76 Flexner, 2:346.

77 *WPLC*, GW to John Sullivan, May 31, 1779, with Instruction.

78 *EAR*, 2:1126–27; Williams, 213–89.

79 *WGW*, 16:267.

80 *EAR*, 2:1126; Williams, 213–89 and 293.

81 *WGW*, 16:347.

82 Williams, 290–96; "Sullivan/Clinton Campaign, Then and Now," at www.sullivanclinton.com; *EAR*, 2:1127–28.

83 Symonds and Clipson, 72–73; *WPLC*, GW to Thomas Jefferson, July 10, 1779.

84 *WPLC*, GW to Benjamin Lincoln, February 27, 1780.

6. THE WAR IN THE SOUTH

1 *PGW*, Revolutionary War Series, 3:474.

2 Symonds and Clipson, *A Battlefield Atlas*, 79.

3 Symonds and Clipson, 79–80.

4 *PGW*, Revolutionary War Series, 2:304, 345, and 469.

5 *EAR*, 2:1095.

6 *PGW*, Revolutionary War Series, 3:326.

7 *PGW*, Revolutionary War Series, 3:435–39, 518–19, and 541 n. 1; Symonds and Clipson, 80.

8 *PGW*, Revolutionary War Series, 3:171 n 8.

9 *PGW*, Revolutionary War Series, 5:168–69.

10 *PGW*, Revolutionary War Series, 5:168–72 and 416; Symonds and Clipson, 83.

11 *WPLC*, GW to Benjamin Lincoln, October 3, 1778.

12 *PGW*, Revolutionary War Series, 18:326–27. (My translation from French.)

13 *PGW*, Revolutionary War Series, 18:327–29 n. 2.

14 *PGW*, Revolutionary War Series, 18:467.

15 *PGW*, Revolutionary War Series, 18:454–56 n. 1.

16 *PGW*, Revolutionary War Series, 18:576–77.

17 Symonds and Clipson, 75; Georgia Historical Commission, 1956, Brier Creek Historical Marker; *WPLC*, GW to Henry Laurens, March 20, 1779; *EAR*, 1:109.

18 *WPLC*, GW to Gouverneur Morris, May 8, 1779.

19 Symonds and Clipson, 75.

20 *WPLC*, GW to Lincoln, July 30, 1779.

21 *WPLC*, GW to Lincoln, September 28, 1779.

22 *New Georgia Encyclopedia*; *WPLC*, GW to Lincoln, September 28, 1779.

23 *WPLC*, GW to George Clinton, October 1, 1779; Symonds and Clipson, 75.

24 *WPLC*, GW to Jonathan Trumbull, November 16, 1779; GW to Philip Schuyler, November 24, 1779; GW to Horatio Gates, November 17, 1779; Symonds and Clipson, 75.

25 *EAR*, 2:1093.

26 *WPLC*, GW to Lincoln, February 27, 1780; GW to Don Juan de Miralles, February 27, 1780; *EAR*, 2:1095.

27 Symonds and Clipson, 79 and 83.

28 *WPLC*, GW to Lincoln, April 15, 1780.

29 *WPLC*, GW to John Laurens, April 26, 1780.

30 *WPLC*, GW to Robert Howe, May 5, 1780.

31 *WPLC*, James Duane to GW, May 5, 1780; Symonds and Clipson, 79 and 83.

32 *WPLC*, GW to James Bowdoin, June 14, 1780.

33 Symonds and Clipson, 85; *EAR*, 2:1145–46.

34 *WPLC*, GW to Congress, August 20, 1780.

35 *WPLC*, GW to comte de Guichen, September 12, 1780; *EAR*, 2:1301.

36 *WPLC*, GW to Guichen, September 12, 1780.

37 *WPLC*, GW to Congress, September 15, 1780.

38 *WPLC*, GW to William Heath, September 26, 1780, and GW to Congress, September 26, 1780.

39 *WPLC*, General Orders, October 27, 1780.

40 *WPLC*, GW to James Clinton, November 5, 1780.

41 *WPLC*, Nathanael Greene to GW, October 31, 1780.

42 *WPLC*, GW to Greene, November 8, 1780.

43 *WPLC*, GW to Thomas Jefferson, November 8, 1780.

44 Symonds and Clipson, 91; *EAR*, 1:278–84 and 2:838; *WPLC*, GW to comte de Rochambeau, January 29, 1781.

45 *WPLC*, GW to Greene, February 2, 1781.

46 *WPLC*, GW to Rochambeau, January 29, 1781.

47 Symonds and Clipson, 91; *EAR*, 1:278–84.

48 *WPLC*, GW to Congress, February 17, 1781.

49 *WPLC*, GW to Lincoln, February 17, 1781; GW to John Laurens, April 9, 1781; Symonds and Clipson, 93.

50 *WPLC*, GW to Greene, March 21, 1781.

51 *WPLC*, GW to Schuyler, March 23, 1781.

52 *WPLC*, GW to Rochambeau, March 31 and April 3, 1781.

53 Symonds and Clipson, 99; *WPLC*, GW to Jefferson, May 16, 1781.

54 *WPLC*, GW to Baron von Steuben, May 16, 1781.

55 Symonds and Clipson, 99.

56 *WPLC*, GW to Greene, April 22, 1781.

57 *WPLC*, GW to Rochambeau, June 2, 1781; Symonds and Clipson, 95.

58 *WPLC*, GW to Francisco Rendon, May 2, June 8, June 21, and July 13, 1781.

59 *WPLC*, GW to Heath, June 14, 1781.

60 *EAR*, 2:1300.

61 *EAR*, 2:1300.

62 *WPLC*, GW to Greene, June 1, 1781.

63 *EAR*, 2:1300–1301.

64 *WPLC*, GW to Rochambeau, June 13, 1781.

65 *WPLC*, GW to Heath, June 14, 1781.

66 Symonds and Clipson, 99.

67 *WPLC*, GW to François Joseph Paul de Grasse, July 21, 1781.

68 *WPLC*, GW to marquis de Lafayette, August 15, 1781; GW to Meshech Weare et al., August 21, 1781.

69 *WPLC*, GW and Rochambeau to de Grasse, August 17, 1781; GW to de Grasse, August 24, 1781.

70 *WPLC*, GW to Rochambeau, August 27, 1781.

71 Symonds and Clipson, 101.

72 *WPLC*, GW to Greene, September 4, 1781.

73 *WPLC*, GW to Congress, September 5, 1781; GW to de Grasse, September 6, 1781; GW to du Portail, September 7, 1781; GW to John Cadwalader, September 7, 1781.

74 *WPLC*, GW to David Forman, September 7, 1781; Symonds and Clipson, 95.

75 *WPLC*, GW to Forman, September 7, 1781.

[76] *WPLC*, GW to Congress, September 15, 1781; GW to Lincoln, September 15, 1781.

[77] *WPLC*, GW to de Grasse, September 17, 1781.

[78] *WPLC*, GW to Heath, September 23 and October 1, 1781.

[79] *WPLC*, GW to de Grasse, October 1, 1781.

[80] *WPLC*, GW to de Grasse, October 3, October 11, and October 16, 1781.

[81] *WPLC*, General Orders, October 6, 1781; Symonds and Clipson, 97.

[82] *WPLC*, GW to Congress, October 12 and October 16, 1781; GW to Greene, October 16, 1781.

[83] *WPLC*, GW to de Grasse, October 16, 1781.

[84] *WPLC*, GW to de Grasse, October 20, 1781; GW to Congress, October 26, 1781; GW to Thomas Nelson Jr., October 27, 1781.

[85] Quoted in Flexner, *George Washington*, 2:469.

[86] *WPLC*, GW to Rochambeau, February 23, 1782.

[87] *WPLC*, GW to Rochambeau, May 28, 1782.

[88] *EAR*, 1:443 and 2:886–87.

[89] *WPLC*, GW to Rochambeau, May 28, 1782.

[90] Quoted in Wall, *George Washington*, 180.

[91] Quoted in Wall, 180–81.

[92] *WGW*, 26:401.

[93] For the following discussion of "Sentiments on a Peace Establishment" and the quoted passages, see Higginbotham, *George Washington*, 37 and 91–114.

[94] *WGW*, 27:122 and 123.

[95] *WGW*, 27:187.

7. AFTER THE REVOLUTION—UNITING AN EXPANDING NATION

[1] *WPLC*, GW to François Jean, comte de Chastellux, October 12, 1783.

[2] *WPLC*, GW to François Jean, comte de Chastellux, October 12, 1783.

[3] Abbot, "George Washington, the West, and the Union," 198.

[4] *WPLC*, GW to James Duane, September 7, 1783.

[5] Barnes, *Historical Atlas*, 224–25.

[6] *WPLC*, GW to Duane, September 7, 1783.

[7] *WPLC*, GW to Duane, September 7, 1783.

[8] Freeman, *George Washington*, 6:8.

[9] *WPLC*, GW to Thomas Lewis, February 1, 1784.

[10] *PGW*, Confederation Series, 1:514.

[11] *PGW*, Confederation Series, 1:216–17.

[12] Abbot, 204–5.

[13] *PGW*, Confederation Series, 1:237–38.

[14] *PGW*, Confederation Series, 1:238.

[15] Abbot, 203.

[16] *DGW*, UPV, 4:1 and 2–3 n. 2.

[17] *DGW*, UPV, 4:4.

[18] Freeman, 6:14.

[19] Abbot, 205–6; *DGW*, UPV 4:6–8.

[20] Achenbach, *The Grand Idea*, 122; *DGW*, UPV, 4:60.

[21] *DGW*, UPV, 4:11–13 n. 4 and 14 n. 6–7.

[22] *DGW*, UPV, 4:60.

[23] *DGW*, UPV, 4:9–13 n. 1.

[24] *DGW*, UPV, 4:14–16 n. 4 and 18–20 n. 1.

[25] *DGW*, UPV, 4:19–20.

[26] *DGW*, UPV, 4:1–2 n.1 and n.18.

[27] *DGW*, UPV, 4:23–24 n. 1 and n. 25.

[28] *DGW*, UPV, 4:21 and 25–31; Freeman, 6:19 n. 111.

[29] The following account of the rest of Washington's trip to the West is drawn from *DGW*, UPV, 4:32–58; Abbot, 203; Freeman, 6:18–22; Achenbach, 114–20.

[30] *PGW*, Confederation Series, 2:89–90. See 1:200 n. 3 for exact titles and dates. See 2:97–98 for the table of distances.

[31] *PGW*, Confederation Series, 2:91–92; Abbot, 203–4 and 206–7; Chase, "A Stake in the West," 184–86.

[32] *PGW*, Confederation Series, 2:86–89 editorial note, and 181–83.

[33] *PGW*, Confederation Series, 2:141

[34] *PGW*, Confederation Series, 2:141.

[35] *PGW*, Confederation Series, 2:181.

[36] *PGW*, Confederation Series, 2:141 n. 1; Presidential Series, 2:293 n. 7.

[37] *PGW*, Confederation Series, 2:372.

[38] *PGW*, Confederation Series, 2:361–62.

[39] *PGW*, Confederation Series, 2:436–37.

[40] *PGW*, Confederation Series, 2:437–38; Barnes, 228, 259.

[41] *DGW*, UPV, 4:170–81.

[42] *PGW*, Confederation Series, 4:6–7 and n. 2 and 73–75.

[43] *PGW*, Confederation Series, 3:152.

[44] Chase, 182.

[45] Wiencek, *An Imperfect God*, 355–58.

[46] *PGW*, Confederation Series, 3:18 n. 1; Freeman, 6:49.

[47] *PGW*, Confederation Series, 3:61–63.

[48] *PGW*, Presidential Series, 2:293 n. 8 and 494–95 editorial note.

[49] *PGW*, Confederation Series, 3:144.

[50] *WPLC*, Barbé-Marbois to GW, June 12, 1785; GW to Barbé-Marbois, June 21, 1785.

[51] Freeman, 7:19.

[52] Freeman, 7:18–19.

[53] *PGW*, Confederation Series, 3:144.

[54] *PGW*, Confederation Series, 3:196.

[55] Freeman, 7:20.

[56] Freeman, 7:19–21.

[57] *PGW*, Confederation Series, 4:63–66.

[58] *PGW*, Confederation Series, 4:169.

[59] *PGW*, Confederation Series, 4:186.

[60] *PGW*, Confederation Series, 4:225 n. 2.

[61] *PGW*, Confederation Series, 4:42–43.

[62] *PGW*, Confederation Series, 3:47–48.

[63] *PGW*, Confederation Series, 3:601.

[64] *PGW*, Confederation Series, 4:55–56.

[65] Freeman, 6:49.

[66] Freeman, 6:125; *DGW*, UPV, 5:178–81; Palmer, *1794*, 120–21.

[67] Freeman, 6:102–3.

[68] Palmer, 147 and n. 1.

[69] *PGW*, Presidential Series, 2:199 editorial note.

[70] *PGW*, Presidential Series, 2:196–200 and 199–200 n. 2.

[71] Freeman, 6:125.

[72] Flexner, *George Washington*, 4:115 and 120.

[73] *PGW*, Confederation Series, 4:43–44; Flexner, 4:119.

[74] Palmer, 145–46; Ferling, *The Ascent of George Washington*, 273–74.

[75] Ferling, 274; Flexner, 3:171.

[76] *DGW*, UPV, 5:445.

[77] The following account of Washington's journey to New York is drawn from *DGW*, UPV, 5:445–48; Freeman, 6:167–84; and Flexner, 3:174–81.

8. DANGER ON THE FRONTIERS, UPHEAVAL IN EUROPE

[1] *WGW*, 30:268.

[2] Palmer, *1794*, 146–48; *WGW*, 30:187.

[3] Palmer, 150.

[4] *PGW*, Presidential Series, 2:196–200 and 199–200 n. 2; Palmer, 151.

[5] Freeman, *George Washington*, 7:13–14.

[6] *PGW*, Presidential Series, 2:494–95 editorial note.

[7] *WGW*, 30:326.

[8] Freeman, 6:271–72.

[9] Palmer, 151.

[10] Palmer, 151–52.

[11] Palmer, 152.

[12] Linklater, *An Artist in Treason*, 97–98.

[13] *WGW*, 30:214.

[14] *WGW*, 30:379 and 383.

[15] Freeman, 6:223–24; Palmer, 151–53.

[16] *WGW*, 31:39.

[17] *WGW*, 30:436.

[18] *WGW*, 31:44.

[19] Freeman, 6:235–37; Palmer, 154–55.

[20] *WGW*, 30:442.

[21] Palmer, 154 and n. 2.

[22] Freeman, 6:238–39.

[23] Freeman, 6:240–42; *DGW*, UPV, 5:462–97.

[24] Palmer, 156 and 160.

[25] Palmer, 156–57.

[26] *WGW*, 31:32.

[27] Freeman, 6:245–46; Palmer, 157.

[28] Palmer, 157–59.

[29] Freeman, 6:269–71.

[30] *WGW*, 31:85.

[31] Freeman, 6:271–72; Palmer, 160–61.

[32] Palmer, 160–61.

[33] Freeman, 6:258–59; Palmer, 161–62.

[34] *WGW*, 31:250.

[35] *DGW*, UPV, 6:85, July 3, 1790.

[36] *WGW*, 31:76.

[37] *WGW*, 31: 77.

[38] *WGW*, 31:74.

[39] Freeman, 7:21.

[40] *WGW*, 31:128.

[41] Palmer, 163.

[42] *WGW*, 31:85.

[43] Freeman, 6:329.

[44] Freeman, 6:271–72; Palmer, 164–68.

[45] *WGW*, 31:143.

[46] *WGW*, 31:144.

[47] *WGW*, 31:156.

[48] *PGW*, Presidential Series, 7:72, Josiah Harmar to Henry Knox, November 4, 1790.

[49] Freeman, 6:284 and 288–89; Palmer, 171–82.

[50] Palmer, 183–86.

[51] Quoted in Palmer, 186–87.

[52] Freeman, 6:298–301.

[53] Freeman, 6:307–8.

[54] *WGW*, 31:267.

[55] *WGW*, 31:273.

[56] Quoted in Freeman, 6:308–9.

[57] Freeman, 6:310–15.

[58] Freeman, 6:316–17.

[59] Freeman, 6:318.

[60] Freeman, 6:318–20.

[61] Freeman, 6:320.

[62] *WGW*, 31:317, GW to David Humphreys, July 20, 1791; Freeman, 6:320–22.

[63] Freeman, 6:320–22.

[64] Palmer, 187–89, 191.

[65] Freeman, 6:324–27 and 335.

[66] *WGW*, 31:386.

[67] *WGW*, 31:326; Freeman, 6:325–28.

[68] Freeman, 6:325–28.

[69] *WGW*, 31:375.

[70] Palmer, 196–201; *WGW*, 31:379.

[71] Freeman, 6:337–39; Palmer, 196–201.

[72] Palmer, 202.

[73] Freeman, 6:340–42; Palmer, 217 and n. 1.

[74] Freeman, 6:340–42; Palmer, 203–6.

[75] Palmer, 208–9.

[76] Palmer, 217–19; *WGW*, 32:103 and 107.

[77] *WGW*, 32:134.

[78] Palmer, 205 and 210–12.

[79] Palmer, 212.

[80] Palmer, 212–14.

[81] *WGW*, 32:117.

[82] Palmer, 214.

[83] Palmer, 214–15; *WGW*, 32:117.

[84] Palmer, 214–15; *WGW*, 32:107 and 117.

[85] Palmer, 214–15.

[86] Palmer, 214–15; Freeman, 6:358–64; *WGW*, 32:125.

[87] *WGW*, 32:113.

[88] Freeman, 7:14.

[89] Palmer, 215–17.

[90] Palmer, 219.

[91] *WGW*, 32:134.

[92] *WGW*, 32:385–86.

[93] Palmer, 212–14.

[94] *WGW*, 32:449–50.

[95] *WGW*, 32:501–2.

9. GAINS IN THE NORTHWEST AND SOUTHWEST, TROUBLE WITH FRANCE

[1] *WGW*, 32:309, GW to Henry Lee, January 20, 1793.

[2] Palmer, *1794*, 220.

[3] Palmer, 220–22; Freeman, *George Washington*, 7:34, 36–37, and 52.

[4] Palmer, 222–23.

[5] Palmer, 223–24 and n. 2.

[6] Palmer, 225–27.

[7] Palmer, 227–28; Freeman, 7:149–50 and 150 n. 12.

[8] Palmer, 228.

[9] Flexner, *George Washington*, 4:112.

[10] Flexner, 4:112–13; Freeman, 7:341–42; Chase, "A Stake in the West," 183; *WPLC*, GW to Tobias Lear, May 6, 1794.

[11] Flexner, 4:122–24.

[12] Flexner, 4:123–25; Wiencek, *An Imperfect God*, 359.

[13] Palmer, 231–33.

[14] Freeman, 7:149–50 and 150 n. 12; Palmer, 238–39.

[15] Freeman, 7:149–50 and 150 n. 12.

[16] Freeman, 7:155–57, 155 n. 60, and 157 n. 76; Palmer, 236–37; *WGW*, 33:304.

[17] Freeman, 7:162–63 and 162 n. 121 and n.125; Palmer, 236.

[18] *WGW*, 33:332.

[19] Freeman, 7:172–73; Palmer, 236.

[20] *WGW*, 33:483.

[21] Freeman, 7:174, 174 n. 231, 179–80, 179 n. 32, and 180 n. 35; Palmer, 237.

[22] Freeman, 7:180–84.

[23] Ambler, *George Washington and the West*, 201–2.

[24] Freeman, 7:184–86, 189, and 196–98.

[25] *DGW*, 4:210; *DGW*, UPV, 6:179.

[26] Palmer, 259.

[27] *DGW*, UPV, 6:179–94; Freeman, 7:210–11.

[28] *DGW*, UPV, 6:197–98; Ferling, *The Ascent of George Washington*, 336–38.

[29] Freeman, 7:217 and 217 n. 25.

[30] *WGW*, 34:15–16.

[31] Freeman, 7:221.

[32] *WGW*, 34:76–77; Freeman, 7:228–29 and 229 n. 104.

[33] Freeman, 7:237–39.

[34] Freeman, 7:240–41.

[35] Freeman, 7:307.

[36] Freeman, 7:326–27.

[37] *WGW*, 34:448; Freeman, 7:340–41.

[38] Freeman, 7:341 and 345–46.

[39] Freeman, 7:382.

[40] Flexner, 4:300–3.

[41] Kaufman, *Washington's Farewell Address*, 20–21.

[42] Flexner, 4:319.

[43] Flexner, 4:325–26.

[44] Flexner, 4:322–24 and 328–29.

[45] *DGW*, UPV, 6:235; Flexner, 4:329–33.

10. BACK TO THE LAND, DIVIDING MOUNT VERNON

[1] *DGW*, UPV, 6:236 and 239–40; GW to James McHenry, April

3, 1797, quoted in *DGW*, UPV, 6:239–40; *WPLC*, GW to James Anderson, November 4, 1797; Flexner, *George Washington*, 4:339.

[2] *WPLC*, GW to McHenry, May 29, 1797.

[3] Niemcewicz, *Under Their Vine*, 102–3, quoted in Wiencek, *An Imperfect God*, 344.

[4] Flexner, 4:354–55; Chadwick, *The General and Mrs. Washington*, 33–34.

[5] *WPLC*, GW to Sarah C. Fairfax, May 16, 1798; Flexner, 4:354–55.

[6] Flexner, 4:371.

[7] Flexner, 4:373–74.

[8] *WGW*, 35:461.

[9] Flexner, 4:374–75; *WPLC*, GW to Fairfax, May 16, 1798.

[10] Flexner, 4:374–75; Ferling, *The Ascent of George Washington*, 351–52.

[11] *WGW*, 36:189.

[12] Flexner, 4:375–77.

[13] *WGW*, 35:446-47.

[14] Quoted in Flexner, 4:380.

[15] Flexner, 4:380; *WGW*, 35:452–53.

[16] Flexner, 4:381; *WGW*, 36:89–90.

[17] *WGW*, 36:92–94.

[18] *WGW*, 36:97.

[19] Flexner, 4:382–83; *WGW*, 36:164.

[20] Flexner, 4:391.

[21] Flexner, 4:391–92; *WGW*, 36:246–47.

[22] Flexner, 4:391–32; Ferling, 352–53.

[23] *WGW*, 36:253.

[24] *PGW*, Retirement Series, 2:351–52 and 359–60.

[25] *PGW*, Retirement Series, 2:368–69.

[26] Flexner, 380, 397; *PGW*, Retirement Series, 2:367 and 368 n.1.

[27] Flexner, 4:397–98, 400, and 402; *PGW*, Retirement Series, 2:397–98; Freeman, *George Washington*, 7:522.

[28] Flexner, 4:402, 407; Ferling, 355–56.

[29] Flexner, 4:379–80 and 406–7; *WGW*, 36: 476–77.

[30] Flexner, 4:407–11; *PGW*, Retirement Series, 3:36–43.

[31] Flexner, 4:413–14.

[32] Flexner, 4:395 and 395 n. 3.

[33] Flexner, 4:417–18; Ferling, 354 and 357.

[34] Flexner, 4:425–26.

[35] Flexner, 4:427.

[36] Flexner, 4:428–29; Ferling, 360–61.

[37] Flexner, 4:428–29; Ferling, 360–62.

[38] Flexner, 4:430–31; Ferling, 360.

[39] Flexner, 4:445; Wiencek, 338–43.

[40] *PGW*, Retirement Series, 4:480; Wiencek, 356.

[41] *PGW*, Retirement Series, 4:479–80; Flexner, 4:453.

[42] *PGW*, Retirement Series, 4:488–89 and 507–8 n. 29; Chase, "A Stake in the West," 183–84.

[43] *PGW*, Retirement Series, 4:488–89 and 508 n. 30.

[44] *PGW*, Retirement Series, 4:487–89 and 508–9 n. 31.

[45] *PGW*, Retirement Series, 4:490 and 508–9 n. 31.

[46] The following account of Washington's final days is drawn from "Tobias Lear's Narrative Accounts of the Death of George Washington," in *PGW*, Retirement Series, 4:542–55; *DGW*, UPV, 378–79; and Flexner, 4:456–62.

BIBLIOGRAPHY

Abbot, W. W. "George Washington, the West, and the Union," in Higginbotham, *George Washington Reconsidered*, 198–211.

Achenbach, Joel. *The Grand Idea: George Washington's Potomac and the Race to the West.* New York: Simon & Schuster, 2004.

Allen, Gardner Weld. *Naval History of the American Revolution.* New York: Russell & Russell, 1962.

Ambler, Charles H. *George Washington and the West.* Chapel Hill: University of North Carolina Press, 1936.

Anderson, Fred. *The War That Made America: A Short History of the French and Indian War.* New York: Viking, 2005.

Augustyn, Robert T., and Paul E. Cohen. *Manhattan in Maps, 1527–1995.* New York: Rizzoli, 1997.

Axelrod, Alan. *Blooding at Great Meadows: Young George Washington and the Battle That Shaped the Man.* Philadelphia: Running Press, 2007.

Barnes, Ian. *Historical Atlas of Native Americans.* Edison, N.J.: Chartwell Books, 2009.

Boston Athenaeum. *A Catalogue of the Washington Collection in the Boston Athenaeum.* Cambridge, Mass.: University Press, J. Wilson and Son, Boston Athenaeum, 1897.

Boudreau, Allan, and Alexander Bleimann. *George Washington in New York.* New York: American Lodge of Research, F. & A.M., 1987.

Bradford, James C., ed. *Atlas of American Military History.* New York: Oxford University Press, 2003.

Brückner, Martin. *The Geographic Revolution in Early America: Maps, Literacy, and National Identity.* Chapel Hill: University of North Carolina Press, 2006.

Burrows, Edwin G. *Forgotten Patriots: The Untold Story of American Prisoners During the Revolutionary War.* New York: Basic Books, 2008.

Calloway, Colin G. *The American Revolution in Indian Country: Crisis and Diversity in Native American Communities.* Cambridge: Cambridge University Press, 1995.

Carnes, Mark C., and John A. Garraty, with Patrick Williams. *Mapping America's Past: A Historical Atlas.* New York: Henry Holt, 1996.

Chadwick, Bruce. *The General and Mrs. Washington.* Naperville, Ill.: Sourcebooks, 2007.

Chase, Philander. "A Stake in the West: George Washington as Backcountry Surveyor and Landholder," in Hofstra, *George Washington and the Virginia Backcountry*, 159–94.

Chernow, Ron. *Alexander Hamilton.* New York: Penguin, 2004.

Clark, Stephen. *Following Their Footsteps: A Travel Guide and History of the 1775 Secret Expedition to Capture Quebec.* Shapleigh, Maine: Clark Books, 2006.

Commager, Henry Steele, and Richard B. Morris, eds. *The Spirit of 'Seventy-six.* New York: Harper & Row, 1967.

Cumming, William Patterson. *British Maps of Colonial America.* Chicago: University of Chicago Press, 1974.

Desjardin, Thomas A. *Through a Howling Wilderness: Benedict Arnold's March to Quebec, 1775.* New York: St. Martin's Press, 2006.

Diamant, Lincoln. *Chaining the Hudson: The Fight for the River in the American Revolution.* New York: Carol Publishing Group, 1989.

Ellis, Joseph. *His Excellency: George Washington.* New York: Knopf, 2004.

Everett, Edward. *Life of George Washington.* New York: Sheldon & Co., 1866.

Faragher, John Mack, ed. *Encyclopedia of Colonial and Revolutionary America.* New York: Da Capo, 1996.

Fausz, J. Frederick. "Engaged in Enterprises Pregnant with Terror: George Washington's Formative Years Among the Indians," in Hofstra, *George Washington and the Virginia Backcountry,* 115–55.

Ferling, John. *The Ascent of George Washington: The Hidden Political Genius of an American Icon.* New York: Bloomsbury Press, 2009.

Flexner, James Thomas. *George Washington.* 4 vols. Boston: Little, Brown, 1965–72.

Fowler, William M., Jr. *Empires at War: The French and Indian War and the Struggle for North America, 1754–1763.* New York: Walker, 2005.

Freeman, Douglas Southall. *George Washington: A Biography.* 7 vols. New York: Charles Scribner's Sons, 1948–57.

Georgia Historical Commission, http://georgiainfo.galileo.usg. edu/gahistmarkers/battlebriercreekhistmarker.htm.

Guthorn, Peter J. *American Maps and Map Makers of the Revolution.* Monmouth Beach, N.J.: Philip Freneau Press, 1966.

Hamilton, Edward P. *Fort Ticonderoga: Key to a Continent.* Fort Ticonderoga, N.Y.: 1995.

Harley, J. B., Barbara Bartz Petchenik, and Lawrence W. Towner. *Mapping the American Revolutionary War.* Chicago: University of Chicago Press, 1978.

Higginbotham, Don. *George Washington: Uniting a Nation.* Lanham, Md.: Rowman & Littlefield, 2002.

———. *George Washington Reconsidered.* Charlottesville: University Press of Virginia, 2001.

Hirschfeld, Fritz. *George Washington and Slavery: A Documentary Portrayal.* Columbia: University of Missouri Press, 1997.

Hoagland, William. *The Whiskey Rebellion.* New York: Scribner, 2006.

Hofstra, Warren R., ed. *George Washington and the Virginia Backcountry.* Madison, Wis.: Madison House, 1998.

Huesser, Albert. *George Washington's Map Maker*. New Brunswick, N.J.: Rutgers University Press, 1966.

Kaufman, Burton Ira. *Washington's Farewell Address*. Chicago: Quadrangle Books, 1969.

Kinnaird, Clark. *George Washington: The Pictorial Biography*. New York: Hastings House, 1967.

Lengel, Edward G. *General George Washington: A Military Life*. New York: Random House, 2005.

Linklater, Andro. *An Artist in Treason: The Extraordinary Double Life of General James Wilkinson*. New York: Walker, 2009.

Marshall, Douglas W., and Howard H. Peckham. *Campaigns of the American Revolution: An Atlas of Manuscript Maps*. Ann Arbor: University of Michigan Press, 1976.

Martin, Lawrence, ed. *The George Washington Atlas*. Washington, D.C.: United States George Washington Bicentennial Commission, 1932.

Nebenzahl, Kenneth, and Don Higginbotham. *Atlas of the American Revolution*. Chicago: Rand McNally, 1974.

New Georgia Encyclopedia. http://www.georgiaencyclopedia. org/nge/Home.jsp.

Niemcewicz, Julien. *Under Vine and Fig Tree: Travels through America in 1797–1799*. Elizabeth, N.J.: Grassman, 1965.

Palmer, Dave Richard. *1794: America, Its Army, and the Birth of the Nation*. Novato, Calif.: Presidio, 1994.

Pedley, Mary. *The Commerce of Cartography: Making and Marketing Maps in Eighteenth-Century France and England*. Chicago: University of Chicago Press, 2005.

————. "Maps, War, and Commerce: Business Correspondence with the London Map Firm of Thomas Jefferys and William Faden." *Imago Mundi* 48 (1996): 161–73.

————."The Map Trade in the Late Eighteenth Century Letters to the London Map Sellers Jefferys and Faden." *Studies on Voltaire and the Eighteenth Century*, 2000:06. Oxford: Voltaire Foundation, 2000.

Pritchard, Margaret Beck, and Henry G. Taliaferro. *Degrees of Latitude: Mapping Colonial America*. Williamsburg, Va.: Colonial Williamsburg Foundation, in association with H. N. Abrams, 2002.

Prussing, Eugene D. *The Estate of George Washington, Deceased*. Boston: Little, Brown, 1927.

Redmond, Edward J. "George Washington: Surveyor and Mapmaker," at George Washington Papers Home Page, Library of Congress, http://memory.loc.gov/ammem/ gwhtml/gwhome.html.

Roberts, Kenneth Lewis. *Arundel*. Garden City, N.Y.: Doubleday, Doran, 1933.

————, ed. *March to Quebec: Journals of the Members of Arnold's Expedition*. New York: Doubleday, Doran, 1938.

————. *Rabble in Arms*. Garden City, N.Y.: Doubleday, 1947.

Schwartz, Seymour I., and Ralph E. Ehrenburg. *The Mapping of America*. New York: H. N. Abrams, 1980.

Selesky, Harold, ed. *Encyclopedia of the American Revolution*. New York: Scribner's/Thomson Gale, 2006.

Short, John R. *Representing the Republic: Mapping the United States, 1600–1900*. London: Reaktion, 2001.

Smith, Justin Harvey. *Arnold's March from Cambridge to Quebec*. New York: G. P. Putnam's Sons, 1903.

————. *Our Struggle for the Fourteenth Colony*. New York: G. P. Putnam's Sons, 1907.

Smith, Thomas H. *The Mapping of Ohio*. Kent, Ohio: Kent State University Press, 1977.

Symonds, Craig L., and William J. Clipson. *A Battlefield Atlas of the American Revolution*. Baltimore: Nautical & Aviation Publishing Company of America, 1986.

Toner, Joseph M. *Some Account of George Washington's Library and Manuscript Records and Their Dispersion from Mount Vernon*. Washington, D.C.: Government Printing Office, 1894.

Tooley, R. V. *The Mapping of America*. London: Holland Press, 1985.

Wall, Charles Cecil. *George Washington: Citizen-Soldier*. Charlottesville: University Press of Virginia, 1980.

Ward, Christopher. *The War of the Revolution*. 2 vols. New York: Macmillan, 1952.

Washington, George. *Diaries of George Washington*. 6 vols. Charlottesville: University Press of Virginia, 1976–79.

————. *Diaries of George Washington, 1748–1799*. 4 vols. Boston: Houghton Mifflin, 1925.

————. *Papers of George Washington*. Charlottesville: University Press of Virginia, 1983–.

————. Papers of George Washington at the Library of Congress, 1741–99, http://memory.loc.gov/ammem/ gwhtml/gwhome.html.

————. *Writings of George Washington from the Original Manuscript Sources, 1745–1799*. Washington, D.C.: Government Printing Office, 1931–44.

Wheeler, Richard. *Voices of 1776*. New York: Penguin, 1991.

Wiencek, Henry. *An Imperfect God: George Washington, His Slaves, and the Creation of America*. New York: Farrar, Straus and Giroux, 2003.

Williams, Glenn F. *Year of the Hangman: George Washington's Campaign Against the Iroquois*. Yardley, Pa.: Westholme, 2005.

ILLUSTRATION CREDITS

Bettman/Corbis: 133

Bibliothèque et Archives nationales du Québec: 53

Boston Public Library: 89 (bottom), 97, 253

Brooklyn Museum: 8

Charles Alan Munn Collection, Fordham University Library, Bronx, New York: 229

Clark Kinnaird, *George Washington: The Pictorial Biography* (New York: Hastings House, 1967): 273

Fort Ligonier: 59 (top right)

The Gilder Lehrman Collection: 80

Courtesy of the artist, Hal Sherman: 240

Historical Society of Pennsylvania: 43 (bottom)

The Huntington Library: 49, 248–49, 256, 269, 270, 271

Independence National Historical Park: 220

Jeffrey L. Ward, cartographer: 65 (left), 94, 107 (bottom), 139 (left), 175 (bottom)

Lawrence Martin, ed., United States George Washington Bicentennial Committee, *The George Washington Atlas* (Washington, D.C.: A. Hoen and Company of Baltimore, 1932): 260

Library of Congress Prints and Photographs Division: 11, 12, 26, 28 (top and bottom), 30, 48, 50, 59 (top left), 60, 64, 77, 82 (top left), 87, 88, 102 (bottom), 104, 108 (top and bottom), 109, 124, 132 (left), 142 (bottom), 155, 174, 195, 196, 198–99, 201, 203, 204, 207, 209, 213, 214, 216, 217, 223, 224, 226, 228, 231, 235, 238, 239, 241 (bottom), 243, 244, 247, 251, 254 (top, middle, and bottom), 261, 263 (right), 264, 265, 267, 272

Library of Virginia: 67

Courtesy of Map Department, Yale University Library: 2–3, 5, 18, 20, 21, 23 (top and bottom), 24–25, 27, 29, 31, 32–33, 34, 35, 36–37, 38, 39, 40, 41 (top and bottom), 43 (top), 46, 55 (top and bottom), 58, 63, 66, 68, 70–71, 72 (top and bottom), 73 (top), 74–75, 76, 78, 79, 83, 85 (top and bottom), 86, 90, 91, 93, 98–99, 100, 101, 102 (top), 103, 111, 112, 113, 114–15, 116, 117, 118, 121, 122, 125, 126, 127, 129, 130, 131, 132 (right), 139 (right), 141, 142 (top), 143, 144, 145 (top and bottom), 146 (bottom), 148, 149 (top and bottom), 150 (top and bottom), 152 (top left and top right), 153, 156, 158, 160–61, 162, 163 (top and bottom), 164, 165, 166, 167, 169, 170, 172, 176, 178, 179 (bottom), 181, 183 (top), 185, 187, 188, 190, 191, 215

Massachusetts Historical Society: 118, 189

Courtesy of Mount Vernon Ladies' Association: 259

Museum of the American Indian: 242

National Geographic Maps: 105

Collection of the New-York Historical Society: 59 (bottom), 106 (top), 134, 136 (top and bottom), 137, 138, 140, 241 (top)

New York Public Library: 22 (top), 31 (bottom), 44, 51, 56, 59 (top center), 61, 62, 73 (bottom), 81, 82 (top left), 89 (top), 106 (bottom), 119, 128, 146 (top), 147 (left and right), 152 (bottom), 154, 157, 173, 175 (top), 177, 179 (top), 182, 183 (bottom), 186, 192, 193, 205 (top and bottom), 221, 227, 232 (bottom), 233, 246, 250, 258, 263

Ohio Historical Society: 232 (top), 237

University of Virginia, Albert and Shirley Small Special Collections Library: 45, 219, 262

Virginia State Library: 210

Washington & Lee University: 57

William L. Clements Library, University of Michigan: 65 (right)

A NOTE ON THE AUTHOR

Historian Barnet Schecter is the author of *The Battle for New York*, about the city's pivotal role in the American Revolution, and *The Devil's Own Work*, a chronicle of the Civil War draft riots in New York. He lives in New York City.